CAMBRIDGE

ENGLISH LANGUAGE AND LITERATURE

A /AS Level for AQA

Student Book

Marcello Giovanelli, Andrea Macrae, Felicity Titjen and Ian Cushing

Series editor: Marcello Giovanelli

CAMBRIDGE
UNIVERSITY PRESS

University Printing House, Cambridge CB2 8BS, United Kingdom

Cambridge University Press is part of the University of Cambridge.

It furthers the University's mission by disseminating knowledge in the pursuit of education, learning and research at the highest international levels of excellence.

www.cambridge.org
Information on this title: www.cambridge.org/ukschools/9781107465664 (Paperback)
www.cambridge.org/ukschools/9781107465671 (Cambridge Elevate-enhanced Edition)
www.cambridge.org/ukschools/9781107465657 (Paperback + Cambridge Elevate-enhanced Edition)

First published 2015

Printed in the United Kingdom by Latimer Trend

A catalogue record for this publication is available from the British Library

ISBN 978-1-107-46566-4 Paperback
ISBN 978-1-107-46567-1 Cambridge Elevate-enhanced Edition
ISBN 978-1-107-46565-7 Paperback + Cambridge Elevate-enhanced Edition

Additional resources for this publication at www.cambridge.org/ukschools

Approval message from AQA

This textbook has been approved by AQA for use with our qualification. This means that we have checked that it broadly covers the specification and we are satisfied with the overall quality. Full details of our approval process can be found on our website.

We approve textbooks because we know how important it is for teachers and students to have the right resources to support their teaching and learning. However, the publisher is ultimately responsible for the editorial control and quality of this book.

Please note that when teaching the AS and A Level English Language and Literature (7706, 7707) course, you must refer to AQA's specification as your definitive source of information. While this book has been written to match the specification, it cannot provide complete coverage of every aspect of the course.

A wide range of other useful resources can be found on the relevant subject pages of our website: aqa.org.uk

Contents

Introduction

Welcome to this student book for your AQA A/AS Level English Language and Literature course!

The AQA English Language and Literature AS/A Level specifications promote a fully integrated vision for the subject where the same methods of analysis, skills and frameworks can be used to explore both literary and non-literary texts. This student book supports AQA's vision by giving you the tools to be able to analyse the language of all kinds of texts, literary and non-literary, precisely and with confidence. Covering the specification, and supported by an enhanced digital edition on the Cambridge Elevate platform, this book also:

- develops your expertise in understanding and discussing the key underpinning principles of the AQA specifications: genre; narrative; point of view; register; representation and the whole question of 'literariness'
- supports the essential skills of text analysis and academic and creative writing in coherent, lively and engaging ways
- supports co-teachability by helping you to work your way through the course in a clear and logical way, whether you are studying AS or A Level.

This student book supports the specifications and helps you to develop the different skills you will be assessed on – skills which will stand you in good stead beyond AS or A Level, whatever you go on to do.

Beginning unit

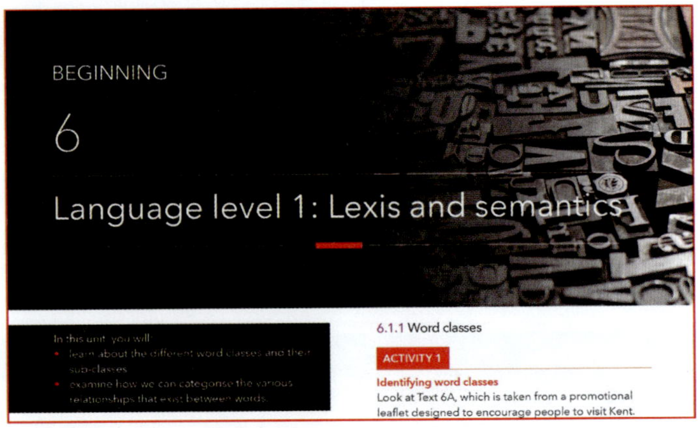
BEGINNING

6

Language level 1: Lexis and semantics

In this unit, you will:
- learn about the different word classes and their sub-classes
- examine how we can categorise the various relationships that exist between words.

6.1.1 Word classes

ACTIVITY 1

Identifying word classes

Look at Text 6A, which is taken from a promotional leaflet designed to encourage people to visit Kent.

Developing unit

DEVELOPING

16

Imagined worlds

In this unit, you will:
- develop your understanding of, and explore the conventions of, the fantasy genre
- learn an extensive analytical toolkit to help you explore narratives
- develop a range of ideas related to the novel that you are studying for this unit
- explore how best to prepare for assessment on this unit.

This relates to 'Views and voices' in the AS Level specification and 'Telling stories' in the A Level specification.

16.1.1 A definition of fantasy

The word 'fantasy' derives from the Latin word *phantasia*, meaning 'the imagination'. The genre's etymology is a good clue to how broad it is since clearly many (if not all) kinds of literature could be defined as imaginative. Indeed, the sheer diversity of different kinds of texts, periods and writers covered by the fantasy genre makes it difficult to pin down more than a few essential characteristics. Even then, the genre is still a fluid one, moving into other genres, having clear exceptions and so on. In Example 1, the literary critics Edward James and Farah Mendlesohn (2012) describe fantasy as follows:

Enriching unit

ENRICHING

25

Dramatic encounters

About the specifications

The AS Level specification has two components:

<u>Paper 1: Views and voices</u>

What it is: *In this component you will learn about how and why views and perspectives of different kinds are shaped and used in narratives.*

You will also learn how language choices help to shape the representations of different worlds and perspectives in prose fiction that constructs imaginary worlds and poetry that constructs a strong sense of personal perspective.

How it is assessed: 1½ hour exam worth 50% of your AS.

Key terms box

Key terms

space: a location in terms of its co-ordinates on a map

place: a location that is given significance and value through being a site of interaction with others, full of important events and personal memories

culture: a set of practices that involve shared ways of thinking and acting and which attach value to material objects of various kinds

society: a group of people working and living in a specific location who act out cultural beliefs and practices

Icons used in the book

- Cross reference
- Key terms
- Glossary
- Check your responses
- Video
- Summary
- Cambridge Elevate 3rd party website

Paper 2: People and places

What it is: *In this component you will learn about the ways in which writers and speakers present narratives about Paris using the AQA Anthology and consider why and how people tell stories about places. You will also produce re-creative work and write a critical reflection on your writing.*

How it is assessed: 1½ hour exam worth 50% of your AS.

The A Level specification has three components:

Paper 1: Telling stories

What it is: *In this component you will learn about how and why stories of different kinds are told and the ways in which writers and speakers present stories. You will explore these questions by studying narratives that construct different views of Paris (using the AQA Anthology), prose fiction that constructs imaginary worlds and poetry that constructs a strong sense of personal perspective.*

How it is assessed: 3 hour exam worth 40% of your A Level.

Paper 2: Exploring conflict

What it is: *In this component you will learn about how language choices help to construct ideas of conflict between people, and between people and their societies. You will explore concepts such as power and identity and analyse the ways that interactions are presented in texts. You will produce re-creative work that seeks to find an absent or underplayed perspective in a novel, write a critical reflection on your work and study drama that explores conflicts at different levels from the domestic to the societal.*

How it is assessed: 2½ hour exam worth 40% of your A Level.

Non-exam assessment: Making connections

What it is: *In this component you will explore language use in different types of text. You will investigate connections between a literary text and some non-literary material based either on a chosen theme or on the idea that particular linguistic strategies and features may occur in the different types of material. You will produce an academic report outlining your research and your findings.*

How it is assessed: one piece of non-exam assessment worth 20% of your A Level.

About this student book

This book follows an innovative three-part structure:

Part 1: Beginning units

These set out the key principles, issues and concepts that underpin the course and support you as you move from GCSE to AS and A Level work. Each Beginning unit contains activities to check understanding and progress, and provides a strong foundation from which to build upwards. The Beginning units can also be used as a stand-alone reference point to which you'll return when studying content in subsequent Developing units, and for revision purposes as you prepare for your exams.

Part 2: Developing units

These longer units are based around the main content in the AS and A Level specifications. They are designed to build on the ideas introduced in the Beginning units, extending knowledge and understanding where appropriate. These units follow the order of topics in the AQA specifications and contain a wider range of activities to develop skills and encourage independence. The start of each Developing unit tells you whether the content is suitable for AS, A Level or both.

Each Developing unit covers the most up-to-date content and research, which is presented in an accessible and engaging way. Many of the activities in these units are supported by commentaries that will support your learning and help you to develop an analytical framework, with which you can consider topic areas more critically and broadly.

These units also contain a 'Bringing it all together' section, which allows you to review key learning for a particular topic and to plan your revision priorities. In addition, practice questions and discussion of the assessment objectives allow you to apply your learning and to think about the demands of individual sections within the exam papers.

Deconstructing exam questions

> Compare and contrast how Duffy presents **time** in these poems.
>
> *This instruction reminds you that you need to compare and contrast. It also contains the focus for the question, here highlighted in bold (time)'.*

Bringing it all together

> **16.6 Bringing it all together: AS Level**
>
> **16.6.1 Self-assessment: check your learning**
>
> For each of the following statements, evaluate your confidence in each topic area:

Topic area	Very con
I understand how fictional worlds are constructed by novelists	
I can identify and comment on narrative structures that are used in the novel I am studying	
I can explain the significance of places in the novel	

End-of-unit summary

> **Summary**
>
> - Texts are part of larger discourse events that involve real-life text producers and receivers communicating and interpreting in specific times and places.
> - Texts can have more than one purpose; it is useful to distinguish between primary and secondary purposes.
> - Text producers and receivers often have constructs called implied readers and writers in mind; in reality, the actual readers and writers may be very different.

A/AS Level English Language and Literature transcription key

Throughout this book the following transcription key is applied:

(.)	indicates a pause of less than a second
(2)	indicates a longer pause (number of seconds indicated)
Bold	indicates stressed syllables or words
: :	indicates elongation of a word
((*italics*))	indicates contextual or additional information
[ ]	indicates the start and end points of simultaneous speech

Tutorial Video available on Cambridge Elevate

Enriching Interview Video available on Cambridge Elevate

Links to video content on Cambridge Elevate

Watch tutorial video, Sounds and Aesthetics, on Cambridge Elevate

Watch Peter Stockwell, Professor of Literary Linguistics at the University of Nottingham, talk about story worlds in science fiction on Cambridge Elevate

Find further examples of intertextuality in advertising via Cambridge Elevate

Part 3: Enriching units

Designed specifically for A Level students but with content that AS Level students will also find useful, these units support your work on the specification and extend your thinking beyond the topics covered in the Developing units in Part 2. These Enriching units contain extension activities on Developing unit topics, as well as ideas for extended independent study, details of wider reading that you will find useful and summaries of recent and relevant research from higher education.

The Enriching units also feature short articles exclusively written for this series by leading academics and professionals, with follow-up questions that offer expert insight into certain aspects of the subject.

About Cambridge Elevate

Cambridge Elevate is the platform which hosts a digital version of this Student Book. If you have access to this digital version you can annotate different parts of the book, send and receive messages to and from your teacher and insert weblinks, among other things. You will also find video content on Cambridge Elevate, specifically:

- Tutorial-style videos, designed to complement material covered in the Developing units and which will refresh your knowledge while broadening your understanding of certain tricky concepts;
- Interviews with leading thinkers and researchers in their fields, which provide a unique resource for stimulating discussion.

I hope you enjoy your AS or A Level Language and Literature course as well as this book, and wish you well for the journey ahead.

Marcello Giovanelli
Series editor

BEGINNING

1

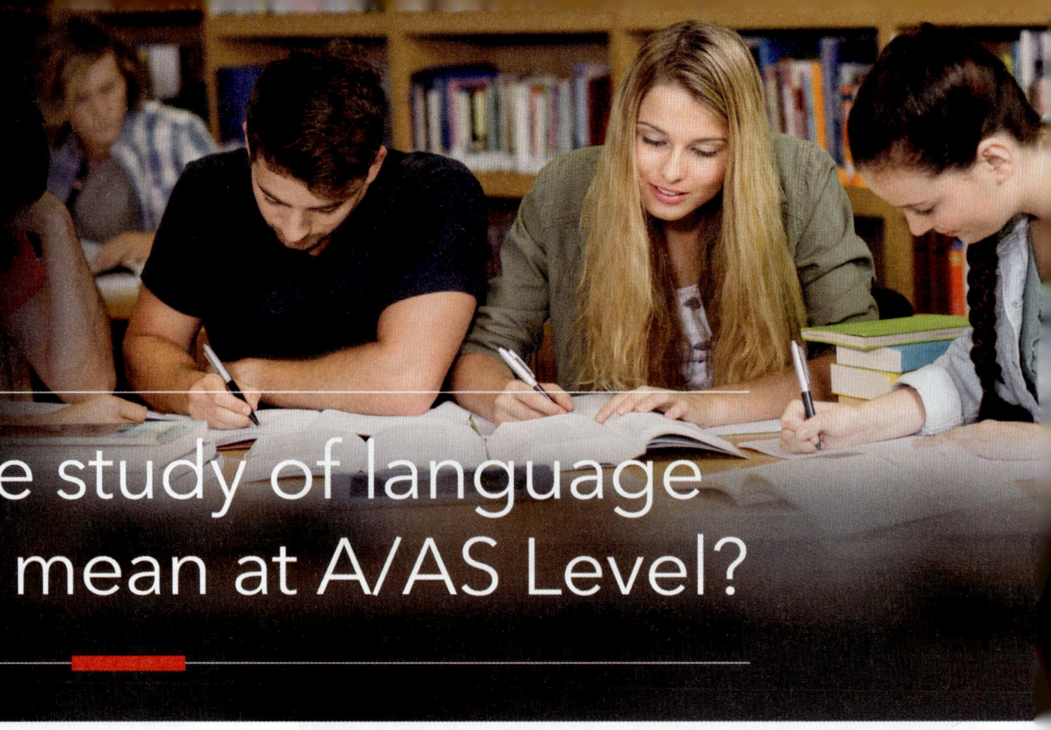

What does the study of language and literature mean at A/AS Level?

In this unit, you will:

- consider what it means to be studying an A Level in language and literature
- understand the assessment objectives against which your learning will be measured.

1.1 Moving from GCSE to A/AS Level

In your previous studies, you may have completed 'language' work and 'literature' work separately, and would have taken individual qualifications in them. You may have preferred one kind of 'English' over another: perhaps you really enjoy reading non-fiction or developing your own writing; on the other hand, you may be an avid reader of literary fiction and enjoy exploring and discussing ideas, themes and characters in the books that you read. At A/AS Level, you will build on all of this work but do so in a way that attempts to find connections between these different types of study, and in doing so present a more holistic and exciting kind of 'English'.

1.2 'Language study' and 'literary study'

A/AS Level English Language and Literature bridges the gap between language study and literary study; indeed, underpinning the course is the idea that this kind of separating of the subject into distinctive areas is potentially unhelpful.

So what is different about this course? To answer this question, it's worth looking at what is studied in the separate A/AS Level qualifications in English Language and in English Literature.

A/AS Level English Language is concerned with discourses (different types of text, context and debate) and explores how these vary according to personal and social factors. It explores the concept of representation (how language is used to present a way of looking at the world), and examines attitudes around language use, and key topics such as how children's language develops and how language changes over time.

On the other hand, A/AS Level English Literature is concerned with the study of literary authors, periods and genres, using historical (how literature has changed over time) or theoretical (ideas about how texts can be understood) perspectives. It tends to privilege certain kinds of texts (the **literary canon**) and dismisses others as not worthy of study. That is, it suggests literature is an exclusive category. However, the notion of what counts as literature and the concept of *literariness* itself are essentially problematic.

See Unit 13 for more on literariness

Traditionally, A/AS Level Language and Literature has been known as a *combined subject* where students have studied a few language topics and a few literature topics. It's now viewed as more of an *integrated* subject where the two strands 'language' and 'literature' are pulled together, and where the analysis of all kinds of text is informed by a secure understanding of how language is constructed and works. Although this concept of the subject is still a little problematic (drawing two things together could be interpreted as still seeing them as separate in some way), the fact that the rigorous study of language is at the heart of the subject gives it a real identity and, as you will discover throughout the course, is very enabling.

1.3 Stylistics

Studying texts by paying close attention to their language is known as **stylistics**. A stylistic analysis uses the best and most recent knowledge about how language operates to present ideas that are:

- **focused and systematic**: the best analyses always focus on language itself, and use methods and models from language study. This means that they don't stray into unnecessary comments about biographies of writers or generalise about what people might have thought, said or done in particular historical periods. As they draw on established ways of working in linguistics, they naturally avoid being simply vague impressionistic claims.
- **transparent**: the best analyses avoid over-the-top 'showing off'. Instead, they concentrate on what's in the text and describe this as transparently as possible so that other readers can understand how that reading was arrived at. The idea of a stylistic analysis is not to show how clever you are but to demonstrate how closely and accurately you can explore features and patterns in the text.
- **interpretative**: the best analyses don't just list language features but also find a motivation for their use. This means that an analysis is always looking for a way to explain features and build these into a wider sense of meaning.

Key terms

literary canon: a collection of authors and texts that is considered 'high status' and especially worthy of study

stylistics: the study of texts focusing carefully on language and providing a rich interpretation of key concerns, themes and possible effects

As an example of what a good analysis might look like, look at Text 1A from Bram Stoker's *Dracula*. In Text 1A, a character called Jonathan Harker is describing his journey by horse and carriage at night to Dracula's castle.

Text 1A

Soon we were hemmed in with trees, which in places arched right over the roadway till we passed as through a tunnel; and again great frowning rocks guarded us boldly on either side.

Source: Bram Stoker, *Dracula*

- A *language approach* might describe the use of prepositions (words that present relationships in space, such as 'in', 'over', 'through'). Although this might be presented as a significant pattern, no real interpretative significance would be attached to it.
- A *literary approach* might comment on a theme such as the fear that Harker experiences as he is travelling, and how he is characterised as being contained. Although some quotation might be used to support these points, they would largely be impressionistic and intuitive, and not make any reference to established ways of talking about language.

- A *language-literature/stylistics approach* would bring the two together to present an analysis that is rooted in the language of the text but has a strong interpretative focus as well. It could draw on the pattern of prepositions to suggest that the narrative demands that the reader shares Harker's point of view. The use of the pronoun 'we' encourages us to adopt the vantage point from which he experiences the events, and the prepositions both mirror the movements the carriage makes and evoke a type of claustrophobic fear, since they all represent the carriage as being contained. In turn, the verbs of containment 'hemmed in' and 'guarded', the latter as part of a metaphor of the rocks being presented as humans, foreground this way of interpreting Text 1A.

See 6.2.3 for more on metaphor

ACTIVITY 1

Stylistics

The stylisticians Peter Stockwell and Sara Whiteley have written that 'Stylistics is the proper study of literature' (*Cambridge Handbook of Stylistics*, 2014: 1). Based on what you have read in this unit, what do you think they mean by this? Would you agree with them or should studying literature also be about other things? Do you think their comment is valid for other kinds of texts as well?

1.4 Assessment objectives and what they mean

Five assessment objectives (AOs) underpin A/AS Level English Language and Literature. These are:

- AO1: apply concepts and methods from integrated linguistic and literary study as appropriate, using associated terminology and coherent written expression
- AO2: analyse ways in which meanings are shaped in texts
- AO3: demonstrate understanding of the significance and influence of contexts in which texts are produced and received
- AO4: explore connections between texts, informed by linguistic and literary concepts and methods
- AO5: demonstrate expertise and creativity in the use of English to communicate in different ways.

Your ability to explain and explore texts using a critical vocabulary in a systematic way is crucial for AO1. This means being able to use appropriate terms at each of the language levels, as well as a wider range of critical ideas and frameworks that you will learn about throughout this book. AO1 also assesses your ability to write clearly and accurately.

See 1.3 for more on appropriate terms at each of the language levels

AO2 is about ensuring a strong interpretative side to your writing when exploring texts. This means that it is not enough simply to use a model of analysis or a set of analytical terms but you should also explain in detail how these contribute to a sense of meaning. Avoiding simply treating texts as data and instead exploring them as inherently rich and meaningful is crucial for this AO.

AO3 assesses your ability to understand how highly influential external factors are in shaping the writing of, speaking about, reading of, and listening to texts . As you will see through the remainder of this book, the study of context can include considering aspects of history, biography, typical features of texts that we can place into groups due to similarities, and the relationships between people involved in creating and consuming them.

AO4 assesses your ability to find connections between different kinds of text. This might be exploring how two extracts are similar and different or thinking about the whole notion of what counts as 'literature' and what kinds of difference exist between so-called 'literary' and 'non-literary texts'.

Finally, AO5 assesses your own creative work. A/AS Level English Language and Literature offers you the opportunity to explore how what you've learnt about how language operates can be put to good use in your own writing. You'll be expected to be able to exploit this in imaginative and interesting ways.

Table 1A shows how each assessment objective is mapped across the different parts of the specification.

Table 1A

	AO1	AO2	AO3	AO4	AO5
AS Level					
Imagined worlds	✓	✓			
Poetic voices	✓	✓		✓	
Remembered places	✓		✓	✓	
Re-creative writing		✓	✓	✓	✓
A Level					
Remembered places	✓		✓	✓	
Imagined worlds	✓	✓	✓		
Poetic voices	✓	✓			
Writing about society		✓		✓	✓
Dramatic encounters	✓	✓	✓		
Making connections	✓	✓	✓	✓	

Summary

- A/AS Level English Language and Literature is an exciting way of looking at all kinds of texts with a strong focus on the language they use.
- A/AS Level English Language and Literature is informed by the discipline of stylistics.
- Assessment objectives are mapped across individual units to allow you to see what is being tested in each part of the specification.

BEGINNING

2

Text producers and receivers

> In this unit, you will:
> - explore the concept of texts as discourse events
> - learn more about the purposes of different texts
> - explore the difference between implied and actual readers and writers.

2.1 Context

At A/AS level, **context** is a very broad term that we use to refer to all of the external factors that shape how texts are written or spoken (the context of production) and read, heard or listened to (the context of reception). All texts have writers/speakers (or **text producers**) and readers/listeners (or **text receivers**). The intentions and motivations of text producers, along with factors such as the time and place in which the text was produced, influence the language choices that they make. Equally, the intentions and motivations of a text receiver, as well as the situation in which reading or listening takes place, influence the way that a reader or listener forms an interpretation.

2.2 Texts and discourse events

As you're working through your A/AS Level studies, it can be tempting to think about the texts that you are exploring and analysing simply as decontextualised extracts on the page. One of the keys to success in more advanced study will be your ability to move beyond thinking about 'texts' in this way, and instead to consider them as rich and complex acts of communication that are part of what we can term a **discourse event** made up of **text producers** (writers or speakers) and **text receivers** (readers or listeners) engaged in the process of making meaning.

> **Key terms**
>
> **context:** the external factors that shape how texts are produced and received
>
> **discourse event:** an act of communication occurring in a specific time and location involving writers/speakers and readers/listeners
>
> **text producer:** the person or people responsible (through writing or speaking) for creating a text
>
> **text receiver:** the person or people interpreting (through reading or listening to) a text

The term 'discourse event' is a useful one as it enables you to explore how texts are produced and received in specific times and places by real people with beliefs and intentions using language to express and understand their ideas and meanings. It adds a strong contextual dimension to any analysis that you might undertake by emphasising the fact that where there is language, there are always language *users*.

Text 2A

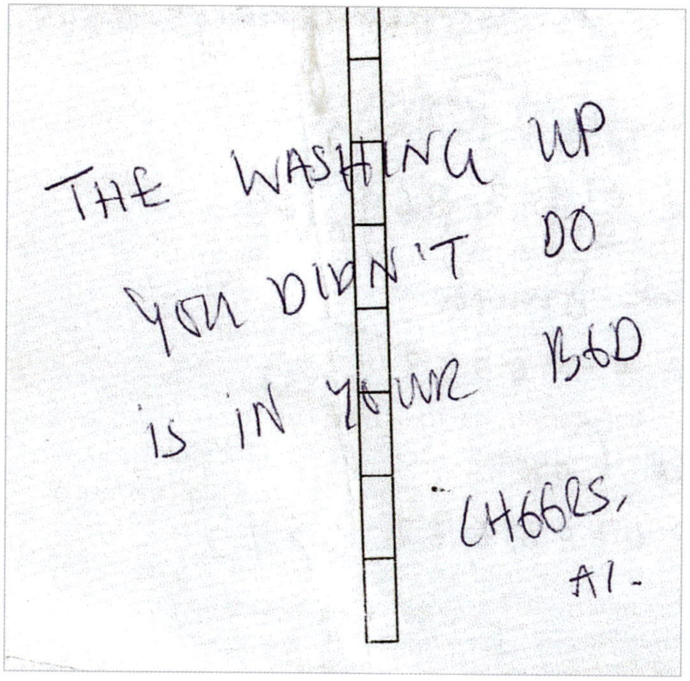

Source: Oonagh O'Hagan, *I Lick My Cheese and Other Notes from the Frontline of Flatsharing*

2.3 Purpose

The concept of a discourse event allows you to explore the familiar terms 'purpose' and 'audience' in more detail. These terms can be explored by considering more closely the kinds of motivations behind writing, speaking and interpreting that producers and receivers might have. As an example of this, look at Text 2A. This note was written by a university student (Al) and addressed to a friend with whom he was sharing a flat.

What's immediately obvious here is that this note has been written for a specific purpose that is motivated very clearly by the text producer's beliefs and emotions: Al is informing his friend of his anger that the washing up hasn't been done. However, we could also imagine another possible purpose to this text, to warn and advise Al's friend that this kind of behaviour will not be tolerated. So, as in this case, a text may have a number of purposes and be what is termed **multi-purpose**. We can also use the terms **primary purpose** (the main and most likely recognisable reason why a text has been produced), and **secondary purpose** (an additional and perhaps more subtle reason why the text has been produced) to differentiate further between types and degrees of textual purposes.

It's also important to consider the impact on the text receiver. In the case of Text 2A, regardless of the producer's original purpose, the impact of the message could well be very different from that originally intended. If Al's friend had simply thrown the note away, the anger and intended warning would have had no impact at all. Regardless of the original purpose, it's also important to explore what in reality a text gets used for; that is to think about its *function*.

Key terms

multi-purpose text: a text that clearly has more than one purpose

primary purpose: the main and most easily recognisable purpose

secondary purpose: an additional and perhaps more subtle purpose

ACTIVITY 1

Identifying purpose

Look at Text 2B, which appeared on Eurostar's website advertising their rail service to Paris. Identify the primary purpose of this text, and any secondary purposes that you can think of.

Check your responses in the Ideas section on Cambridge Elevate

Text 2B

> **FIND YOUR £69 RETURN TO PARIS**
>
> VIEW DATES & PRICES
>
> Set off from London St Pancras International and arrive in Paris Gare Du Nord in just over 2 hours via high-speed train with Eurostar. Our fares start from as little as **£69 return in Standard Class**, or you can upgrade to Standard Premier or Business Premier class for a little luxury.
>
> Whether you're after a weekend of romance or just an evening of fun, song and dance, Eurostar will take you straight to the heart of Europe's finest capital cities to soak up the true soul of the continent.

Source: www.eurostar.com

ACTIVITY 2

Interpreting texts

Find an example of a text, for example, an advertisement or lines from a literary text or song that has been used in a very different way (and in consequence has a different purpose) to that which was originally intended for it. What does this suggest to you about how and why text receivers interpret texts to suit their own needs?

2.4 Audience

It's clear from looking at Texts 2A and 2B that there are some more complex issues around the notion of the person (or people) for whom a text is produced. The term 'audience' is again likely to be one that you are familiar with. However at A/AS Level, it's useful to distinguish more closely between an idealised version of an audience that a producer has in mind and the readers or listeners who in reality will encounter, and engage with, a text in specific situations.

Looking at Text 2B again, we could suggest that the text producer of this leaflet has a particular kind of reader in mind and makes language choices accordingly. In fact this **implied reader** is a constructed image of a reader who best fits the central message, beliefs and world-views the text is presenting. In this instance, the implied reader is someone who likes to travel to Europe.

In reality, of course, a text may have many different **actual readers**, each reading and interpreting in different contexts, and influenced by their own belief systems. The potential number of actual readers of any text will depend on how private or public the text is. For example, Text 2A clearly has a potentially smaller number of actual readers compared to Text 2B. Actual readers may of course also choose to resist any kinds of identity and ideology that are projected and constructed for them by a text producer. For example, a reader who doesn't like travelling is unlikely simply to be swayed or to 'buy into' what's being offered as a result of reading this advertisement.

In turn, a reader will have a constructed version of an **implied writer** in their mind when reading a text. In the case of Text 2B, this may be a constructed image of a local person, who knows Paris well and/or is a seasoned traveller. The **actual writer**, however, is likely to be a professional copywriter.

Finally, we can categorise larger groups of readers who might be drawn to reading texts in particular ways, with shared beliefs, interests and intentions as members of a particular **discourse community**. In the case of Text 2B, these readers are likely to be people who like to travel and share an interest in Paris as a city of culture. The concept of a discourse community offers a way of understanding how people form socially oriented groups, with common interests, purposes and strategies for reading and responding to texts. Discourse communities can be large (e.g., One Direction fans) or small (e.g., members of a village book club), and each community will have its own agreed conventions for communicating and sharing ideas.

Key terms

implied reader: a constructed image of an idealised reader

actual reader: any person or groups of people who engage with and interpret a text

implied writer: a constructed image of an idealised writer

actual writer: the 'real' person or people responsible for text production

discourse community: a group of people with shared interests and belief systems who are likely to respond to texts in similar ways

ACTIVITY 3

Images of readers

Find examples of written and spoken texts. Identify their primary and secondary purposes, and their implied readerships. Can you identify how they begin to construct an image of an idealised reader who fits their own belief systems, or any messages about the company and their products that they want to portray?

ACTIVITY 4

Discourse communities

Find examples of specific discourse communities and try to identify how they have shared and agreed conventions for interpreting and communicating. You could start by looking at message boards or Twitter posts related to fans of pop groups to see how these communities operate.

Summary

- Texts are part of larger discourse events that involve real-life text producers and receivers communicating and interpreting in specific times and places.
- Texts can have more than one purpose; it is useful to distinguish between primary and secondary purposes.
- Text producers and receivers often have constructs called implied readers and writers in mind; in reality, the actual readers and writers may be very different.

BEGINNING

3

Mode and genre

In this unit, you will:

- learn about how we can distinguish between the modes of speech and writing
- explore how we classify text types using the notion of genre.

3.1 Mode

We can make very obvious distinctions between texts based on whether they were originally examples of speech or writing. In doing so, we are drawing attention to different channels or **modes** of communication.

3.1.1 The oppositional view

There are several ways of thinking about the differences between speech and writing. The most straightforward way is to consider them in opposition, by defining them broadly as having completely different characteristics. This is known as the **oppositional view** as shown in Table 3A.

This view, presented in Table 3A, is attractive in some ways because it offers a neat way of categorising language, and in many cases texts will fit the characteristics of each mode in a relatively straightforward way.

Table 3A

Writing is:	Speech is:
objective	interpersonal
a monologue	a dialogue
durable	ephemeral
planned	spontaneous
highly structured	loosely structured
grammatically complex	grammatically simple
concerned with the past and future	concerned with the present
formal	informal
decontextualised	contextualised

Source: adapted from Naomi Baron (2001)

Key terms

mode: the physical channel of communication: either speech or writing

oppositional view: a way of defining the difference between modes by arguing that they have completely different features

continuum: a sequence in which elements that are next to each other are not noticeably different but elements at the opposite ends are very different from each other

blended-mode: a text which contains conventional elements of both speech and writing

Text 3A

ALICE: hello didn't see you in there uh (.) you OK
GILL: that was so great (.) you had such a good time didn't you Michael (1) did you like that Luke ((*Luke nods*))
ALICE: which one did you go to
GILL: the ninky nonk (.) you
ALICE: yeah (.) too (.) it's so good here (.) the way they've done the tent and all (.) really good
GILL: really impressive
ALICE: and you know the price is good for us all
GILL: mmm (.) definitely (.) amazing (.)

Source: private data

Text 3B

In the Night Garden Live

It is sometimes helpful to call on a toddler for reviewing advice, especially when faced with the task of identifying the likes of Igglepiggle, Pinky Ponk, Makka Pakka and the rest, from *In the Night Garden Live*. Taking place in a purpose-built dome, the show is an enchanting experience for preschoolers, in which the characters of the *CBeebies* programme are given the live theatre treatment.

The arrival of the stars of the show is greeted with recognition and delight – kids are enthralled at seeing their favourites in front of them, and the mood, costumes and sounds replicated from the television show seem to be authentic enough as to convince them the characters are real.

The Stage, 2 August 2010

ACTIVITY 1

Exploring the oppositional view

Look at Text 3A, where two speakers, Alice and Gill, are discussing taking their children to a live performance of the children's TV show *In the Night Garden*, and Text 3B, which is a written review of the same show. To what extent do these texts reflect the oppositional view of speech and writing?

3.1.2 Blended-mode texts

However, many texts do not fit into the neat distinction proposed by the oppositional view. For example, a birthday card sent by one friend to another is clearly interpersonal, a political speech by the prime minister is not a dialogue, graffiti found on a school corridor is clearly not durable since it is likely to be washed off, and a telephone conversation between two friends about a holiday is more than likely to be just as concerned with the past (talking about the holiday) as the present.

An alternative way that avoids some of the problems inherent in the oppositional model is to consider speech and writing as ends of a **continuum**. This is a more attractive way of thinking about how many texts contain elements that might be traditionally associated with both speech and writing, what we can term **blended-mode texts**. For example, Text 3C, which is taken from a message board discussion of the *In the Night Garden* show, clearly has elements of both speech and writing and could be placed at the centre of the continuum (see Figure 3A) to show that it is a blended-mode text.

'...kids are enthralled at seeing their favourites in front of them.'

The Stage

Text 3C

Date March 12th, 2010, 10:52 AM

Originally posted by
DynoMite123:

Bloody tickets cost a bomb ☹ cant wait tho. The gigs going to be awesome ☺

BaBs98

Yeah expensive tickets but will be worth it. Who needs food lol. Last time they played there was amazing.

Source: private data

Figure 3A

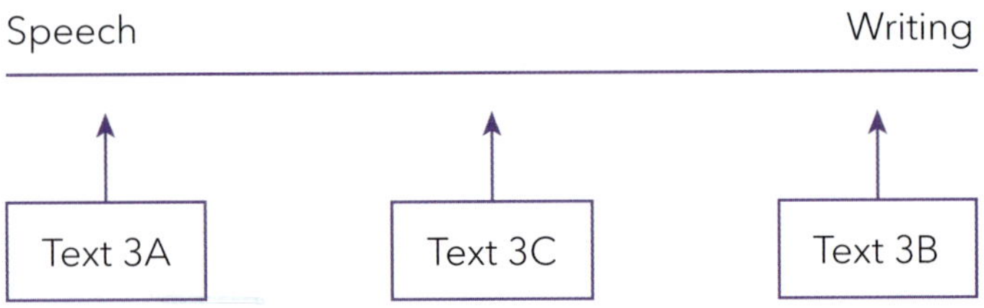

3.1.3 The prototype model

A final way of thinking about mode and distinguishing between types and degrees of speech and writing borrows ideas from psychology, and in particular the idea that humans generally categorise and classify based on a **prototype model**. This suggests that for any given category (e.g., the mode of speech) we can identify examples that are prototypes (typical or 'good members') and examples that are 'less good' or 'less typical members'. A conventional way of showing this distinction is by placing the prototype at the centre of a radial structure, and other examples moving outwards from it; the greater the distance from the centre indicates that a text is less of a fit (see Figure 3B). So, looking at Texts 3A, 3B and 3C again, we could say that 3A is a strong example of speech (a prototype), while 3C has conventional elements of speech and could be placed on an outer ring; however, Text 3B has very little if anything that we would associate with speech and therefore sits on the very outer ring.

Figure 3B

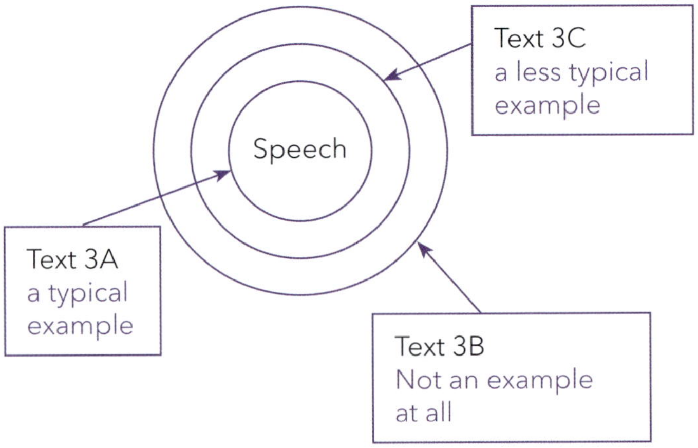

Key terms

prototype model: a model of looking at differences within a category or mode by thinking about typical and less typical examples

ACTIVITY 2

Exploring mode

Explore the ideas that have been discussed about mode in this unit by collecting some texts of your own and exploring their features. You could look at obvious examples of blended-mode texts, such as Facebook posts, tweets and text messages, and think about why the text producers have decided to use the features that they have. Think about:

1. how spoken-mode features in writing help to convey meaning
2. how the language choices that text producers make depend on the conventions of the medium they are writing in
3. how the language choices text producers make depend on their own purposes for communicating.

3.2 Genre

Like mode, **genre** is an important concept in the study of language since it enables us to group texts based on shared characteristics and expected textual conventions. For example, within the genre of advertising, we would expect to find details of a product that a company or individual would like us to buy, persuasive language used to tempt us into buying into the lifestyle associated with the product and to see the benefits of making a purchase. In the case of written advertisements, we would expect to see the use of images designed to make us think in a positive manner about the product on offer, and to encourage us to want to buy it.

Advertising offers a good way of exploring how text producers can exploit generic conventions in innovative ways to make their texts and the products that they are advertising memorable. Text 3D, an advertisement for a Virgin media cable TV package, 'borrows' conventions from another type of text (a receipt) to emphasis the exceptional value offered by the company: the text looks like a receipt in itemising purchase units and their costs, and even contains the words, 'Please keep receipt for your records.' This kind of **intertextuality** is an example of the way that text producers can use what readers know about different kinds of genres in creative and novel ways.

Key terms

genre: a way of grouping texts based on expected shared conventions

intertextuality: a process by which texts borrow from or refer to conventions of other texts for a specific purpose and effect

ACTIVITY 3

Intertextuality

Find other examples of texts that have very obvious intertextual links within the genre of advertising. Which aspects of other genres do they 'borrow' and why? How do they exploit what readers will know and understand?

See further examples of intertextuality in advertising via Cambridge Elevate

3.2.1 Literary genres

Literary texts can be classified into one of the three main literary genres of prose, poetry and drama. Although these may appear to be very general headings – and some models of thinking would argue that these are not really genres at all but *literary forms* – they do provide

Text 3D

Source: Virgin Media

a starting point for considering the characteristics of different types of writing. You will explore these in much more detail in your work on *Imagined worlds*, *Poetic voices* and *Dramatic encounters*.

Summary

- We can make a basic distinction between the modes of speech and writing but there are many examples of blended-mode texts that use elements of both speech and writing to create meaning.
- It is useful to think of degrees of difference between and within modes rather than holding a strictly oppositional view.
- A genre is a way of categorising texts based on expected shared conventions.

BEGINNING

4 Variation, register and representation

In this unit, you will:

- learn about the key concept of variation
- explore the notions of register and representation.

In Unit 2, we drew attention to the importance of thinking about language as part of a larger discourse event, involving text producers (writers or speakers) and text receivers (readers or listeners). We identified that a fundamental part of thinking about language use is to consider the role of language users in context.

One of the key characteristics of both language use and language users is **variation**. In language study, this term refers to differences associated with particular instances of language use and between groups of language users.

4.1 Language use

As you saw in Unit 2, language users vary their use of language depending on a number of contextual factors (such as audience and purpose, the specific times and places where they are speaking or writing, and a range of personal beliefs and motivations). This means that language variation is always systematic in that language choices are always influenced by contextual factors.

4.1.1 Register

In your work on mode in Unit 3, you explored one of the most basic distinctions we can make between variation in language, that of speech and writing. We can develop our understanding of variation by thinking about the term **register**.

A register is a variety of language that is associated with a particular **situation of use**. So, for example, a teacher taking a sixth-form class might speak in an academic spoken register; someone writing a review of a hotel they had been to might use an informative written register; someone going to the chip shop to buy some food might use a register associated with what we call 'service encounters'. As you can see, registers can be either spoken or written.

Exploring texts from a register perspective always begins with considering those key aspects of context, what we can term **situational characteristics**, and exploring the relationship between these and a text's linguistic features.

Key terms

variation: the differences associated with particular instances of language use and between groups of language users

register: a variety of language that is associated with a particular situation of use

situation of use: a specific place, time and context in which communication takes place

situational characteristic: a key characteristic of the time, place and contexts in which communication takes place

When thinking about situational characteristics we can ask ourselves the following questions:

- Who are the people communicating?
- What is their relationship?
- Where is the setting?
- Are they communicating face to face or are they separated in time and place (e.g., communicating by email, telephone, letter)?
- What is the purpose of the communication?

The relationship between these situational characteristics and language choices is crucial since the situational characteristics motivate a speaker or writer to adopt a certain register.

As a way of exploring the notion of register as a variety of language, we can look back at the text in Unit 3 which features two speakers discussing *In the Night Garden*. It is reprinted here as Text 4A.

Text 4A

ALICE: hello didn't see you in there uh (.) you OK
GILL: that was so great (.) you had such a good time didn't you Michael (1) did you like that Luke ((*Luke nods*))
ALICE: which one did you go to
GILL: the ninky nonk (.) you
ALICE: yeah (.) too (.) it's so good here (.) the way they've done the tent and all (.) really good
GILL: really impressive
ALICE: and you know the price is good for us all
GILL: mmm (.) definitely (.) amazing (.)

Source: private data

In this extract the situational characteristics are that Alice and Gill know each other and each other's children and they are speaking face to face, having both just seen the show. Their speech is therefore spontaneous and their conversation is a social or interactional one focusing on personal aspects. This motivates the use of a conversational register, where they take turns to speak; use key features of spoken language, such as pauses and responses designed to provide support and encouragement (e.g., 'mmm', 'definitely', 'amazing'); and miss out words that would normally be present in written language (e.g., 'really impressive' instead of '*it is* really impressive'). This then can be understood as an example of a specific register that the speakers are using to match a specific situation of use.

ACTIVITY 1

Exploring register

Look back at Texts 3B and 3C in Unit 3. How would you describe the register that each writer uses? How is each motivated by situational characteristics? What key language features are there?

Check your responses in the Ideas section on Cambridge Elevate

The relationship between these situational characteristics and language choices is crucial...

4.2 Representation

Language use may vary in terms of how events, people and circumstances are represented by different users, in different texts, and with different motivating factors. **Representation** can be defined as the way in which events, people and circumstances are portrayed through language and other meaning-making resources (e.g., images and sound).

Key terms

representation: the portrayal of events, people and circumstances through language and other meaning-making resources (e.g., images and sound) to create a way of seeing the world

A straightforward example of representation can be seen in Text 4B, two pages from a book written for children called *The Tiger Who Came to Tea*, which was originally published in 1968. On the first page, the female character (who has just had to deal with a tiger arriving at her house and eating all of her food!) is represented through the way she looks (the type of clothes she is wearing), the actions she undertakes, the setting she is in (clearing up in the kitchen) and the speech she uses (uncertain, worried about how she will look after her husband). On the second page, the way in which the male character is positioned in the centre of the page, while the female character and her daughter are on the outside, portrays the male as a potentially much stronger and more influential figure in the story. In all, we could argue that this text represents males as strong and females as weak, and projects a certain way of looking at a family unit; other texts of course offer different ways of representing families.

It's worth remembering that representation can be very much a result of wider societal values and a way of 'seeing the world' that is particular to an era or certain culture. You could explore this by searching online for advertisements from the 1970s and 1980s and looking at how people and events are represented there. Clearly then, exploring representation involves considering how a certain way of seeing the world is projected.

ACTIVITY 2

Rewriting a text

Experiment with *The Tiger Who Came to Tea* pages in Text 4B by rewriting and redesigning them so that they represent male and female characters and family units in different ways, such as the father undertaking domestic duties.

You might also like to explore how female characters are portrayed in more recently published children's fiction. If you have younger brothers or sisters, you could look at their books or use preview facilities on Amazon, Google Books or publishers' websites.

ACTIVITY 3

Representing groups

You will explore representation in more detail throughout this book and the concept is an important one across your A/AS Level study. As a starting point, find an example of a text that represents a group of people in a very clearly defined way. How are they represented? How does the text producer do this?

Text 4B

Sophie's mummy said, "I don't know what to do. I've got nothing for Daddy's supper, the tiger has eaten it all."

So Sophie and her mummy told him what had happened, and how the tiger had eaten all the food and drunk all the drink.

Source: HarperCollins UK

Summary

- Variation is a key term in language study.
- Registers are specific varieties or uses of language.
- Representation is an important concept to explore how text producers present ways of looking at the world (people, events and circumstances).

BEGINNING

5 Narrative

In this unit, you will:

- explore the key components of narrative
- learn how readers use their own knowledge to help build up narrative worlds.

5.1 Narratives and narrators

One of the most fundamental and most interesting human characteristics is our capacity for storytelling. We organise our experiences of events, people, time and places into structures that we relate to others for various purposes and in various forms. These structures are called **narratives**, the people who write or speak them are called **narrators** and the people to whom these are told are called **narratees**.

Our deeply embedded capacity to produce and understand narratives means that we make sense of even static images within some kind of narrative frame. For example, if you look at Figure 5A, it's very difficult not to view this as part of an ongoing narrative sequence.

At a simple level, most people asked to describe this image will interpret it by focusing on the action of the man smashing the window (you could test this out by asking friends and family). Typically, a description might be something like:

The man smashed the window.

At an explicit level this sentence organises the event (the smashing of the window) and the entities involved (the man and the window) into a certain way of looking at what's going on; in this instance the positioning of the man at the front of the sentence suggests that he is the dominant force in the event. The use of the past tense adds a dimension of time, giving the impression that the narrator is looking back on something that happened before the act of speaking. This ability to position events within **time frames** is an important part of narratives. We could also have altered the tense in the following ways, so that a very different sense of time is evoked.

Figure 5A

1 The man smashes the window. (the time of telling is the same as the time of action)

2 The man will smash the window. (the time of telling is before the time of action)

We could do much more with our emerging narrative. We could specify time even more by adding a particular indicator *'at six o'clock*, the man smashed the window'; manipulate time by presenting the events as a flashback or flashforwards: 'the man remembered the day that he smashed the car window' or 'of course, one day he would see a car, check that nobody was looking and smash its window'. We could introduce specific reasons, emotions and additional events that feed into the main action: *'after ten minutes of trying to force the lock, the man gave up* and smashed the window'. We could even move beyond the limits of our own world by imagining a reality where windows talk and feel pain, '"Ouch!" said the car window, as the man smashed it.' In all of these examples, the narrative has been fleshed out to give a much richer sense of meaning.

See 16.2.3 for more on giving a richer sense of meaning in narratives

Key terms

narrative: writing or speech that presents a series of events, characters and places in a coherent form

narrator: a person responsible for writing or speaking a narrative

narratee: the person to whom a narrative is told

time frame: the positioning of a narrative in the past, present or future

5.1.1 Story and narrative discourse

This discussion naturally leads to thinking about categorising two distinctive aspects of a narrative: the building blocks (the events, characters and setting) and the way in which these are represented and organised through language. A useful distinction suggested by Porter Abbott (2008) involves using the terms **story** and **narrative discourse**. A model for thinking about narrative using these terms is shown in Figure 5B.

Figure 5B

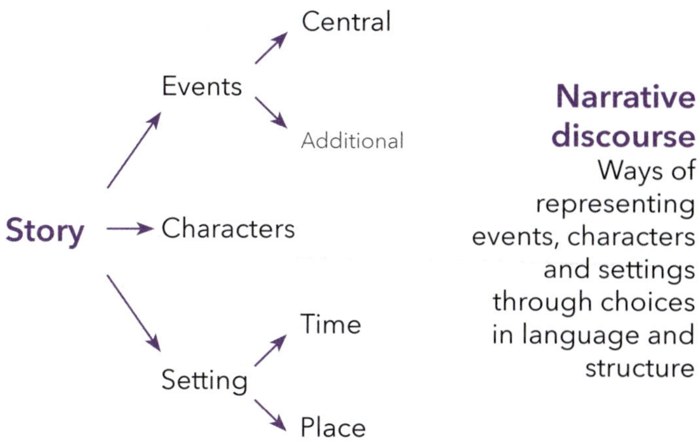

Figure 5B highlights the distinction in a narrative between what happens (the story) and how this gets narrated (the narrative discourse). You'll also notice that we can further classify events as either **central** (main and important to the overall story) or **additional** (less important in terms of the overall story). This distinction is an interesting one since if additional events are included in a narrative, there is probably a very good reason why a narrator has chosen to do so. In other words, foregrounding additional events is a deliberate narrative ploy, driven by contextual factors or some kind of explicit purpose.

Key terms

story: the building blocks of a narrative in terms of events, characters, time and place

narrative discourse: the shaping of the story through choices in language and structure

central events: main events that are crucial to the overall story

additional events: secondary events that are not necessarily crucial to the overall story but through being included may have been highlighted as important

5.1.2 Gap-filling

One other important aspect of a narrative is the way that we use our own stores of knowledge to 'fill in the gaps' as we follow a narrative. Clearly not all of the information that we need to interpret a text comes from the text itself, and we frequently rely on mental maps or **knowledge frames** built up through our general awareness of, and interaction with, the world to help us make meaning. At a global level, this could involve having narrative templates for understanding how certain kinds of stories are structured and operate. For example, Disney's 2013 animated film *Frozen* relies on its viewers understanding the basic structure of fairy stories, as well as having some knowledge of the events and characterisation of Hans Christian Anderson's *The Snow Queen*. At a more local level, we consistently engage in **gap-filling**, drawing on our everyday knowledge to help us make sense of individual words in their context, adding meaning beyond what is explicitly stated in the text. The fact that we do so explains both why communication is possible at all (since if we didn't writers and speakers would need to explain almost every word they wrote or said), and why different interpretations of a text are possible, since different readers will gap-fill in different ways depending on their own background and experience.

Key terms

knowledge frame: a mental store of knowledge about the world gained through experience

gap-filling: the act of adding a rich sense of meaning to individual words and phrases based on our own knowledge and the context in which they appear

ACTIVITY 1

Building a narrative

Read through Text 5A, the opening to the Prologue of *The Suspicions of Mr Whicher, or The Murder of Road Hill House*. Can you identify key elements of the story and the ways in which they are presented? What kinds of gap-filling does a reader need to do in order to construct and understand this narrative?

Text 5A

On Sunday, 15 July 1860, Detective-Inspector Jonathan Whicher of Scotland Yard paid two shillings for a hansom cab to take him from Millbank, just west of Westminster, to Paddington station, the London terminus of the Great Western Railway. There he bought two rail tickets: one to Chippenham, Wiltshire, ninety-four miles away, for 7s.10d., another from Chippenham to Trowbridge, about twenty miles on, for 1s.6d. The day was warm: for the first time that summer, the temperature in London had nudged into the seventies.

Kate Summerscale, *The Suspicions of Mr Whicher, or The Murder of Road Hill House*

Check your answers in the Ideas section on Cambridge Elevate

5.2 Tellability

One of the most important questions to ask is why do narrators narrate? What makes someone want to tell a story? Why is it worth reading and listening to?

The sociolinguist William Labov (1972) coined the term **tellability** to identify the features of a narrative that make it worth telling. He argued that as narratives were the organisation of personal experience, they had to be tellable; that is, there should be a strong reason for people wanting to read, listen and relate to them. Generally, narratives have **high tellability** if they present interesting and engaging material in a compelling style, and **low tellability** if the material is uninteresting and/or the way it is presented is uninspiring.

Tellability can also be understood in the context of the more familiar terms *audience* and *purpose*. If a narrative has a very strong and identifiable purpose or strongly motivates its reader or listener to find one, it is likely to have more tellability than a narrative where the purpose is either so obvious it's not worth paying attention to, or is too obscure and difficult to follow. Equally, a writer or speaker's concept of what is worth telling will to a large extent depend on to whom they are speaking or writing; clearly then, tellability is to some extent both *context specific* and *culturally dependent*.

For example, look at Text 5B, the headline and first lines of a story that appeared on the website of *Hello* magazine.

Key terms

tellability: the features of a story that make it worth telling to an audience

high tellability: the characteristic of a narrative that presents interesting material in an engaging way

low tellability: the characteristic of a narrative that presents uninteresting material in an uninspiring way

Text 5B

The Duke and Duchess of Cambridge remember the fallen on ANZAC day

The Duke and Duchess of Cambridge carried out the final official engagement of their tour of New Zealand and Australia on Friday morning.

William and Kate paid their respects to fallen soldiers by attending the ANZAC Day march and a commemorative service in Canberra before visiting the Australian War Memorial in the country's capital.

Source: Hello magazine

In this case, the story of William and Kate visiting Australia is inherently tellable since their status as members of the British royal family, and the recent birth of their first child, George, meant they had a very high profile. Furthermore, since this was their first visit to Australia and New Zealand, there was also great interest in those countries - possibly even more so than in the UK. The added fact that they attended a march on ANZAC Day (a national day of remembrance in memory of all Australian and New Zealand soldiers who died in conflict around the world) was likely to make this story interesting to an Australian/ New Zealander audience.

ACTIVITY 2

Exploring tellability

Read the following two texts. Text 5C is part of a story about a motorcyclist that was told by a teenage boy to his friends. Text 5D is the opening to a short story called 'The falling dog' by Donald Barthelme that appeared in his 1970 collection *City Life*. What do you think makes these stories tellable? How do the narrators shape and present their tales?

Text 5C

The strange motorcyclist

er (.) there's this um (.) there's this sort of pool in the river in my dad's quarry and um (.) it's really deep and there's this about (.) twenty foot cliff above it and people jump dive off that (.) straight into the water (.) AB (.) he um (.) went up there with a motorcycle (.) and he wore his motorcycle helmet and the superman cape [small laugh] and dived in with um helmet and the superman [laughs] cape (.) cape (.) but um that um story's also been exaggerated and people say that he was trying to kill himself and but he came up for air (1) um (.) he's done some pretty stupid things um (.) with the law as well he (.) stole a gate from the fire brigade place (.) and um (.) cut the gate up and used the bars to (.) um (.) build the go-kart (.) with a welder (.) and stuck a motorcycle engine on it and he got in some pretty deep trouble for that.

Source: N. Coupland, P. Garrett and A. Williams, 'Narrative demands, cultural performance and evaluation: teenage boys' stories for their age peers' in Joanna Thornborrow and Jennifer Coates (eds) *The Sociolinguistics of Narrative*, 2005, pp. 76–77.

Text 5D

The falling dog

Yes, a dog jumped on me out of a high window. I think it was the third floor, or the fourth floor. Or the third floor. Well, it knocked me down. I had my chin on the concrete. Well, he didn't bark before he jumped. It was a silent dog. I was stretched out on the concrete with the dog on my back. The dog was looking at me, his muzzle curled round my ear, his breath was bad, I said, 'Get off!'

He did. He walked away looking back over his shoulder. 'Christ' I said. Crumbs of concrete had been driven into my chin. 'For God's sake', I said. The dog was four or five meters down the sidewalk, standing still. Looking back at me over his shoulder.

Source: Donald Barthelme, *City Life*

Check your answers in the Ideas section on Cambridge Elevate

Summary

- We can distinguish between two key components of a narrative: the story and the narrative discourse.
- We rely on knowledge frames and a process of gap-filling to help us interpret and gain meaning from narratives.
- Narratives need to have high tellability so that readers and listeners will be interested in them and see a value in giving them their attention.

BEGINNING

6

Language level 1: Lexis and semantics

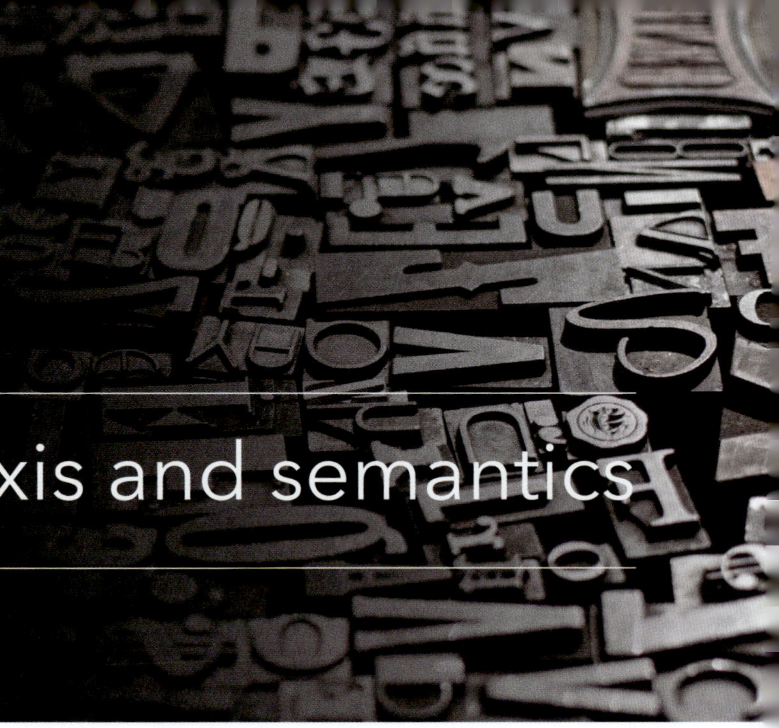

In this unit, you will:

- learn about the different word classes and their sub-classes
- examine how we can categorise the various relationships that exist between words.

6.1 Lexis

Lexis is the term that we use in language studies and linguistics to refer to vocabulary. We group words together on the basis of the particular roles and functions they play both in written and spoken modes of language. These groups are known as **word classes**.

Key terms

word class: a group of words that fulfil the same kind of role and function in speech and writing

noun: a word that names a thing or concept

verb: a word that shows a state of being, action or concept

adjective: a word that modifies a noun

adverb: a word that modifies a verb, an adjective or another adverb

6.1.1 Word classes

ACTIVITY 1

Identifying word classes

Look at Text 6A, which is taken from a promotional leaflet designed to encourage people to visit Kent.

Taking each word in red in turn, describe its function in the sentence as a whole.

Together these categories form three of the four main word classes – **nouns**, **verbs** and **adjectives:**

- **noun:** a word that names a thing or concept
- **verb:** a word that shows a state of being, action or event (we can call this a *process*)
- **adjective:** a word that modifies a noun.

In addition, a fourth major class of word is the **adverb**. Adverbs act in a similar manner to adjectives, but they modify verbs, adjectives or other adverbs, for example:

He ran quickly (adverb modifying the verb 'ran').

It was a very slow game (adverb modifying the adjective 'slow').

They were incredibly well organised (adverb modifying another adverb 'well').

Text 6A

Source: Kent Tourist Board

These four word classes have the most members and are generally open to new membership. Nearly every new word that comes into the English language can be placed in one of these classes. Consequently, the noun, verb, adjective and adverb word classes are known as **open** or **lexical word classes**.

In contrast, a smaller group of word classes exists that tend to have a much smaller membership, have fewer new members and tend to be used to provide connections and cohesion between other words. The following are known as **closed** or **grammatical word classes**:

- **pronoun:** substitutes for a noun, often referring back or forwards to them (e.g., 'he', 'she', 'they', 'it')
- **determiner:** adds detail or clarity to nouns (e.g., 'the', 'my', 'some')
- **preposition:** provides connections between words, often showing a sense of place or time (e.g., 'in', 'on', 'between', 'during')
- **conjunction:** provides connections between the larger structures, phrases, clauses and sentences (see Unit 6, e.g., 'and', 'but', 'because').

Key terms

open (or lexical) word class: a word class that is generally open to new membership

closed (or grammatical) word class: a word class which doesn't readily admit new members; a word class that is generally open to new membership

pronoun: a word that substitutes for a noun

determiner: a word that adds detail or clarity to a noun

preposition: a word that shows connections between other words often showing a sense of place or time

conjunction: a word that connects larger structures such as phrases, clauses and sentences

6.1.2 Sub-classes

Most word classes can also be further examined and broken down into sub-classes. This is useful because it helps you both to understand some subtle differences within the broad word class categories and to fine-tune your identification of a particular feature in order to explain how and why it operates in a text. Table 6A provides details of how we might sub-classify each word class discussed in section 6.1.1.

Table 6A

Word class	Sub-class	Description	Example
Nouns	Proper	Refer to names of people or places	James, England
	Abstract	Refer to states, feelings and concepts that do not have a physical existence	love, anger
	Concrete	Refer to objects that have a physical existence	countable (can be pluralised, e.g., cup) non-countable (do not take a plural form, e.g., furniture)
Verbs	Material	Show actions or events	hit, jump, wash, build
	Relational	Identify properties or show states of being	be, appear, seem, become
	Mental	Show internal processes such as thinking	think, believe, wish
	Verbal	Show external processes of communicating through speech	say, shout, scream, whisper
Adjectives and adverbs	Base	The basic form of an adjective or adverb, modifying another word	big, interesting, carefully
	Comparative	A form used to compare two instances either adding '-er' or using 'more'	The parcel was bigger. That was a more interesting game. He read more carefully.
	Superlative	A form used to compare more than two instances, identifying a best example	That was the biggest parcel. The most interesting game. It was the most carefully he had ever read.
Pronouns	Personal	Refer to people and are differentiated in terms of person (1st, 2nd, 3rd), number (singular or plural) and gender (male or female)	I (1st person singular), you (2nd person singular/plural), she (3rd person, singular, feminine), they (3rd person, plural)
	Demonstrative	Orientate the reader or listener towards a person, object or idea, either nearby or further away	this, these, that, those
	Indefinite	Refer to a person, object or idea that is non-specific	someone, anybody, everything
Determiners	Articles	Show that something is definite or indefinite	the (definite), a/an (indefinite)
	Possessives	Show ownership	my, your, her, our
	Quantifiers	Show either specific or non-specific quantities of a noun	one, two (specific), some, any, a few (non-specific)
Conjunctions	Co-ordinating	Link words or larger structures such as phrases and clauses together where they are equal (see also Unit 6)	and, but, or, yet
	Sub-ordinating	Link clauses together to show one is dependent on another (see also Unit 6)	because, although, while, for

6.1.3 Using word classes to help support descriptive linguistic analysis

It is important to be able to label language as accurately as you can. Indeed, becoming an A/AS Level student means becoming a linguist and joining a community that uses a common metalanguage. This means you need to be precise and avoid making impressionistic comments that are not supported by close attention to language features.

On the other hand, you should remember that your A/AS Level study is about much more than being able to label features outside their context. A descriptive analytical approach always has a strong interpretative element to it. That is, whenever you identify a feature, you should always be trying to say something about its meaning and significance to the text as a whole, drawing on any contextual influences and ideas about mode, genre and register.

ACTIVITY 2

Exploring sub-classes

Using what you have learnt about word classes in sections 6.1.1 and 6.1.2, look at Text 6B. Taking one word class at a time, identify sub-classes and explain why you think these are used in the text.

You could repeat this activity with other texts that you find in order to build up your skills in both identifying world classes accurately, and thinking about how word choices are influenced by contextual factors.

Text 6B

Source: Bowers and Wilkins Group Ltd

6.2 Semantics

Semantics is the study of *meaning* in language. At a straightforward level, this is concerned with what words actually refer to in the real world.

For example, the word 'table' refers to an item of furniture, usually with four legs, that is used by someone sitting at it to undertake some kind of task (e.g., eating or working). This would be a standard dictionary definition. However, within this sense of meaning, there are some blurred edges. For example, people tend to stand rather than sit at a pool table, and sometimes the word is extended into a metaphor as in the newspaper headline 'Arsenal table bid for French striker'.

Equally, words often have very striking meanings when they are used in specific contexts that may be far richer than their dictionary definition. For example, the word 'beautiful' has a pretty standard dictionary definition of 'being attractive', but in specific instances of use, it can have a much more developed sense of meaning, for example when used in an advertisement for a mobile phone to describe its screen as 'vivid deep beautiful'.

6.2.1 Semantic fields and collocations

We can also explore the meanings of words by considering how they combine with other words. At a general level, we can talk of a group of words that are based around a topic or theme as being part of the same **semantic field**. For example, 'player', 'team' and 'ball' are all from the semantic field of sport. Semantic fields can be very broad (as in the example above) or more narrowly defined (for example, we could speak of a more defined semantic field of football containing words such as 'goalpost', 'penalty' and so on). Some words are also commonly associated with other words and can often be found in use with them. For example, words such as 'cosmetic' and 'surgery' are frequently used together in the phrase 'cosmetic surgery' and are known as **collocates**. Some examples of collocations end up becoming what we term **fixed expressions**, with words occurring together so regularly that they become accepted as one long structure rather than separate words, for example, 'at the end of the day', 'see you later' and so on.

Key terms

semantic field: a group of words that fulfil the same kind of role and function in speech and writing

collocates: words that typically appear together

fixed expression: a well-used group of words that becomes accepted and used as one long structure

synonym: a word that has equivalent meaning to another word

euphemism: a more socially acceptable word or phrase

dysphemism: using a blunt or direct word instead of a more polite or indirect alternative, close to taboo

6.2.2 Synonymy, antonymy and hyponymy

Another way that we can explore sense relations between words is by looking in more detail at the relationships between words in terms of meaning. **Synonyms** are words that have largely equivalent meanings but may be used in different ways depending on various contextual factors. Some synonyms are related to regional use and decreased formality (e.g., 'mate' used for 'friend') while others have varying degrees of acceptability within particular contexts. In addition, writers and speakers may choose to use **euphemisms** (more socially acceptable words or phrases) or **dysphemisms** (harsher, more blunt and probably taboo words or phrases). As always, the choice depends on a range of contextual factors.

ACTIVITY 3

Using a thesaurus

Go to a good online dictionary or thesaurus and explore synonymy, euphemism and dysphemism. Choose a fairly neutral word, for example 'toilet', and look at the number of synonyms available. Which of these are clearly euphemistic and which are dysphemistic? In what circumstances might you expect a writer or speaker to use one over another?

Text 6C

Source: Samsung

In contrast to synonyms, **antonyms** are words that have opposite meanings. Some antonyms are complete opposites or *complementary* (such as 'alive' and 'dead' - a person can only be one or the other), while others are *gradable* (such as 'long' and 'short' - something could conceivably be quite short or quite long).

A final relationship is that of **hyponymy**. If we take a word such as 'computer', we can say that it is a more general way of referring to more specific items, such as 'laptop' and 'PC'. In turn, computer could be referred to by a more general term such as 'hardware' (which would include other more specific items such as 'printer' and 'scanner'). So, we have a kind of chain set up along which we can choose to use more or less specific words that are all semantically related. As shown in Figure 6A, a higher word in the chain is seen to be superordinate to a lower level subordinate one.

Figure 6A

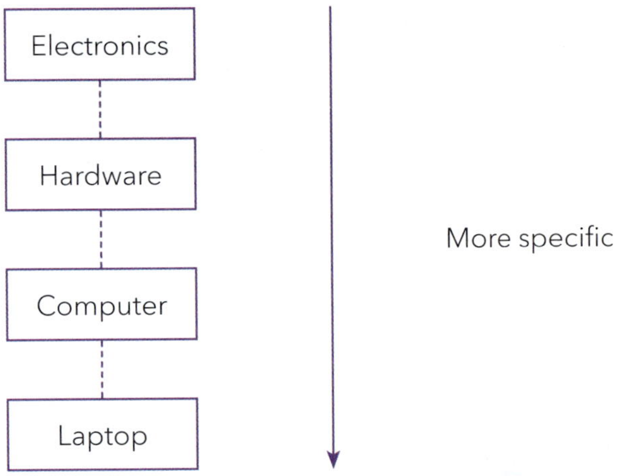

Specificity is often very important to advertisers wanting to sell their products. For example, for a leading camera manufacturer, using the more specific camera model in the advertising copy 'The new and easy to use D3300' is likely to be more effective than the superordinate terms 'camera' or 'electronic equipment'!

6.2.3 Metaphor

A final, useful and very interesting aspect of semantics relates to the way in which we can understand an object, idea or concept metaphorically in terms of something else.

Although you might think that **metaphors** are only to be found in literary texts, much of the everyday language we use is rich in metaphorical constructions. Indeed, much of the way we conceptualise and view the world can be understood in terms of metaphor.

Key terms

antonyms: words that have opposite meanings

hyponymy: the way of viewing the relationship between more general and specific words

metaphor: a structure that presents one thing in terms of another

For example, we typically understand abstract concepts, such as our lives and emotions, by seeing them in more concrete physical terms. Expressions such as 'heading in the right direction', 'moving on with my life', and 'going sideways' are all examples of a broad metaphor that *life is a journey*. Equally, talking of being 'boiling with rage' expresses an emotion (anger) as a physical entity (liquid), while sayings such as 'I'm on a high' or 'I feel low' rely on a very conventional way of expressing feelings based on vertical orientation (here feeling good is understood with reference to standing up straight, while being physically low gives a kind of structure for understanding being emotionally low).

ACTIVITY 4

Metaphor in advertising

Look at the advertisement in Text 6C. How would you describe the use of metaphor here? Explain how you think the advertisement works and what associations the reader is expected to make.

Summary

- We can distinguish between words based on their role and function. We call these categories word classes.
- Word classes can be divided into sub-classes to give a more focused set of categories.
- Semantics is the study of what words mean and the relationships that exist between words.

BEGINNING

7 Language level 2: Grammar

In this unit, you will:

- learn about the ways that words form larger structures within utterances and texts
- examine and explore the constituent elements of phrases, clauses and sentences.

7.1 The rank scale

The rank scale offers a neat way of explaining how language is systematic. Broadly speaking, it provides a model for explaining how larger language units are built up from smaller ones. Figure 7A shows this relationship.

Figure 7A: The linguistic rank scale

morpheme	word	phrase	clause	sentence	text

smaller units ⟶ **larger units**

In this unit, we will be concerned with two elements of grammar: the study of the morpheme (**morphology**) and the study of phrases, clauses and sentences (**syntax**).

During this unit (and indeed throughout the rest of this book), we will also be stressing the importance of taking a **descriptive** approach to language study that draws attention to how language is actually used. The term 'grammar' can often be associated with more **prescriptive** approaches that emphasise rules and notions of correctness, and that view language as deficient if it doesn't follow these rules.

Key terms

morphology: the study of word formation

syntax: the study of how words form larger structures such as phrases, clauses and sentences

descriptive: taking an approach to language study that focuses on how language is actually used

prescriptive: taking an approach to language study that focuses on rules and notions of correctness

7.2 Morphology

Morphology is the study of how words are formed. For example, a noun in its plural form such as *apples*, is made up of two morphemes, a base or **root** *apple*, and an ending or **suffix** *-s*. In some words, the root has an element added before it, for example the adjective *unhealthy* has a **prefix** *un-* added to its root *healthy*. Together prefixes and suffixes are known as **affixes**.

Some affixes have an **inflectional function** as they show the tense of verbs and the plural form of nouns (for example *-s*). Others have a **derivational function** as they help to form a new word by being added to a root (for example *un-*).

ACTIVITY 1

Forming words

Look at the following prefixes, all of which have a derivational function in word formation. What meanings do these prefixes hold? How many words can you think of that start with these? Using a dictionary, find out which ones are the most common in the English vocabulary system. Are there particular types of word that each prefix tends to attach to, to form a new one?

1 ab-	6 de-	11 pre-
2 anti-	7 ex-	12 pro-
3 bi-	8 inter-	13 semi-
4 cent-	9 mono-	14 trans-
5 contra-	10 post-	15 uni-

Key terms

root: a morpheme that can stand on its own and can usually form a word in its own right

suffix: a morpheme that comes after a root word to modify its meaning

prefix: a morpheme that goes before a root word to modify its meaning

affix: the overall term for an addition to a root (a prefix or suffix) to modify its meaning or create a new word (Cf. **infix**: an affix inserted inside a root word to create a new word or modify its meaning (eg. abso-blooming-lutely))

inflectional function: the way that an affix shows a grammatical category such as a verb tense or a plural noun

derivational function: the way that an affix helps form a new word by attaching itself to a root

7.3 Phrases

As we saw in Unit 5, words can be categorised into word classes related to the function they serve and the kinds of characteristics group members display. Moving up the rank scale, these words can form larger structures called phrases. In this section, we will concentrate on the two most important type of phrase: the **noun phrase** and the **verb phrase**.

7.3.1 Noun phrases

Noun phrases are groups of words centred round a noun that acts as the 'head' of the phrase. Other words in the phrase fulfil certain functions in relation to this head.

For example, the noun *television* can form the larger structure *the television*, which is a noun phrase with a **head word** *television* and a determiner *the*. It can also form a longer noun phrase, *the expensive television* (this time containing a determiner and a **pre-modifier**, *expensive*). And, it can form an even longer noun phrase – *the expensive television in the corner* (this time adding a **qualifier** that doesn't modify the quality of the television itself but rather gives information as to its location as a **post-modifier**). Together then a noun phrase's constituent elements are:

- head word (h)
- determiner (d)
- modifier (m)
- qualifier (q).

Noun phrases can then be labelled using the following notation.

d	m	h	q		
The	expensive	television	in	the	corner

Key terms

noun phrase: a group of words built around a noun

verb phrase: a group of words built around a head (main) verb

head word: the main noun in the phrase

pre-modifier: a word that goes before the head noun to add detail or clarify some aspect of it

qualifier: an additional word or phrase that adds some further detail to the noun

post-modifier: a word that comes after the head noun to add detail or clarify some aspect of it

ACTIVITY 2

Connecting noun phrases to readership and purpose

Look at Text 7A. This appeared in a lifestyle magazine aimed at adult female readers. What can you say about the use of noun phrases in this text? How does this relate to the text's implied readership and purpose?

Check your responses in the Ideas section on Cambridge Elevate

Text 7A

Source: Advertising Archive Ltd

7.3.2 Verb phrases

In a similar way to a noun phrase, a verb phrase is built around a head word, the main verb. Verb phrases are generally less complex than noun phrases but can, in addition to main verbs, include auxiliary verbs that help to show either tense (the **primary auxiliary verbs** *be*, *do* and *have*), or show someone's degree of commitment towards an event or person (the **modal auxiliary verbs** such as *may*, *could*, *must*).

Key terms

primary auxiliary verb: an auxiliary verb that joins with a main verb to show tense

modal auxiliary verb: an auxiliary verb that joins with a main verb to show the degree of commitment towards an event or person that a speaker holds

ACTIVITY 3

Modal auxiliary verbs and commitment

It is possible to place modal auxiliary verbs along a continuum to show degrees of strength towards a commitment. Look at the modal auxiliaries (in red) in the sentences below, which all relate to degrees of possibility. Using the contextual detail provided, place the modal auxiliaries in order of modal force. Are there occasions when a speaker might choose one form over another? What might influence their choice?

Context: two friends discussing a football match

1 Liverpool should beat Man City.
2 Liverpool will beat Man City.
3 Liverpool might beat Man City.
4 Liverpool must beat Man City.

7.4 Clauses

In the same way that words form phrases, phrases form larger structures called **clauses**. These are groups of words centred round a verb phrase.

Clauses also have constituent elements that we can label and comment on depending on their function. In a clause, the verb phrase combines with other phrases as shown in Table 7A.

Table 7A

Constituent element	Description
Subject (S): usually a noun phrase	Acts as the key focus of the clause and is often the focus of a relational verb process or the agent of a material verb process
Object (O): usually a noun phrase	Identifies the entity being acted on by the action of a verb process
Complement (C): usually a noun phrase	Is the attribute of a subject in a relational verb process
Adverbial (A): usually an adverb or prepositional phrase	Identifies the circumstances of a verb process in terms of time, place or manner

In the examples, we can label the constituent elements:

S V
1 I awoke

S V O
2 I turned on the television

S V C
3 I was tired

S V O O
4 I lent my friend my iPad

S V O A
5 I put the book on the floor

Notice that example 4 has two objects (a verb like *lent* needs both a *direct object* – the object being lent; and an *indirect object* – the person receiving the object).

7.4.1 Multi-clause structures

In turn, clauses can form larger multi-clause structures through the processes of **coordination** and **subordination**.

Coordinated clauses are joined by the coordinating conjunctions *and*, *but*, *or* and are independent in so far as they can stand on their own and make complete sense. For example, the multi-clause structure *I went into town and met my friends* contains two single clauses that could stand on their own if the coordinator were not there – *I went into town* and *I met my friends*. Traditional grammar calls these single clause structures 'simple sentences' and coordinated clauses 'compound sentences' and these may well be terms you are familiar with from your previous studies.

Subordinated clauses are a little more complicated since the process of subordination means there will always be a main clause (a unit that can stand on its own and make complete sense) and any number of subordinate clauses (that depend on the addition of a main clause to make complete sense). Again, the term 'complex sentence' to describe subordinated clauses will probably be a term you are familiar with from your previous studies.

In fact, a subordinate clause fulfils the role of a constituent element within the main clause. The most common role is that of an adverbial using a subordinating conjunction. In the following example, the subordinate clause functions as an **adverbial clause**.

A S V O
Although I went into town, I didn't meet my friends (adverbial clause)

Subordinate clauses can also function as **noun clauses** that act as a subject, object or complement, for example:

S V C
Meeting my friends was not planned for (noun clause acting as subject)

S V C
I did not know *that I could meet my friends* (noun clause acting as complement)

Key terms

clause: groups of words centred around a verb phrase

coordination: the joining of two clauses that gives them equal weighting

subordination: the joining of two clauses that gives one clause (the main clause) more weighting than another clause - or clauses (the subordinate clause(s))

adverbial clause: a subordinate clause that functions as an adverbial

noun clause: a subordinate clause that functions as a subject, object or complement

7.4.2 Active and passive voice

Within a clause, agency can be emphasised or downplayed by presenting an event in either the **active** or **passive voice**.

Look at the examples below, taken from two newspaper headlines, after a fox had attacked a young baby in London:

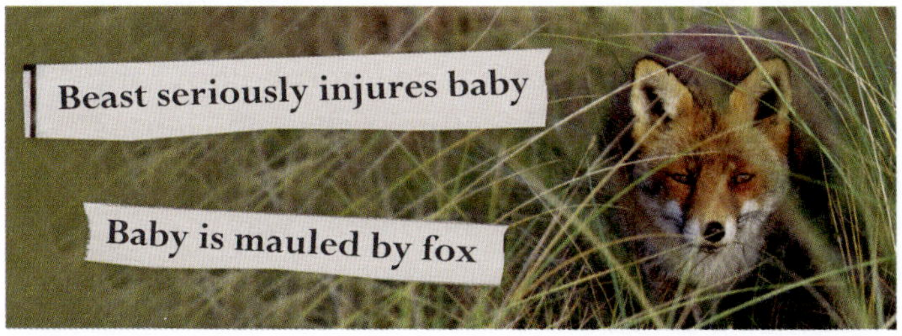

In the first example, written in the active voice, the entity responsible for carrying out the verb (the agent) is placed in the subject position of the clause. This gives prominence to the fox and its action (emphasised by the verb phrase being modified by the adverb *seriously*).

In the second example, written in the passive voice, the entity affected by the verb (in this case the baby) is placed in the subject position in the clause, and the agent positioned at end of the clause. In this case, prominence is given to the victim of the attack.

In fact, some passive constructions omit the agent entirely. This can have the effect of placing even more emphasis on the entity affected by the verb and/or avoiding drawing attention to the person or group responsible for the action. Text producers may choose to use this form for a number of different purposes, for example to sensationalise an event or to tactfully avoid identifying the cause of an action. For example, look at the difference between the following two ways of presenting the same event:

1 The council closed the children's playground (active).
2 The children's playground was closed (passive).

In the first, the blame for the closure is emphasised; in the second, agency is removed so that the focus is just on the event itself. In fact a third possible way of representing this event goes even further to remove any possible sense of agency or blame by showing the closure as a completed action.

3 The children's playground closed.

Key terms

active voice: agent in subject position for prominence; verb phrase in present or past tense

passive voice: agent omitted or placed later in the clause using a prepositional phrase; verb phrase changes to a form of *to be* + participle form (verb root + en/ed)

ACTIVITY 4

Active and passive in newspaper headlines

Find a selection of newspaper headlines and consider how they present events in either the active or passive voice. Why might the writers want to either emphasise or downplay agency? Re-write the headlines from the active to the passive or the passive to the active. What is the effect?

7.5 Sentences

As we saw in section 7.4, the terms simple, compound and complex sentences can be used to describe single or multi-clause structures. This fits in with the traditional definition of the sentence as having to contain a verb. However in Text 7B, taken from the ghost story *The Woman in Black* by Susan Hill, the sentences towards the end do not contain a verb, but are recognised as such through the use of a capital letter and full stop. These **orthographic sentences** are a common feature in written texts and are often used to give a punchy, emphatic stress to an idea or feeling. In Text 7B, the orthographic sentences might be said to emphasise the increasing sound of a strange noise that the narrator has heard and his own increasing terror.

Key terms

orthographic sentence: a 'sentence' marked by a capital letter and full stop but containing no verb

Text 7B

There was something in that room and I could not get to it, nor would I dare to, if I were able. I told myself it was a rat or trapped bird, fallen down the chimney into the hearth and unable to get out again. But the sound was not that of some small panic-stricken creature. Bump bump. Pause. Bump bump. Pause. Bump bump. Bump bump. Bump bump.

Susan Hill, *The Woman in Black*

7.5.1 Sentence functions

In use, clauses and sentences have one of four functions:

1 forming statements (e.g., *I read a ghost story.*)
2 forming questions (e.g., *Did you read that ghost story?*)
3 giving commands (e.g., *Read that ghost story!*)
4 making exclamations (e.g., *What a scary ghost story!*)

These functions tend to be associated with a particular grammatical form, although there are of course many exceptions to this. Statements tend to have a straightforward subject-verb-object/complement structure; questions begin with primary or modal auxiliaries or wh- words; commands start with a verb phrase and have no subject; while exclamations usually start with a wh- word and then a noun phrase.

Sometimes there is a tension between a sentence's grammatical form and its actual function. For example, think of all of the ways that you might ask someone to shut a door that has been left open. You might use one of the following:

1 Shut the door (grammatical form = command).
2 Can you shut the door (grammatical form = question)?
3 The door is open (grammatical form = statement).
4 What a terrible draught (grammatical form = exclamative)!

While all of these sentences have different forms, they all essentially function as commands. Their use would depend on the context in which they were being spoken and, above all, the relationship between you and the person you were speaking to. Examples 1 and 2 are more direct and might be used if you knew someone well, whereas 3 and 4 are more indirect and potentially less likely to cause offence (although both could well be used in a very sarcastic way!). These examples show that there is not always a straightforward relationship between form and function.

Summary

- The study of grammar can be divided into looking at word formation (morphology) and looking at larger structures (phrases, clauses and sentences).
- The linguistic rank scale offers a way of explaining how larger elements are built out of smaller ones.
- Text producers often manipulate and shape grammatical forms for specific effects.

BEGINNING

8

Language level 3: Phonetics, phonology and prosodics

In this unit, you will:

- learn about some basic components of the sound system and how it is used
- learn about how different aspects of the sound system play a role in making meaning.

8.1 Definitions of phonetics, phonology and prosodics

'**Phonetics**' and '**phonology**' both refer to areas of language study that focus on sound. They are in fact very closely related terms and can sometimes be difficult to distinguish. However, generally, we can say that phonology is the area of study that refers to the abstract sound system, while phonetics is concerned with investigating how sounds are actually produced by language users. In turn, **prosodics** is the study of how speakers can shape meanings through emphasising certain aspects of intonation, speed and volume.

8.2 The IPA

The **International Phonetic Alphabet (IPA)** is a system for showing the different sounds that we use in English in a way that the conventional alphabet for written language cannot do. For example, think about the words 'laughter' and 'naughty', where the 'augh' is pronounced in very different ways. Equally, whole words such as 'row' (an argument) and 'row' (something you do in a boat) have exactly the same spelling but are pronounced in very different ways. Pairs of words like these are known as **heterophones** (in contrast **homophones** are words that are pronounced identically but have different meanings and often spellings).

Key terms

phonetics: the area of study that is concerned with investigating how sounds are actually produced by language users

phonology: the area of study that refers to the more abstract sound system

prosodics: the study of how speakers can shape meanings through emphasising certain aspects of intonation, speed and volume

International Phonetic Alphabet (IPA): a system for showing the different sounds possible

heterophones: words that have the same spelling but very different pronunciations and meanings

homophones: words that are pronounced the same but have a different meaning and may have different spellings; e.g., there and their

The IPA therefore allows us to distinguish between sounds so that we can describe how they are used in specific instances more easily and systematically. As A/AS Level students, you'll find this useful in helping you to explore data (either for exam units or non-examined assessment) where pronunciation or the representation of pronunciation is important to understanding an utterance or a text. The IPA is also useful in bringing together phonology and phonetics into a single area of studying the significance of sound in the making of meaning.

There are many examples of the IPA available online, and some of them are very complex. As an A/AS Level student, you only need to have a working knowledge of a table like the one provided in Figure 8A. The underlined part of each word corresponds to the IPA symbol but note that this is how the word would be pronounced in received pronunciation (RP); for example, the vowel in the word 'bath' is pronounced as /ɑː/ in RP but in many parts of the country, and by many users, as /æ/.

ACTIVITY 1

Exploring using the IPA

One of the easiest ways to explore how the IPA works is to practise using it. Transcribe your name and those of your family and friends, as you would say them, using the IPA symbols. Now transcribe this sentence about the singer Rihanna.

Rihanna has sold over 30 million albums and 120 million singles worldwide.

Compare your transcriptions with another student. Do you notice any differences? Can any of these differences be explained in terms of people's linguistic backgrounds?

8.2.1 Consonants

The consonant sounds shown in the IPA table can be grouped in terms of how they are articulated in the mouth. All consonant sounds involve the restriction of airflow by **articulators**: either the lips coming together (labial), or the tongue being positioned against the teeth (dental) or in some part of the roof of the mouth (alveolar ridge, hard and soft palate) as shown in Figure 8B.

Key terms

articulators: the vocal organs above the larynx, including the lips, teeth, tongue and hard palate that help to form consonant sounds

Figure 8A: The International Phonetic Alphabet (IPA)

Consonants

p	pip	ʒ	measure
b	bib	h	hen
t	ten	tʃ	church
d	den	dʒ	judge
k	cat	m	man
g	get	n	now
f	fish	ŋ	sing
θ	thigh	l	let
ð	this	r	ride
s	set	w	wet
z	zoo	j	yet
ʃ	ship		

Vowels

Short vowels		Long vowels		Diphthongs	
ɪ	pit	iː	bean	aɪ	bite
e	pet	ɜː	burn	eɪ	bait
æ	pat	ɑː	barn	ɔɪ	boy
ɒ	pot	ɔː	born	əʊ	toe
ʌ	but	uː	boon	aʊ	house
ʊ	book			ʊə	poor
ə	mother			ɪə	ear
				eə	air

Figure 8B

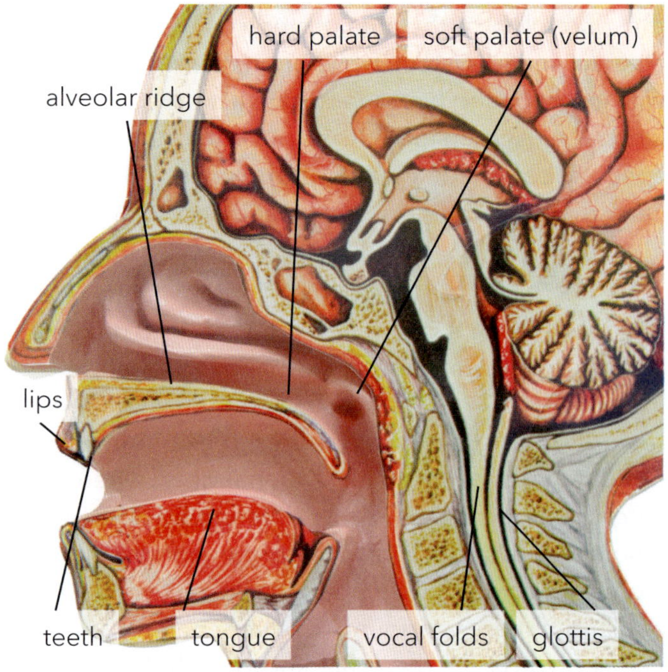

These consonant sounds can be categorised as in Table 8A.

Table 8A: Consonant sounds

Consonant group	Description	Members
Plosive	Produced by the articulators coming together to stop the airflow and then being released	b, p (labial); t, d (alveolar); k, g (soft palate)
Fricative	Produced by the articulators positioned together but a small gap remaining through which the sound comes	θ, ð (dental) f, v (labio-dental: lower lip against upper teeth) s, z (alveolar)
Affricate	Produced by the articulators coming together, then released but in a way that is similar to the friction sound of a fricative	dʒ, tʃ (hard palate)
Nasal	Produced by articulators stopping the airflow with a release through the nose	m (labial); n (alveolar); ŋ (soft palate)
Lateral	Produced by articulators coming together and air being released over the sides of the tongue	l (alveolar)
Approximant	Produced in a similar way to other consonant sounds but without the articulators fully coming together	w (labial); r (alveolar); j (hard palate)

8.2.2 Vowels

Vowels, on the other hand, do not involve any restriction and release of airflow in the mouth. Vowels can be grouped depending on whether they are short, long or are **diphthongs** (a combination of two sounds where a speaker moves from an initial sound to a second sound across the vowel). You can see how the vowel sounds in English are categorised by looking back at the IPA in Figure 8A.

8.3 Sound iconicity

Text producers use sound patterns in the same way as other language features to help create effects. Often this involves using patterns where sounds mirror the actions they describe, or which are intended to draw attention to some relationship between sound and form. This is known as **sound iconicity**.

Key terms

diphthong: a vowel sound that is the combination of two separate sounds, where a speaker moves from one to another

sound iconicity: the matching of sound to an aspect of meaning

8.3.1 Sound patterns in literature

Literary texts often make extensive use of sound iconicity. Read Text 8A, an extract from a poem by the First World War poet Siegfried Sassoon, which describes a group of soldiers in the trenches. Think about the poet's use of sound as you read these lines and try to picture the context in which they were written.

Text 8A

Stepping along the barred trench-board, often splashing
Wretchedly where the sludge was ankle-deep

Siegfried Sassoon, 'A Working Party'

We can explore the ways in which Sassoon uses sound to mirror the scene in the trenches as follows:

- The repetition of the plosive sounds /p/ and /b/ mirror the thudding of the soldiers' boots on the trench-board. A repeated set of consonant sounds for effect is also known as **consonance**.
- The initial consistent patterning of vowel sounds: /e/, /ɪ/, /æ/, /ɒ/, /ə/ (short), /ɑː/ (long), /e/ (short), /ɔː/ (long), again possibly mirrors the marching boots; a string of short vowels /ɒ/, /e/, /æ/, /ɪ/, /e/, /e/, long vowels /iː/, /ɛə/, short vowels, /ə/, /ʌ/, /ɒ/, /æ/ and two final long vowels /ɔː/ and /iː/ represent a more frantic movement and then the sense of the boots taking a long time to be removed from the increasing sludge. A repeated set of vowel sounds for effect is also known as **assonance**.
- Fricative and affricate sounds /s/, /tʃ/, /ʃ/, and /dʒ/ mimic the sound of the mud and water in the environment of the trench. These kinds of repeated fricative sounds are also known as **sibilance**.

Some of these patterns rely on **lexical onomatopoeia**, where there is a clear association between the sound of a word and its meaning. A word like 'sludge', for example, works on our ability to draw some kind of association between the /dʒ/ sound and the messy, thick mud of the trench. Text producers may also use **non-lexical onomatopoeia** to create similar effects. This involves using 'non-words' whose sounds nonetheless are intended to signify some meaning, for example 'brrrm' to describe the noise of a car or 'jger-jger-jger-jger' to describe the rhythm of a moving train.

Key terms

consonance: a pattern of repeated consonant sounds for effect

assonance: a pattern of repeated vowel sounds for effect

sibilance: a pattern of repeated fricative sounds, especially /s/, for effect

lexical onomatopoeia: words that have some associated meaning between their sound and what they represent

non-lexical onomatopoeia: 'non-words' that nonetheless are intended to signify some meaning through their sound

8.3.2 Sound patterns in non-literary texts

Text producers often rely on both very obvious and more subtle kinds of sound patterns, depending on the product they are advertising. Brand names in particular can provide very fruitful opportunities to explore how sounds are used in innovative ways.

ACTIVITY 2

Maluma and Takete

Look at the two shapes in Figure 8C. Which do you think best fits with the word 'Maluma' and which with 'Takete'? Give reasons for your decision.

Check your responses in the Ideas section on Cambridge Elevate

'... where the sludge was ankle-deep'

'A Working Party', Siegfried Sassoon

Figure 8C

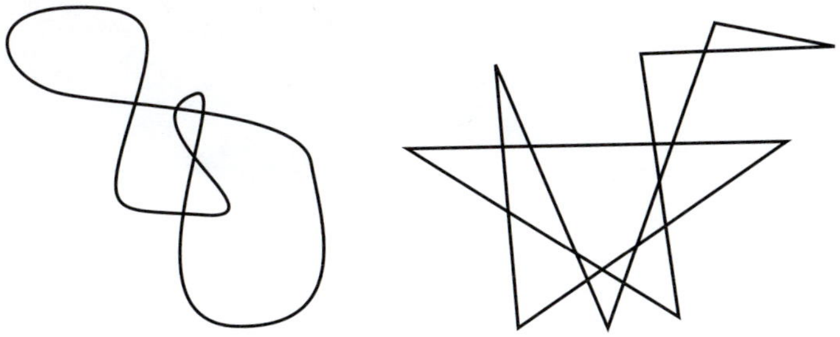

Jokes are another genre that rely on the manipulation of sound patterns for effects. The notoriously bad jokes that appear inside Christmas crackers use a range of strategies to produce comic effects. You can find many examples of these online. For instance, the website for 'pun of the day' has plenty of jokes that you could explore in terms of **phonological manipulation**. See Text 8B for one example.

Find examples of puns via Cambridge Elevate

Text 8B

I keep reading The Lord of the Rings *over and over.*
I guess it's just force of hobbit.

Source: punoftheday

The joke 'works' here through a process of substitution, 'hobbit' for 'habit', with one phoneme /ɒ/ replacing another /æ/, to make a different word. It is the fact that 'hobbit' is associated with *The Lord of the Rings*, whereas 'habit' is part of the fixed expression 'force of habit', that is the basis for the humour. In fact many jokes rely on this kind of very simple substitution involving **minimal pairs** like 'hobbit' and 'habit'.

Key terms

phonological manipulation: making creative changes in sound patterns to give certain effects

minimal pair: two words that differ in only one single sound

8.4 Prosodics

Prosodic features provide non-verbal meaning, relying not on what speakers say but how they say it. The following sections show ways in which speakers vary what they say as a way of expressing meaning in non-verbal ways.

8.4.1 Variation in pitch and intonation

Differences in pitch can often signal important emotional aspects behind meaning. For example, a speaker lowering or raising the pitch of their voice can show different attitudes, while rising or falling intonation can often be an important indicator of meaning, for example, the rising intonation in the final part of the utterance 'I loved that film, didn't you?' would suggest that a speaker is seeking agreement.

8.4.2 Variation in volume

Differences in volume can convey a number of possible emotions as well as emphasising certain parts of words that a speaker wants to emphasise.

8.4.3 Variation in speed

Speeding up might convey a speaker's excitement or anger, while slowing down might convey their uncertainty or a lack of commitment towards a proposition.

ACTIVITY 3

Thinking about prosodics

As you work through the course and explore spoken language (and its representation in written texts), make a note of how speakers use pitch, intonation, volume and speed to help emphasise meaning. You could make a start by looking at some political speeches on the official White House YouTube channel. It contains a wide range of speeches by the current US president, as well as others by important American politicians and social commentators.

Watch videos of speeches by the American president via Cambridge Elevate

Summary

- We can study how sound works in speech and writing by looking at it both as a system and how it is employed by actual users, and at how non-verbal aspects of meaning are conveyed through prosodic features.
- The study of the sound system can enable us to say important things about how meaning is shaped in a variety of texts and discourses.

BEGINNING

9 Language level 4: Graphology

In this unit, you will:

- learn the key aspects of graphology
- explore how multimodal texts rely on readers and listeners working with writing, images and sound to make meaning.

9.1 Understanding graphology

Many texts rely on the use of layout, space, images, colour and different font types to help convey their meaning. Often, these can be used in very obvious ways to help support meaning; at other times, their use may be more subtle. In all cases, graphological features tend to combine with other language levels to help support interpretation.

An obvious example of a text that relies on graphological features is shown in Text 9A, a page from a story for very young children, *How to Catch a Star*, by Oliver Jeffers.

In Text 9A, the author has set out the page following the conventions of a picture book with the text being supported by images. These images are focused and straightforward (there aren't too many of them), and the space around ensures that they are seen as important. They are also in colour to give them more prominence. The images largely represent the things they stand for in very straightforward ways (a spaceship and a boy), and support the accompanying writing that is likely to be read with them. The images convey meaning in their own right; the boy's hand drawn towards his face suggests pensiveness (linking to the verb 'thought' in the main body of the writing). The writing itself uses a font that has childish associations, is fairly large, and is spaced out evenly across the top of the page. Of course, the layout and set of features are heavily determined by the text's intended audience (young children) and the context in which reading takes place (likely to be read by a parent to a child, possibly at bedtime).

Text 9A

He thought he could fly up in his spaceship and just grab the star. But his spaceship had run out of petrol last Tuesday when he flew to the moon.

Source: Oliver Jeffers, *How to Catch a Star*

Text 9A gives a quick flavour of the kinds of features associated with graphology. In the following sections, we will revisit each of these in turn.

9.2 Types of graphological features

9.2.1 Layout, shape and space

The **layout** of a text is often related to its genre. For example, shopping lists, emails, menus and advertisements all tend to have prototypical layout features so that they are visually easily recognisable.

See 3.2 for more on genre

See 3.1.3 for more on prototype models

ACTIVITY 1

Layout, space and shape

Find some examples of texts from specific genres that make unconventional use of layout, shape and space. Can you account for these in terms of the text's audience, purpose and the ways in which meaning is likely to be understood? Do any of these texts rely on readers making intertextual links?

9.2.2 Icons and symbols

Largely speaking, images are signs of things (they represent things that are in the real world). If we look again at the images in Text 9A, we can see that the image of the rocket is a direct picture of the thing that it represents. These kinds of signs are **iconic**. On the other hand, the image of the boy whilst clearly standing iconically as a representation of a young male child, has, as we saw, a more associative meaning. In this case, the image also functions symbolically to convey a certain emotion or state of mind. Of course, the way that we make the association between the image and its **symbolic** meaning is always bound by some kind of cultural, social or cognitive convention. In this case, the shared understanding of our bodies acting in a certain way when we are thinking (arms crossed, eyes looking downwards) helps us to make sense of the image and attach a sense of meaning to it.

Another conventional way in which signs act symbolically is when they make use of colours that are strongly associative. For example, red is seen in some cultures as a sign of danger (ironically many cultures also perceive this as a sign of passion!). Text producers often make use of this kind of general knowledge, as well as expecting readers or listeners to draw on any highly personal associations that might come from their own experience.

9.2.3 Typography

Typographical features are those related to the way that fonts are used and set out in texts. These may include aspects of type, size, colour, effects (for example, using bold, underlined or italicised font), the choice of background against which a font is set, and any spacing that is used. The careful use of typographical features can help readers to follow writing clearly, highlight important points and produce dramatic effects.

9.2.4 Multimodal texts

Many of the texts we read rely on an interaction of written and visual codes. This is especially the case in certain genres, such as young children's literature (Text 9A) and advertising (Text 9B), where meaning is often dependent on the interplay of writing and images. Texts that rely on more than one code or mode are known as **multimodal texts**.

Key terms

layout: the physical organisation of a text

iconic sign: a sign or image that is a direct picture of the thing it represents

symbolic sign: a sign or image where an associated meaning is drawn from some shared degree of knowledge

typographical feature: a feature related to the use of fonts in texts

multimodal text: a text that relies on the interplay of different codes (e.g., the visual and the written) to help shape meaning

We encounter multimodal texts all the time and develop our ability to work with the conventions of different codes very quickly, to the point where we do it with very little effort whatsoever. For example, look at Text 9B, which is part of a larger map outlining key bus routes in central London.

To read Text 9B, we have to work with both written and visual codes. Visually, we rely on our understanding that the different coloured lines represent different bus routes (there is actually a key explaining this on another part of the map). We also 'read' the London underground and national rail icons as representing parts of the routes where there are stations (for example, Paddington, Marble Arch and Baker Street). Furthermore, a shaded green area represents a park, and iconic images are used to show areas of interest: Lord's Cricket Ground, Sherlock Holmes Museum, London Zoo and Madame Tussauds. These are all used in conjunction with writing that lists the names of key places, stops and stations, and numbers that represent the different routes (linked to the coloured line that shows its direction).

ACTIVITY 2

Multimodal texts

You could explore multimodal texts in more detail by finding further examples that rely on the interplay of written and visual codes, and explaining how these

Text 9B

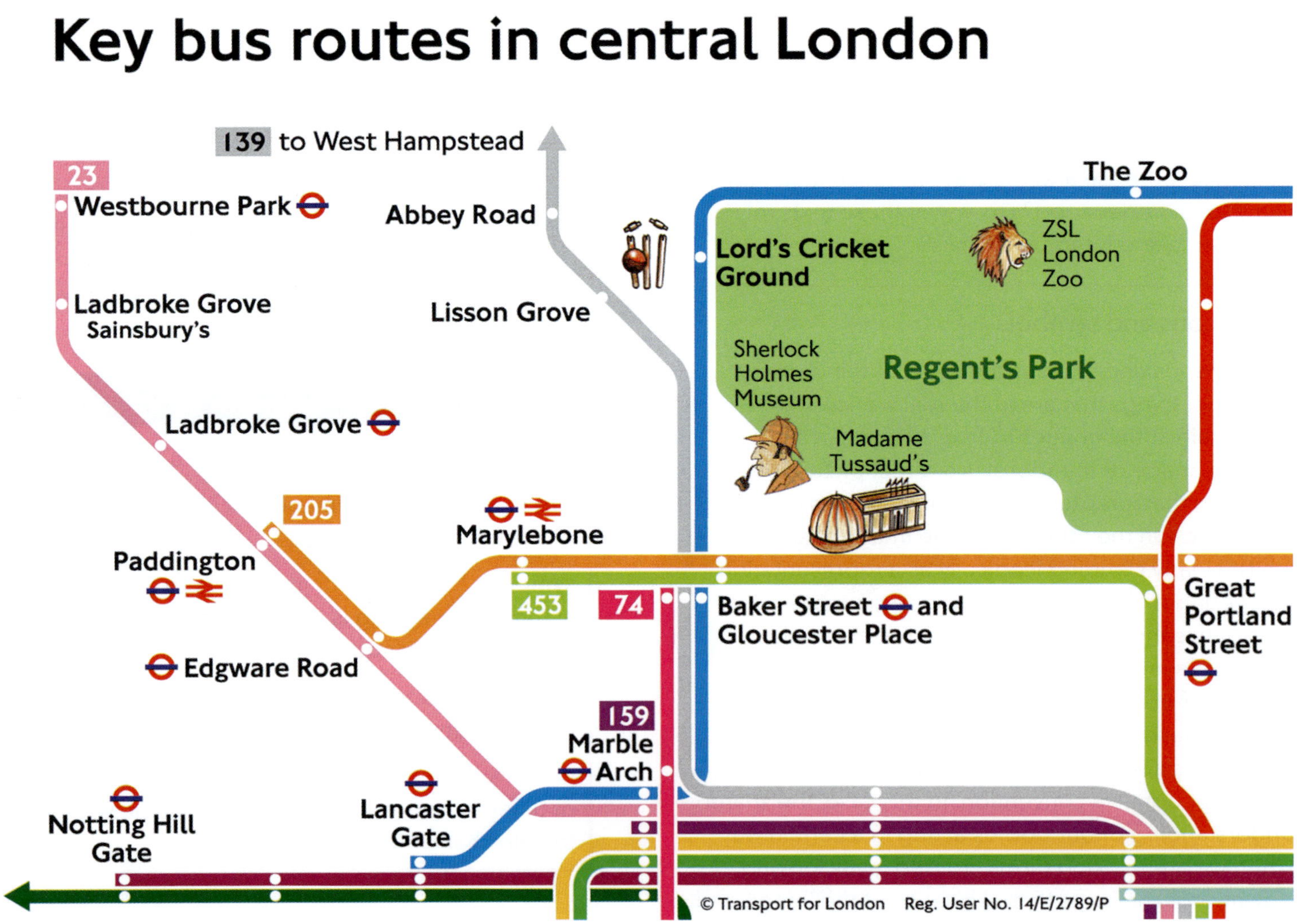

Source: Transport for London

work to help create meaning. You could look online to see how video advertising makes use of a third type of code (sound) to support words and visuals.

Explore the LonelyPlanet YouTube channel via Cambridge Elevate for examples of the interplay of written and visual codes

ACTIVITY 3

Graphology and other language levels

Draw together your learning on this unit by looking at Text 9C. This leaflet was produced by the Nottinghamshire Healthcare NHS Trust to encourage dental health in children. How does the text producer use graphological features? How do these features combine with features at the other language levels?

Text 9C

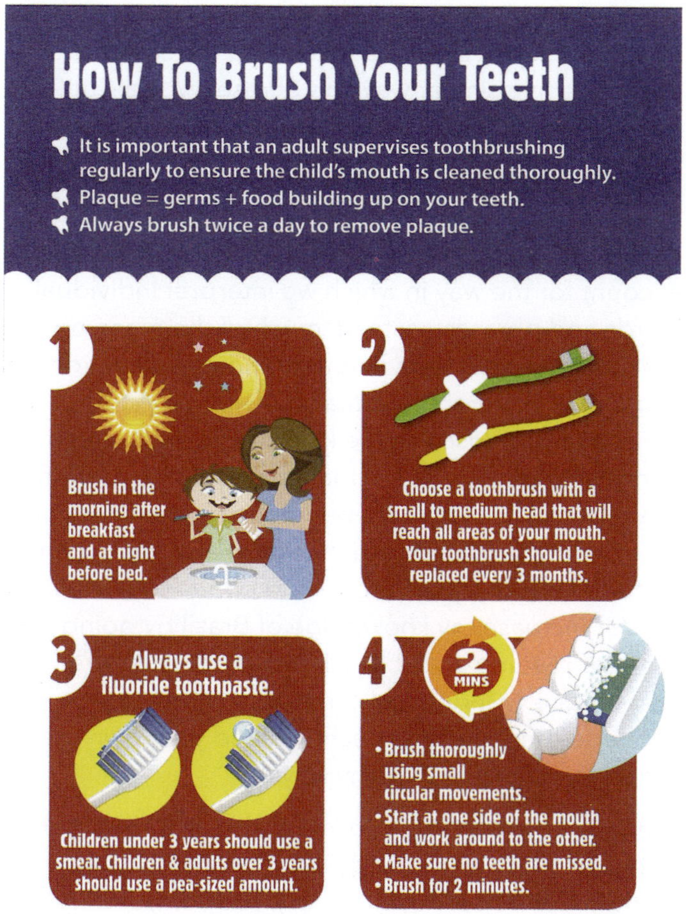

Source: Nottinghamshire Healthcare NHS Trust

Check your responses in the Ideas section on Cambridge Elevate

Summary

- Graphological features can play a key role in shaping meaning.
- A large number of texts are multimodal, relying on a combination of written and visual codes.
- It is important to consider how graphological features combine with features at other language levels.

BEGINNING

10

Language level 5: Pragmatics

In this unit, you will:

- learn that contextual factors are an important part of how meaning is generated
- be introduced to the key pragmatic principles of cooperation, politeness and deixis.

10.1 Background knowledge

Pragmatics is the area of language study associated with exploring how contextual factors influence meaning. One way of looking at this is to explore how the act of interpretation itself relies on all kinds of background knowledge about the world that text producers and receivers hold. For example, look at Text 10A, which appeared in a top-selling gadgets magazine.

Text 10A

YOUR MONTH JUNE

Why fly to Brazil for the World Cup? We've got two of 'em right here in Europe!

Source: *Stuff Magazine*, July 2014

In order to understand this text, a reader needs to do more than decode the semantic meaning of individual words. In fact, each word evokes a rich store of knowledge that we make use of in the act of interpretation. Reading the word 'Brazil', for example, evokes more than just the name of a country in South America, instead drawing on a range of other knowledge a reader might have about the country, its people, its culture, its geography, its politics and so on. Some of this knowledge may be **embodied** (the smells, sights, noises) gained from physically visiting the country, and of course all of this knowledge will vary from person to person: one individual's 'Brazil' can never be the same as another's. In a similar way, the phrase 'World Cup' will evoke different types and degrees of knowledge that a reader would use to help form an interpretation.

There are two key points here. The first is that dictionary definitions in themselves can never really account for the way in which we interpret individual words and phrases; instead, much of the meaning that we gain from texts and utterances is reliant on *contextual* rather than *textual* knowledge. A term we can use to describe the kind of knowledge of a concept, person or event that is triggered by a word is a **schema**. Schemas are bundles of information built up from our experience in the world and are dynamic in that they can be amended and added to (I can alter and/or increase my knowledge of Brazil by going there or reading about it). Although schemas are also unique to individuals, they also share common properties (so my 'Brazil' schema and your own are going to be similar in many ways).

Clearly not everything you know about Brazil is going to be useful when reading Text 10A (in fact some of it will not be very useful at all). The surrounding text, or **co-text**, acts as a kind of filter to ensure that we largely draw on what's relevant. In this instance, since the focus is on the World Cup, we would only be expected to think about Brazil as the host for the tournament, the stadia, the players and so on.

Key terms

embodied knowledge: knowledge that is associated with memories of physically experiencing something, for example the sights and smells of visiting a city

schema: a bundle of knowledge about a concept, person or event

co-text: other words or phrases surrounding a word in a text

ACTIVITY 1

Your schematic knowledge

You can test your own schematic knowledge by looking at the following list of countries. What do you think of when you read the name of each? What differences are there between the kinds of knowledge you hold for each? For which countries do you have a rich schema, and for which a relatively poor one? What might have influenced this? Think about those you might have visited, read about, seen on television and so on.

- France
- Spain
- Algeria
- Australia
- Japan
- Honduras.

10.2 Conversational maxims

One of the things we can assume when someone speaks to us is that they intend to convey some kind of meaning, and therefore that communication is essentially a cooperative enterprise between speaker and listener.

One of the ways that language study has explained this **cooperative principle** is through the use of what the linguist and philosopher Paul Grice (1975) called **conversational maxims**:

The maxim of quantity: do not say too little or too much.

The maxim of quality: speak the truth.

The maxim of relevance: keep what is being discussed relevant to the topic in hand.

The maxim of manner: be clear and avoid ambiguity.

Grice didn't claim that these maxims acted as rigid rules but rather that when they were broken (as often happens when we speak to each other) they gave rise to what he called **implicatures**, implied meanings that listeners were intended to infer from speakers' comments. In the following exchanges in Texts 10B and 10C, speakers are discussing Collabro, an all-male singing group who won the 2014 *Britain's Got Talent* show. In responding to the question posed, Speaker B breaks one of the conversational maxims, with the result that certain implicatures need to be inferred by Speaker A.

Key terms

cooperative principle: the general principle that people work together to communicate

conversational maxims: explicit principles that provide a backdrop for conversation to take place so that speakers can easily understand one another

implicature: an implied meaning that has to be inferred by a speaker as a result of one of the maxims being broken

Text 10B

A: What did you think of Collabro?
B: What time did you say we were leaving?

Source: private data

In Text 10B, Speaker B breaks the maxim of relevance by changing the topic of conversation. The implicature inferred here by Speaker A could be that Speaker A does not like Collabro.

Text 10C

A: What did you think of Collabro?
B: Well they can sing.

Source: private data

In Text 10C, Speaker B breaks the maxim of manner in that her response is ambiguous (is she commenting on their vocal prowess or being ironic?). The implicature inferred here by Speaker A would no doubt depend on the way in which Speaker B utters the words (are they spoken in an obviously ironic way?).

10.3 Politeness

Another way that speakers support communication with each other is through what might be called a 'super-maxim': being polite by being mindful of others' personal or face needs.

In face theory, first developed by the sociologist Erving Goffman (1955), an individual has both **positive and negative face needs**. Positive face needs are those associated with feeling appreciated and valued, while negative face needs are the desire to feel independent and not be imposed upon. Interactions between people therefore have the potential to be **face-threatening acts** (FTAs), and consequently speakers can choose from a range of politeness strategies to minimise this loss of face.

For example, imagine a situation where someone (A) is reading quietly on a train and another person (B) next to them decides to turn up their mp3 player so that the noise begins to interfere with A's ability to concentrate. Given that saying something is likely to threaten B's face needs (i.e. A's utterance will no doubt be an FTA), A now has a number of choices:

- Threaten face by using a direct request addressing the problem and not worrying about B's reaction: 'Turn that music down!'
- Use a positive **politeness strategy** that addresses B's positive face needs. This might include saying something at the start that is complimentary to B such as: 'That's a great album isn't it …'
- Use a negative politeness strategy that addresses B's negative face needs. This might include apologising before speaking: 'I'm really sorry to ask you this but …', or trying to minimise the level of imposition: 'Can you just turn the music down a little?'
- Use an indirect request that avoids being explicit and therefore tries to minimise any threat to face, for example by saying: 'This is a great book I'm reading.'

Key terms

positive face need: a universal human need to feel valued and appreciated

negative face need: a universal human need to feel independent and not be imposed upon

face threatening act: a speech act that has the potential to damage someone's self-esteem either in terms of positive or negative face

politeness strategies: distinctive ways in which speakers can choose to speak to avoid threatening face

A final option would be to say nothing at all since the risk of threatening face, and any unwelcome consequences might be so high that A simply puts up with the unwanted noise.

These options are summarised in Figure 10A.

Figure 10A: Politeness options

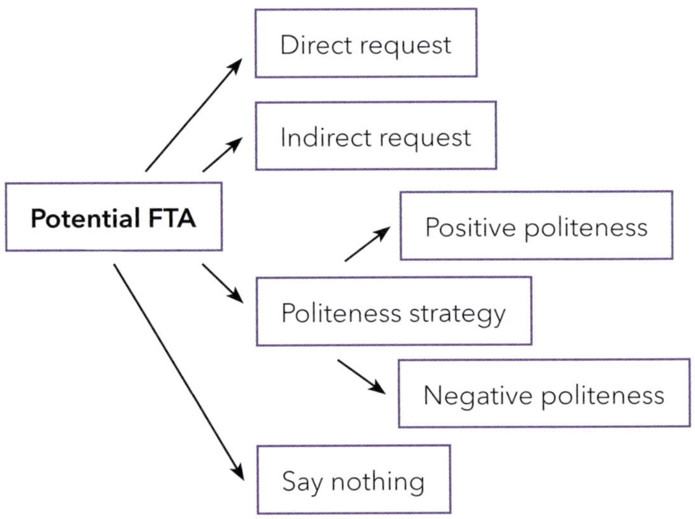

ACTIVITY 2

Working with your own data

Record some short conversations between friends and family members (do ask for permission from those you record) and think about the ways in which speakers break conversational maxims and their reasons for doing so. Alternatively, search YouTube to find examples of debates and interviews on TV programmes and identify the various politeness strategies (or lack of them) that speakers use where there are clear face-threatening acts.

10.4 Deixis

A final important area of study in pragmatics is **deixis**. Deictic words are words that are context-bound in so far as their meaning depends on who is using them, where they are using them and when they are using them.

Deictic terms belong to one of a number of **deictic categories**, the three main ones being:

- **Person deixis** (names and personal pronouns)
- **Spatial deixis** (adverbs of place such as 'here', 'there', demonstratives showing location such as 'this' and 'that', orientational words such as 'left' and 'right', and deictic verbs such as 'come' and 'go')
- **Temporal deixis** (adverbs of time such as 'today', 'yesterday' and 'tomorrow'). Each of these both locates a speaker in and points from a particular deictic centre.

So, for example, if I say the words 'I am here today' sitting at Euston station in London on 7 July 2014, my lexical choices point out from the centre of a person (me), place (Euston station) and time (7 July 2014). But, if I say those words in a different place and at a different time, then the words 'here' and 'today' will obviously locate me in a different set of parameters. If instead of me, someone else says those words then the time and place to which they refer will differ again.

Deictic expressions are commonly used when speakers share the same time and space since they can point to objects and refer to events that can commonly be understood. For example, look at Text 10D, part of the opening dialogue between a window cleaning canvasser (Speaker A) and a customer (Speaker B).

Text 10D

A: Oh hi (.) I was wondering if you'd like a reliable window cleaner at all (.) I don't know if that's something you might have thought about

B: We have been thinking about it (.) yes

A: Well um (.) we've just signed up the house there (.) we're doing that every eight weeks (.) and what I can do is these windows here now for you and then come back tomorrow for the top ones

B: OK

Source: private data

Here Speaker A is able to use the deictic expressions 'there' and 'here' that point towards specific objects in the speakers' shared physical space and so are contextually understood. He also uses the temporal deictic terms 'now' and 'tomorrow' to point towards specific time frames. Both of these pairs contain one term that is close to the speakers ('here' and 'now'), and one term that is a little more distant to the speakers ('there' and 'tomorrow'). These terms are known as **proximal** and **distal deixis** respectively.

Key terms

deixis: words that are context-bound and whose meaning depends on who is using them, and where and when they are being used

deictic categories: types of deictic expressions (**person**, **spatial** and **temporal**)

proximal deixis: deictic expressions that refer to concepts, events or people close to the speaker

distal deixis: deictic expressions that refer to concepts, events or people at a distance from the speaker

ACTIVITY 3

Deixis in tour guides

Look at Text 10E taken from an internet tour guide to Paris. Identify all of the deictic terms used in this text. Why do you think texts like this tend to use these kinds of expressions?

Text 10E

You say good-bye to Notre-Dame and walk towards Rue de la Cité, turn right, then left and you'll arrive at Boulevard du Palais. There's so many things to see here, you might think of visiting 'la Sainte Chapelle' but you only have a day, remember? So skip it, turn right into Boulevard du Palais and find on your left hand side the Palais de Justice, the Paris High Court. Have a look: it was here, to the right of the majestic stairways, where the carts containing condemned men and woman during the French revolution left the Palais, heading for the Guillotine.

It was here, too, in a vast labyrinth of palaces, where French kings held court during medieval times and for many centuries afterwards. Go straight down the Boulevard du Palais and find yet another bridge over the Seine river, 'le Pont au Change.' A first bridge was built here around the year 1000, destroyed in 1280, then rebuilt, then destroyed again and rebuilt, and so on, but anyway: step onto this bridge and you'll have a nice view of the famous Pont Neuf right down the river. It was built in 1578 and is the oldest bridge of Paris still standing. So what you see is still the real thing, you're looking 450 years back in time. Take a photo, this is a memorable moment. And then: move on!

Source: Mad about Paris website

Check your responses in the Ideas section on Cambridge Elevate

Summary

- Background knowledge, held in schemas, plays an important role in how meanings are arrived at.
- The principles of cooperation and politeness can explain the decisions speakers make when communicating with each other.
- Deictic expressions are frequently used to refer to things within a shared context.

'Take a photo, this is a memorable moment.'
madaboutparis.com

BEGINNING

11 Language level 6: Discourse

In this unit, you will:

- learn about ways of describing and analysing spoken narratives
- explore the typical structure and some key features of conversations.

11.1 Types of discourse

Discourse is the level of language concerned with larger stretches of text. Since the main focus in previous units has largely been on written discourse, here we will focus exclusively on spoken discourse as a way of introducing some key concepts and analytical methods to explore both storytelling and multi-speaker interaction.

11.2 Storytelling

11.2.1 Labov's narrative categories

The sociolinguist William Labov (1972) suggested a structure for explaining how speakers gave accounts of personal experiences based on fieldwork he had carried out in New York. He suggested that one-speaker narratives largely followed this order of elements:

- Abstract (A): an indication that the speaker wants a listener's attention and is signalling the start of the narrative
- Orientation (O): the 'who', 'where', 'what' and 'why' – that sets the scene and provides background information that the speaker sees as important
- Complicating action (CA): the main body of the narrative
- Resolution (R): the ending of the narrative that ties up loose ends and provides closure
- Coda (C): a signal that the narrative has ended.

These categories have been highlighted in Text 11A, part of an account given by a teacher explaining what she had done at the weekend.

Text 11A

Abstract → Well (.) at the weekend I went to get my hair done at the salon (.) ← Orientation when I was there (.) I saw my friend who gave me an invitation for her wedding (1) it was lovely to see her (.) and a surprise to hear that she was getting married (.) which we will look forward to going to in a couple of weeks (1) after that I went to the shops (.) and did some shopping with my partner Craig (.) ← Complicating action then we went home and had the very boring task of putting it all away (.) not my favourite thing to do (.) ← Resolution anyway that's all really ← Coda

Source: private data

In addition, Labov suggested that at any point in a narrative, speakers could include what he called evaluation, additions to the narrative that the speaker felt were worth mentioning. In Text 11A we can see that the speaker moves outside of the main narrative detail to provide her opinion on meeting her friend, and her attitude towards the forthcoming wedding:

---

it was lovely to see her (.) and a surprise to hear that she was getting married (.) which we will look forward to going to in a couple of weeks

---

This is an example of what Labov called **internal evaluation**, where the speaker stands back from the action but makes comments that are within the same time frame as the main narrative. In contrast, speakers may also add opinions and attitudes at the time of telling that are not part of the sequence of events in any way. In the extract we have been looking at, the words 'not my favourite thing to do', where the speaker 'stands back' from the action and simply expresses an attitude towards the events she is talking about, are an example of **external evaluation**.

Key terms

internal evaluation: an expression of attitude towards the events in a narrative that occur in the same time frame as the main action

external evaluation: an expression of attitude where the speaker 'stands back' from the main action

turn-taking: the process by which speakers co-construct conversation

adjacency pair: a simple structure of two turns

Labov's narrative categories are summarised in Figure 11A, which is based on Labov's own diagrammatic representation of his work. Evaluation is represented in the middle of the diamond to show that it can occur at any point during the narrative.

Figure 11A: Labov's narrative categories

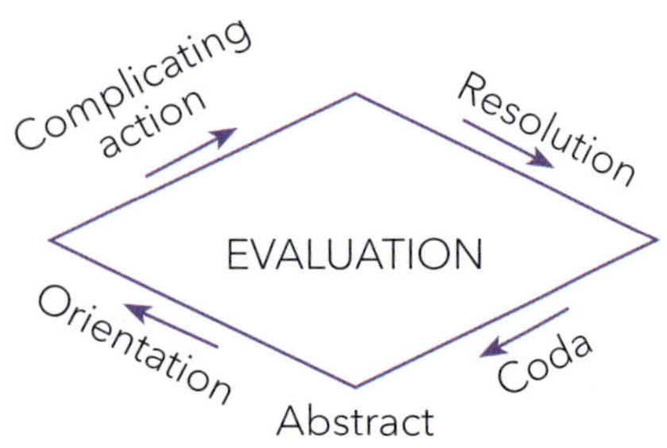

ACTIVITY 1

Working with Labov's categories

Look at Text 11B, an extract from a recount by a sixth form student of what she did at the weekend. Label this recount using Labov's narrative categories.

Text 11B

OK let me tell you about my weekend (1) I went to Maidstone (.) with two of my friends (1) I drove around the one way system which was quite scary (.) and then I managed to get a ticket from the little car park machine (.) without stalling my car (.) or letting it roll forward (1) that's quite an accomplishment for me (.) I then attempted to do some Christmas shopping (.) but saw this really nice dress I thought would be perfect for my birthday and I ran out of money and couldn't do any Christmas shopping so had to come home (1) it makes me laugh when I think of it now (1) there you go

Source: private data

Check your responses in the Ideas section on Cambridge Elevate

11.2.2 Goodwin's story structure

Many narratives, of course, do not get told by a single speaker to an audience who simply listen without participating in any way. For example, in the following extract, the story told by Speaker A depends on Speaker B working with her to both encourage her to tell her story and help to move it forwards:

A: well I've often found Rob rude
B: why (.) what has he done to you
A: do you (.) want (.) really want to know
B: yes tell me
A: OK (.) well …

The linguist Charles Goodwin (1984) has proposed an alternative model for analysing narratives that highlights this interactive nature of storytelling. He suggested that there are six interactional techniques that speakers use when building narratives together:

- **story preface:** a signal that a speaker wants to tell a story and an invitation for others to show interest

- **story solicit:** a response from someone else that they want to listen to the story
- **preliminary to the story:** background information to the story in the form of the 'who', 'where', 'what' and 'why'
- **story action:** the main body of the narrative
- **story climax:** the conclusion of the narrative
- **story appreciation:** signals from the audience that communicate their response to the narrative. This might be at several points during the story or at the end and could consist of questions, agreements and laughter or other signs of emotions.

In addition, a speaker might add what Goodwin calls parenthesis (more background information) at any point in the narrative where she feels that this is appropriate. Goodwin suggests that this could be used to clarify any details that have already been stated or to add information to particular descriptions of events and/or people to make them more vivid.

Turning to the short extract in Text 11C, the value of looking at these kinds of narratives using Goodwin's model becomes clear. Here we can see A's preface to the story in the comment about Rob's rudeness, to which B responds with a story solicit both encouraging further information and consequently leading into the remainder of the story.

ACTIVITY 2

Exploring Goodwin's model

Look at Text 11C, which contains the rest of the narrative discussed. Analyse this using Goodwin's model, giving reasons for your labelling of different sections.

Text 11C

A: well I've often found Rob rude
B: why (.) what has he done to you
A: do you (.) want (.) really want to know
B: yes tell me
A: OK (.) well (.) I had this new sofa and he just came in
B: yeah
A: put his feet all over it (.) you know we had only just got it
B: right
A: I told him (.) get your feet off (.) and he laughed
B: how rude
A: yeah (.) loser
B: ha ha ((*laughs*))

Source: private data

Check your responses in the Ideas section on Cambridge Elevate

11.3 Multi-speaker interaction

Unit 11.2 focused on one particular kind of speech (storytelling), but of course the analysis of conversation more broadly is an important part of language study.

A useful framework for looking at multi-speaker interaction is based around the idea of a conversational turn. In a similar way to how we take turns when we play sport (for example, hitting a tennis ball, going into bat at cricket or performing during a gymnastics competition), or play cards or wait to be served in a supermarket queue, conversations involve people negotiating and managing opportunities for individuals to share speaking time to create a successful conversation.

'I then attempted to do some Christmas shopping…'

11.3.1 The structure of turns

The most simple structure in **turn-taking** is the **adjacency pair**, which consists of two turns uttered by different speakers, one in response to the other, as in the following:

A: Would you like to come with me to the cinema tonight?
B: Yes!

This is a very straightforward example of a *question–answer* adjacency pair. In this instance, B responds in an expected manner, and probably in line with what A wanted her to say. In other words, B's response is what we can call a **preferred response**. Alternatively, had B responded with 'no' or been ambiguous or even answered irrelevantly, this would have been a **dispreferred response**.

However, conversations are rarely as straightforward as consisting of neat pairs of turns, and often additional turns are added before the sequence is completed. In this instance, we can label these additional parts an **insertion sequence**:

A: Would you like to come with me to the cinema tonight?
B: Why what's on?
A: *Dawn of the Planet of the Apes.*
B: Yes!

Here A and B insert an additional sequence 'Why what's on/*Dawn of the Planet of the Apes*' before the original adjacency pair is completed. Together the adjacency pair and insertion sequence form an overall **exchange structure** between the speakers.

11.3.2 Allocating turns

There are usually three ways in which turns get allocated and different speakers have an opportunity to speak:

1 If the current speaker is asking a question to a specific individual, as in the exchange about the cinema, then it is clear that he is selecting another speaker. If there is more than one person who could respond, then this speaker selection could be by naming the next speaker (e.g., 'Would you like to come to the cinema with me tonight, Sophia?') or by some non-verbal cue such as gesturing towards or pointing at the preferred next speaker.

2 If the current speaker does not select another, then at an appropriate point, or **transition relevance place**, another speaker can self-select to take a turn.

3 If no one takes this opportunity to take their turn, then the third option is that the current speaker carries on with another turn.

Many things can influence the taking of turns, not least the relationship between the speakers and their relative status in terms of power. For example, a teacher or parent talking to a young teenager will be able to apply **constraints** on the selection of turns.

Key terms

preferred response: a second part of an adjacency pair that fits in with what the speaker of the first part wants to hear

dispreferred response: a second part of an adjacency pair that doesn't fit in with what the speaker of the first part wants to hear

insertion sequence: an additional sequence between the two parts of an adjacency pair

exchange structure: sequence of turns between speakers

transition relevance place: a point where it is natural for another speaker to take a turn

constraint: the influence a more powerful speaker can have on another speaker

ACTIVITY 3

Analysing turns

Record a short conversation between two or more people (do ask for their permission to record them). Analyse this in terms of exchange structures and the allocation of terms. What do you notice? How are turns allocated and what strategies do speakers use to select and manage speech?

11.3.3 Other spoken language features

There are many more features that can be typically found in natural or represented speech and conversations. Table 11A lists some of the most important ones for you to learn and be able to use when exploring spoken discourse.

Table 11A

Feature	Definition	Example(s)
Filler	a non-verbal sound that acts like a pause – either to signal uncertainty or simply as a 'breathing space' for the speaker	Er, erm
False start	when a speaker begins to speak, stops and then starts again	A: Well I was (1) well I was going to the shops
Repair	when a speaker corrects some aspect of what they have said – the error might be a grammatical one or the use of a wrong word, either by accident or mentioning something that is inappropriate	A: We was (.) were going out (grammatical repair: 'was' to 'were') A: I really want England to lose (.) I mean win (word repair 'lose' to 'win')
Skip-connector	a word or phrase that returns the conversation to a previous topic	Anyway, coming back to our original discussion
Ellipsis	the omission of words for economical reasons and/or because the context means that the person listening understands the shortened utterance	A: What do you want for lunch? B: ham sandwich ('I would like' is ellipted)
Speaker support	words or phrases (both verbal and non-verbal) that show attention or agreement, and encourage a speaker to carry on talking	Mmm, yeah, OK

ACTIVITY 4

Annotating a transcript

Use all of your learning in this unit to analyse Texts 11D and 11E. Think about how:

- the conversation is structured
- how turns are selected
- the speakers use typical features of spoken discourse.

Text 11D

Context: a conversation between a teacher (A) and a student (B)

A: So you didn't do your homework today
B: No
A: And you got sent out of maths
B: Yea
A: Well what was the other reason
B: Because I didn't do my homework
A: Well who sent you out
B: Mrs Lawrence
A: Well where are you going now
B: In the computer room
A: To
B: To do some other work
A: What work
B: My maths homework
A: well you best get to it then hadn't you

Source: private data

Text 11E

Context: a conversation between four sixth-form students

A: Why is everyone in here
B: Katherine has been all on her own
A: Awww (.) poor Katherine (.) Where you going
C: We have (.) general studies ((*Katherine is packing up her bag*))
B: What you doing
D: Sod it I only have one lesson (.) I'm going home
B: What did you say
D: I have one lesson (.) I'm going home ((*laughs*))
A: What you doing here
C: We were allowed a short break from English ((*Katherine leaves*))

Source: private data

Summary

- We can describe and examine the structure of one-speaker narratives using the models suggested by Labov and Goodwin.
- The analysis of conversations allows us to explore how speakers manage speech by negotiating the taking of turns.
- There are some key typical features of spoken discourse that are important when analysing speech.

BEGINNING

12 Analysing texts

In this unit, you will:

- learn about and explore foregrounding in texts
- consider some key principles to remember that can help you to analyse texts.

12.1 Attention and foregrounding

Look carefully at Figure 12A. Here, you will see either a framed *black cross* against a white background, or *four white boxes* against a black background. One part of the image will always stand out to you against the background of the other and it's impossible to see both at the same time (you can try to do this but you'll end up frustrated!). This basic pattern forms the basis for how we organise everything in our visual field; without this, our worlds would exist in disorganised chaos!

Figure 12A

Of course, visually, objects can draw our attention to them by moving, making noises, being more sharply defined against backgrounds, or by simply being constant and not going away. In written texts too, these kinds of distinctions can be made. Put simply, writers can manipulate what they want us to focus our attention on, and what they want to remain in the background. A simple example of this can be seen in Text 12A, the opening of a short story.

Text 12A

There was a hill, and on the hill there was a road. The road was narrow and straight and it went straight up the side of the hill. The road was broken, with ruts, and holes, and streaks of mud where tractors or tracked vehicles must have turned in or out of the fields on either side.

Source: 'I remember there was a hill', in Jon McGregor (2013) *This isn't the Sort of Thing that Happens to Someone Like You*, Bloomsbury

Here, McGregor manipulates the way our attention is drawn to the landscape. He introduces the hill, through two noun phrases, firstly pre-modified with an indefinite article 'a hill' (it could be any hill), and then with a definite article 'the hill', to anchor our attention to a specific location. This pattern is mirrored in 'a road'/'the road', which links the end of the first sentence to the beginning of the second sentence. The maintained emphasis on 'the road' (repeated and given page space in the third sentence) distracts our attention from the hill and 'drills down' to its finer details (the streaks of mud from the farm vehicles), which the writer wants us to focus on.

This notion of focusing attention is commonly known as **foregrounding**. Foregrounding is a process by which writers draw our attention to key ideas in their texts through their intentional and strategic use of language. There are two main types:

- **Parallelism**: this involves the setting up of patterns through the repeated use of one or more of the language levels that were discussed in earlier units in this book. Text 12A contained an example of lexical and syntactical parallelism with the parallel noun phrases 'a hill'/'the hill', 'a road'/'the road'.
- **Deviation**: this involves breaking patterns so that language used is seen as distinctly different from an established norm. The effect here is therefore one of explicit distraction. The stylistician Mick Short (1996) suggests that there are two ways in which deviation can occur: **external deviation**, where there is a break from the normal conventions of language use, such as the use of nonsense words, or a convention not usually associated with a particular genre; and **internal deviation**, where there is a break from some existing pattern that has been already been set up in the text, such as a string of plosive sounds in a line of verse being broken by the insertion of a fricative sound.

Key terms

foregrounding: drawing attention to a key aspect in a text

parallelism: foregrounding through repetition at any one of the language levels

external deviation: a break from the normal conventions of language use that exist beyond the text itself

internal deviation: a break from some kind of pattern that has been set up within the text

ACTIVITY 1

Internal and external deviation

Look at Texts 12B and 12C. Which text has an example of external deviation and which has an example of internal deviation? Can you comment on the effect that each type of deviation produces?

Text 12B

Celia, Celia

When I am sad and weary,
When I think all hope has gone,
When I walk along High Holborn
I think of you with nothing on.

Source: Adrian Mitchell (1991), *Greatest Hits*, Bloodaxe

Text 12C

'Twas brillig, and the slithy toves
Did gyre and gimble in the wabe;
All mimsy were the borogoves,
And the mome raths outgrabe.

Source: Lewis Carroll (1871), 'Jaberwocky', in *Through the Looking-Glass, and What Alice Found There*, Macmillan

Check your responses in the Ideas section on Cambridge Elevate

12.2 Key principles of stylistic analysis

In Unit 1, we emphasised some important points about analysing texts on a language-literature specification, drawing attention to the fact that it is important to be systematic, clear and focused both in identifying language *and* providing an interpretation at all times. The following sections provide some more guidance for you on this, which you will find useful as you progress through this course.

12.2.1 Avoiding impressionism and intuitive comments

Read Text 12D, 'Ozymandias' by the nineteenth-century poet Percy Bysshe Shelley (if necessary, do some background research on the poem), and then read Texts 12E and 12F, extracts from two student responses to Text 12D.

Text 12D

Ozymandias

I met a traveller from an antique land,
Who said – 'Two vast and trunkless legs of stone
Stand in the desert ... Near them, on the sand,
Half sunk a shattered visage lies, whose frown,
And wrinkled lip, and sneer of cold command,
Tell that its sculptor well those passions read
Which yet survive, stamped on these lifeless things,
The hand that mocked them, and the heart that fed;

And on the pedestal, these words appear:
My name is Ozymandias, King of Kings,
Look on my Works, ye Mighty, and despair!
Nothing beside remains. Round the decay
Of that colossal Wreck, boundless and bare
The lone and level sands stretch far away.'

Source: Percy Bysshe Shelley 'Ozymandias'

Text 12E

'Ozymandias' is clearly a poem about death, and it may be that Shelley was trying to give his view on what happens to us all eventually. It seems as though all the characters in the poem are important in helping us understand this in some way.

One of the key things you will need to avoid when writing about texts is falling back on **impressionistic** or intuitive comments, which have very little focus on the language of the text itself. At one extreme they may just be comments on 'hunches' you might have as in Text 12E; at the other extreme, they may be attempts to show off and be coloured by flowery rhetoric and pretentious language, as in Text 12F.

Text 12F

The ending of the poem relies on a sense of movement away across the 'lone and level sands'. The landscape opens up to represent the emptiness and futility of Ozymandias's kingdom, a place that seemed to stand outside time but ultimately is seen as another victim of an increasingly fragile human existence. The statue remains a mere shadow in the burning sun of the dusty desert; the poem, like Ozymandias himself, drifts away until it disappears into the eternal universe.

There are two ways of avoiding this and making your work with texts and your writing on texts better. The first is to start by making some initial thoughts on a text, and then standing back and objectively working out which language features you feel are responsible for the comments you have made. In this way, you can pinpoint precisely which features you feel are important to write about, and make sure you give these coverage.

The second way is to start by closely looking for specific patterns of language use and then start to build some interpretative comments around these. This is a good approach to use to ensure that you have a strong language focus from the beginning. Although either one of these ways to explore texts is fine, you will probably find that you use the first way more initially before you build up your confidence with language and its terminology.

To help you structure your ideas, you could use a table like Table 12A. If you take the 'thoughts-first' approach then fill in the left-hand column first; if you take the 'language features-first' approach then you should initially fill in the right-hand column. You should ensure the two columns match up clearly and precisely, whichever approach you take.

Key terms

impressionistic: a response to a text that is rooted in very subjective terms and is not focused carefully on language use

Table 12A

Thoughts	Language features

ACTIVITY 2

Rewriting to avoid impressionism

Take Texts 12E and 12F and rewrite each so that the writer's points are less impressionistic and more in line with the kind of response you should make at A/AS level. Experiment with the two ways of approaching textual analysis described above to see which way works best for you.

12.2.2 Thinking about writing

As you develop your ideas into more fully formed answers, you will need to show both an understanding of the texts that you are studying and an ability to write about those texts in a logical and structured manner. As you progress through the course, you will have plenty of opportunity to practise writing short responses, longer written responses and examination-style responses. The activities in later units of this book will help to build up your skills in these key areas, but the following are offered as an initial starting point to help you to think about what writing means at A/AS Level.

1 Remember that there are many different types of writing that you will undertake. You need to develop expertise in note-taking and annotation around texts as well as in writing responses to them. Try to develop a 'writer's mind-set' by keeping a notebook in to which you can add thoughts as you read and/or keep a blog or other virtual space.

See Unit 14 for more information on keeping a scrapbook of annotated texts

2 When you are planning for longer pieces of writing, try to cluster ideas into themes or focal points that you can devote a set amount of space to (e.g. one or two paragraphs). You can use a table similar to Table 12A to help you with this.

3 As you move from pre- to post-16 study, try to experiment more with your writing style so that you move away from the *point-evidence-explain* formula of writing that is often held up as good practice for younger students. Of course, you need to be clear and focused at all times, but try to develop your own writing style and voice; much of this will come from reading other examples of academic writing (further reading suggestions in the 'enriching' units in this book will support you with this), and from writing frequently in a variety of forms and for a variety of reasons as described above.

Summary

- One of the most useful tools for text analysis is the notion of foregrounding through parallelism and deviation.
- Foregrounding offers us a way to explore how writers draw our attention to key aspects in texts.
- It is important to retain a strong language and interpretative focus when writing, and to avoid simply making impressionistic comments.
- There are a number of ways you can build and develop your writing skills as you progress through the course.

BEGINNING

13

Literature and literariness

In this unit, you will:

- think about what we mean when we use the term 'literature'
- explore the notion of 'literariness'.

13.1 What is literature?

Many of the texts that you will be studying in your A/AS Level course will be 'literary texts', and your non-examination assessment 'Making connections' (see Unit 20) will involve you drawing together literary and non-literary material around an analysis of a theme or a linguistic concept or issue. One of the central (and most interesting) questions as you work through the course will be to think about what the term 'literature' actually means.

ACTIVITY 1

What do you understand by the term 'literature'?

What do you think 'literature' is? What distinguishes 'literary' material from 'non-literary' material? Are the texts listed in examples 1–5 'literature'? Why?

1 *King Lear*, William Shakespeare

2 *The Hunger Games*, Suzanne Collins

3 *Tom Gates: A Little Bit Lucky*, Liz Pichon

4 *The Official Highway Code*

5 *The King James Bible*

This is a tricky question to answer, not least because the term 'literature' can mean many different things to different people. However, you may have discussed some of the following:

- *King Lear* is literature as this is by an established canonical author. In this instance, you might have explored how 'literature' equates to so-called 'classic' or 'serious' 'works of art'.
- *The Hunger Games* and *Tom Gates: A Little Bit Lucky* could be considered 'children's literature', but is this a term which simply refers to a genre rather than to 'literature' in the same sense as *King Lear*?
- For some people *The King James Bible* might be literature, or at least share some of the same kind of qualities as literary texts, and often the term 'literature' can simply be used to refer to anything that's published in a certain field. So, *The Official Highway Code* could well be classified as 'official government literature' and so on.
- The slippery nature of the term means that often literature is what people think or say it is, rather than being clearly or sharply defined. In many cases, 'literature' becomes a value judgement or a mindset from which attitudes towards certain kinds of writing can be made.

One very famous example of the final bullet point is detailed by the literary scholar Stanley Fish (1980) in his book *Is There a Text in This Class?* Fish recounts how he had written a list of five names of famous linguists on the board during a previous lesson, and left it there for the next class to see. He told this incoming group of students that it was a religious poem, from which they proceeded to treat the list of names as though it were a literary text, finding significance in patterns of all kinds and assigning various complex meanings. In other words, they chose to see it as literature, and treated it in a way that they used when working with that form of writing.

13.1.1 Literature as deviation

Literature can also be seen as a particular kind of deviation that separates it from everyday language. In fact, some of the very early attempts to work with literature using language-based approaches in the twentieth-century equated 'being literary' with being far removed from the ordinariness and norms of everyday language.

13.1.2 Literature as aesthetics

Literature has also been viewed as something that is aesthetically beyond normal everyday language. The Romantic poet John Keats, writing to his friend John Taylor in 1818 (Text 13A), saw literature (essentially poetry) as a magical, beautiful entity.

Text 13A

I think Poetry should surprise by a fine excess and not by singularity – it should strike the reader as a wording of his own highest thoughts, and appear almost a remembrance – Its touches of Beauty should never be halfway thereby making the reader breathless instead of content: the rise, the progress, the setting of imagery should like the Sun come natural to him – shine over him and set soberly although in magnificence leaving him in the luxury of twilight – but it is easier to think what Poetry should be than to write it – and this leads me on to another axiom. That if Poetry comes not as naturally as the leaves to a tree it had better not come at all.

Source: John Keats, Letters, 27 February 1818

13.1.3 Literature as politics

Finally, the term 'literature' has always been highly political. In compulsory education there has been a continual debate about what should count as 'literature' and therefore be worthy of study by schoolchildren in the context of improving attainment, raising standards, and allowing children to enjoy reading. For example, read Text 13B, part of a speech made by Michael Gove, who was the Secretary of State for Education from 2010–14.

Text 13B

Stephenie Meyer cannot hold a flaming pitch torch to George Eliot. There is a Great Tradition of English Literature – a Canon of transcendent works – and *Breaking Dawn* is not part of it.

Source: Rt Hon. Michael Gove MP

13.2 Literature or 'literariness'?

It is clearly problematic to label something as 'literature' and 'literary' or 'non-literary'. Equally, it is easy to see how the more deviant and aesthetic features of language that have been exclusively claimed for 'literary' texts can also occur in non-literary material. For example, many advertising texts, newspaper headlines and social media postings display the kinds of lexical and semantic innovation and phonological patterning that can be found in the most complex poetry. And, as the linguists George

Lakoff and Mark Johnson (1980) have demonstrated, a so-called 'literary trope' like metaphor actually underpins much of our everyday language.

See 6.2.3 for more on everyday language

For these reasons, the stylisticians Ron Carter and Walter Nash (1990) suggest that rather than think of 'literary texts' and 'non-literary texts' as absolute opposites, we should instead think of **literariness** as a continuum (Figure 13A), along which we can place any number of texts, with some of them showing more or less 'literary' properties than others.

Figure 13A: Literariness as a continuum

Non-literary ←——————→ Literary

But just what defines 'literary' if, as we have discussed, the term itself is difficult to pin down, prone to individual interpretations and has been highly politicised? Carter and Nash suggest that one of the key linguistic features of a literary text is its degree of **semantic density**, the way in which different levels of language work together to produce certain effects across the text as a whole. So, for example, a more literary text might have foregrounded features at the levels of phonology, syntax and lexis all working together to create a rich and complex set of effects. In Text 13C, the first stanza from John Keats' poem 'La belle dame sans merci', there are prominent language features at the levels of *discourse* (set out as a poem of four-line stanzas), *phonology* (the foregrounded /l/ sound and the broken pattern of syllables from lines 1–3 to line 4), and *lexis-semantics* (the semantic field of emptiness and negation), all of which give high semantic density. In contrast, Text 13D, taken from the Parisinfo website for visitors to Paris, only has patterning at the level of syntax (the parallel noun phrases 'all budgets'/'all tastes').

Text 13C

O what can ail thee, knight-at-arms,
Alone and palely loitering?
The sedge has withered from the lake,
And no birds sing.

Source: John Keats, 'La belle dame sans merci'

Text 13D

Where to sleep in Paris?

From hotels to camping, Paris boasts a wide range of accommodation for all budgets and all tastes.

Key terms

literariness: the degree to which a text displays 'literary' qualities along a continuum rather than being absolutely 'literary' or 'non-literary'

semantic density: different levels of language working together to produce certain effects across the text as a whole

ACTIVITY 2

Attitudes to literature

Ask your friends and family what they understand by the term 'literature'. How might you categorise and summarise the responses they make? How is 'literature' defined by booksellers (including online retailers), and in press coverage of debates about education?

ACTIVITY 3

Exploring semantic density

Explore the notion of semantic density by discussing texts that you have collected and analysed yourself. To what extent do you think this is a useful way of thinking about literariness?

ACTIVITY 4

Making connections

What connections can you make between the ways that texts with different degrees of literariness treat the same topic matter or make use of a similar linguistic feature? In what ways are they different? In what ways are they similar? You should keep a record of any reading you do and observations you make since these may well be useful when it comes to choosing a focus for your personal investigation (see Unit 20).

Summary

- 'Literature' is notoriously difficult to define and is often a matter of personal preference and stance.
- The terms 'literary' and 'non-literary' are also problematic and are best replaced by a more/less model of 'literariness'.

BEGINNING

14 Becoming an investigator

In this unit, you will:

- learn about some key ways in which you can build your skills as an investigator by keeping a scrapbook and keeping a record of any material you read.

14.1 Keeping a scrapbook

One of the most important things that you need to be able to do as you work your way through your AS/A Level course is to practise the knowledge and the skills that you have learnt by finding and analysing your own examples of texts and applying what you know. Keeping a record of these texts, complete with your annotations, will help you to assess your own progress, give you material that you can use in class to discuss with fellow students and your teacher, and provide ample revision material in preparation for your exams.

In line with the principles behind this course, which were discussed in Units 1, 12 and 13, you should aim to collect a range of literary and non-literary material, and both describe language features and interpret their significance in terms of shaping meaning. This will give you the opportunity to think of ways in which you can explore the literary and non-literary and find meaningful connections between them. This will provide excellent preparation for your non-examination assessment.

See Unit 20 for more on preparing for your non-examination assessment

There are a number of ways that you can collect, annotate and keep material. For example, you could:

- keep a hard-copy scrapbook, using an A3 art pad (or similar), sticking texts in with glue, labelling key language features and summarising their effects
- use your school/college's VLE to upload material that you have scanned in and annotated (either by hand or using a feature such as 'comment box' in Word). You might be able to store these in a shared area so that other students can access them and share their thoughts. This is a good way to build up a dialogue about language and the way it shapes meaning. You will also be able to upload speech and video files using this method.
- use a web-based space such as a padlet wall. This will allow you to upload texts, add annotations, audio and video files and links to other documents and websites.

Find out more about padlet walls via Cambridge Elevate

14.2 Keeping a record of references

As you work through the course, you will also be finding and completing new reading to supplement this book and recommendations from your teacher. There is an established way of referencing in academic work. However, what you can do from a very early stage is keep a record of everything you have read, and a summary of its key points. This will prove invaluable when it comes to thinking about background reading for your own investigation. It will also ensure that you don't forget the original source of some information you want to use. At this stage, although it doesn't matter how you record this information, you should remember to keep the following details:

- **for books**: the name of the author(s), the year of publication and the publisher and place of publication (these can usually be found on the 'copyright' page at the beginning of the book)
- **for articles from journals or magazines**: the name of the author(s), the year of publication, the title of the article, journal/magazine and page numbers
- **for reading from the internet**: the name of the author(s), the date you accessed it and the web address.

See Unit 20 for more on referencing academic work

You should also remember to include any quotations from these publications in quotation marks so that you do not accidentally use them as your own!

Summary

- Keeping a scrapbook (either in hard copy or virtual format) will help you to develop your skills and knowledge as you progress through the course.
- It is important to keep a record of any reading you undertake, including page numbers, so that you can refer back to this accurately at a later date.

DEVELOPING

Introduction to *Telling stories*

What will you study?

In this part of the course, you will explore the ways that writers and speakers present stories by constructing narratives of various types. Each of the texts that you will study involves writers or speakers presenting their experiences in ways that draw attention to the act of storytelling as an important and fundamentally human characteristic.

This relates to 'Views and Voices' and 'People and places' at AS level, and 'Telling stories' at A level.

See Unit 5 for more on constructing narratives

ACTIVITY 1

Thinking about narratives

Drawing on your learning from Unit 5, think about the different types of narrative that there are. For example, what might make the texts in Figure A narratives of one sort or another, and what similarities and differences do they have?

Figure A

- novels
- short stories
- sports commentaries
- facebook posts
- obituaries
- a ballet show
- a postcard written whilst on holiday
- a conversation between friends
- advertisements

Can you think of any texts that couldn't be considered narrative in any way? What about, for example, a bank statement or a parking ticket?

ACTIVITY 2

Literary or non-literary?

As a further introductory activity, think about what makes the narratives you have discussed either more or less literary or non-literary. Use ideas on literariness to help you with this.

See Unit 13 for more on literariness

As you work your way through the three units in this section, you will draw on a number of models from linguistics, stylistics and narrative study to explore the following key questions.

- Why do people tell stories?
- How do we tell stories? What makes a good narrator?
- How do we characterise a narrative? What does it need to have?
- How do narratives work in specific genres (e.g. advertising, stories for children, newspapers, comics)?
- How are identities constructed and stories told in online environments (e.g. on message boards)?
- What are some of the differences and similarities between spoken and written narratives?

- How are events, people, times and places in narratives represented by narrators/speakers and authors according to their purposes, audiences and the contexts in which they appear?
- How do narrators connect to other stories in the same genre and in other genres?
- What strategies do readers and listeners use to make meaning? What else goes on beyond the 'words on the page'?
- Is there a special kind of narrative called 'literature?' How does this work?

You'll also build on Unit 5, thinking critically and deeply about why stories are worth telling, and how writers and speakers persuade their audiences that they should read or listen to them, how and why different points of view are used in texts, how characters in fiction are introduced and developed, and how writers manipulate the presentation of time and space in both fiction and non-fiction texts. You'll also think closely about the structure of narrative discourse, including exploring aspects of genre and intertextuality, specific conventions (e.g. turn taking and co-construction in dialogue), and the structure of different kinds of literary and non-literary discourse. In all of this the focus will be on the fact that narratives can be found everywhere!

ACTIVITY 3

Narratives and you

Think about your views on narrative.

- How do you use narrative as a way of understanding yourself?
- How do you use narrative as a way of representing yourself to the world?
- How do those narratives differ according to whom you're telling them and why you're telling them?

Section A: *Remembered places* (Unit 15)

In Unit 15 you will study an anthology of wide-ranging non-literary material where writers and speakers have represented the city of Paris in different ways. Unit 15 will allow you to draw on the concept of representation to examine ways in which Paris has been presented by different people, writing at different times, with different purposes and in a range of different genres.

See Unit 4 for more on representation

Section B: *Imagined worlds* (Unit 16)

In Unit 16 you will study one of the following four novels from the fantasy genre:

1. Mary Shelley, *Frankenstein* (Penguin)
2. Bram Stoker, *Dracula* (Penguin)
3. Alice Sebold, *The Lovely Bones* (Picador)
4. Margaret Atwood, *The Handmaid's Tale* (Virago).

You will explore the various narrative techniques that the writers use to present the fictional worlds of the novels, and the characters, places and events within them. You will also explore the extent to which writers make use of the conventions of the fantasy genre in their writing.

Section C: *Poetic voices* (Unit 17)

In Unit 17 you will study a selection of poems from one of the following poets:

- John Donne
- Robert Browning
- Carol Ann Duffy
- Seamus Heaney.

These all appear in the *AQA Anthology: Poetic voices*. The poetry question will be more broadly focused on the nature and function of poetic voice in the telling of events and the presentation of people, times and places in specific poems.

What knowledge and skills will you develop?

Whichever texts you study, you will develop your understanding of narrative and support work that you will undertake on other areas of the course, particularly your own investigative project in *Making connections*. As you work through the different units, you'll build up an extensive set of analytical tools with which you'll be able to explore texts from any period or genre in a focused and systematic way.

DEVELOPING

15

Remembered places

In this unit, you will:

- develop your understanding and explore the conventions of travel narratives
- learn a range of concepts and frameworks to examine the representation of Paris in different kinds of texts
- explore how best to prepare for assessment on this unit.

This relates to 'People and places' in the specification for AS Level and to 'Telling stories' in the specification for A Level

15.1 Introduction to the anthology

The *AQA Anthology: Paris* is a collection of non-literary material consisting of a range of texts from different genres written and spoken for a variety of different purposes. The anthology offers you the opportunity to both build on and further develop all of the skills and knowledge you encountered in the Beginning units. In particular, the texts in the anthology allow for a close examination of:

- representation and tellability by exploring the ways that places in and around Paris, people visiting or living in the city, and events that take place in the city are portrayed;
- how texts represent the key concepts of culture, society and memories that become associated with travelling to, or living in, Paris;
- how texts about Paris rely on metaphor to present people and events, and how writing itself can often be seen as a metaphorical journey;
- the affordances (possibilities) and constraints (limitations) offered by different types and genres of communication;
- the reasons why different writers and speakers present their ideas as they do and the vast array of contextual factors that influence those decisions.

The anthology thus focuses on the following concepts that underpin the entire specification:

- genre
- narrative and point of view
- register
- representation
- literariness.

As well as these key areas of focus, the anthology is also designed to support your study in some additional ways. First, although the texts in the anthology are classified as non-literary, you will be able to explore to what extent they exhibit degrees of 'literariness'. This will allow you to develop your understanding of how so-called non-literary texts often display examples of what we might term 'literary' features and to be aware of the literary/non-literary distinction as points on a continuum rather than binary absolutes.

ACTIVITY 1

Exploring literariness

You can think about this question by examining short extracts from anthology texts and highlighting any literary qualities and characteristics that you think they might have. On first reading through the anthology are there some texts that you might expect to be more literary than others? Why do you think this might be?

The anthology can also support your studies by encouraging you to make links with literary texts in other units on the specification. This will be useful in its own right to develop your analytical skills across a broad range of texts, but particularly useful if you are following the full two-year A Level course where you have to submit a personal investigation as part of your non-exam assessment (NEA). In the spirit of this specification, which promotes an integrated study of language and literature, exploring connections between literary and non-literary material is very important. If you are following the full A Level course, you might begin to think about distinctive areas of focus that could be of interest as you work through the anthology; for example, the representation of children, or of travelling, or of metaphor or deixis as structuring and cohesive devices. Of course, whilst you cannot use any of the anthology material in your NEA, you should be able to get some ideas of a potential representation or language feature that you can explore in more detail through wider reading.

There are two further points that are worth noting here. The first concerns how you should approach the reading and annotating of your anthology. Clearly, you are going to need to read these texts several times; with each reading, you will develop your previous readings as well as explore potentially new avenues of meaning. Therefore, it would be a very good idea to return to your anthology texts regularly even as you move on to other units on the specification, aiming to make connections between previous and current readings and between other texts that you come across.

Second, if you are following the AS course, then the assessment on this unit is considerably different to the full A Level. In this instance, you should also ensure that you read Sections 15.4 and 15.8 in this unit carefully.

15.2 Why Paris?

Paris is an important European capital city for all sorts of reasons. It has a worldwide place in the imagination due to its history and reputation and due to its cultural, social and philosophical influences. Here are two research tasks to start you thinking about the city and its significance.

ACTIVITY 2

What do you know?

What do you already know about Paris? What knowledge do you have of the city? Think of landmarks, famous people and places, and activities that Paris is well known for. Think about how Paris is represented in literature, film, television, song lyrics and so on.

When you have gathered your ideas, divide them into two groups.

1 Actual knowledge/experience
2 Second-hand (received) knowledge

Then sub-divide the second group into where that knowledge comes from. Discuss your findings with the rest of the class. Here are some questions that you might consider:

- Do certain topics come up again and again? What are these? Food? Love and romance? Fashion?
- Were real experiences of Paris very different to second-hand ones?
- Is there a certain way of thinking about the city and its people?

ACTIVITY 3

Researching Paris

In order to better understand the various contexts of the city, it would also be a useful idea to do some more extensive research. Select two or three from this initial list as a starting point.

- The French Revolution
- The 1968 Paris Riots
- Fashion
- French philosophy and philosophers, e.g. Jean-Paul Sartre and Simone de Beauvoir
- Artists and musicians
- Writers
- The history of travelling to Paris
- The cemeteries of Paris
- Tourism in Paris.

15.3 Remembering places

15.3.1 Representation: selection and subjectivity

All of the texts in the anthology are broadly concerned with the representations of the concepts of place, memories, self and others. In Unit 4, we defined representation as the way in which events, people and places are portrayed through language and other meaning-making resources, for example, images and sound. The concept of representation is clearly linked to the notion of **point of view**, the particular perspective through which a text presents its version of reality. In Unit 4 we saw how the same event can be represented in a number of different ways depending on which aspects of that event a text producer wants to emphasise and which they want to downplay or omit. All narratives are of course highly selective in terms of what they reveal and what they conceal. Consequently writers and speakers make specific choices when they present their narratives. In other words, all representations display high **subjectivity** and are never neutral. This idea has important implications for your work on the texts in the anthology.

Key terms

point of view: the perspective used in a text through which a version of reality is presented

subjectivity: the characteristic of being seen from a particular perspective

Look at Text 15A, where the narrator is describing a group of tourist walkers in Paris.

Text 15A

Uncertain, they loiter at the foot of our street, at the corner of the Boulevard Saint-Germain, one of the busiest on this side of the Seine. Couples, usually, they're dressed in the seasonal variation of what is almost a uniform – beige raincoat or jacket, cotton or corduroy trousers, and sensible shoes.

Source: John Baxter (2013), *The Most Beautiful Walk in the World*

It is evident from Text 15A that the description of people and places is highly selective; they are both represented in ways that steer the reader towards viewing the situation in a particular way. In this extract, the narrating voice has selected a specific part of the location (the corner of the boulevard) and specific attributes of the walkers (their uncertainty, their movements and their clothing) to focus on. The latter is particularly subjective even though the narrator's reading of their feelings and movements are presented as facts; the particular attention to their clothes, described as a 'uniform', represents them rather negatively as a faceless group, lacking any individuality. This is exemplified in the fact that only 'raincoat or jacket' is modified by a colour and that the colour chosen is 'beige', which has conventional connotations of being uninspiring and mundane. The narrator could have chosen to mention the colours of other items or clothing, or perhaps the street, where, for example, we might imagine there to be a multitude of colours, but chooses not to do so. Instead this group of walkers - and by extension other tourists on walking guides through Paris - is being intentionally represented in a certain way. In this instance, it's not so much being told about the walkers that is important, but *how* we are told about them.

ACTIVITY 4

Selection

Read Text 15B, where the narrator describes the Bastille (a fortress and prison in Paris). How is an aspect of Paris represented in this extract? What has she selected to focus on?

Text 15B

We saw the hooks of those chains by which the prisoners were fastened, round the neck, to the walls of their cells; many of which, being below the level of the water, are in a constant state of humidity; and a noxious vapour issued from them, which more than once extinguished the candle, and was so insufferable that it required a strong spirit of curiosity to tempt one to enter.

Source: Helen Maria Williams, *Letters from France 1790–1796*

Check your responses in the Ideas section on Cambridge Elevate

15.3.2 Discourses of travel

One key aspect that links all of the anthology texts is that they all involve either directly or indirectly the idea of journeys to, from or within Paris. Broadly speaking then, all of the texts are concerned with travel and as such can be considered as members of the travel genre.

Travel as a narrative genre has a long history. Indeed, accounts of travel have been found on artefacts and literature from ancient Egypt, Greece and Rome. And of course, since composing and reading or listening to narratives is a universal human phenomenon, we can assume that whenever people have made journeys - however short these journeys may have been - they have told others about them.

ACTIVITY 5

Journeys

Think of a recent journey or number of journeys that you have made. These could be long journeys (perhaps on holiday to another country) or much shorter ones (perhaps an evening or a weekend away or even a day out shopping or attending a sporting event). Now think of examples of narratives you have told about these journeys around the following questions.

- To whom did you speak and/or write?
- What format/medium did you use?
- What was the purpose of your communication?
- What aspects of your journey did you emphasise?
- What kind of register did you use for each account?

Of course, some of the texts in the anthology are not examples of writing but are either speech, or blended mode texts that make use of new technologies such as blogging and discussion fora. However, these will still retain some of the key characteristics that are typical of the genre. In aiming for a definition, the literary scholar Carl Thompson (2011) suggests that travel narratives have the following defining features:

- they may focus on either complex or simple journeys but there is always a sense of moving into or out of a physical space that is at the heart of the narrative;

- they often involve an account of meeting and interacting with people, places and cultures that are unknown;
- they function either to give a literal account of the journey or to emphasise some kind of learning experience or revelation that has taken place from that journey;
- they offer an additional insight into the attitudes and belief systems of the writers/speakers themselves as well as their background and culture.

You can test these against examples of texts in the anthology to see the extent to which they adhere to these characteristics. For example, if you were to look at the extract from Ernest Hemingway's 'American Bohemians in Paris', taken from *Ernest Hemingway on Paris*, you could comment on the following:

- the extract details events following a journey made to Paris by Hemingway to live in the city and consequent visits to the Latin Quarter (an area renowned for its lively atmosphere) that he made;
- it focuses on the Café Rotonde, the people who frequent it, the events that take place there and the kind of culture associated with it;
- it functions to provide some kind of revelation about the Rotonde and its customers, their life histories and motivations;
- it offers a tremendous amount of detail on Hemingway's own perspective on the Rotonde and the people there, evident in strongly evaluative and attitudinal lexis and a generally negative portrayal.

The example from 'American Bohemians in Paris' demonstrates that representations of people, places and events often fit together as grand and coherent ways of thinking, talking and writing about the world.

The linguist James Paul Gee (2012) calls this a type of *Discourse* (the capital 'D' is intentional to show how important and pervasive in our society Discourses are). In 'American Bohemians in Paris', Hemingway adopts a written journalistic register to project a clearly defined way of viewing and thinking about specific people, places and societies. In this view of the world, Hemingway deliberately positions himself as an outsider. In contrast, if you were to look at a text such as Text 15O from the *Gransnet* forum, you would see a very different kind of Discourse operating, with participants interacting and behaving in much more collaborative ways. In Unit 2, we referred to this type of close-knit community, often found on specialist message boards, as a discourse community.

15.3.3 Writers, narrators, audiences and purposes

The types of language choices that text producers make and their overall motivation for representing places, people and events in certain ways is of course influenced by a vast range of contextual factors. One important question you will need to consider as you explore the texts in the anthology is the extent to which broad framing contextual factors such as the period in which the text was written and the gender and social class of the writer/speaker may have influenced its production and reception.

One of the most interesting angles to take might be to explore the actual and perceived influence of the gender of the writer/speaker on texts from the anthology. Historically, travel narrative has tended to be a more male-dominated genre, centred around traditionally stereotypical male-centred stories of adventure, discovery and reclamation of land. Indeed, restrictions on what was deemed acceptable female behaviour meant that when women did travel, they did so under tight restrictions regarding where and with whom they could go, and were often accompanied by chaperones. Carl Thompson (2011) suggests that women's status as writers of and about travel prior to the seventeenth century was limited since their relative lack of education compared to men meant that even if they did travel, they might not have the literacy skills to be able to record their experiences. However, restrictions and stereotyping began to dissolve, and the feminist movement in the 1960s and 1970s led to more female travel writing and a re-evaluation of the perception of the genre as male-centred. This led to a new focus on how travel narratives written by women might represent distinctive female perspectives.

ACTIVITY 6

Gender and perspective

Read the following quotations, the first from the travel writer Mary Morris (2007) and the second from the travel writers and broadcasters Dea Birkett and Sara Wheeler (1998).

'Women move through the world differently than men.'

'The emotional terrain is traditionally seen as the territory of women writers.'

Using any number of the following texts from the anthology, explore to what extent you agree or disagree with these ways of thinking about women's narratives. Do you think they represent distinctively female ways of seeing the world? Why? How?

- Nancy Miller, *Breathless: An American Girl in Paris*
- Natasha Fraser-Cavassoni, 'Understanding chic'
- Helen Maria Williams, *Letters from France 1790–1796*
- Anna and Zara's personal narratives
- Lucy Knisley, *French Milk*
- Jennifer Cox, *Around the World in 80 Dates.*

Researchers working in the field of language and gender studies have opposed a crude notion of difference between male and female uses of language. For example, work on gendered language has moved away from categorising male and female speech styles as polarised and driven by biological differences, instead focusing on how speakers (and of course writers) construct and perform gendered identities for themselves, which may either draw on or challenge perceived stereotypes. The idea that gender is something that speakers and writers 'do' as part of a deliberate projecting of identity is critical of a so-called **difference theory of language** where males and females are understood in similar terms to those suggested by Morris, and Birkett and Wheeler. The psychologist Janet Hyde (2005) actually proposes a **gender similarities hypothesis**, claiming that in fact there are substantially more similarities than there are differences between male and female language.

She argues that where there are differences, these may be due to a number of other variables. You can check these by returning to Activity 6 and thinking about how the age, background (born in Paris? European? Travelling from a different continent?), status/occupation, and education of the writers and speakers and so on could influence the content and style of those narratives.

Key terms

difference theory of language: the belief that men and women have innate differences in the style and function of their speech and writing

gender similarities hypothesis: a way of thinking that argues for more similarities than differences in male and female speech and writing

Finally, two of the most important contextual factors to consider are audience and purpose. You could return to Unit 2 to review key learning around these terms: in particular, the notions of actual and implied readers and of single and multipurposes. As you read and reflect on the texts in the anthology, keep in mind the extent to which the following influence the ways in which these texts are produced and received.

- **Audience**: who is the implied reader/listener? Who might the actual reader/listener(s) be? In what kinds of places and situations might these texts be read and/or heard?
- **Purpose**: are the texts single or multipurpose texts? Might they get used in different ways from that originally intended? How does this affect language choices?

15.4 Re-creative writing and *Remembered places*

So far in this unit, you have looked at texts in different genres and thought about different modes, and you have considered the role of point of view, audience and purpose. Now we are going to explore these aspects of texts through a method called **re-creative writing**. If you are following the AS specification, you will need to complete a re-creative writing task on one of your examination papers. If you are following the A Level specification, then this introduction to re-creative writing will support your work on *Writing about society* (Unit 18) where you will explore characterisation and narrative voice in literary texts. Here, though, we will be using it to analyse and comment on aspects of mode, genre, point of view, context, audience and purpose in the kinds of texts you're studying in the anthology. This work will enrich your understanding of the anthology texts whichever pathway you are following.

See 15.8.2 for a re-creative writing task

Re-creative writing can be thought of as a three-part analytical process of studying a text. Let's think through this process in relation to Text 15C.

Text 15C

St-Jacques was so long and crooked that it had the character of three or four streets: a ragged place with dank laneways and jutting decayed houses … The street became a sedate cobbled stretch … further along … little groceries and bakeries appeared … Finally, it came up to the sweaty, grey … church of St-Jacques.

Source: Peter Lennon, *Foreign Correspondent: Paris in the Sixties*

Firstly, we need to look at the 'what', the 'how' and the 'why' of the text.

- What is the text about? What is the text producer trying to communicate? What details, opinions, etc. are the main focus of the writing?
- How is the text producer conveying the content – the 'what' of the text? What language is used and with what interpretative effects? What mode and genre is the text producer using?
- Why is the text producer communicating in this way? What is the purpose of the text? What audience are they trying to appeal to and what kinds of overall effects are they trying to produce?

So, let's look at the 'what', 'how' and 'why' of Text 15C. This text is a description of Rue St-Jacques, focusing particularly on the changing character of the street as you walk from one end to another. The differences in the character of street are conveyed using adjectives that range from 'long', 'crooked', 'ragged', 'dank' and 'decayed' initially, to 'sedate', 'cobbled' and 'little', and then to 'sweaty' and 'grey', shifting from a sense of decay, to attractive and ornate, and back to dismal. The nouns mark a change in focus from the 'laneways' and 'houses' to the 'groceries and bakeries' to the 'church'. The participial adjective 'jutting' suggests a kind of disordered protrusion, and works with some of the adjectives and some of the other verbs (like 'appeared' and 'became') to give the street a chaotic and animate, dynamic quality. The description of the church as 'sweaty' adds to this a sense of **anthropomorphism**. The length of the street is emphasised through the adverb 'so' in 'so long', the spatial implications of the noun 'stretch', and the adverb 'finally', suggesting the journey down the street has taken quite some time. The text is a memoir and seems designed to give a detailed and atmospheric impression of Rue St-Jacques to its readers, guiding them along it as if they were there, and illustrating the contrasting gloomy and quaint character of the street.

Secondly, we need to use our understanding of the text to compose a re-creative version of it, adapting it to new purposes. This act of re-creative writing demonstrates your understanding of how the original text works – and of the relationship between language and meaning more broadly – and demonstrates your creative flair in effectively recasting and repurposing the original.

'…a ragged place with dank laneways and jutting decayed houses…'

***Foreign Correspondent: Paris in the Sixties*, Peter Lennon**

- One act of re-creative writing could be to recast the original text (referred to as the **base text**) as spoken directions given in response to someone asking the way to the church of St-Jacques. The recast text might be something like Text 15D.

Key terms

re-creative writing: the deliberate act of transforming a text so as to present it from a different perspective and/or in a different genre

anthropomorphism: the attributing of human characteristics to non-human entities

base text: the original text from which the act of re-creative writing takes place

Text 15D

Right, OK, well we're at the top of Rue St-Jacques now, right, and the church is all the way at the other end. It's a really long street, and it changes quite a bit as you walk down it – it's pretty slummy up this end but further down it becomes cobbled and quite quaint for a bit. You'll go past a few little grocery shops and bakeries. Keep going and you'll see it get a bit more grim again as you get nearer to the church. It's grey – you shouldn't miss it.

Text 15D demonstrates one way in which the Text 15C could be recast. Now complete Activity 7, thinking about how you might describe a hotel in the area.

ACTIVITY 7

Recasting a base text

The hotel Dagmar is situated opposite the church of St-Jacques. Transform the base text into part of a radio advertisement for the hotel describing its location. Write about 200 words.

You might consider:

- what the managers of the hotel (the Dagmar) think will appeal to visitors about the location
- how the hotel will describe the local area positively.

The third step is to provide a commentary on the re-creative writing, to explain the 'what', 'how' and 'why' of the new text, but with an emphasis on 'how'. The commentary is in effect an analysis of the recast text, illustrating your thinking behind your language choices, and your understanding of how the language you've chosen shapes the meaning you intend to create. So, in your commentary, you need to select some features of language in your rewrite and explain your reasons for using them. For example, a commentary on the recast Text 15D might discuss some of the following aspects of language use.

- **The colloquial register** (with simple and imprecise lexis and phrasing like 'quite a bit', 'a few' and 'pretty slummy', and fillers like 'well' and 'right'), suggesting the spoken mode and an informal, everyday context.
- **The use of pronouns** – the first-person plural 'we' in situating the addresser and addressee together initially, and then the second-person pronoun 'you' in describing what the addresser will see on his/her route.
- **The use of orienting spatial language**, including some deixis, to describe the addressee's journey and the different markers of the route.
- **The use of adverbs and adjectives** to convey the length of the street and aspects of its varied character, and to hedge some of the assertions the speaker is making (such as 'all the way', 'really long', 'quite a bit' 'pretty slummy', 'quite quaint', and 'a bit more grim').

There are a few other elements of language use which could be discussed, but you aren't expected to provide a fully comprehensive analysis. Rather, your ability to select interesting and interpretatively significant features for discussion helps to illustrate your analytical skill and linguistic understanding. Along with being selective, organising your thinking clearly and logically, providing examples, and explaining the relationship between language and effect are crucial aspects of a successful commentary.

ACTIVITY 8

Writing a commentary on a recast text

Write a commentary on the recast text you created in Activity 7. Identify four specific examples of language in your writing and explain your reasons for using them. Write about 200 words.

The re-creative writing process is a really useful analytical tool. Approaching texts in this way helps to develop your skills in understanding how texts work, and in controlling interpretative effects in your own writing.

You've now explored this process step by step. You can repeat this process with any of the extracts you look at in this unit and think about how and why you might make certain choices. Activity 31 at the end of the unit gives you the opportunity to try it out all together as you would if you were taking the AS exam.

15.5 Places, people and events

15.5.1 Space and place

All of the texts in the anthology are concerned with locations, either broadly focusing on Paris (for example the extract from *The Sweet Life in Paris* by David Lebovitz), or more specifically on a particular area of the city (for example *Neither Here Nor There: Travels in Europe* by Bill Bryson), or even more specifically on a unique landmark (for example Isabelle's narrative about le Parc Monceau). A useful distinction to make when thinking about the importance of locations is between the concepts of **space** and **place**.

Geographers commonly use this distinction to signify the difference between a set of co-ordinates on a map (space) and a location that is given significance and value through its use as a site of human activity filled with interaction with others, important events and personal memories (place). The geographer Mike Crang (1998) describes how a place comes into being in the following way:

> Spaces become places as they become 'time-thickened'. They have a past and a future that binds people round them.

The concept of 'time-thickened' is interesting here. Crang suggests that the layering of events and the building of memories around a physical location gradually result in a 'dot on a map' evolving into a significant part of someone's life, forever associated with a feeling, emotion, set of events or group of people. Crang also argues that a place usually has a series of narratives attached to it, marking when, how and why it became significant, and tracing its value as a site of significance.

A good example of the concept of 'time-thickening' can be seen in Isabelle's narrative about le Parc Monceau. In this extract Isabelle recounts how the park gathered a significance over time from her early days playing there as a young girl, taking pony rides, going there as a schoolchild and then as an older college student with friends. This is an excellent example of Crang's term 'time-thickened'. In the course of her narrative, Isabelle uses temporal and spatial deixis; for example, 'we used to go' and 'near a bilingual school', to anchor her experiences around particular times and landmarks; this also has the effect of creating the sense of 'thickening'.

Isabelle's experience and her account of the park is an embodied one drawing on a range of sensory experiences. She refers to sights (e.g. the ruins), touch (sitting on the benches), sound (the waterfall) and smell (cigarettes) to evoke a representation of a place that is full of personal significance.

ACTIVITY 9

Significant places

Think about a place that is significant to you in the same way as le Parc Monceau is to Isabelle. Draw a picture of that place in as much detail as you can, outlining the full range of embodied knowledge that you have of it in terms of sights, sounds, texture, smells and so on. Compare and discuss your place with someone else. How is your place 'time-thickened'?

Now think about and explore other texts in the anthology that 'thicken' time in the creation of a place in a similar way. You could start by looking at the following places in these texts:

- Jennifer Cox, *Around the World in 80 Dates* (on Père Lachaise cemetery)
- Peter Lennon, *Foreign Correspondent: Paris in the Sixties* (on the area around the Hôtel du Maréchal Ney)
- Helen Maria Williams, *Letters from France 1790–1796* (on le Champ de Mars).

15.5.2 Culture and society

As well as drawing attention to significant places, travel narratives also explore aspects of **culture** and **society**, and in the case of the texts in the anthology, those of France and Paris. Culture can be defined as a set of practices that involve shared ways of thinking and acting, and which attach value to material objects of various kinds. On the other hand, a society can be viewed as the acting out of these cultural beliefs and practices by a group of people working and living in a specific location.

See 15.3.2 for more on Discourse

Representations of cultures and societies can be both positive and negative, drawing on aspects of cultural beliefs and practices that appear both attractive and not so appealing. In some instances these can present themselves as **stereotypes**, broad representations of a group of people around exaggerated perceived common characteristics. You might have identified some of these commonly held stereotypes about Parisians in the research you undertook in Section 15.2 of this unit.

Key terms

space: a location in terms of its co-ordinates on a map

place: a location that is given significance and value through being a site of interaction with others, full of important events and personal memories

culture: a set of practices that involve shared ways of thinking and acting and which attach value to material objects of various kinds

society: a group of people working and living in a specific location who act out cultural beliefs and practices

stereotype: a broad representation of a group of people around exaggerated perceived common characteristics

A good example of a stereotype can be seen in Text 15E, where the narrator is writing about traffic congestion around the Arc de Triomphe.

Text 15E

Here you have a city with the world's most pathologically aggressive drivers – drivers who in other circumstances would be given injections of thorazine from syringes the size of bicycle pumps and confined to their beds with leather straps – and you give them an open space where they can all try to go in any of thirteen directions at once.

Source: Bill Bryson, *Neither Here Nor There: Travels in Europe*

In Text 15E, the stereotype of Parisian drivers that Bryson presents is informed by his own Paris schema, first- and second-hand knowledge that he has built up over many years. The stereotype is evident in the pre-modified noun phrase 'most pathologically aggressive drivers' with strong negative connotations, and the analogy of a patient needing a heavy dose of thorazine (an anti-psychotic drug).

It can sometimes be very difficult to pin down exactly how schemas come into being since they can have many influences and are prone to change over time. In fact, in some cases, we can build up very detailed schemas without being conscious of how complex they are. What is clear is people (and consequently writers and speakers in the anthology) may have very strong ideas about a society and its people even before they travel and experience it first-hand for themselves.

ACTIVITY 10

Paris schemas

Using texts from the anthology, explore the assumptions and stereotypes held by writers and speakers before they set off on their travels. What were they expecting? How do they represent the societies that they are about to visit? What do their Paris schemas consist of?

Stereotyping is not always negative. In Section 15.2, you may have discovered that a very powerful and enduring stereotype of Paris is that it is a 'city of love' as Text 15F demonstrates.

Text 15F

Paris is often called the most Romantic city in the world, and it's easy to see why. It has been this way for centuries, with the French capital starring in countless poems, plays, books and movies about love.

Source: *Not for Parents: Paris*

A strange but fascinating consequence of such positive stereotyping of Paris can be found in what has become known as 'Paris syndrome'. This is a disorder where tourists visiting Paris with expectations fuelled by positive representations of the city and its people in their own popular culture are overcome by feelings of immense disappointment when the reality of experiencing the city is very different to what they had believed to be the case. Indeed, a BBC report in 2006 on the condition suggested that the Japanese embassy even had a dedicated 24-hour helpline to support any tourists suffering from it!

'Paris is often called the most Romantic city in the world...'

Not for Parents: Paris

Read about 'Paris syndrome' via Cambridge Elevate

15.5.3 Moving to Paris

'Paris syndrome' is an example of what is known as **culture shock**, defined by the sociologist John Macionis (2008) as 'personal disorientation when experiencing another way of life'. This can manifest itself in several ways but often includes negative feelings towards cultural practices and language, being bored and homesick, and in extreme cases, feeling anxiety and a sense of danger.

ACTIVITY 11

Culture shock

Find explicit examples of evidence of culture shock in texts from the anthology. How do writers and/or speakers frame their responses through particular language choices (lexis and syntax) to the environments they find themselves in?

It has been suggested that culture shock occurs in the following stages:

1. **honeymoon stage:** feeling excitement and being intrigued by the new culture and society
2. **anxiety stage:** beginning to feel a sense of disillusionment, disappointment or fear about the new culture and society. It is here where the majority of negative feelings are experienced
3. **coping stage:** developing strategies to deal with the demands of living in a new culture or society
4. **settled in stage:** a final stage where the traveller feels comfortable in their new surroundings.

Can you trace these stages in any of the texts in the anthology? Again, examine how these feelings are presented through the language choices writers and speakers make.

Moving to a new environment can also be understood as part of a grander narrative structure. The literary scholar Tim Youngs (2013) suggests that the **quest narrative** is central to the travel genre. It involves a hero (the traveller) embarking on a journey that contains the following elements:

- it focuses on a search for something or someone unavailable in the hero's present culture/society
- it is almost exclusively from the traveller's perspective and so presents a very subjective way of seeing the world
- characters and objects within the narrative are seen as obstructions that need to be overcome
- readers and/or listeners are positioned to follow the narrative in certain ways so as to accept a particular point of view – that of the traveller
- the 'questers' use the journeys they take for their own purposes as a way of promoting a certain world-view and often centred round a narrative of self-discovery.

Key terms

culture shock: the sense of personal disappointment that may be felt when experiencing another culture

quest narrative: a grand narrative design involving a 'hero' undertaking a journey into a foreign land that underpins much of the travel genre

ACTIVITY 12

Quest narratives

You can explore the typical characteristics of a quest narrative by examining to what extent they can apply to relevant texts in the anthology. It would be particularly useful to explore how other people, their cultures and societies are presented as part of larger narrative structures. This type of representation is known as **othering**, a way of presenting differences between cultures, often in a negative way – think back to Text 15E.

A particular kind of quest is captured in the term **flâneur**, a French word referring to an individual immersed in the everyday events and activities of a particular culture, and particularly those around urban and highly populated areas, as a way of interacting with a particular cultural space and finding out about its practices. In English, flâneur is loosely translated as 'stroller', an outsider who wanders into a location and remarks on the culture and society there. This definition and description would certainly fit Bryson's narrator. Are there other narrators in texts in the anthology that could be described in the same way?

Key terms

othering: a way of presenting differences between cultures, often in a negative way

flâneur: a French term for a 'stroller', an individual who observes and experiences the practices of a culture and society

15.5.4 Memories

ACTIVITY 13

Memories

Think of a place that you have strong memories of as a child. What are those memories? Why do you have them? What are they connected with? Do you think those memories have changed over time?

The concept of memory and the act of recollecting memories are important areas to consider in travel narratives. In completing Activity 11, you may have thought about how memories necessarily fade over time and how they might take on an additional or very different significance as you get older. Indeed, memories are so fragile, and our cognitive capacity for remembering relatively limited, that we often rely on material objects like postcards and souvenirs from holidays and trips to preserve our sense of events of a particular place in the past. Advances in technology and social media mean that these physical reminders can now be in virtual form such as message board posts, blogs and photographs in shared spaces and tweets, all of which are instantly recoverable unless deleted. And, memories are often embodied in a range of sensory experiences such as sight, taste and smell. You might want to refer back to Isabelle's narrative about le Parc Monceau for an example of how memories are often associated with experiences beyond language. In fact all memory is a form of reconstruction, a way of representing the past and making sense of events, people and places using a range of strategies motivated by the current context.

In this way, memory is itself a form of **narrative discourse**.

See 15.5.1 for more on Isabelle's narrative about le Parc Monceau

As you explore the texts in the anthology, it would also be useful to think about the ways that language is used to present both memories and the act of remembering itself. Some of the ways that memories may be represented include:

- narrative structures that follow a Labovian pattern with scene-setting, and orientating details before outlining memories which may be evaluated in the present time frame by the narrator
- analogies to the present time to emphasise the significance of a memory in the current context
- the use of the past tense to set up a distant time frame within which events occur
- the use of mental verb processes
- a reliance on verbs of perception and sensory experience
- the use of epistemic modality to stress degrees of certainty towards memories and their significance.

See 16.4.2 for more on degrees of certainty and their significance

As an example, look at Text 15G, taken from Zara's personal narrative about Paris.

Text 15G

there was a time when we (.) went on holiday and my parents heard me saying in the night to my sister, (1) 'What is this? This isn't the real Paris. This isn't Disneyland Paris.' (.) Erm. So, I think it just, I guess as a small child it's a bit, (1) you don't get as excited in the same way by things unless they're (.) rollercoasters or something.

Here, Zara uses a structure that sets the scene for the narrative that continues, the past tense to anchor the narrative in a different time frame, a number of verbs of perception, 'guess', 'think', 'know', and reference to sensory experience, and the experience of *Disneyland* and rollercoasters to help introduce the memories that she continues to explore in the remainder of the extract. You could explore how she uses language in the act of remembering and presenting her memories by reading and commenting on the rest of the extract in your anthology.

ACTIVITY 14

Memories

How are memories explored in the following texts? Think about the range of strategies text producers use to portray significant events that have occurred in the past and the people that took part in them?

- Bill Bryson, *Neither Here Nor There: Travels in Europe*
- Trip Advisor message board posts, 'What do you wish someone had told you?'
- Ernest Hemingway, *Ernest Hemingway on Paris*
- Mike and Sophia, 'Visiting Paris'
- Sophia talking about travelling from Charles de Gaulle airport to central Paris by train ('Memories of places in Paris').

15.6 Metaphor

Metaphor involves describing one thing in terms of another. In Unit 6 we also saw that metaphors are not only confined to literary texts; indeed much non-literary material is rich in metaphorical language.

Metaphor works by making explicit connections between two different concepts so that we understand one more fully. These connections may be presented directly or indirectly but always involve the transferring of attributes from one concept or thing to another. For example, in Text 15H the reader is being asked to think about the product (Samsung Audio Dock) through another concept/object: chocolate. The metaphor works by presenting the sound that a consumer will get from this product through the features of chocolate. This is emphasised both verbally though the phrase 'a new flavour of sound' and visually through the image of the musical note (a crotchet) 'dripping' with chocolate.

The metaphor becomes understood by a reader knowing that sound does not usually either have a flavour or drip chocolate and therefore realising that a connection is being made between the two to influence our reaction to the qualities of the audio dock. In this instance we are able to draw on our knowledge of what 'chocolate' is like and transfer these attributes over to 'sound' so as to enrich our understanding of what the Samsung device will sound like. You will have explored some of the associations that we might be expected to make in Activity 2 in Unit 6 but here are some potential characteristics of chocolate and how we might be expected to understand the audio dock in these terms.

Watch tutorial video, Metaphor, on Cambridge Elevate

Table 15A: The metaphor 'sound is chocolate'

Characteristics of chocolate	Understood qualities of sound through the metaphor
Luxurious	Has a significant quality and texture that provides the listener with the same positive feeling and sensual pleasure as indulging in eating a luxurious bar of chocolate
Tasty	
Has a smooth texture	
Has a distinctive smell	
Melting chocolate is warm	
Provides a feeling of well-being to the consumer	

This metaphor follows a very conventional pattern of using a more concrete/physical entity (chocolate) to understand something that is more abstract (sound). In fact, sound is often understood in terms more related to physical entities such as in expressions like 'a warm sound'. However, in this particular example, the metaphor is made much more explicit in drawing on something a bit more unconventional, and the text producer clearly has a vision of how readers might respond to this and the associations that they will make viewing this product in such a way.

Text 15H

Source: Samsung

Another very common metaphor is one which presents life as a type of journey. Again, as we saw in Unit 6, this is present in everyday expressions such 'heading in the right direction', 'moving on with my life', and 'going sideways'. Furthermore we conceptualise our lives in terms of stages and milestones such as anniversaries, birthdays and significant events such as starting and leaving school, learning to drive, getting a job and so on, all of which are viewed as points along a timeline. It's clear that our abstract concept of life is understood as a series of movements along a path from birth to death in the same way as we physically undertake a journey from point A to point B. As you might imagine, this metaphor is significant in the context of writing about travel or place since the journey can take on significant meaning and hold wider symbolic value. Indeed the often autobiographical and revelatory nature of some travel narratives means that the act of writing itself is often seen as a kind of journey moving from one life stage to another. In fact, the literary critic and philosopher Michel de Certeau (2001) argues that all writing is actually a form of travel writing since the act of composition necessarily involves taking the writer on a journey either within an imaginative world or exploring him or herself.

ACTIVITY 15

Metaphors of journeys

Find examples of the metaphors 'life is a journey' and 'writing is a journey' in different kinds of spoken, written and blended mode texts, including any in this anthology. How do writers and speakers use this metaphor? Can you find examples of unconventional or particularly creative variations of this?

15.6.1 The double-journey

Text 15I provides a good example of how travel narratives draw on life being understood metaphorically as a journey, where the journey taken - and written about - in the travel narrative assumes additional significance.

Text 15I

Like so many others, David Lebovitz dreamed about living in Paris ever since he first visited the city in the 1980s. Finally, after a nearly two-decade career as a pastry chef and cookbook author, he moved to Paris to start a new life. Having crammed all his worldly belongings into three suitcases, he arrived, hopes high, at his new apartment in the lively Bastille neighborhood.

Source: David Lebovitz, *The Sweet Life in Paris*, blurb

Many narratives about travel involve a type of **double-journey** like this one, where the writer or speaker is not only relaying the events of a physical journey they have made but also describing a psychological journey, usually involving some kind of self-discovery, reinvention of the self or personal quest. In some instances, the psychological journey becomes the central focus of the writing so much so that the physical journey is downplayed and given less significance. Indeed the travel writers and broadcasters Dea Birkett and Sarah Wheeler (1998) argue that 'the writer's inner journey is the most important part - and certainly the most interesting part of any travel book'.

Key terms

narrative discourse: the shaping of the story through choices in language and structure

double-journey: a narrative that relays both the events of a physical journey and a psychological one that the narrator has undertaken

A good example of the double-journey can be seen in Text 15J.

Text 15J

Paris was my first taste of a Latin country. I was thirteen and went with my godmother, Marigold Johnson, and her three teenage children. We travelled by car. I cannot remember crossing the channel – we were coming from England – but I do recall a noisy traffic jam caused by a motor bike accident. It was a hazy afternoon, our car windows were rolled down, and I was struck by the smell of baked baguettes wafting along the street, the feisty honking of cars, and a toddler with a blunt fringe catching my eye and slowly sucking on her lollipop. The Parisians were different, I quickly registered.

A few hours later, I poured water and shook sugar into my first *citron presse*. The next morning, I found myself admiring the clipped lawns of the jardins du Luxembourg. Topping everything off was the discovery of school notebooks packed with cubed pages as opposed to lined ones. I remember gliding my hand down their brightly colored covers and liking the rainbowlike array they formed in my suitcase.

Ten days later, I returned to my family and became a Paris Bore. Every conversation became an occasion to slip in tales from my Parisian adventure.

Source: Natasha Fraser-Cavassoni, 'Understanding chic'

In Text 15J, Fraser-Cavassoni is clearly recounting a physical journey (travelling to Paris for the first time as a child) but the journey as recounted in this memoir is also a psychological one as it marks an important stage in her growing up and making sense of the world. The physical journey is told largely through the use of temporal deixis (for example, the use of the past tense to anchor the events of the journey in the past) and spatial deixis (for example, 'crossing the channel' and 'we were coming from' that position events around particular locations). In contrast, in the first paragraph, the use of verbs of perception and focus on sensory experiences to describe Paris and the people within it have a revelatory aspect that suggest the psychological journey that the narrator is also undertaking.

This pattern continues in the second paragraph where Fraser-Cavassoni intersperses details of her physical journey with details of how she becomes immersed into French culture. This culminates in a sense of her having established a strong mental connection with Paris and the sense that the physical journey that she has undertaken has also acted metaphorically as a journey of discovery both about Paris, its culture and its people, and about herself. This is made clear at the beginning of the third paragraph where she recounts returning home and being perceived as a 'Paris Bore'. The physical journey in this case has resulted in a significant change in the way the narrator views the world; here, writing becomes a vehicle for a process of self-reflection and discovery.

ACTIVITY 16

Exploring 'double-journeys'

Read the anthology extract from Nancy Miller's 'Waiting for Godard' taken from *Breathless: An American Girl in Paris*. How might you read this extract through the lens of a 'double-journey'?

Check your responses in the Ideas section on Cambridge Elevate

ACTIVITY 17

Examining metaphor across the anthology

How do other texts in the anthology make use of metaphor at this similar kind of global level? What similarities and differences can you find between them in the way that metaphor is used to organise ideas around physical and psychological journeys? As a starting point, you could explore and comment on these texts:

- David Lebovitz, *A Sweet Life in Paris*
- Anna and Zara's personal narratives
- Lucy Knisley, *French Milk*
- Jennifer Cox, *Around the World in 80 Dates*.

15.6.2 Understanding the unknown

Metaphors are often used by writers and speakers of travel narratives to present events, people and customs that are unusual and unfamiliar in terms of something that is known and familiar. These types of metaphorical construction can be realised in a number of different forms including **simile**, **personification** and **allegory**, all of which represent different surface forms of metaphor. A simile draws attention to the connection made by using the words 'like' or 'as'; personification involves a non-human entity being understood in human terms; and allegory involves metaphorical connections being made between two larger narrative structures so that one is understood in terms of another.

Key terms

simile: a form that draws attention to a connection between two concepts or things by using the words 'like' or 'as'

personification: representing a non-human entity in human terms

allegory: a metaphorical connection that is made between two larger narrative structures so that one is understood in terms of another

ACTIVITY 18

Metaphor: places, people and events

Writers and speakers also use metaphor to make their description of places, people and events interesting and engaging. Look at Text 15K, which describes the interior of the Café Rotonde. What metaphors does Hemingway use to describe the Rotonde? How are they realised and what effect do you think they are intended to have?

Text 15K

A first look into the smoky, high-ceilinged, table-crammed interior of the Rotonde gives you the same feeling that hits you as you step into the bird-house at the zoo. There seems to be a tremendous, raucous, many-pitched squawking going on, broken up by many waiters who fly around through the smoke like so many black and white magpies.

Source: Ernest Hemingway, *Ernest Hemingway on Paris*

Check your responses in the Ideas section on Cambridge Elevate

The metaphor in Text 15K is an example of what is known as an **extended metaphor** or **megametaphor**, a construction that carries on beyond one example and provides a structural frame for the way that we view and respond to places, people and events. The letters in Nancy Miller's 'Waiting for Godard' operate in a similar way. Look back at your work on Activity 14 and think about how this metaphor is used by Miller in her writing.

Key terms

extended metaphor/megametaphor: a metaphor that continues beyond just one example and provides a structural frame for viewing places, people and events

fuzziness: the characteristic of not neatly fitting into one category; in the case of texts, not neatly fitting into one genre

15.7 Genre

15.7.1 Revisiting the notion of genre

One of the most important ways that you can study the texts in this anthology is by thinking carefully about genre. As we saw in Unit 3, categorising texts according to their genre is useful since it enables us to explore shared characteristics and expected textual conventions. However, as we also saw in that unit, genres are fluid and dynamic, and often it can be difficult to pin down some texts as being exclusively of a particular genre. A useful way of thinking is therefore to adopt a prototype model whereby texts are seen as excellent, good, satisfactory or poor examples of a particular genre. This can help you to think about both how to cope with **fuzziness** when it

'...the smoky, high-ceilinged, table-crammed interior of the Rotonde...'

Ernest Hemingway on Paris, **Ernest Hemingway**

comes to categorising – for example with multimodal or blended mode texts – and give you a useful way in to thinking about the complexities and intricacies associated with different types of texts.

In the sections that follow we explore the characteristics of a number of different genres that are represented in the anthology. This will allow you to consider how well texts exemplify a particular genre. You should also think about to what extent generic conventions hold an important influence on the choices that writers and speakers make in terms of their affordances and constraints.

An **affordance** is a term that refers to the properties or characteristics associated with a particular genre or mode that dictate how it might be used. For example, the Eurostar advertisement 'Stories are waiting in Paris' is both an advertisement and crucially an example of a text that uses verbal and visual codes. This means that the text producer (Eurostar) is able to draw on the conventions associated with advertising as a genre and specifically the affordances associated with using a visual code in a format that can be easily viewed and shared. This advertisement was hosted on the company's official *YouTube* channel so is both easily accessible and able to be further shared through various social media. These offer a range of possibilities as to how this text might be received and the situations in which it might be viewed (on a computer, laptop, tablet, mobile phone; at home, travelling and so on).

In contrast, a **constraint** refers to properties or characteristics that limit its potential uses. In the case of the Eurostar advertisement, a very obvious physical constraint is that a screen and sound are required in order to 'read' the advertisement. Furthermore, one of its affordances (portability) is also dependent on having an internet connection of some kind; consequently this might actually prove to be a very serious and limiting constraint.

Key terms

affordance: a property or characteristic of a particular genre or mode that dictates how it might be used

constraint: a property or characteristic that limits potential uses

15.7.2 First-person narratives

Examples of these include:

- Peter Lennon, *Foreign Correspondent: Paris in the Sixties*
- David Lebovitz, *The Sweet Life in Paris*
- Helen Maria Williams, *Letters from France 1790–1796*
- Anna and Zara's narratives
- Natasha Fraser-Cavassoni, 'Understanding chic'
- Lucy Knisley, *French Milk*
- Isabelle and Sophia, 'Memories of places in Paris'.

The first-person narrative, told through the use of a first-person pronoun, is a very broad genre that incorporates a number of different types of text such as autobiography (e.g. Peter Lennon), memoir (e.g. Bill Bryson), political reportage (e.g. Helen Maria Williams) and spoken monologues (e.g. Anna and Zara). Clearly first-person narratives can function as a **sub-genre** within other genres as well. For example Lucy's Knisley's *French Milk* can also be understood as graphic non-fiction, and consequently has many characteristics associated with that genre. First-person narratives contain some of the following features:

- **strong tellability** in so far as the narrative will represent events that the narrator believes are important to narrate
- **extensive use of the first-person** singular and plural pronouns 'I' and 'we' to shape the narrative from a particular perspective
- **a register or registers normally associated with the narrator**, including the use of particular words, phrases and syntax and patterns of linguistic behaviour, for example the tendency to exaggerate, understate, make attempts at humour, engage or disengage the reader

- **verbs of perception and modality that frame the narrator's character** (e.g. insightful, ignorant, uncertain, proud, arrogant) and their view of people, or places and events
- **references back through time** (marked through temporal deixis) to previous experiences or memories that may be personal to them and have some connection to the current narrative
- **an ability to step outside the narrative** to provide evaluations on narrative events.

Key terms

sub-genre: a further division of a genre into an additional category

See 15.7.4 for more on genre

As the events in a first-person narrative are filtered through the perspective of the narrator who assumes the 'I' of the narrative, they will be largely subjective and present views of people, places and events that, despite being extremely idiosyncratic, may be presented in a way that positions the reader to accept them as facts. Look at Texts 15L(a) and (b), which are from Texts 15A and 15E.

See 15.3.1 for more on subjective narrative

Text 15L

(a)

Uncertain, they loiter at the foot of our street, at the corner of the Boulevard Saint-Germain, one of the busiest on this side of the Seine. Couples, usually, they're dressed in the seasonal variation of what is almost a uniform – beige raincoat or jacket, cotton or corduroy trousers, and sensible shoes.

Source: John Baxter, *The Most Beautiful Walk in the World*

(b)

Here you have a city with the world's most pathologically aggressive drivers – drivers who in other circumstances would be given injections of thorazine from syringes the size of bicycle pumps and confined to their beds with leather straps – and you give them an open space where they can all try to go in any of thirteen directions at once.

Source: Bill Bryson, *Neither Here Nor There: Travels in Europe*

In your previous work on these texts, you may have highlighted the highly subjective way that John Baxter chooses to focus on the clothing of the walkers, and particular lexical and syntactic choices that present his 'view of the world'. Bryson, as we have already seen, chooses to play on a stereotype of Parisians as fast and not particularly careful drivers. You might have noticed that Bryson makes use of specific modifiers and analogies to describe the drivers and draws on a more casual conversational register, which is maintained throughout most of this book and is often seen as a marker of his unique style. He also uses the second-person pronoun 'you' generically in expressions such as 'you have' and 'you give' rather than speaking to a specific addressee. However, the intention here may be to promote a sense of familiarity and proximity.

ACTIVITY 19

Rewriting perspectives

Take one of Text 15L(a) and (b) and rewrite them for a different audience and purpose so that they represent a different perspective on the events they describe. Think about how these might be reshaped to provide an alternative lens on the same events. These are genres you would not be expected to write on in this specification, but they will provide good practice in exploring how point of view operates.

- Text 15L(a) - a transcript from a radio programme interviewing the chairperson of the *Paris Walkers* association, a group dedicated to walking around Paris, trying to attract new members
- Text 15L(b) - a series of tweets by a Parisian describing how non-Parisians should approach the Arc de Triomphe roundabout when driving in Paris (you might need to undertake some further research on the roundabout to complete this task).

15.7.3 Information texts

Examples of these include:

- Rough Guides, *The Rough Guide to Paris*
- Alastair Horne, *Seven Ages of Paris*
- Klay Lamprell, *Not For Parents: Paris, Everything You Ever Wanted to Know*
- Reginald Piggott and Matt Thompson, *Mile By Mile London to Paris*
- Lonely Planet travel videos on *YouTube*
- Rick Steves, *Paris Audio Tours – The Louvre Podcast* and accompanying map

The texts in the anthology that might be considered information texts also include a wide range of sub-genres, and are written for a range of different audiences and purposes. This can be demonstrated by looking at the examples in this section, all of which do more than simply give information. For example, the Rick Steves audioguide is designed to promote Rick Steves' company and its services, and to present his products as both highly practical and highly attractive to a tourist. Given that this is one of several podcasts that Rick Steves has placed on his website, and given that his website also includes an extensive array of other guidebooks, DVDs, maps, travel accessories and gift sets that can be purchased, the text is clearly designed to encourage travellers to 'buy in' to the Rick Steves brand. In this instance a subtle additional purpose for this text is to persuade, and the situation in which this text might be encountered and used by an individual or group of people means that it is clearly put to use and functions in a similar way to the genre of advertising.

ACTIVITY 20

Multipurpose texts

Look carefully at the other texts given as examples at the start of this section. To what extent might they function in additional or more complex ways than simply being information texts?

Check your responses in the Ideas section on Cambridge Elevate

ACTIVITY 21

Multimodal texts

Think about the extent to which producers of information texts utilise the affordances of multimodality, drawing on visual and verbal codes, and sometimes sound, to communicate and generate meanings. Although multimodality and the use of visuals as a narrating device are explored in the section that follows, you could think about the extent to which images support textual detail.

Check your responses in the Ideas section on Cambridge Elevate

15.7.4 Visual narratives

Examples of these include:

- Lucy Knisley, *French Milk*
- Rough Guides, *The Rough Guide to Paris*
- Klay Lamprell, *Not For Parents: Paris, Everything You Ever Wanted to Know*
- Reginald Piggott and Matt Thompson, *Mile By Mile London to Paris*
- Rick Steves, *Paris Audio Tours – The Louvre Podcast* and accompanying map

As we saw when looking at Texts 15M(a) and (b), representation is not simply confined to writing; indeed, places, people and events can be represented in very striking and idiosyncratic ways in visual media. The representation of the Eiffel Tower in Text 15M(a) is of course equally as subjective as a written description or narrative of the landmark. In the case of Text 15M(a), a very different Eiffel Tower could have been represented (perhaps in the rain, or on a cloudy day, or focusing on a part of it covered in graffiti, or surrounded by rubbish and so on). Clearly here the lens through which the Eiffel Tower has been shown is one perspective amongst many; test this by researching other visual images of the Eiffel Tower and thinking about how they represent the landmark in different ways to the Lonely Planet *Paris City Guide*. What 'version' of the Eiffel Tower do they promote?

Maps are also representational since they present a particular perspective on a place or series of places, and will of course vary according to the purpose of the text into which they are incorporated. You can explore this by looking at the maps in Reginald Piggott and Matt Thompson's, *Mile By Mile London to Paris* and comparing both the style and use of these to the maps that accompany Rick Steves' *Paris Audio Tours – The Louvre Podcast*.

Two texts, Lucy Knisley's *French Milk* and to a lesser extent Klay Lamprell's *Not For Parents: Paris, Everything You Ever Wanted to Know*, draw on the conventions of graphic novels, a genre whose narratives are often more complex than conventional prose.

The narratologist Pascal Lefèvre (2011) suggests that narratives that rely on hand-drawn graphics tend to be different from those that use photographic or cinematic images since the hand-drawings of the author/artist will be highly stylised and personal, again with a heightened sense of subjectivity in the shaping and recounting of narrative events. Drawings will necessarily omit certain characteristics and attributes of places and people, foreground others, and project a highly idiosyncratic representation of reality through aspects of these **mise en scène** (what's included or left out in a particular drawing), page layout and use and manipulation of typography. And of course, over time and a series of books, a style of drawing becomes recognised as the work of a particular author/artist or publisher.

Key terms

mise en scène: a term to define what's included in, or put into, a particular visual representation

Visual narratives will also handle the representation of narrative time in a different way. Look at Text 15M, which depicts Lucy's frustration at her mother's incessant talking. Here, a significant amount of time – enough for Lucy's mother to speak on six separate occasions and for Lucy to respond three times – is compressed into a single image. This makes it much harder to follow the passing of time compared to how a cinematic narrative might portray these events. In this case, the reader is expected to make sense of the temporal organisation of the narrative by assigning Lucy's responses to individual questions her mother asks and by 'filling in' narrative gaps to draw out the emotions that the characters might be feeling and any understood movements that they might make. For example, at what point in the narrative sequence might Lucy be understood as turning her head on to her pillow and covering her ears? This means that a text like *French Milk* relies heavily on readers using their own background schematic knowledge to construct a narrative and to make connections between verbal and visual codes. Of course, the fact that the medium cannot portray and project time in the same way as a moving image is an important constraint.

ACTIVITY 22

The handling of narrative time

Take another extract of your choice from *French Milk* and think about how it handles narrative time. How can you explain this in terms of affordances and constraints of the genre?

Text 15M

Source: Lucy Knisley, *French Milk*

15.7.5 New technologies

Examples of these include:

- Posts on the *Trip Advisor* Paris discussion forum
- Lonely Planet travel videos on *YouTube*
- British Pathé video of 1968 Paris Riots
- Posts on the *Gransnet* discussion forum
- *Just Another American in Paris* blog

In previous sections, we have already explored some of the affordances and constraints of texts that rely on new technologies. Of course the term 'new technologies' is a relative one since technologies are constantly being developed that open up new possibilities for – and limit – the ways that we can interact and communicate with others. Think, for example, about the telephone, television, the internet, and text messaging, all of which would now be considered established technologies but, when they first arrived, opened up a number of new ways for information to be shared and people to interact.

An interesting example of what you might not consider to have ever been a new technology is the picture postcard, which was first introduced in the late nineteenth century and which, with the development of and access to postal services, quickly became a popular way of sharing information and particularly experiences of visiting places. In effect, the picture postcard can be viewed as a very early form of social media! According to the historian James Walvin (1988), by 1914, over one billion postcards were sent annually to homes in England and Wales. In Paris, a big increase in the production and sending of picture postcards coincided with the building and completion of the Eiffel Tower in 1889.

As should now be clear from your studies on this unit, a postcard, like any form of communication, is a representation of a place, people, events, and a society and culture; a picture postcard typically represents a sense of 'otherness'.

See 15.5.3 for more on otherness

ACTIVITY 23

Postcards and Paris

Find examples (either on the internet or from people you know who may have received them) of picture postcards sent from Paris. How do these represent the city? What kinds of narratives do writers of these postcards construct? How does what they write depend on to whom they are writing? You should draw here on all your previous learning in this unit to think about how places, events, people and memories are presented linguistically.

Recent advances in social media have opened up new ways for expressing ideas on and memories of travel. For example, applications such as *Twitter*, *Facebook* and *Instagram* offer users a number of affordances in terms of how narratives can be shaped and how the sharing of experiences can take place. Equally, mobile devices such as smartphones, tablets and laptops are used in diverse ways to exploit their potential in producing, receiving, storing, re-viewing and redistributing information.

A sub-genre that has become increasingly popular over time is the blog (an abbreviation of web log), a web-based medium that allows users to set up a series of posts split into various categories that they wish to share with readers. Blogs also allow comments from other users who register on the hosting site and so can be interactive: bloggers can write about their experiences but also receive comments from others, and in some cases feedback and advice on questions they may have asked.

Although the version of the blog in the anthology does not include the comments that other users have posted, you could extend your study of this text by looking at the original version online.

Find and read the blog 'Just Another American in Paris' via Cambridge Elevate

ACTIVITY 24

Interactivity in blogs

One of the affordances of the blog is that bloggers can request responses and thoughts from interested followers and readers. This can create a series of **asynchronous** interactions, where there are delays between the turns that participants take, as opposed to **synchronous** interactions that take place in real time.

Explore how this interactivity is managed in one section of a blog of your choice. How do users who post comments in responses present themselves and interact? What do you notice about the use of politeness strategies that they use to meet face needs? If you are an A Level student, this could be useful preparation for your NEA.

Key terms

asynchronous interaction: interaction between discourse participants that involves delays between turns that they take

synchronous interaction: interaction that takes place in real time

discussion forum: an online environment where members of a community can communicate with each other by posting messages and responding to those of others

Another sub-genre that affords asynchronous interaction is the message board or **discussion forum**, an archived virtual space to which members sign up and engage in discussions about topics that interest them and are generally centred around a shared set of interests or topic.

A member can create their own username which - complete with other information that they want other members to see such as age, gender, location - and the number of posts that they have made to the forum in the past appears alongside each post that they make. Discussion fora operate like any other discourse community in that there is usually a kind of hierarchy amongst members. This can either be explicit, with some members holding the roles of **administrators** (responsible for the organisation and running of the forum) and **moderators** (responsible for monitoring and editing posts if required), or more implicit in the sense that over time, some posters assume seniority through the number of posts that they have made or by peer-recognition of their knowledge of a particular topic.

It is important to be aware of the discourse structure of the forum, and the expected linguistic behaviour that takes place within it. Although the mode of communication is clearly writing, discussion forum posts and interactions are often closer both in features and structure to prototypical speech. Consequently, as with face-to-face spoken language, even though interaction takes place in non-physical virtual spaces, posters will try to be co-operative and pay attention to others' face needs. Look at Text 15N, which is a short extract taken from the *Gransnet* forum.

Key terms

administrator: a senior member responsible for the organisation and running of the forum

moderator: a senior member responsible for monitoring, managing and sometimes editing posts made by contributors to a discussion forum

Text 15N

JaneAnn Mon 20-May-13 16:30:46

Hello everyone

I am planning to take my grandchildren to Paris – singly – starting with the 12 year old. I thought we would stay for three nights, in the centre somewhere and I would love to hear about other people's experience and to have some advice about things to do

Text 15N is the first post (or **seed message**) in what is known as a **thread**, and is followed by a group of responses by and exchanges between other posters that follow it. Sometimes, these responses include parts of a previous poster's comments that are either fully or partially quoted as part of the response. On other occasions, posters may introduce **embedded stories** into the main narrative thread. Embedded stories tend to be different in content but serve to maintain group identity and solidarity by focusing on, and therefore asserting and preserving, shared points of interest or value.

Key terms

seed message: the first post in a thread on a discussion forum

thread: a group of posts in a discussion forum initiated by a seed message

embedded story: a story that is introduced into a narrative that is different in content but serves to maintain group identity and solidarity by focusing on and therefore asserting and preserving shared points of interest or value

Since users are members of a particular discourse community they will tend to adhere to others' face needs and draw on a range of positive and negative politeness strategies. As part of what can be potentially large online communities, posters may project an identity that can be very different from their 'physical' self. Depending on the context, they may attempt to present themselves with varying degrees of expertise on the topic they are starting or joining. In Text 15N, JaneAnn positions herself as less knowledgeable compared to other members of the community whom she is asking for help. This is evident in her opening (virtual) address, 'hello everyone' and by her appeal to others' expertise in the topic she is posting about. Both of these comments pay attention to the positive face needs of her fellow *Gransnet* community members, and consequently are likely to help her obtain responses from others and be able to take away some useful information.

ACTIVITY 25

Exploring the *Gransnet* discussion forum

Read the remainder of the *Gransnet* discussion forum text. What can you say about the subsequent posts to JaneAnn's in terms of how they present information about Paris and form part of an interactive discourse space in which posters project identities and are aware of the face needs of others?

Check your responses in the Ideas section on Cambridge Elevate

15.7.6 Spoken discourse

Examples of these include:

One-speaker narratives

- Rick Steves, *Paris Audio Tours - The Louvre Podcast* and accompanying map
- Anna and Zara's narratives
- Isabelle and Sophia, 'Memories of places in Paris'

Multispeaker narratives

- Mike and Sophia, 'Visiting Paris'
- Isabelle, Mike and Sophia, 'Eating in Paris'

There are other texts in the anthology that contain instances of speech but these are examples of represented or fictionalised speech rather than natural speech, which is the focus of this section. You could, however, explore some of the differences between natural and represented speech by comparing texts like Lucy Knisley's *French Milk* or Bill Bryson's *Neither Here Nor There: Travels in Europe* with the examples of texts given at the start of this section.

See 16.3.4 for more on the differences between natural and represented/ fictionalised speech

In the remainder of this section, you will return to some of the ideas discussed in Unit 11. It would be a good idea at this stage to remind yourself of the key features of both one-speaker and multispeaker discourse before you read on.

ACTIVITY 26

Paris as personal 'remembered history'

Oral narratives, where speakers reminisce about their pasts, are often inextricably linked with a sense of place so that the memories and events associated with that place form an important part of that speaker's identity. Look at Isabelle's narrative on Le Parc Monceau again. To what extent can you say that this is the case with her narrative? How is le Parc Monceau an important part of her life story?

You can also explore this narrative and other one-speaker narratives (involving Anna, Zara, Isabelle and Sophia) in terms of how speakers organise their narrative content. In Unit 11, you explored how Labov's narrative categories can be used to explain and analyse the structure of one-speaker narratives. Can you apply this to the one-speaker texts in the anthology? For example, how would you analyse the first two paragraphs of Isabelle's narrative, beginning 'One of the places in Paris that's always meant a lot to me' and ending 'but it was nice back then to be able to sit on a pony and go riding'.

Of course, other spoken texts involve more than one speaker, and with these texts you will need to able to analyse not just how aspects of Paris are represented but how the speakers interact, shape their narratives and perform important aspects of identity work.

There are two main areas that you need to be able to explore successfully in this respect. First, as you think about the ways that speakers present versions of themselves when they talk to others, you should be mindful of the fact that this type of *identity work* is a performance. In other words, speakers undertake a projection of a self through a range of linguistic strategies that promote a certain way of seeing the world and certain attitudes towards places, people and events. These have been discussed in Section 15.5 but include features such as the use of a first-person narrative, a dependence on modality and verbs of perception and knowledge, and the use of evaluative adjectives and adverbs to emphasise a personal stance. You can also think about how a speaker in a spoken interaction positions themselves in relation to other concepts we have discussed in this unit such as the *quest narrative* and *othering* and the *double-journey*.

See 15.5.3 for more on the quest narrative and othering

See 15.6.1 for more on the double-journey

Second, you should explore how speakers perform relational work in tending to the needs of others. This is undertaken in Unit 11 through:

- keeping to conversational maxims
- acknowledging and paying attention to the face needs of others and using appropriate politeness strategies
- adhering to discourse norms such as exchange structure patterns, turn taking, and not interrupting
- helping to maintain conversation through the use of speaker support and preferred responses.

A further important way in which speakers support each other is by shaping their own evaluations or judgements in responses to each other, what the linguist Anita Pomerantz (1984) calls **assessment making**. Pomerantz argues that when a first speaker makes an assessment, their preferred response is clearly that the second speaker agrees with their initial assessment. Pomerantz suggests that even when there is some disagreement a second speaker will either **upgrade** (add intensity) or **downgrade** (lower the intensity) of the initial assessment in order to show a difference in agreement but to avoid a completely dispreferred response and potentially a threat to face. These can be seen in the exchanges between Isabelle and Sophia in Text 15O.

Text 15O

(a)

ISABELLE: Paris is a good city to visit
SOPHIA: Paris is the best city to visit!

(b)

SOPHIA: If you like shopping you've got to visit Le Marché Rétro d'Oberkampf for a real bargain
ISABELLE: It's OK there (.) you can get a few good deals

In Text 15O(a) Isabelle's 'good' is upgraded by Sophia to 'best', whereas in Text 15O(b) Sophia's 'a real bargain' is downgraded by Isabelle to 'a few good deals'.

ACTIVITY 27

Investigating dialogue

Look at Text 15P. This is taken from a stretch of dialogue between two friends, Mike and Sophia, who are talking about their experiences of visiting Paris. An earlier part of this dialogue appears in your anthology as Mike and Sophia, 'Visiting Paris'.

Using all of your learning from Unit 11 and from this unit, explore how Mike and Sophia represent and evaluate Parisian people and culture, and how they work together to structure and share their experiences.

Key terms

assessment making: the act of evaluating something or someone when talking to others

upgrade: the raising of the intensity of a speaker's assessment in a response to it

downgrade: the lowering of the intensity of a speaker's assessment in a response to it

Text 15P

SOPHIA: But (.) erm (.) yeah (.) in (.) in comparison to the tourists (.) or (.) when I was walking through the streets (.) I noticed how (.) all the Parisians kind of (1) even though life is quite fast paced
MIKE: Hmm
SOPHIA: They always take time to have (.) their lunch sessions for about two hours
MIKE: Yeah (.) they t- all the shops are closed at lunch aren't they
SOPHIA: Yeah (.) and they just
MIKE: Yeah (.) you can't go anywhere
SOPHIA: Yeah (.) have about a five-course meal
MIKE: Yeah
SOPHIA: At lunchtime (.) which is nice
MIKE: It's really great (.) the thing is (.) the cafés are open still
SOPHIA: Yeah
MIKE: It's just all of the shops are shut (.) so if you're (.) there at a (.) the wrong time you're not going to get anything
SOPHIA: Yeah (.) you're not going to get that much (.) yeah

MIKE: Yeah ((*laughter*))
SOPHIA: **Exactly** (.) and I think (.) well unless you're going to have a big sit-down meal at lunchtime (.) you have to deal with (.) just having a (.) baguette
MIKE: Baguette and cheese
SOPHIA: Yeah (.) ((*laughter*)) or a salad

Check your responses in the Ideas section on Cambridge Elevate

ACTIVITY 28

Storytelling

Explore Charles Goodwin's model for analysing the structure of storytelling. Apply this to an extract from one of the example texts given at the start of this section and comment on your findings.

Another text that is fascinating to explore is Rick Steves' podcast on the Louvre. To fully appreciate the context and the situational aspect of this text, it would be worth spending some time looking at Rick Steves' website and thinking about how a reader/listener might come across the podcast, how they might use it and how it fits in to a wider set of services that Rick Steves provides for the traveller.

Read Rick Steves' podcast on the Louvre via Cambridge Elevate

Since the podcast is designed to be listened to as walkers are touring the Louvre, it exists as a **mobile narrative** that can be listened to on a variety of devices. And of course, listeners are able to control the pace of what they hear through pausing, and revisiting parts of the recording as they require. A podcast like this forms part of an integrated and interactive embodied experience for the listener: its focus on transmitting information aurally integrates with the listener's visual experience as she or he tours the Louvre. The listener is therefore very much an active participant in imagining and bringing to life the world that is being described in the podcast. This type of immersive experience has developed considerably since the advent of technology that affords this kind of mobile and interactive narrative. In fact, the mobile narrative provides a new dimension to the experience of the flâneur.

See 15.5.3 for more on the flâneur

If you are interested in finding out a little more about this kind of narrative experience (for example, if you are an A Level student you might be interested in narratives like this for your NEA project) then you could start by looking at more radical examples of mobile narratives that allow users to construct and shape their experiences. One example is the *Walking Stories* experience, an immersive and highly interactive group audio-walk for parks.

Find and read about the *Walking Stories* experience via Cambridge Elevate

Key terms

mobile narrative: a narrative that is designed accommodate a listener's movement in and around locations that are described as part of the narrative

exophoric storytelling: when a narrative is told in a different location to where the narrated events actually took place

endophoric storytelling: when a narrative is told in the same location as the narrated events actually took place

Finally, a very useful way of distinguishing between types of spoken text is a framework developed by the narratologist Ruth Page (2012). Page suggests that we can classify how narratives operate by distinguishing between synchronous and asynchronous interaction (look back at section 15.7.5) and then between two terms coined by the narratologist David Herman, **exophoric** and **endophoric storytelling**. Exophoric storytelling occurs when a narrative is told in a different location to where the narrated events actually took place: a good example of this would be Isabelle's account of le Parc Monceau, which took place in the UK. On the other hand, endophoric storytelling takes place in the same location as the narrated events; an example of this would be Sophia's account of her train journey which takes place on the site of the journey in Paris. Another good example of exophoric storytelling would be someone downloading and listening to Rick Steves' podcast in their own home, although in this instance the interaction between speaker and listener is asynchronous. Equally asynchronous but this time endophoric would of course be someone listening to the Rick Steves' podcast while walking in the Louvre. Figure 15A shows how these distinctions provide a neat way of categorising different types of spoken narrative.

Figure 15A: Types of storytelling

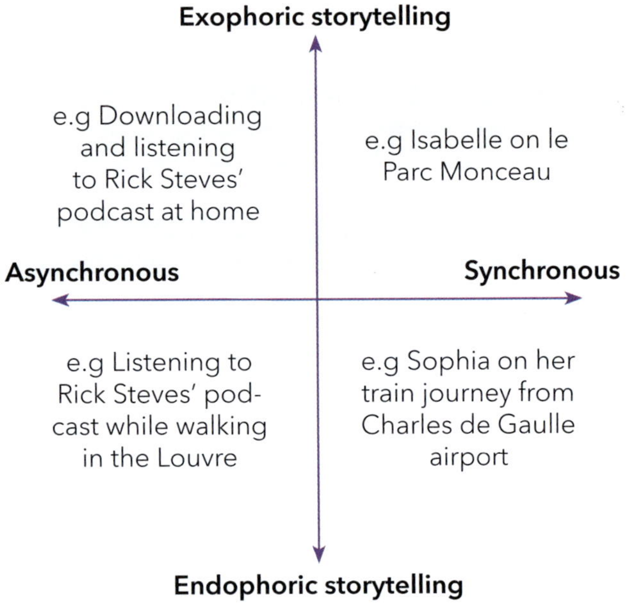

Adapted from Ruth Page (2012), *Stories and Social Media: Identities and Interaction*, Routledge, p. 146

ACTIVITY 29

Exploring deixis

A text like Rick Steves' podcast will rely on an abundance of deictic forms to orientate the listener perceptually, temporally and spatially. Review the section on deixis and then look at Activity 3 in Unit 10 for a short example of deixis in action in an audio guide. Now choose an extract from the podcast to analyse. How do deictic terms operate in this text? Do you think that listening to this in the Louvre or at home (or on the bus, train, etc.) makes any difference to how these deictic terms are interpreted?

See 10.4 for more on deixis

15.8 Bringing it all together: AS Level

15.8.1 Self-assessment: check your learning

For each of the statements in Table 15B, evaluate your confidence in each topic area.

Remembered places is assessed on Paper 2 of the AS Level examination across three questions. All exam questions follow the same format. Questions 1 and 2 are presented in two parts and question 3 asks for a commentary.

Explaining the assessment objectives

For question 1 there are three assessment objectives tested and they carry different weightings as shown here.

- **AO1** (10 marks): Apply concepts and methods from integrated linguistic and literary study as appropriate, using associated terminology and coherent written expression

> The key elements are your:
> - clear expression of ideas
> - accurate use of terminology
> - reference to and use of various levels of language analysis to explain and comment on effects of particular choices that text producers have made
> - good stylistic analysis.

- **AO3** (20 marks): Demonstrate understanding of the significance and influence of the contexts in which texts are produced and received

> You need to consider the impact of the following:
> - **audience** – for whom the text was written or spoken and who is likely to read it
> - **purpose** – why the text was produced, including any important information about the text producer and their relationship with their audience
> - **mode and genre** – any aspects of mode and genre in terms of conventions and affordances and constraints that are relevant and ought to be discussed.

Topic area	Very confident	Some knowledge	Need to revise
I understand the nature of representation			
I understand the key concepts around the nature of journeys and travel			
I can explain the various ways in which speakers and writers present subjective perspectives through narratives about Paris			
I can identify and comment on the representation of place, people, events, societies and cultures			
I can explore how narrators emphasise the importance of memories in texts in the anthology			
I understand and can explain the conventions of different genres and the importance of a range of contextual factors on the shaping of meaning			
I understand how to reshape a text to provide a new perspective on events for a particular audience and purpose			
I am able to identify language choices I have made in my own writing and comment on why I have chosen them			

- **AO4** (10 marks): Explore connections across texts, informed by linguistic and literary concepts and methods

You need to think about:

- **similarities** – how texts are similar in the ways that they represent places, people, events, culture, society and memories
- **differences** – how texts are different in the ways that they represent places, people, events, culture, society and memories
- **narrative connections** – how the texts can be connected in terms of how they represent aspects of Paris through the writer and/or speaker's shaping of experiences and the use of narrative conventions.

15.8.2 Exploring possible AS questions

Question 1

In question 1 you will need to compare two extracts from the anthology. Question 1 will follow the same format as here:

This is the question together with the instruction to compare and contrast

Compare and contrast how the writers and speakers in these extracts present Paris. You should refer to both extracts in your answer and consider:

- the language choices made and their likely effects
- the different audiences and purposes of the texts
- aspects of mode.

These bullet points guide you to what you need to focus on and discuss in your answer

You can plan for question 1 by thinking carefully about the following key questions. As you do so, identify particular parts of the texts that you are going to comment on in detail when you come to write up your answer.

Questions on representation and language

- How is the narrative told? What distinctive features of storytelling are present and why have these been chosen?
- How does each narrator provide a particular perspective on events? What language features do they use and why do you think they use them?
- How is Paris defined as a place?
- What do the writers and speakers of these texts have to say about Parisian culture and society?
- What events do they show and why do they think they are important?
- Are there references to memories? What are they?

Questions on contextual factors

- How important are the audience and purpose of each text?
- How important are genre and mode? How do the texts draw on the conventions of each?

Questions on connections

- How might you summarise any similarities or differences between the two texts in terms of how they represent Paris?
- What connections can be made between the two texts in terms of how the writers and/or speakers tell their stories?

Questions 2 and 3

In question 2, you will need to rewrite the base text (this will be one of the extracts in question 1) according to a given brief that specifies a particular genre, audience and purpose. You will then need to explain the choices that you have made in a commentary for question 3. The questions will follow this format.

This is the question together with the instruction to compare and contrast

2. Refer to **Text A** from *The Most Beautiful Walk in the World: A Pedestrian in Paris* by John Baxter.

Recast this as the section of the Café Danton's website where the café's location in Paris is described.

This is what you need to recast this text into

These are your specific instructions regarding what to include

You might consider:

- what will appeal to visitors about the location
- how the local area might be best described.

3. Identify four **different** examples of language features in your writing and explain your reasons for using them.

This is the instruction for what you need to do for the commentary

You should write about 200 words.
In your commentary you should:

- consider the importance of purpose, audience, mode and genre in your language choices
- consider how you have used language to shape your intended meaning
- structure your writing clearly to express your ideas.

Explaining the assessment objectives

There are three assessment objectives tested on questions 2 and 3, and they all carry different weightings as shown here.

Question 2

- **AO5** (15 marks): Demonstrate expertise and creativity in the use of English to communicate in different ways

> You need to be able to demonstrate that you can:
> - follow the brief in the question and follow the instructions
> - respond imaginatively and creatively to the task that you have been given.

Question 3

- **AO2** (5 marks): Analyse the ways that meanings are shaped in texts

> Here you need to:
> - select four **different** examples of language that you have consciously used in your rewriting
> - think about how these language choices help to shape meaning.

- **AO3** (10 marks): Demonstrate understanding of the significance and influence of the contexts in which texts are produced and received

> Here you need to consider:
> - **the audience** for whom your text is being written and who is likely to read it
> - **purpose** – the reason why your text is being written
> - **mode and genre** – any aspects of mode and genre in terms of conventions, affordances and constraints that you feel are relevant and ought to be discussed in the light of language choices you have made.

- **AO5** (5 marks): Demonstrate expertise and creativity in the use of English to communicate in different ways

You need to be able to demonstrate that you can:
- follow the brief in the question and follow the instructions
- respond imaginatively and creatively to the task that you have been given.

ACTIVITY 30

Practice questions

a You can practise and prepare for question 1 by choosing short extracts from any two texts in the anthology and comparing and contrasting them using the focuses and advice outlined in this unit. For questions 2 and 3, complete the following task on Text 15Q, which is the same stretch of dialogue between Mike and Sophia that you used in Activity 27.

Recast this as the opening of a TV documentary about shopping in Paris at lunchtime. You might consider:
- how trying to shop in Paris at lunchtime might be best described
- what impressions of Parisian culture might be suggested.

b Identify four specific examples of language in your writing and explain your reasons for using them. You should write about 200 words.

Text 15Q

SOPHIA: But (.) erm (.) yeah (.) in (.) in comparison to the tourists (.) or (.) when I was walking through the streets (.) I noticed how (.) all the Parisians kind of (1) even though life is quite fast paced
MIKE: Hmm
SOPHIA: They always take time to have (.) their lunch sessions for about two hours
MIKE: Yeah (.) they t- all the shops are closed at lunch aren't they
SOPHIA: Yeah (.) and they just
MIKE: Yeah (.) you can't go anywhere
SOPHIA: Yeah (.) have about a five-course meal
MIKE: Yeah
SOPHIA: At lunchtime (.) which is nice
MIKE: It's really great (.) the thing is (.) the cafés are open still
SOPHIA: Yeah
MIKE: It's just all of the shops are shut (.) so if you're (.) there at a (.) the wrong time you're not going to get anything
SOPHIA: Yeah (.) you're not going to get that much (.) yeah
MIKE: Yeah ((*laughter*))
SOPHIA: **Exactly** (.) and I think (.) well unless you're going to have a big sit-down meal at lunchtime (.) you have to deal with (.) just having a (.) baguette
MIKE: Baguette and cheese
SOPHIA: Yeah (.) ((*laughter*)) or a salad

15.9 Bringing it all together: A Level

15.9.1 Self-assessment: check your learning

For each of the statements in Table 15C, evaluate your confidence in each topic area.

Remembered places is assessed on Paper 1 Section A of the A Level examination.

For this question you will need to compare two texts from the anthology on a given focus.

Explaining the assessment objectives

There are three assessment objectives tested on this question and these carry different weightings.

- **AO1** (15 marks): Apply concepts and methods from integrated linguistic and literary study as appropriate, using associated terminology and coherent written expression

The key elements are your:
- clear expression of your ideas
- accurate use of terminology
- reference to and use of the various levels of language analysis to explain your ideas and comment on effects of particular choices that text producers have made
- good stylistic analysis.

- **AO3** (15 marks): Demonstrate understanding of the significance and influence of the contexts in which texts are produced and received

> You need to consider the impact of the following:
> - **audience** – for whom the text was written or spoken and who is likely to read it (look back at the notions of *implied* and *actual readers/ listeners* in Unit 2)
> - **purpose** – the reason why the text was produced including any important information about the text producer and their relationship with their audience
> - **mode and genre** – any aspects of mode and genre in terms of conventions, affordances and constraints that you feel are relevant and ought to be discussed.

- **AO4** (10 marks): Explore connections across texts, informed by linguistic and literary concepts and methods

> You need to think about:
> - **similarities** – how texts are similar in the ways that they represent places, people, events, culture, society and memories
> - **differences** – how texts are different in the ways that they represent places, people, events, culture, society and memories
> - **narrative connections** – how the texts can be connected in terms of how they represent aspects of Paris through the writer and/or speaker's shaping of experiences and the use of narrative conventions.

You can plan for this by thinking carefully about the following key questions. As you do so, identify particular parts of the texts that you are going to comment on in detail when you come to write up your answer.

15.9.2 Exploring possible A Level questions

Question 1

The question will follow the same format as detailed here.

This is the question together with the instruction to compare and contrast. This part of the question also gives you the focus, here highlighted in bold

Compare and contrast how the writers and/or speakers of these texts express their ideas about **people living in or visiting Paris**.

- You should refer to both texts in your answer.

This part of the question reminds you that you must look at both texts

Questions on representation and language

- How is the narrative told? What distinctive features of storytelling are present and why have these been chosen?
- How does each narrator provide a particular perspective on events? What language features do they use and why do you think they use them?
- How is Paris defined as a place?
- What do the writers and speakers of these texts have to say about Parisian culture and society?

Topic area	Very confident	Some knowledge	Need to revise
I understand the nature of representation			
I understand the key concepts around the nature of journeys and travel			
I can explain the various ways in which speakers and writers present subjective perspectives through narratives about Paris			
I can identify and comment on the representation of place, people, events, societies and cultures			
I can explore how narrators emphasise the importance of memories in texts in the anthology			
I understand and can explain the conventions of different genres and the importance of a range of contextual factors on the shaping of meaning			

- What events do they show and why do they think they are important?
- Are there references to memories? What are they?

Questions on contextual factors

- How important are the audience and purpose of each text?
- How important are genre and mode? How do the texts draw on the conventions of each?

Questions on connections

- How might you summarise any similarities or differences between the two texts in terms of how they represent Paris?
- What connections can be made between the two texts in terms of how the writers and/or speakers tell their stories?

ACTIVITY 31

Practice question

You can practise and prepare for this question by looking at the question we discussed earlier in this unit and applying it to Texts 15R and 15S.

Text 15R

Paris was my first taste of a Latin country. I was thirteen and went with my godmother, Marigold Johnson, and her three teenage children. We traveled by car. I cannot remember crossing the channel – we were coming from England – but I do recall a noisy traffic jam caused by a motor bike accident. It was a hazy afternoon, our car windows were rolled down, and I was struck by the smell of baked baguettes wafting along the street, the feisty honking of cars, and a toddler with a blunt fringe catching my eye and slowly sucking on her lollipop. The Parisians were different, I quickly registered.

A few hours later, I poured water and shook sugar into my first *citron presse*. The next morning, I found myself admiring the clipped lawns of the jardins du Luxembourg. Topping everything off was the discovery of school notebooks packed with cubed pages as opposed to lined ones. I remember gliding my hand down their brightly colored covers and liking the rainbowlike array they formed in my suitcase.

Ten days later, I returned to my family and became a Paris Bore. Every conversation became an occasion to slip in tales from my Parisian adventure. Someone adult pointed out that I had been to Paris in August and that 'no one chic ever stays there then.' I refused to give the woman's remark much credence. Besides, what on earth was 'chic'? Undaunted, I bounced along in my enthusiasm. Paris was hard to fault. Unlike London of the mid-1970s, it basked in the beauty of tradition – the ritual and order were an indication of that – and there was a respect for vegetables. In shop windows, polished tomatoes were lined up like jewels. French civic pride.

Visiting the Chateau de Versailles, I briefly stepped on the cordoned-off lawn, an easy enough mistake that had a shocking consequence. A Frenchman – not a guard – came forward and slapped me full in the face. Whatever prompted him to *gifler* (slap) an ungainly teenager was his problem – but it became briefly mine. I burst into quick, embarrassed tears. My godmother quickly admonished him, as did the rest of the family, a brave brood when tangled with. Apparently, we all hugged afterward. I write 'apparently' because I mentally zapped this drama from start to finish, only to be reminded of it thirty-three years later. (No doubt I did this because the horrible man and his offending *gifle* did not fit into my perfect, picture-postcard memories.)

In retrospect, I doubt whether the experience would have put me off. Still, it might have prepared me for how tricky the French can be. Am I suggesting that behind every French person lies an unexpected slap? That would be unfair. But my experience with the Parisians is that, mentally, there is a slap instinct – mild in some, more fervent in others. Defensive, they tend to attack. The briefest grasp of their city's history offers reason for this: being besieged several times leaves its mark. Yet that very 'slap instinct' is both the Parisians' strength and their weakness.

It also explains why Paris remains the fashion capital. Fashion, when exciting, is all about the shock of the new – the equivalent of a swift slap. And being chic can be viewed as a visual slap enforced by the wearer's character, taste, eye. It's being au courant and yet daring to be different.

Source: Natasha Fraser-Cavassoni, 'Understanding chic'

Text 15S

Paris Hotels Flights Holiday Rentals Restaurants Things to Do Trending Now

Europe > France > Paris > Paris travel forum

Browse all 99,033 Paris topics »

7. Re: What do you wish someone had told you?

15 August 2011, 20:35

Wow,, so many little tips, many of them learned here. You don't have to get a Musuem pass to avoid long lines in many places, there are alternate entrances and online tickets and a bunch of other tricks.

Having a pen and paper easy to get to is handy if you want to write down a number or have a shop keeper do so,, I know french numbers up to a hundred or so , but when they speak quickly I can get confused.

Ignore ignore ignore,, I knew this one from relatives, but I really think its something that every first time visitor should learn to do when confronted by strangers wanting to "chat" have you sign a clip board, or give you a ring.. lol.People from big cities usually know this, but people from smaller cities and towns may feel they are being rude. They are not, they are being smart .

Hotel rooms with shower only usually have the type of shower I am used to, the mounted one in a stall,, ones with tub and shower often have a hand held shower and no shower curtain, so you have to sit in tub and "shower" or get room soaking. I try to reserve shower only rooms.

French people are not cold or rude, but, they are not bubbly "hi I'm Jeff your waiter for tonight " types either,, they are warm and wonderful with family and close friends, but there is a reserve that is cultural and does not mean they hate you,, just like you are not crazy cause you smile at passerbys(they think its weird there) ,, they are not mean cause they don't. Showing respect is important there, always greet(bonjour madame or monsieur) shopkeeper or clerk before asking for anything,, they are not your servants and feel very much to be at same standing as you,, the revolution meant something to them,, lol so just walking up and demanding something is a no no.. (hey they will likely give it to you, but there will be an air about it),, and metro kiosk workers can actually just ignore you (I have seen them close a window on a rude demanding tourist once,, he just kept yelling at them louder and louder in english,, thinking that would help,, lol)

Try the stinky cheeses(being from Netherlands you probaly know this one) , they are often the tastiest.

Pops and juices are expensive in restos.. get house wine and tap water.

Its worth the metro trip out to St Denis, I guess I should be happy its not a crowded place like Notre Dame, but its so worth seeing if you have any interest in French history.. I loved my day there.

You can't just sit on the grass anywhere in Luxembourg gardens,, there are signs everywhere , but I just thought this was weird,, so plan to picnic on a bench,, there is sitting grass, but on hot days its crowded.

Source: *Trip Advisor* discussion board

DEVELOPING

16 Imagined worlds

In this unit, you will:

- develop your understanding of, and explore the conventions of, the fantasy genre
- learn an extensive analytical toolkit to help you explore narratives
- develop a range of ideas related to the novel that you are studying for this unit
- explore how best to prepare for assessment on this unit.

This relates to 'Views and voices' in the AS Level specification and 'Telling stories' in the A Level specification.

16.1 The fantasy genre

In Unit 3 you explored the notion of genre, working with a definition of the term as a way of grouping texts based on expected shared conventions. As we saw in that unit, although texts can vary in their degrees of prototypicality, the idea of having some kind of reference point against which to measure group membership can be useful. In this unit, the concept of genre is important since all of the novels (from which you will be studying one) can be considered as members of the fantasy genre. Although this is a very broad term and can include several different types and styles of writing, there are some agreed shared conventions that will be useful to you as you develop your ideas and respond to these texts.

16.1.1 A definition of fantasy

The word 'fantasy' derives from the Latin word *phantasia*, meaning 'the imagination'. The genre's etymology is a good clue to how broad it is since clearly many (if not all) kinds of literature could be defined as imaginative. Indeed, the sheer diversity of different kinds of texts, periods and writers covered by the fantasy genre makes it difficult to pin down more than a few essential characteristics. Even then, the genre is still a fluid one, moving into other genres, having clear exceptions and so on. In Example 1, the literary critics Edward James and Farah Mendlesohn (2012) describe fantasy as follows:

---

1 'Fantasy is not so much a mansion as a row of terraced houses, such as the one that entranced us in C. S. Lewis's *The Magician's Nephew* with its connecting attics, each with a door that leads into another world. There are shared walls, and a certain level of consensus around the basis bricks, but the internal décor can differ wildly, and the lives lived in these terraced houses are discrete yet overheard.'

Source: Edward James and Farah Mendlesohn, 'Introduction' in *The Cambridge Companion to Fantasy Literature*, 2012, Cambridge University Press.

One of the ways of dealing with this potential problem is to adopt the prototype/radial structure model as a way of exploring how different texts may display varying degrees of these characteristics. As you work through your chosen novel, you should consider to what extent it is a more or less central member in terms of the characteristics that are offered in 16.1.2–16.1.3, as a starting point for thinking about the genre.

16.1.2 Characteristics of fantasy

The fantasy genre is often characterised by its strong focus on **anti-realism**: that is, texts within this genre will often portray places, events and characters that are not usually found in the 'real world'. Consequently, fantasy literature is freed from the constraints of what might be possible in the 'real world' (see 16.2.1). Building on this, the literary scholar Brian Attebery (1992) suggests that generally fiction in the fantasy genre tends to have the following characteristics:

- some violation of what is possible in the real world
- a basic narrative structure that begins with a problem and ends in resolution
- a sense of reader wonder at the strangeness of the events in the fictional world, making us think closely about our own real world as a result.

In addition, the literary scholar Rosemary Jackson (1981) suggests that fiction in the fantasy genre will:

- dissolve the usual laws of time and space so that time travel is possible, and places take on extreme significance
- have themes such as the transformation of people, the exploration of 'otherness' and the notion of good versus evil
- be essentially subversive in that it expresses and explores the types of desires that have been repressed by society.

Key terms

anti-realism: a focus on places, events and characters that are not present in the 'real world'

Watch tutorial video, Fantasy, on Cambridge Elevate

16.1.3 Other genres

A consequence of working with a very broad set of definitions for fantasy is that, frequently, an understanding of how the genre relates to other genres will be very helpful. Some closely associated genres are given and briefly discussed below.

Science fiction: this has a long history dating back to the nineteenth century, and is a hugely popular genre across a wide range of media (novels, short stories, graphic fiction, TV and cinema). A great deal of science fiction is concerned with the advent of technology, and the implications it might have on society, often presenting alternative worlds where an aspect of technology has improved, or made worse, the lives of people living there. In this sense, one of the defining features of the genre is that it deals with actions and events that are not yet possible in the 'real world'.

Political allegory: an allegory is a long-established literary trope (dating back to Ancient Greece) that involves the subtle understanding of one narrative event in terms of another (in other words, it is like a sustained metaphor). A political allegory is, therefore, a narrative (usually fantastical) through which we are asked to interpret the characters and events in a particular historical event from a certain ideological stance. One of the most famous political allegories is George Orwell's (1945) *Animal Farm*, which comments on the Russian revolution and subsequent events in the Soviet Union, and criticises the Soviet leader Joseph Stalin.

...fantasy literature is freed from the contraints of what might be possible in the 'real world'...

Dystopian fiction: deals with a speculative world in which society has been reduced to an undesirable state (crime, poverty, disease, lack of freedom), usually due to some practice that it has itself introduced. In turn, dystopian fiction often warns readers about the danger of following a certain political or ideological policy in the 'real world'. A recent, and very successful, example of dystopian fiction is Suzanne Collins' *Hunger Games* trilogy, set in a society called 'Panem', but with very clear parallels to modern-day America.

The Gothic: gothic fiction became popular in the late eighteenth century, where it was characterised by clearly defined settings (dark castles and spooky landscapes), characters (shadowy male villains, female heroines, ghosts and monsters), and plots (involving the mysterious, unexplained and supernatural). Famous examples include Horace Walpole's (1763) *The Castle of Otranto*, and Ann Radcliffe's (1794) *The Mysteries of Udolpho*. The sheer volume of stock gothic novels at that time led to Jane Austen famously parodying the genre in *Northanger Abbey*, written in 1798 but not published until twenty years later. During the nineteenth century, gothic fiction fused the supernatural with the scientific, and is still incredibly popular today in the work of modern horror fiction writers.

Magic realism: a genre where one substantial fantastical element is introduced into an otherwise realistic fictional world. This might involve one character being able to break the rules of the 'real world' by doing something that is impossible in 'real world' terms. In contrast, the other characters remain bound by the constraints of the 'real world'. An example of magic realism is Angela Carter's (1984) *Nights at the Circus*.

ACTIVITY 1

Developing reading around genre

You can explore the novel and its relationship with other genres in more detail as you work through the course (you may already be thinking about how what you are reading fits into one or more of the genres discussed above). As a starting point, you could read the article by Margaret Atwood on science fiction that appeared in *The Guardian* in 2005.

Find and read *The Guardian* article 'Aliens have taken the place of angels', by Margaret Atwood, via Cambridge Elevate

See Unit 22 for additional reading around the fantasy and associated genres

16.1.4 Finding out about your set texts and their place within the genre

As you will have seen from the discussion in 16.1.3, the notion of genre is intrinsically linked to other contextual factors such as the biographical details of the writer; the social, cultural, political and historical contexts in which works of fiction are produced; and the social, cultural, political and historical contexts in which they are read and interpreted. One of the ways that you can support your study of your chosen novel is to begin to explore these important contexts of production and reception. Indeed, you will need to think about selecting important aspects of these when you come to the assessment section of this unit.

See 16.5 for selected important aspects of production and reception

ACTIVITY 2

Contexts

To start thinking about some important contextual factors related to the reading, undertake some research on your chosen novel. Some ideas for where you might start to do preliminary reading are listed below but this is not an exhaustive list and you should develop your own reading and ask your teacher for any further suggestions.

- *Frankenstein*: Mary Shelley's life and background, including her parents (William Godwin and Mary Wollstonecraft) and husband (Percy Bysshe Shelley); the influence of the gothic novel and Romanticism on her thinking; the *Prometheus* myth; early nineteenth-century concerns with radical science, the supernatural and the search for knowledge.
- *Dracula*: Bram Stoker's life and background, his employment with Henry Irving in the world of London theatre; the history and development of the vampire short story and novel; vampires, the supernatural and technology in Victorian literature.

- *The Handmaid's Tale*: Margaret Atwood starting the novel in Berlin in the mid-1980s, political dictators and oppressive regimes in the twentieth-century, theocracies, feminism and the influence of other dystopian novels such as *Nineteen Eighty-Four* (George Orwell), *Brave New World* (Aldous Huxley), *Fahrenheit 451* (Ray Bradbury).
- *The Lovely Bones*: Alice Sebold's own influence for writing the novel (her memoir *Lucky* is an important, though harrowing, read); her experiences with becoming a writer; gothic and feminist influences on her writing; the popularity of 'life' and 'overcoming adversity' narratives as genres in the 1990s/2000s (e.g. on chat shows, in popular culture, and magazine features and problem pages).

16.2 Setting up fictional worlds

16.2.1 Impossible worlds

The world of the fantasy genre is generally set up to be understood as strange, unusual or impossible in relation to how we understand the real world. In 16.1, the anti-realist nature of the genre was discussed as one of its defining features.

The world that is set up in the novel you are reading might of course be the same as the one in which we live in some ways, perhaps involving the same places, historical events and so on, but made fantastical by something that isn't possible in the 'real world' (for example, the creation of life from dead body parts in *Frankenstein*, vampires moving to London in *Dracula*). On the other hand, the world of the novel itself may be something very far removed from what we know (such as the descriptions of Gilead in *The Handmaid's Tale*, Susie's descriptions of heaven in *The Lovely Bones*). Of course, the novel may move between realism and fantasy, synthesising various elements of the possible and the impossible into a singular narrative space.

As you progress through the rest of this unit, your focus should be on understanding the ways in which authors build rich fictional worlds, populating them with places, characters and events. All of the novels in this unit present impossible worlds relative to the 'real world' that nonetheless we are asked to immerse ourselves in as we read. Two of them, *Frankenstein* and *The Lovely Bones* (although you could argue this is the case for *The Handmaid's Tale* as well), have impossible acts of narration (the Creature and Susie – a dead man and girl – respectively).

16.2.2 World-building

In Unit 5 you explored how narratives indicate aspects of time, place and characters, and provide details of both central and additional events. At this point, it is worth revisiting that unit and, in particular, Activity 1 in that unit, to remind yourself of these key points.

We can now develop these ideas in more detail to provide a way of looking at how authors set up and flesh out a rich narrative world within which the events of the novel take place and develop. We can label this rich fictional space a **storyworld**.

Key terms

storyworld: the fictional world that is shaped and framed by the narrative

Look at Text 16A, from near the opening of *Dracula*. The narrator Jonathan Harker is describing his journey to Dracula's castle.

Text 16A

Soon we were hemmed in with trees, which in places arched right over the roadway till we passed as through a tunnel; and again great frowning rocks guarded us boldly on either side. Though we were in shelter, we could hear the rising wind, for it moaned and whistled through the rocks, and the branches of trees crashed together as we swept along. It grew colder and colder still, and fine, powdery snow began to fall, so that soon we and all around us were covered with a white blanket. The keen wind still covered the howling of the dogs, though this grew fainter as we went on our way.

Source: Bram Stoker, *Dracula*

In Text 16A we can highlight the characters (Harker and his travelling companions), the time (in the past – specified earlier in the novel as 5 May), the place (Carpathian mountains on the way to Dracula's castle), central events (the coach journey and the storm) and additional events (snow, the howling of dogs).

In addition, one of the ways that we could explore the fleshing out of the storyworld in more detail is by focusing carefully on the kinds of textual detail that Stoker has included. So, we can start by looking at the use of verb phrases and how these contribute to the way in which the storyworld is set up. As we saw in Unit 7.3.2, verb phrases detail different types of process (material, relational, mental or verbal). Consequently, the relative balance given to each of these by an author will provide a certain 'feeling' to the storyworld. In Text 16A, most of the processes are material, 'arched', 'passed through', 'guarded', 'crashed', 'swept', 'to fall', 'went'. This emphasis on actions gives the sense of a storyworld that is dynamic, and iconically ensures that the reader's processing of the passage is similar to the movement of the carriage through the Carpathian landscape.

As discussed in Unit 1.3, *Dracula* positions us as readers to experience the events from the vantage point of Harker and his fellow passengers both through the use of the first-person pronoun 'we', and prepositions that are suggestive of imaginatively experienced movements. In addition, we could now argue that the use of a distinctive type of verb process centred around verbs of motion helps to provide a kind of immersive reading experience in an enriched narrative space. At other times, of course, authors will choose to use a different kind of verb patterning to either emphasise description over action (with relational processes), or a character's inner thoughts or feelings (with mental processes).

ACTIVITY 3

Exploring verb processes

An extended extract where a certain kind of verb process dominates can give rise to certain effects as we saw in Text 16A. As a way of exploring this in more detail, rewrite Text 16A so that there are fewer material processes and more relational ones. What is the effect of these changes? How does Text 16A 'feel' after you have done this?

Now take an extract of around the same length from the novel you are studying (or, if you are studying *Dracula*, another part of that novel). What kind of verb process dominates in your extract? Why do you think that is? What effect do you think this has?

You could also rewrite your extract, experimenting with different verb patterns. What do your choices emphasise and what do they relegate to the background?

The use of a certain type of verb process in developing a storyworld is also a way in which an author can emphasise *time*, since verbs indicate a time frame (in their tense), and the number of actions can give an indication of how quickly time moves; generally speaking, the more actions described, the greater the sense of time moving we have. There are, of course, other ways that an author can develop a storyworld to give a greater sense of the expansiveness of the setting. Returning to Text 16A, we can see the fleshing out of physical space through the use of noun phrases with pre-modified head nouns, 'great frowning rocks', 'rising wind', 'fine, powdery snow', 'white blanket'. These noun phrases provide a much richer and sharper resolution to the objects described: imagine, for example, the difference it would make to your reading of Text 16A if it simply read 'and snow began to fall'.

Overall, then, the kind of world-building that occurs in Text 16A is a way of developing a rich fictional world where elements of time and space

'The keen wind still covered the howling of the dogs...'

***Dracula*, Bram Stoker**

are identified, developed, and within which we are invited to immerse ourselves as readers of the fiction. And, as we have seen, in Text 16A the world-building is geared towards the reader being positioned in an active experiencing role.

16.2.3 Authors and narrators

In Unit 5 you learnt how 'narrator' is the term we use to describe the voice responsible for conveying the details of a narrative to us. In some cases, this is also likely to be the author of the narrative. In Example 2, taken from an autobiography by the comedian John Bishop, the narrator and author are the same entity, which we assume to be the real person John Bishop.

---

2 I entered the world at Mill Road Hospital in Liverpool on 30 November 1966.

Source: John Bishop, *How Did All This Happen*, HarperCollins

---

However, for many narratives it is problematic to equate the narrator with the author. For example, each of your set text options opens with a narrating voice, which is clearly not that of the author:

- *Frankenstein*: Robert Walton
- *Dracula*: Jonathan Harker
- *The Handmaid's Tale*: Offred
- *The Lovely Bones*: Susie Salmon.

In spite of this, authors clearly have overall control over what is being narrated; narrators, after all, are characters either in or associated with the action of the novel and are not real people. Consequently, they are, of course, under the control of an author. Indeed, when we talk or write about Robert Walton's words at the beginning of *Frankenstein*, we are very unlikely to mention that they are the product of Walton himself but rather that Mary Shelley is using this narrative voice for a particular reason. That is, we assign a degree of **intentionality** to the use of a particular narrator and that intentionality comes from our concept of what we think the author might be trying to say. However, even this is a little problematic. Who exactly is the Mary Shelley that we think is speaking to us by using Walton as a narrating vehicle? Unless we know authors personally (highly unlikely in most books that we read and impossible for the author of *Frankenstein*, given that Mary Shelley died in 1851), then when we talk about authors in a writing sense, we are only talking about a very small part of their identity.

As you saw in Unit 2, we can distinguish between a real writer and an implied writer. This distinction helps us to remember that the writer we have in mind when we read a text is necessarily a very different entity to the real-life writer. We can add the term 'narrator' to these to provide a model for thinking about the relationship between the narrative voice and the person (i.e. the author) responsible for the overall shaping of the narrative.

In Figure 16A we highlight the differences between different levels of real-life and fictional entities (note the terms real writer and implied writer have been replaced in the model in Figure 16A by the terms **real author** and **implied author**).

Figure 16A

Real author ⟶ Implied author ⟶ Narrator

Key terms

intentionality: the idea that the author has a reason for shaping a narrative in a particular way

real author: the real-life human entity responsible for writing a piece of fiction

implied author: the conceptual entity that a reader creates and has in mind when they read a particular piece of fiction

Returning to *Frankenstein* and Mary Shelley, we can now draw important distinctions between:

- the real author: the real person Mary Shelley, daughter of William Godwin and Mary Wollstonecraft, and wife of the poet Percy Shelley. The only access that we, as readers in the twenty-first century, have to Mary Shelley is through biographies and other encyclopaedic information either in books or online.
- the implied author of *Frankenstein*: the Mary Shelley we associate with writing *Frankenstein*. Again, much of this information is second-hand to us but might include more specific knowledge around the composition of the novel: for example, the Shelleys' summer in Geneva with Lord Byron, John Polidori and Claire Claremont, telling each other ghost stories at the Villa Diodati that led to

the writing of *Frankenstein*. This 'version' of Mary Shelley will be the one that we have created in our minds and use when we read *Frankenstein*, and will be different to the implied author of her other work, such as the novel *The Last Man*.
- the narrators of *Frankenstein*: Walton, Frankenstein and the Creature. These are all, of course, under the control of Mary Shelley and we associate intentionality around what they say and do with Mary Shelley, the implied author of the novel.

Drawing attention to the differences between these three concepts enables you to not only understand and explore narrative voices as constructs but also to see the potential irony when perceived differences between the intention of a narrator and an implied author controlling that narrative voice are drawn to our attention. Two examples of this are Atwood's positioning of 'Historical notes', which calls into question the reliability of Offred's narrative in *The Handmaid's Tale*, and Victor's first narrative in *Frankenstein*, which contains philosophies that readers might see as in contrast to those of Mary Shelley.

ACTIVITY 4

Real and implied authors

Explore your understanding of the terms *real author* and *implied author* by sketching out what you know about each for the novel you are studying. What sorts of information about each of these entities do you hold? How have you 'created' your implied author for your text?

16.2.4 Narrative structures: temporal, spatial and perceptual dimensions

So far, we have looked at how storyworlds are developed from relatively small amounts of language detail. However, these shorter extracts fit into a larger narrative structure across a whole text and, as they do so, the parameters of the storyworld may change. For example, another character might start speaking or be described by the narrator, or there could be shifts in the location in which the action takes place. Another very common type of shift is in time. This can occur when the action naturally moves forwards, or when a specific narrator/character decides to narrate details from an earlier time frame known as **analepsis**. Alternatively, a narrator/character might imagine a future time frame or be able to travel into one, known as **prolepsis**. There are a variety of ways in which an author can signal such temporal shifts. For instance:

- **temporal adverbs**: e.g. 'later', 'tomorrow', 'yesterday'
- **prepositional phrases that evoke certain time frames**: e.g. 'in the evening', 'at four o'clock'
- **verbs of perception or desire that show a character or narrator thinking back or projecting forwards**: e.g. 'remember', 'recall', 'imagine', 'wish'.

Key terms

analepsis: a shift made by a narrator back to an earlier time frame

prolepsis: a projection forwards that a narrator makes to a future time

Sometimes the most striking shifts can be very rapid ones that are designed to draw attention to a particular idea or to achieve a particular effect. In Text 16B there are lines alternating from different deictic centres in terms of place (from the Salmon family home to Harvey's hiding place) and in terms of perception (from the speech of Susie's mother, to Susie's narration of the events with Harvey). Here, the quickfire spatial and perceptual shifts draw the reader's attention to the horror of Susie's experience in contrast to the safety and ignorance of the family environment.

Text 16B

"Susie! Susie!" I heard my mother calling. "Dinner is ready."

He was inside me. He was grunting.

"We're having string beans and lamb."

I was the mortar, he was the pestle.

"Your brother has a new finger painting, and I made apple crumb cake."

Source: Alice Sebold *The Lovely Bones*, Chapter 1

One of the most obvious ways that a narrative can shift temporally and spatially is through the introduction of a perceptual shift within the global narrative structure, where the responsibility for narration is distributed across several characters.

This is the case for two of the set texts on this unit, *Frankenstein* and *Dracula*, but even if you are studying *The Handmaid's Tale* or *The Lovely Bones*, you may well be studying other texts during other parts of the course that contain similarly divergent structures.

In *Frankenstein*, Shelley employs a set of narrative frames, which are summarised in Figure 16B. The opening narrator Walton gives way to Frankenstein, whose narrative in turn leads to that of the Creature. This central narrative then moves out again back to Frankenstein and then finally Walton, who closes the novel. Since each narrative is positioned within the frame of the preceding one, Walton's narrative becomes central to understanding the novel; the quest he embarks on at the novel's opening and terminates at the end provide bookends for reading the central concerns both of the narratives of Frankenstein and the Creature, and the wider themes and issues of the novel itself.

Figure 16B

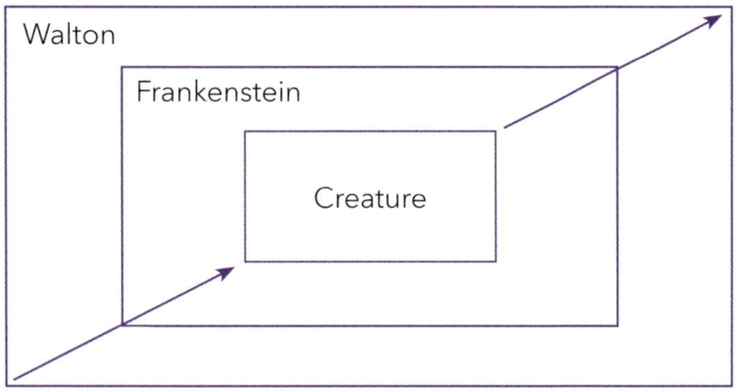

Dracula is narrated by different characters within the storyworld through the letters, diaries and journals they keep (summarised in Figure 16C). These, together with some press cuttings and ships' logs, make up the individual chapters in the novel. The novel follows an epistolary format, where each chapter shifts its deictic parameters to a new narrating voice, in new temporal and spatial locations. The reader is essentially asked to piece all of this together into some coherent whole.

Figure 16C

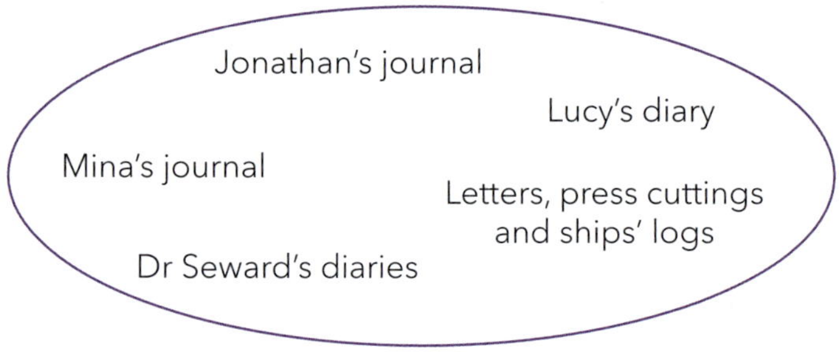

ACTIVITY 5

Narrative structures

If you are studying either *Frankenstein* or *Dracula*, use either Figure 16B or 16C to explore in more detail the significance of the global narrative structure. What do you notice about the ways that perceptual shifts in narration occur? What do you think is the significance of any patterns that you can see? If you are studying *The Handmaid's Tale* or *The Lovely Bones*, can you sketch that novel's narrative structure visually? Although there are fewer perceptual shifts in these novels (apart from younger and older versions of Offred and Susie, and the 'Historical notes' that frame *The Handmaid's Tale*), there are many temporal and spatial shifts that are important to each novel's overall structure. How are these mapped out across the novel you are studying? What do you think is significant about any patterns that you can find?

16.2.5 Filling in gaps

As we saw in Unit 5, a universal strategy that readers have to undertake is to gap-fill, drawing on their encyclopaedic knowledge to enhance explicit textual detail. In fact, much of this work happens so quickly and so effortlessly that readers are often not conscious of doing it. In Unit 5, you learnt how this kind of knowledge was held in structures called schemas that are built up from our everyday interaction with the world, the people we speak to, and the books, films and other media that we consume. Authors make use of this schematic knowledge and rely on it when setting up and developing storyworlds. They work on the basis of utilising both readers' existing knowledge structures and new ones that they build and maintain as they progress through their reading.

Schemas can contain different kinds of knowledge, either about the real world and how it operates, or about the fictional world and the events and characters that are introduced within it by the author.

As an example, look at Text 16C, where the narrator, Offred, is describing walking along a street in Gilead.

Text 16C

Doubled, I walked the street. Though we are no longer in the Commanders' compound, there are large houses here also. In front of one of them a Guardian is mowing the lawn.

Source: Margaret Atwood, *The Handmaid's Tale*, Chapter 5

In reading Text 16C we have to draw on our real-world knowledge of what a 'street' and a 'house' are, as well as our knowledge of what 'mowing the grass' involves. In addition, we use our fictional world knowledge, gained from reading the novel so far, to understand who the 'Commanders' and 'Guardian' are, and why Offred is 'doubled' and walking along the street. A great part of this fictional knowledge of course is dynamic and evolves as we read the novel. So, our knowledge of characters and places is built up on successive mentions of them and their changing statuses and roles as the novel progresses.

ACTIVITY 6

Exploring fictional knowledge

Take short extracts from the beginning, the middle and the end of your chosen novel that focus on the same character and/or place, and explore the kinds of knowledge you have to draw on to help build a rich storyworld. How much of this is real and how much of this is fictional-world knowledge? How do you think that your fictional-world knowledge has changed at later stages of the novel? How does this influence your understanding of character and place?

16.2.6 Focus and motifs

One of the ways in which an author can assign prominence to a character, event or place in a storyworld is to give it a significant amount of attention or **focus**. Clearly, leading characters in a novel receive a great deal of 'page space' simply because they are at the heart of the story; equally central events by their definition will have more time spent on them than additional ones.

Put simply, if an episode is narrated in detail, and a great deal of narrative time is spent on it, then it is being signalled as important and worthy of a reader drawing some interpretative significance from it. On the other hand, events that are simply glossed over, downplayed or marginalised are (in the narrator's eyes) at least seen as being less significant and less worthy of our attention.

As an example of this, look at Text 16D. Here, Susie narrates an episode where her father, Jack, is speaking to George Harvey. The men have been building the structure for a tent and Harvey has gone to fetch some white cotton sheets, which he hands to Jack.

Key terms

focus: the amount of attention given to an event or a character in any part of a text

Text 16D

My father and Mr Harvey spread the sheets over the domed arch, anchoring them along the square formed by the crossbars that linked the forked posts. Then they hung the remaining sheets straight down from these crossbars so that the bottoms of the sheets brushed the ground.

Source: Alice Sebold, *The Lovely Bones*, Chapter 4

In *Frankenstein*, Shelley employs a set of narrative frames…

In Text 16D, the time afforded to the description of the sheets and the tent that the two men construct suggests that they hold some kind of interpretative significance. The sheets remain in our attention by having our focus maintained on them through the repeated lexis 'sheets', and the details of what the men are doing with them. This foregrounding of the 'white sheets' might be interpreted by a reader in a number of ways, perhaps signifying the innocence of Susie, the irony of Harvey's criminal thoughts as they are building the tent, the tent itself as an enclosed and dangerous space reminiscent of the hiding place in which Susie is killed, or the enlightenment that comes over Jack as he begins to suspect that George Harvey knows something about Susie's murder.

When something is repeated across a larger section of a novel or occurs more frequently throughout the storyworld, we can say that it becomes either a **theme** or a **motif**. The narratologist Porter Abbott (2008) offers this useful distinction between the two:

- **Theme:** an abstract idea e.g. violence, love, families, war
- **Motif:** a repeated concrete object, place or phrase e.g. a rose, a kitchen, a garden, words that a character speaks.

Abbott argues that themes are implicit in motifs (for example, the repeated mentioning of a rose might suggest the theme of love) but that motifs are not implicit in themes (so the theme of love does not necessarily mean that it will always be signified by a rose).

In Text 16D, the sheets act as a motif that evoke the themes of innocence, entrapment, danger or enlightenment, depending on which particular interpretation of their significance a reader might be drawn to.

ACTIVITY 7

Themes and motifs

Keep a track of any motifs that occur in the novel you are studying and explain how these relate to both major and minor themes. You could keep a record of how many times a motif occurs; any particular chapters or parts of the novel it appears in most; and whether it is associated with a particular character, event or location.

Key terms

theme: a repeated abstract idea or concept in a work of fiction

motif: a repeated concrete object, place or phrase which occurs in a work of fiction and is related to a particular theme

16.2.7 Locations

Locations can be one of the most important motifs in narrative, drawing attention to certain themes and ideas round them, and helping to influence readers' interpretations. For example, some of the most important locations in the four novels on this unit are:

- *Frankenstein*: St Petersburgh/Archangel, Geneva, Ingolstadt, the region around Mont Blanc, the Orkney Islands
- *Dracula*: Dracula's castle, Transylvania, Whitby, London
- *The Handmaid's Tale*: the city of Gilead, the Commander's house, Offred's former home, 'Jezebel's'
- *The Lovely Bones*: The Salmon family home, Harvey's house, Harvey's hiding place, the hospital, heaven, the abandoned house that Lindsey and Samuel find.

On the one hand, places can be viewed as a very general motif. For example, in *Frankenstein* the constant shifting in location highlights the novel's concerns with the theme of journey and exploration. On the other hand, locations can act as more local and specific motifs. In *The Lovely Bones*, the abandoned house that Lindsey and Samuel find becomes representative of salvation and regeneration, both central themes in the novel.

ACTIVITY 8

The importance of locations

Take one example of a location that has repeated coverage in the novel you are studying and explore its significance. You should think about:

- how it is described
- what events take place there

- what wider significance it has in the novel, either as a local and specific or as a more general motif.

16.2.8 Beginnings and endings

If you think about your favourite film or novel and identify its most memorable part, it's very likely that this will be either the beginning or the ending. These generally will contain some of the most dramatic and emotionally charged events. The beginning and ending of a novel are automatically foregrounded to us because of their position: a beginning will always stand out because nothing precedes it, whilst an ending has the same effect because it marks the end of the narrative, with nothing to follow. Beginnings and endings also have to be attention-grabbing in their own right, to engage a reader in exactly the same way as a spoken narrative.

The narratologist Peter Rabinowitz (2002) has argued that beginnings and endings have what he calls 'privileged positions' in prose fiction for these very reasons. This means that anything that gets textually foregrounded in the beginning or the ending is essentially double-foregrounded in that our attention is also drawn to it because of the fact that it exists in this privileged position.

ACTIVITY 9

Early foregrounding

Look at the first sentence from your chosen novel (listed together as Text 16E). What do you think each is foregrounding? How does this relate to the wider concerns and themes of the novel?

Text 16E

Frankenstein

'You will rejoice to hear that no disaster has accompanied the commencement of an enterprise which you have regarded with such evil forebodings.'

Dracula

'Left Munich at 8.35pm on 1st May, arriving at Vienna early next morning; should have arrived at 6.46, but train was an hour late.'

The Handmaid's Tale

'We slept in what had once been the gymnasium.'

The Lovely Bones

'My name was Salmon, like the fish; first name Susie.'

ACTIVITY 10

Titles

Rabinowitz argues that titles occupy a privileged position in that they can immediately direct the reader towards a particular character or idea. Look at the following titles of books, which were all in the top 10 fiction list on Amazon during July 2014. What would you expect each of these novels to be about? What do you think they might be drawing attention to and foregrounding for the reader?

1 *Bite*
2 *The Fault in our Stars*
3 *Sycamore Row*
4 *The Cuckoo's Calling*
5 *The Summer Child*
6 *The Knot*
7 *Hotel on the Corner of Bitter and Sweet*
8 *The Silkworm*
9 *Abducted*
10 *The Villa*

Check your responses in the Ideas section on Cambridge Elevate

ACTIVITY 11

Alternative titles

What difference do you think it would make if your chosen novel was known by the following title? All were either considered by the author at one point or, in the case of *Frankenstein*, is its full (if not always widely acknowledged) title.

- *Frankenstein*: *Frankenstein Or, The Modern Prometheus* (full title)
- *Dracula*: *The Un-dead* (considered title, changed before publication)
- *The Handmaid's Tale*: *Offred* (considered title, changed before publication)
- *The Lovely Bones*: *Monsters* and *This Wide Heaven* (both considered titles, changed before publication).

As you learnt in categorising spoken narratives, endings are also important since they work to signal a sense of closure to the listener/reader.

Conventional endings in prose fiction will tie up loose ends, reveal any aspects of plot that need to be resolved and provide details of the narrator(s)' and characters' thoughts on the events of the novel. However, some novels do not have this kind of conventional ending, and may leave questions unanswered. This lack of closure is more typical of certain types of genre (for example, horror fiction, where the killer might remain undiscovered, or a monster comes back from the dead and anticipates further victims). Here, the intended effect might be to prolong suspense or provoke further questions from the reader. In some cases, the lack of closure might motivate us to doubt the validity of what we have been told at certain points in the novel, and even question our perception of what really happened in the fictional world. This can be a very powerful conclusion to a novel indeed.

ACTIVITY 12

Exploring endings

Look carefully at the ending of your chosen novel. To what extent does it operate as a conclusion to the novel? Think about:

- how conventional the ending is in drawing together loose ends and aspects of plot
- how much closure there is - is there anything that gets unresolved? Why do you think this is? Is there anything that you think a reader is left thinking about having put the book down?

16.3 Characterisation

In this section we will look at some aspects of the ways that authors use characters in setting up and developing the storyworld. One important distinction you should be able to make is between the term **character**, which refers to a participant in the storyworld, and **characterisation**, which refers to the range of strategies authors and their readers use to build, maintain and develop these participants.

Watch tutorial video, Characterisation, on Cambridge Elevate

Key terms

conventional ending: a prototypical ending in which the plot is resolved and any loose ends are tied up

character: a participant in the storyworld

characterisation: the range of strategies authors and readers use to build, maintain and develop characters

16.3.1 Constructing and tracking characters

As we saw in 16.2.5, our understanding of fictional texts comes from a combination of the words on the page and various types of background knowledge that we bring to the reading experience in the form of schemas. In that section, we drew a distinction between two types of knowledge: real-world knowledge and fictional-world knowledge.

The way that we build our ideas about characters is also dependent on using this kind of knowledge and undertaking a tremendous amount of inferring through gap-filling. Look at the opening to *The Lovely Bones* in Text 16F.

Text 16F

My name was Salmon, like the fish; first name, Susie. I was fourteen when I was murdered on December 6, 1973. In newspaper photos of missing girls from the seventies, most looked like me: white girls with mousy brown hair.

Source: Alice Sebold, *The Lovely Bones*, Chapter 1

If you were asked to draw a picture of what Susie looks like, you would probably find this very easy despite the fact that only two aspects of her physical appearance (her skin colour and her hair colour) are mentioned. It is unlikely, for example, that you would draw her with three eyes, or four legs, or a tail. This is because we begin with a default mental impression of what a fourteen-year-old girl must look like, built out of own experience, and used as the basis for interpreting and imagining a fictional character.

You can test this by making some very small changes to the text, such as:

- 'I was forty when I was murdered'
- 'In newspaper photos of missing boys from the seventies, most looked like me'
- 'white girls with blonde hair'

Effectively then, this means that any textual detail that an author provides us with is crucial in terms of both triggering and augmenting any pre-existing knowledge about characters that we might use to build up a picture of them. These details could include:

- what characters look like
- how they act, speak and think
- how they interact with other characters
- what other characters say about them
- how they present themselves to other characters
- how they present themselves to the reader (if acting as a narrator).

We can summarise the process of characterisation in Figure 16D.

Figure 16D: The process of categorisation

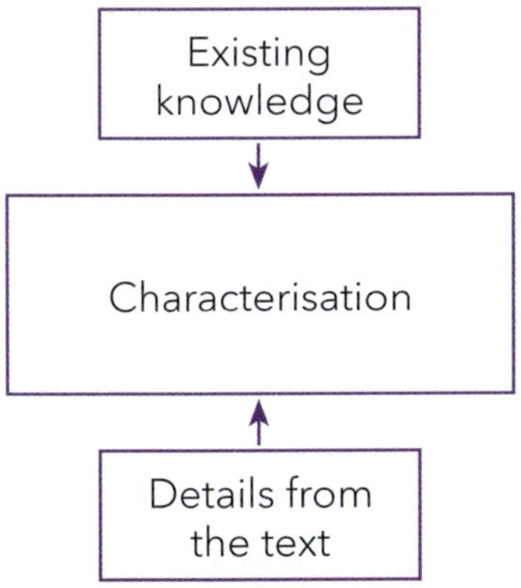

Just as in real life, characters in the storyworld aren't simply static entities; they develop and change over time and readers need to be able to track these changes, often being asked to consider some crucial difference between a character in an early part of the novel, and that same character at a later stage, possibly many years down the line. Indeed, one particular type of novel, the ***bildungsroman*** (a coming of age story) explicitly charts the life of its central character from early childhood to adulthood, asking the reader to follow significant changes in that character over time as they reach maturity (classic examples of the *bildungsroman* novel would include Charles Dickens's *Great Expectations* and *David Copperfield*).

Frankenstein can also be considered a *bildungsroman* novel as it maps out the life history of two characters, Frankenstein and the Creature. If you are studying this novel, you could explore significant points in the 'life history' for each of these characters, identifying what for you are foregrounded as being most important by Mary Shelley. Equally, although in *The Lovely Bones* Susie is dead at the beginning, the novel still charts the various journeys of her family, not least Buckley and Lindsey, as well as the 'ghost version' of Susie herself as she both watches them grow up and finds her own maturity of sorts in Harvey's death at the end of the novel.

Key terms

***bildungsroman*:** a fictional work that charts the development of a central character through time, usually from childhood to adulthood

ACTIVITY 13

Tracking characters

You can undertake some interesting work based on how different 'versions' of characters are presented to us, whichever novel you are studying. Choose one character and explore characterisation as the novel progresses, using evidence from either the character's own narrative and descriptions, or those of others. You can set up a 'character log' to trace and keep a record of how these versions develop. Start by identifying some key episodes for that character in the novel and then explore:

- how the character is presented at each of these stages
- who is narrating/describing the character (it may be the same narrator, of course, across the novel)
- what significant events have occurred between episodes
- what kinds of fictional world knowledge a reader is asked to draw on at various stages.

For example, if you are studying *The Lovely Bones* you might take Jack Salmon and identify the following key episodes for analysis:

- learning of Susie's death in chapter 2
- playing with Buckley in chapter 3
- talking to Len in chapter 5
- going to the cornfield in chapter 11
- talking to Lindsey in chapter 13
- looking at photographs in chapter 17
- after his heart attack in chapter 19
- with Abigail in chapter 20.

16.3.2 Types of characters

Within the storyworld, it is useful to distinguish between different types of character, and there are several ways of doing this. One straightforward way would be to distinguish between the main and additional characters in the same way as we suggested was possible with events. This would depend on analysing how much page space is given to them, and how they are related to the main events in the novel. Another related way would be to consider how much **depth** each character has. This concept was explored by the novelist and literary critic E. M. Forster, in his book *Aspects of the Novel* (1927). Forster distinguished between what he called **flat characters** and **round characters**. For Forster, flat characters were one-dimensional and could be summarised in a single sentence, whilst round characters were more complex, and were closer to real-life people in their qualities and imperfections, which made it difficult to summarise them so easily and briefly. Depth is therefore a key feature of a round character but not a flat one.

Another way of differentiating between types of characters is to consider them in functional terms, looking at the kinds of roles they undertake in the storyworld. There are a number of models for doing this. Two that you might find useful are those proposed by the Russian narratologist Vladimir Propp (1928) and the French linguist Algirdas Julien Greimas (1966).

In his work exploring patterns in Russian fairytales, Propp developed a list of plot elements that he felt typified the events and their sequence in the narrative. In addition, he suggested that there were seven character types, each of which plays a particular function in the storyworld. These are listed in Table 16A.

Table 16A: Propp's seven character types

Character type	Function
villain	represents wrong-doing or evil
hero	stands in opposition to the villain and represents good
donor/ provider	provides the hero with some kind of tool to help him
dispatcher	sets the hero a task to complete
helper	accompanies and supports the hero
princess	the romantic interest of the hero, usually associated with the task itself (e.g. needs saving from the villain)
false hero	originally seen as good but then develops villainous tendencies

If we use these with reference to *Dracula*, we might tentatively identify some of the characters in that novel as follows:

- **villain**: Dracula
- **hero**: Abraham Van Helsing, Quincey Morris
- **donor/provider**: Abraham Van Helsing, John Seward
- **dispatcher**: John Seward
- **helper**: John Seward, Jonathan Harker, Arthur Holmwood, Quincey Morris
- **princess**: Mina
- **false hero**: Lucy (good at first but then becomes the 'Bloofer lady' attacking children).

Greimas' model has one less character role (he called these **actants**). These are outlined in Table 16B; you can hopefully see the overlap between these and Propp's model.

Table 16B: Greimas' character roles

Character type	Function
giver	sets a task for the subject to complete
receiver	the character who stands to benefit from the task
subject	the central character in the narrative
object	the object of the character's quest (could be a person or the realisation of an event)
helper	accompanies and supports the hero
opponent	the villain of the narrative

Using Greimas' model we might suggest the following characters fit these roles:

- **giver**: John Seward, Abraham Van Helsing
- **receiver**: all characters in the novel
- **subject**: Abraham Van Helsing
- **object**: the death of Dracula
- **helper**: John Seward, Jonathan Harker, Arthur Holmwood, Quincey Morris
- **opponent**: Dracula, Lucy.

Of course, merely labelling the characters in line with these proposed roles or functions is not sufficient. You need to be able to explore how thinking of characterisation in these **structuralist models** helps you to provide a developed analysis and interpretation of the novel and any extract you are studying.

ACTIVITY 14

Character roles

If you are studying *Dracula*, look at the examples of the character roles listed above and decide whether you agree with them. Are there other characters that you feel fulfil the roles suggested by Propp and Greimas? If you are studying a different novel, try a similar exercise with the characters in that particular text. You could start by thinking about the roles of the following characters.

- *Frankenstein*: Frankenstein, Walton, the Creature, Clerval, Elizabeth, Frankenstein's father, De Lacey
- *The Handmaid's Tale*: Offred, Luke, the Commander, Serena Joy, Nick, Moira, Aunt Lydia, the two Offglens
- *The Lovely Bones*: Susie, Jack, Abigail, Lindsey, Buckley, George Harvey, Grandma Lynn, Len Fenerman, Ruth Simmons, Ray Singh

Now, taking each of the characters in turn, find evidence from the text itself to support your classification. For example, what aspects of the storyworld and descriptions of characters mark them in certain roles? In some cases, this should be straightforward (for example, Dracula and George Harvey as villains), but in other cases, categorisation may be less clear-cut. For example, who is the villain in *Frankenstein*? And is Offred the only contender for the role of hero in *The Handmaid's Tale*?

Key terms

actant: a person, creature or object with an active role in a narrative

depth: the complexity associated with a round character

flat character: a character that is simplistic and can be easily and very quickly summarised

round character: a more complex character, more difficult to summarise

structuralist model: a model that explains aspects of a work of fiction in terms of how they provide an overall structure for the text

16.3.3 Representing actions

Examining the kinds of actions characters are involved in is also a useful way of exploring characterisation at a specific point in the novel. It will also help you to think about how particular incidents might form larger patterns with interpretative significance across the novel as a whole.

Within the storyworld, it is useful to distinguish between different types of character...

As you learnt in Units 6 and 7, a verb process is the grammatical unit that shows actions, states of being, and mental operations. In Text 16G, where Samuel and Lindsey find an abandoned house, the verb processes have been underlined.

Text 16G

'Happy graduation,' he said

He tightened his hold on her

Their boots crunched down on top of tin cans

It was dark except for Samuel's safety light

She imagined trees split down the middle and houses on fire

Samuel shut off the safety light immediately

Source: Alice Sebold, *The Lovely Bones*, Chapter 17

As you learnt in Unit 6, one way of distinguishing between types of verb is to do with their semantic properties. We explained that we can generally split verb processes into material ones (denoting actions), relational ones (denoting states of being), mental ones (denoting psychological operations), and verbal ones (denoting speech). We can now categorise the examples in Text 16G as follows:

- **material processes**: grabbed, tightened, crunched, shut off
- **relational process**: was
- **mental process**: imagined
- **verbal process**: said.

This kind of categorisation can be very useful when looking at how characters are represented both in selective episodes in the novel, and in larger-scale patterns across the whole text. For example, characters who are largely represented by mental processes might be being characterised as thoughtful or introverted; those who are largely represented through relational processes might be unable to act of their own accord and so on. Conversely, very powerful characters will often be represented through material processes and clauses that demonstrate their ability to have active agency.

ACTIVITY 15

Processes and characters

Read Text 16H, taken from early on in *Dracula* when Jonathan Harker meets Dracula for the first time. What do you notice about the clauses and the verb processes in them? What do these suggest about the way that Dracula and Harker are being portrayed in Text 16H?

Text 16H

The Count halted, putting down my bags, closed the door, and crossing the room, opened another door, which led into a small octagonal room lit by a single lamp, and seemingly without a window of any sort. Passing through this, he opened another door, and motioned me to enter. It was a welcome sight; for here was a great bedroom well lighted and warmed with another log fire, which sent a hollow roar up the wide chimney. The Count himself left my luggage inside and withdrew, saying, before he closed the door:-

'You will need, after your journey, to refresh yourself by making your toilet. I trust you will find all you wish. When you are ready come into the other room, where you will find your supper prepared.'

Source: Bram Stoker, *Dracula*

You can undertake a similar type of analysis to this with any part of the novel you are studying. Search for patterns in the kinds of processes that are used to describe characters and relate this to what we know about them and their relative status in the storyworld. You might find that specific patterns are replicated across the novel for certain characters, whilst for others the kind of representation may vary according to the context for the action. So, for example, a character may well be highly active in one part of the novel, and pensive and introverted in another. Equally, characters might be represented in different ways depending on with whom they are interacting. As always, ensure that you attach some interpretative significance to any patterns that you find.

Check your responses in the Ideas section on Cambridge Elevate

16.3.4 Representing speech and thought

ACTIVITY 16

Speech in life and fiction

In order to think about the relationship between natural speech and represented speech in prose fiction, read Text 16I, part of an interview between a police officer (P) and a suspect (S) who has been arrested on suspicion of breaking and entering a shop. Then read Text 16J, some dialogue between George Harvey and Len from *The Lovely Bones*. What similarities and differences do you notice?

Text 16I

P: As you've come out there you've turned left onto Tyne so you've started walking up Turner (.) and (.) you've got the shops on your right hand side (.) the LowPrice dry cleaners newsagents on your right hand side haven't you (0.2)

S: yeah

P: did you go anywhere near there (0.2)

S: no (0.4) not anywhere here at all near there (0.2)

P: not anywhere at all

S: no (0.5) just (0.8) out of the subway and round the corner

Source: Elisabeth Carter, *Analysing Police Interviews*, Continuum, page 46 (emphasised words are underlined)

Text 16J

'Have you talked to the Ellis boy?' Mr Harvey asked.

'We talked to the family.'

'He's hurt some animals in the neighbourhood, I hear.'

'He sounds like a bad kid, I grant you,' said Len, 'but he was working in the mall at the time.'

'Witnesses?'

'Yes.'

Source: Alice Sebold, *The Lovely Bones*, Chaper 5

Check your responses in the Ideas section on Cambridge Elevate

One of the most fruitful ways of exploring what characters say in novels is to consider their language choices at a lexical level. This can involve looking at specific instances of language that form a character's **personal vocabulary**, such as:

- lexis that is related to a *character's age or ideology*, and consequently provides evidence of a particular world-view. For example, Buckley in *The Lovely Bones* uses a simple vocabulary that projects his child-like naïve view of the world; the Commander in *The Handmaid's Tale* has a vocabulary which is in keeping with his powerful status in the novel.
- lexis related to a *character's regional background*. For example, Quincey Morris in *Dracula* has a vocabulary that partly reflects his Texan roots, whilst parts of the novel contain characters speaking in a London dialect, with variant spelling used by Stoker to replicate their London accents.
- lexis that is more idiosyncratic, relating to a *character's idiolect*. This might include the use of particular metaphors, personal discourse markers, non-fluency features and politeness strategies. A character's idiolect can also extend into syntax: for example, in a particular way of ordering words, or the framing of questions.

As well as analysing speech in these terms, we can also explore the options that authors have when framing a character's speech through a narrating voice. Look at Example 3, spoken by Serena Joy in *The Handmaid's Tale*.

3 'I want to see as little of you as possible,' she said.

This is just one of a number of ways that Serena's words could have been presented to us by Margaret Atwood. In Example 3, Serena's words are told to us by Offred (the narrating voice), who provides her exact words, indicated by the speech marks and the speech clause 'she said'. This is known as **direct speech** (DS). On the other hand, Atwood could have presented Serena Joy's words in one of the ways in Examples 4–8.

Key terms

personal vocabulary: the individual words that make up a character's speech

4 'I want to see as little of you as possible': the speech clause is removed so that only the character's actual words remain, without any framing by the narrator. This is known as **free direct speech** (FDS).

5 'She said that she wanted to see as little of me as possible': the speech clause introduces most of what Serena said, but here verb tense 'wanted' and pronouns 'I' to 'she' and 'you' to 'me' are reconfigured from the narrator's perspective so that the speech has greater narrator framing. This is known as **indirect speech** (IS).

6 'She wanted to see as little of her as possible': there is no direct presentation of the words, and the pronoun 'I' has been replaced by 'She' as in Example 5. However, the use of 'her' positions this from Serena's, rather than Offred's, perspective, even though the narrator still provides a frame for the speech. This is known as **free indirect speech** (FIS).

7 'She spoke negatively towards me': the speech has been summarised by the narrator to provide a flavour of what Serena Joy said but to avoid providing any of her actual words. This is known as **narrator's representation of speech act** (NRSA).

8 'She said something': the speech has been summarised to the point where all we know is that Serena spoke. This is known as **narrator's representation of speech** (NRS).

In Examples 4–8 we can see that some of the options, FDS, DS and to a point FIS, remain close to Serena Joy's original words, with no or little narrator intervention, whilst IS, NRSA and NS work in the opposite way, and they filter what was said through the narrator. FIS is often seen as a kind of 'halfway house' since it combines a character's original words with some degree of narrator filtering. These options can be shown as a continuum of speech presentation as in Figure 16E.

Figure 16E: A continuum of speech presentation

FDS DS FIS IS NRSA NRS

← →

Character emphasis **Narrator emphasis**

The stylisticians Geoffrey Leech and Mick Short (1981) have suggested that authors can manipulate these speech categories so as to provide the sense of either character or narrator control. As we move along the figure, from left to right, we move away from more character-oriented ways of presenting speech to more narrator-oriented ones. We could argue that the further left on the figure we are, the more we are likely to empathise with a character or characters, whose words have been given directly to us. This can be seen in Text 16K, where Alice Sebold does not have her narrator Susie interfere in or mediate any of the dialogue between Buckley and Jack.

Text 16K

'See this shoe?' my father said. (direct speech)

Buckley nodded his head.

'I want you to listen to everything I say about it, okay?' (free direct speech)

'Susie?' my brother asked, somehow connecting the two. (direct speech)

'Yes, I'm going to tell you where Susie is' (free direct speech)

Source: Alice Sebold, *The Lovely Bones*, Chapter 5

In contrast, the further right we go, the more we are likely to view the storyworld from the perspective of a biased narrator who is controlling what we know about what characters have said. This can be seen in Text 16L, where Offred is recounting an incident in a supermarket with Luke. Here Luke's actual words are largely filtered through Offred's narration, giving her close control in revealing what was said.

Text 16L

There are some differences he said (direct speech). He was fond of saying that (narrator's representation of speech), as if I was trying to prove there weren't. But mostly he said it when my mother was there (narrator's representation of speech). He liked to tease her (narrator's representation of speech act).

Source: Margaret Atwood, *The Handmaid's Tale*

ACTIVITY 17

Character or narrator emphasis?
Choose a section (around half a page to a page in length) of the novel that you are studying where either one of the ways of presenting speech highlighted in Examples 4–8 dominates, or where the author uses a combination of approaches at different points. What is the effect of presenting speech in this way? How does this relate to the ways that characters and narrators present speech in the novel more generally?

ACTIVITY 18

Exploring the presentation of thought in prose fiction
The continuum in Figure 16E can also be used to explain and explore the different options authors have in presenting characters' thoughts. Moving from a character-oriented to narrator-oriented options, we can trace the following speech categories:

- **Free direct thought** (FDT)
- **Direct thought** (DT)
- **Free indirect thought** (FIT)
- **Indirect thought** (IT)
- **Narrator's representation of thought act** (NRTA)
- **Narrator's representation of thought** (NRT)

Can you find examples of thought presentation in the novel you are studying and explore their significance in the same way as for Activity 17?

Key terms

free direct speech/thought: speech or thought that is presented word-for-word with no speech/ thought clause added by the narrator

direct speech/thought: speech or thought that is presented word-for-word but with a speech/ thought clause added by the narrator

free indirect speech/thought: speech or thought that is a hybrid of character and narrator representation of what was said

indirect speech/thought: speech or thought that is framed by the narrator but retains an element of what was said by the character

Key terms

narrator's representation of speech/thought act: speech or thought that is presented as a summary by the narrator

narrator's representation of speech/thought: speech or thought that is presented by the narrator as simply an indication that a character was speaking or thinking

16.3.5 Body language

Another way that we can explore characterisation is by examining characters' **body language** in those key scenes where they are described to us. We use body language in our own day-to-day interactions and behaviours: for example, to read or display emotions. In a similar way, authors assign characters in fictional texts a range of non-verbal cues and moves. And, just as with represented speech, these are designed to be recognised by a reader as significant, and worthy of some interpretative comment.

Key terms

body language: non-verbal communication given to characters in the storyworld

The framework that follows is taken from the work of the literary scholar Barbara Korte (1997) who has devised a model for thinking about the various types of body language that characters may display in fiction. Korte suggests that body language can be categorised as shown in Table 16C. The third column in the table gives examples of each of the categories from one of the set texts.

ACTIVITY 19

Exploring the effects of body language
Take one category of body language and find examples of this in the novel that you are studying. Comment on the significance you feel readers are being asked to draw from the specific body language that characters exhibit.

Table 16C: Categories of body language

Category	Definition and types	Examples	Commentary
kinesics	gestures, postures, eye and facial movements, other body movements due to feelings or emotions e.g. trembling	'Now I shift my gaze. What I see is not the machines, but Ofglen, reflected in the glass of the window. She's looking straight at me. We can see into each other's eyes. This is the first time I've ever seen Ofglen's eyes, directly, steadily, not aslant.' (Chapter 27 of *The Handmaid's Tale*, where Offred and Ofglen are standing outside Soul Scrolls looking through the windows.)	In this extract, the eye contact between Offred and Ofglen is significant as a communicative tool that draws the characters together and initiates Offred into the world of the underground movement.
		'My <u>heart palpitated</u> in the sickness of fear; and I hurried on with <u>irregular steps</u>, not daring <u>to look about me'</u> (Chapter 4 of *Frankenstein*, describing Frankenstein following completing work on the Creature).	Here, Frankenstein's fear and horror on realising the implications of his work manifest themselves in a physical way.
haptics	touching another person: e.g. holding, shaking hands, kissing, pushing, punching	'She and I would <u>tuck</u> Lindsey in together. I stood by the bed as she <u>kissed</u> my sister on her forehead and <u>brushed back</u> her hair from her face' (Chapter 12 of *The Lovely Bones*, where Susie describes the bath-time routine that she, Lindsey and her mother shared)	The descriptions of touching and closeness signify the intimacy that existed between mother and daughters and the nostalgia with which Susie looks back on that episode.
proxemics	movement in relation to another character's personal space e.g. moving closer to, further away from	'The fair girl advanced and bent over me till I could feel the movement of her breath upon me' (Chapter 3 of *Dracula*, where Jonathan Harker is approached by one of the 'three young women' in Dracula's castle).	Here the aggressive sexuality of the women and their movement into Harker's personal space signify an inherent danger; the taking over of personal space (the body) by Dracula and his followers is a central concern of the novel.

We can also draw attention to a further aspect of body language: the relationship between body language and the representation of speech. In fiction, body language can accompany and enrich, as well as replace, speech. Examples 9 and 10, from the episode in chapter 4 of *The Lovely Bones*, where Jack is talking to George Harvey (Text 16B), show how both of these are possible.

---

9 'You know something', my father said.
He met my father's eyes, held them, but did not speak.

10 Standing inside the tent, Mr Harvey thought of how the virgin bride would be brought to a member of the Imezzureg on a camel. When my father made a move toward him, Mr Harvey put his palm up.
'That's enough now' he said. 'Why don't you go on home?'

Source: Alice Sebold, *The Lovely Bones*, Chapter 4

In Example 9, the eye contact between the two characters suggests some communication based on the question that Jack has just asked. The significance of Harvey not responding verbally but clearly articulating some kind of response through gaze sets up the tension for the remainder of Text 16B.

In Example 10, the attempt Jack makes to approach Harvey is thwarted not only by Harvey's words but by his action, a gesture which signifies that Jack cannot physically move into his personal space. The gesture could also be read as the way in which Harvey's power over Jack is enacted in the novel. Jack rightly believes that Harvey knows something about Susie's disappearance (the eye contact which occurred previously has confirmed this) but is unable to find any concrete evidence to support his 'father's hunch'.

One further interesting way in which speech and body language interact is in the form of what the literary scholar Mark Lambert (1981) calls the **suspended quotation**. This is where a character's speech is interrupted with at least five words of narrative, which provides some character description, often in the form of body language, before returning to complete the speech within the same orthographic sentence. In Example 11, Frankenstein meets Clerval shortly after completing his work on the Creature. Clerval, worried by his friend's looks and behaviour, asks him what is wrong. The underlined narration – including the movements Frankenstein makes due to his extreme fear – suspends the speech, in this instance to give a greater intensity to the realisation of horror that Frankenstein now feels.

---

11 'Do not ask me,' cried I, putting my hands before my eyes, for I thought I saw the dreaded spectre glide into the room; 'he can tell – oh save me! save me!.'

Source: Mary Shelley, *Frankenstein*, Volume I, Chapter 4

16.4 Point of view

In the study of narratives, the term **point of view** is used to refer to the perspective(s) from which the narrative unfolds and the consciousness through which action, events and characters are filtered.

One way that we can understand point of view is by thinking about it in visual terms. Texts 16M, 16N and 16O are taken from Matt Madden's *99 Ways to Tell a Story: Exercises in Style* (2006). Madden (borrowing from an earlier idea by the French writer Raymond Queneau) reworks a story (Text 16M) about a man taking a break from work and going to his fridge into a further ninety-eight ways of telling the same event either by shifting perspective or genre. In Text 16N the same event is seen from a different spatial perspective (upstairs) involving another previously unseen character, whilst in Text 16O, the perspective is of a 'voyeur' looking at the events through a pair of binoculars. In each of Text 16N and Text 16O the same event has been presented in a very different way, with different objects given prominence whilst others remain sidelined. This visual representation of how perspective works is a useful way of thinking about how narrative point of view generally operates.

Key terms

suspended quotation: an instance where a character's speech is interrupted with at least five words of narrative within the same orthographic sentence

point of view: the perspective from which the narrative unfolds

Text 16M: Going to the fridge 1 (viewed from downstairs)

Source: Matt Madden, *99 Ways to Tell a Story: Exercises in Style*, 2006

Text 16N: Going to the fridge 2 (viewed from upstairs)

Source: Matt Madden, *99 Ways to Tell a Story: Exercises in Style*, 2006

Text 16O: Going to the fridge 3 (viewed from a different location and through a pair of binoculars)

Source: Matt Madden, *99 Ways to Tell a Story: Exercises in Style*, 2006

16.4.1 Types of narration

One way that we can explore different points of view from a linguistic perspective is to make a basic distinction between types of narration. **Homodiegetic narratives** are those that are told from a first person perspective, such as in Text 16M. These are presented through the use of the first-person pronouns 'I' and 'we'. Alternatively, heterodiegetic narratives are told in the third person and so rely on the third-person pronouns 'he', 'she' and 'they'.

An example of a homodiegetic narrative is shown in Text 16P, from *Frankenstein*. In Text 16P, Frankenstein has met the Creature at the summit of a mountain.

Text 16P

We crossed the ice, therefore, and ascended the opposite rock. The air was cold, and the rain again began to descend: we entered the hut, the fiend with an air of exultation, I with a heavy heart, and depressed spirits. But I consented to listen; and, seating myself by the fire which my odious companion had lighted, he thus began his tale.

Source: Mary Shelley, *Frankenstein*, Volume 2 Chapter 2

We can list some of the linguistic features that mark this homodiegetic narrative.

- The use of the first-person plural and singular pronouns 'we' and 'I', which anchor the narrative to a particular psychological viewpoint as well as situating that viewpoint to a particular place: the mountain and surrounding area.
- A very subjective feel since the narrative is filtered through one sole viewpoint and therefore offers a rather narrow version of events. In Text 16P this is shown linguistically through the use of specific lexical choices that mark the register within which Frankenstein shapes his version of this event, such as the evaluative adjective 'odious' and the relational deictic term 'fiend' to describe the Creature; the verb processes 'crossed', 'ascended', 'entered' and 'consented'; and the modified noun phrases 'heavy heart' and 'depressed spirits'.

ACTIVITY 20

Re-positioning point of view

One of the best ways to explore the particular effect of point of view is to rewrite an extract from a different vantage point. Imagine that Text 16P was being narrated by the Creature instead of by Frankenstein. How would you show the very subjective nature of the narrative through specific language choices? If you are not studying *Frankenstein*, then you could take an extract from your own text, and experiment with changing the viewpoint to another heterodiegetic narrator.

Each of the possible text choices for 'Imagined worlds' has a homodiegetic narrator. However, some of the texts that you will study on other parts of the course – for example, the *AQA Anthology: Paris* – will have a different type of narration, and when you explore your final literary text as part of your non-examined assessment, you may well need to examine and comment on heterodiegetic narration.

In contrast to homodiegetic narratives, heterodiegetic narratives have a narrator who is not a character in the storyworld. Unlike the very subjective homodiegetic narration, these can therefore appear to be a more rounded version of events since they can take in a number of perspectives. We can distinguish between two types of heterodiegetic narration: **external** and **internal**. Example 12 demonstrates an external narrative, where the narrator is describing a courtroom scene.

12 The accused man, Kabuo Miyamotot, sat proudly upright with a rigid grace, his palms placed softly on the defendant's table – the posture of a man who has detached himself insofar as this is possible at his own trial.

Source: David Guterson, *Snow Falling on Cedars*

Key terms

homodiegetic narrative: a first-person narrative where the narrator is usually also a character in the storyworld

external heterodiegetic narrative: a third-person narrative where the narrator is outside of the events of the storyworld

internal heterodiegetic narrative: a third-person account where the narrator filters their account through the consciousness of a particular character

Here the narrator (at the very beginning of the novel) holds a position outside of the events of the story and offers a 'bird's eye' view of those events. There are some evaluative comments on characters and action, but here the focus is on merely telling those events, and the description stands outside the consciousness of the character Kabuo Miyamotot. Internal narratives, in contrast, have a narrator who, despite being outside of the narrative events, holds a more privileged position since the narrative is filtered through a particular character's consciousness and is able to show what that character is thinking or feeling.

In Text 16Q, the narrative is told in the third person but filtered through the consciousness of Emma.

Text 16Q

At 7 p.m., Emma takes one last look in the mirror to ensure that it doesn't seem as if she has made any kind of effort. The mirror leans precariously against the wall and she knows that it has a foreshortening, hall-of-mirrors effect, but even so she clicks her tongue at her hips, the short legs below her denim skirt. It's too warm for

tights but she can't bear the sight of her red scuffed knees so is wearing them anyway.

Source: David Nicholls, *One Day*, Hodder and Stoughton

Here, the narrator gives us access to Emma's consciousness through the use of verb phrases such as 'to ensure it doesn't seem', 'she knows' and 'she can't bear', all of which provide privileged information that a conventional external narrator would not be able to provide. The effect here is that the reader, given an insight into a character's thoughts and feelings, is more likely to empathise with that character. Indeed, internal heterodiegetic narrators are often referred to as **omniscient narrators** since their 'all-knowing' narration means that they are able to weave in and out of different characters' minds and to some extent control readers' sympathies and reactions to them.

It is possible for narrative types to shift during the course of a novel, from heterodegetic (third person) to homodiegetic (first person), from homodiegetic (first person) to heterodiegetic (third person), or within the heterodiegetic (third person) category from internal to external. Within homodiegetic (first person) narratives, a shift in person deixis may signal a different narrating voice, so that the 'I' of the narrative refers to a different narrator, with a different point of view and consciousness.

Key terms

omniscient narrator: a heterodiegetic narrator who can move freely across the storyworld, entering the consciousness of different characters and being aware of all events that occur

ACTIVITY 21

Switches in narrative

Look back at Text 16P. The next section of the novel shifts into the Creature's homodiegetic narrative; the final part of Frankenstein's narrative, and first part of the Creature's are reprinted as Text 16R. What do you notice about the way that the shift in point of view is handled?

Text 16R

...and, seating myself by the fire which my odious companion had lighted, he thus began his tale.

CHAPTER III

'It is with considerable difficulty that I remember the original era of my being: all the events of that period appear confused and indistinct. A strange multiplicity of sensations seized me ...'

Source: Mary Shelley, *Frankenstein*

Check your responses in the Ideas section on Cambridge Elevate

16.4.2 Modality

Modality is the term used to describe language that presents a speaker or writer's opinions, attitude and commitment towards any state of affairs, including those involving events, objects and people. For this reason, modality is sometimes known as 'attitudinal' language. Modality can be expressed through a range of linguistic forms such as:

- **Modal auxiliary verbs** e.g. 'must', 'will', 'might'
- **Modal lexical verbs** e.g. 'like', 'hope', 'believe'
- **Modal adjectives** e.g. 'sure', 'certain', 'doubtful'
- **Modal adverbs** e.g. 'perhaps', 'possibly', 'maybe'
- **Modal tags** e.g. 'I guess'

Broadly speaking, we can classify examples of modality into one of three modal domains, each of which functions to represent a different concept:

1. **Deontic modality**: expressions that highlight a sense of obligation or necessity
   - 'You must come back' (modal auxiliary verb)
   - 'It is necessary for you to come back' (modal adjective)
2. **Boulomaic modality**: expressions that highlight aspects of desire
   - 'I hope you will come back' (modal lexical verb)
   - 'Hopefully, you will come back' (modal adverb)
3. **Epistemic modality**: expressions that highlight degrees of belief, certainty or perception.
   - 'You might come back' (modal auxiliary verb)
   - 'I think you'll come back' (modal lexical verb)
   - 'You'll come back, I guess' (modal tag)
   - 'It's clear that you are coming back' (modal adjective).

The stylistician Paul Simpson (1993) provides a very useful model for exploring the likely effects when narratives are dominated by one particular modal domain. He suggests that narratives can be classified based on a particular kind of **modal shading** that they display.

- **Positive shading**: the prominent use of deontic and boulomaic forms (expressions that show necessity and desire), and/or epistemic forms that show strong certainty together with evaluative adjectives and adverbs
- **Negative shading**: the prominent use of epistemic forms that display uncertainty and a general feeling of anxiety
- **Neutral shading**: a flat narrative with little or no modalised expressions.

As an example, look at Text 16S. Here the narrator (Frankenstein) recounts his childhood memories of his cousin Elizabeth.

Text 16S

She was docile and good tempered, yet gay and playful as a summer insect. Although she was lively and animated, her feelings were strong and deep, and her disposition uncommonly affectionate. No one could better enjoy liberty, yet no one could submit with more grace than she did to constraint …

Source: Mary Shelley, *Frankenstein*, Volume 1, Chapter 1

Key terms

modality: the term used to describe language that presents degrees of attitude or commitment

deontic modality: expressions that highlight a sense of obligation or necessity

boulomaic modality: expressions that highlight aspects of desire

epistemic modality: expressions that highlight degrees of belief, certainty or perception

modal shading: the dominant type of modality that an extract or text displays

In Text 16S, evaluative adjectives such as 'docile', 'lively' and 'animated' show strong certainty, and the repeated modal form 'could' is suggestive of certainty, emphasising the speaker's strong commitment and belief. Frankenstein's voice as captured at this point in the novel is strong and confident.

ACTIVITY 22

The effect of different modal domains

To see the effect of different modal domains, look at the effect of shifting from positive to negative shading. Continue to rewrite Text 16S (started for you in the box below) so that it is *negatively* shaded. What effect does your rewriting have?

It was perhaps from this time that Elizabeth Lavenza became my playfellow, and it seemed as we grew older, my friend …

ACTIVITY 23

Modality in *Frankenstein*

Read Text 16T, where Frankenstein is contemplating the current and future implications of bringing the Creature to life. What can you say about the use of modality in Text 16T? How does this influence your understanding of the character of Frankenstein?

Text 16T

About this time we retired to our house at Belrive. This change was particularly agreeable to me. The shutting of the gates regularly at ten o'clock, and the impossibility of remaining on the lake after that hour, had rendered our residence within the walls of Geneva very irksome to me. I was now free. Often, after the rest of the family had retired for the night, I took the boat, and passed many hours upon the water. Sometimes, with my sails set, I was carried by the wind; and sometimes, after rowing into the middle of the lake, I left the boat to pursue its own course, and gave way to my own miserable reflections. I was often tempted, when all was at peace around me, and the only unquiet thing that wandered restless in a scene so beautiful and heavenly, if I except some bat, or the frogs, whose harsh and interrupted croaking was heard only when I approached the shore – often, I say, I was tempted to plunge into the silent lake, that the waters might close over me and my calamities for ever. But I was restrained, when I thought of the heroic and suffering Elizabeth, whom I tenderly loved, and whose existence was bound up in mine. I thought also of my father, and surviving brother: should I by my base desertion leave them exposed and unprotected to the malice of the fiend whom I had let loose among them?

At these moments I wept bitterly, and wished that peace would revisit my mind only that I might afford them consolation and happiness. But that could not be. Remorse extinguished every hope. I had been the author of unalterable evils; and I lived in daily fear, lest the monster whom I had created should perpetrate some new wickedness. I had an obscure feeling that all was not over, and that he would still commit some signal crime, which by its enormity should almost efface the recollection of the past. There was always scope for fear, so long as any thing I loved remained behind. My abhorrence of this fiend cannot be conceived. When I thought of him, I gnashed my teeth, my eyes became inflamed, and I ardently wished to extinguish that life which I had so thoughtlessly bestowed. When I reflected on his crimes and malice, my hatred and revenge burst all bounds of moderation. I would have made a pilgrimage to the highest peak of the Andes, could I, when there, have precipitated him to their base. I wished to see him again, that I might wreak the utmost extent of anger on his head, and avenge the deaths of William and Justine.

Source: Mary Shelley, *Frankenstein*, Volume 2, Chapter 1

Check your responses in the Ideas section on Cambridge Elevate

16.4.3 Reliability

One important question in any narrative concerns the reliability of the narrative voice. Of course, any narration will always have a certain subjectivity about it, but a narrative can be said to have an **unreliable narrator** when that shaping of events is a distortion of the actual events in the storyworld. In other words, we cease to believe that the narrator is providing an accurate version of what actually happened.

Reliability can often be measured by comparing what the narrator is telling us with what we can reasonably assume is the actual version of events. In other words, we notice an irony in what the narrator is telling us, as we are aware of a discrepancy between their version and a more plausible version that we think is closer to the truth.

ACTIVITY 24

Reliable narrators?

Imagine that there has been a car accident and a number of people have been interviewed by the police at the scene. How might each of the interviewees in the list potentially give an unreliable account of what had actually happened?

- a passenger in the car whose driver was at fault for the accident
- a bus driver who turned a corner in his vehicle and saw the two cars just before the collision
- a ten-year-old child who was waiting for his mother outside a shop
- a road engineer who was digging the road nearby wearing safety goggles and ear protectors.

We can summarise the ways in which narrators might be unreliable as follows:

- They have limited knowledge of the events they are narrating. They may have missed out on some important event or have only partial knowledge that means that they cannot provide a reliable version of events.
- Their understanding – and consequently their narration – is compromised by a factor such as age or some mental deficiency.
- They have a strong emotional involvement that means the narrative is very subjective and reliability can be called into question.
- And finally, they might deliberately not be telling the truth.

If we turn to *The Handmaid's Tale*, we can identify some ways in which Offred might be determined an unreliable narrator, and use these as the basis for further exploration.

- There are constant references to her position and role as a storyteller, and a clear tension between the imaginative and the actual: for example, her thoughts on storytelling in chapter 7, her desire to construct possible scenarios for what happened to Luke in chapter 18, and her comment that her narrative 'is a reconstruction' at the beginning of chapter 23.
- She is often unable to remember things precisely: for example, the murals in the university in chapter 27 or what's happened to her at the end of chapter 46.

- Her narrative is heavily subjective with a great deal of emotional investment in her family: for example, in chapter 28.
- The 'Historical notes' at the end of the novel, in which Margaret Atwood, as the implied author, draws our attention to the origins of Offred's narrative, its authenticity, and problems around her very identity, and the naming of and comments on other characters mentioned by her.

Check your responses in the Ideas section on Cambridge Elevate

ACTIVITY 25

Developing ideas on unreliable narrators

You can explore and debate how reliable the narrator(s) are in your chosen text. If you are studying *The Handmaid's Tale*, then you can further develop the ideas outlined for you here (as well as your own) to explore Offred's (un)reliability as a narrator. If you are studying a different novel, find evidence that might call the following narrators' reliability into question.

- *Dracula*: Jonathan Harker
- *Frankenstein*: The Creature
- *The Lovely Bones*: Susie Salmon.

Key terms

unreliable narrator: a narrator whose shaping of events is a distortion of actual events in the storyworld

16.5 Interpretations of fantasy

In 16.1.4, you began to explore some of the important contextual influences on the novel you are studying. You were encouraged to keep thinking about these as you worked your way through the remainder of the activities in this unit. These were largely based around the context of production, factors that potentially influenced the author at the time of composition. However, a more rounded, and useful, exploration of context should also consider aspects of the novel's *reception*. This will also provide some additional material in terms of the study of genre.

16.5.1 Literary criticism

One of the most obvious ways to explore the context of reception is to look at how your novel has been treated by academics working in literary theory, stylistics and narratology. There has, of course, been much more work published on *Frankenstein* and *Dracula* than on *The Handmaid's Tale*, and certainly on *The Lovely Bones*, and the sheer wealth of literature on these texts means that it is relatively easy to find material, although you will need to think carefully about how suitable and useful it might be for you.

Some of the obvious places to start are your school library, local libraries and online resources such as Google Books and Google Scholar. Of particular use would be:

- books that offer a range of critical readings of the novel, from different periods and critical positions
- books and resources that take a genre-based and/or narrative approach to text analysis
- books and resources that explore the novel through various literary-critical perspectives (e.g. feminist, historical)
- articles written especially for A/AS Level students such as those found in *emagazine* and *The English Review* (you could check if your school/college subscribes to these).

Find and read *The Guardian*'s article on the gothic novel via Cambridge Elevate

Find and read *The Guardian*'s article on *The Lovely Bones* via Cambridge Elevate

Find and read *The Guardian*'s article on *The Handmaid's Tale* via Cambridge Elevate

See Unit 22 for some additional useful and accessible references for A Level study around these novels

16.5.2 Responses from 'real readers'

Another interesting and useful activity is to explore how 'real' (i.e. non-academic) readers have responded to these novels. These interpretations can be as insightful and valid as those made by literary critics. The best place to find these is in review pages on online booksellers such as Amazon and Waterstones, and on reading group/book club pages such as Goodreads.

Find out more about Goodreads via Cambridge Elevate

ACTIVITY 26

Literary debates

Find an example of a comment or short analysis of the novel you are studying on a review/reading group page. To what extent do you (and others in your class) agree with this particular interpretation? Can you justify this reader's response in less impressionistic terms by drawing on your now-expert knowledge of stylistics and how to read a text?

Now try to match this reader's response up with an established (published) critical response on the novel. Can you find some published criticism that supports what the reader is saying?

16.5.3 Adaptations in artistic and popular culture

A final way of exploring your novel is to consider its 'afterlife', the extent to which it has influenced subsequent both artistic and popular culture following its publication. Many novels in the fantasy genre generate expanded fictional worlds in their own right (for example, the characters, events and places in the original *Star Wars* films have been developed beyond recognition to allow for unlimited fictional possibilities in spin-off films, TV series, novels, graphic fiction, computer games and so on).

Unsurprisingly, *Frankenstein* and *Dracula* have spawned a huge number of sequels, prequels and adaptations, ranging from literary fiction through to radio and theatre plays, graphic fiction, young adult fiction, popular novels, musicals and TV series. Both were given a central place in modern cinema with releases from Universal Studios (USA) in the 1930s and from Hammer Film Productions (UK) in the 1950s, 1960s and 1970s, and have found their way into popular entertainment and culture through appearances in children's TV shows (e.g. *Sesame Street*, *The Muppet Show*, *Scooby Doo* and *The Simpsons*), video games and toys, rock songs, and even cereals (an American food company called General Mills produces varieties called 'Frankenberry' and 'Count Chocula'!). Needless to say, the characters of the Creature and Dracula have reached iconic status.

Both *The Handmaid's Tale* (dir. Volker Schlöndorff) and *The Lovely Bones* (dir. Peter Jackson) have received big screen treatment, and *The Handmaid's Tale* has also been adapted for radio, the stage, opera and ballet versions.

ACTIVITY 27

Adaptations

Find out as much as you can about the impact of the novel you are studying on artistic and popular culture. Even if you are studying *The Lovely Bones*, you could explore fanfiction websites, where readers continue to expand the storyworld of the novel in their own imaginative ways.

Find out more about fanfiction websites via Cambridge Elevate

16.6 Bringing it all together: AS Level

16.6.1 Self-assessment: check your learning

For each of the following statements, evaluate your confidence in each topic area:

Topic area	Very confident	Some knowledge	Need to revise
I understand how fictional worlds are constructed by novelists			
I can identify and comment on narrative structures that are used in the novel I am studying			
I can explain the significance of places in the novel I am studying			
I am able to explore the processes by which novelists shape and present characters			
I can explore the effects of the various ways of presenting time - and time switches - points of view, and speech and thought in the novel I am studying			
I can explore the effects of using specific types of narration in the novel I am studying			

16.6.2 The examination

Imagined worlds is assessed on Paper 1 of the AS Level examination.

On this question you will need to analyse one extract from the novel that you are studying. The questions will always focus on one aspect of the following:

- Point of view
- Characterisation
- The presentation of time and place/space
- Narrative structure

The question will follow the same format as detailed below. The example here is from *Dracula*.

Read the extract printed below. Examine how Stoker presents **Dracula** in this extract.

This is the focus for the question, here highlighted in bold (characterisation)

Explaining the assessment objectives

There are two assessment objectives tested on this question and these carry different weightings:

- **AO1** (20 marks): Apply concepts and methods from integrated linguistic and literary study as appropriate, using associated terminology and coherent written expression

Here you need to:

- Express your ideas clearly
- Use terminology associated with this topic and the question focuses accurately
- Make reference to and use the various levels of language analysis as you explain your ideas and comment on effects of particular choices and narrative strategies that the novelist has used
- Undertake a good stylistic analysis (read Unit 12.2 again to remind you of the principles behind how you should respond to texts on this specification)

- **AO2** (15 marks): Analyse the ways that meanings are shaped in texts

Here you need to:

- Address the focus of the question carefully and in a sustained way
- Comment in detail on the interpretative effects caused by specific lexical, grammatical, phonological and discourse patterns used by the novelist
- Select parts of the extract carefully and comment on these in detail to support the points you are making

You can plan for this by thinking carefully about the following key questions.

Questions on narrative style

- How are fictional worlds set up and maintained throughout the novel?
- What narrative structures are used at a global and more local level?
- How are places presented?
- How do novelists characterise? What techniques do they use to establish and develop aspects of characters?
- How are different points of view set up? How are perspectives presented in the novel?
- How are speech and thought controlled in the novel?
- What types of narrating voices dominate? Are there shifts in style?

Questions on interpretative effects

- What effects are created by specific choices that have been made by the novelist?
- How do these effects help to develop themes, characterisation, narrative structure and the importance of locations?

ACTIVITY 28

Practice questions

You can practise and prepare for this paper by looking at the following questions on the novel that you are studying.

Frankenstein

Read the extract, Text 16U. Examine how Shelley presents Frankenstein in this extract.

Text 16U

About this time we retired to our house at Belrive. This change was particularly agreeable to me. The shutting of the gates regularly at ten o'clock, and the impossibility of remaining on the lake after that hour, had rendered our residence within the walls of Geneva very irksome to me. I was now free. Often, after the rest of the family had retired for the night, I took the boat, and passed many hours upon the water. Sometimes, with my sails set, I was carried by the wind; and sometimes, after rowing into the middle of the lake, I left the boat to pursue its own course, and gave way to my own miserable reflections. I was often tempted, when all was at peace around me, and I the only unquiet thing that wandered restless in a scene so beautiful and heavenly, if I except some bat, or the frogs, whose harsh and interrupted croaking was heard only when I approached the shore--often, I say, I was tempted to plunge into the silent lake, that the waters might close over me and my calamities for ever. But I was restrained, when I thought of the heroic and suffering Elizabeth, whom I tenderly loved, and whose existence was bound up in mine. I thought also of my father, and surviving brother: should I by my base desertion leave them exposed and unprotected to the malice of the fiend whom I had let loose among them?

At these moments I wept bitterly, and wished that peace would revisit my mind only that I might afford them consolation and happiness. But that could not be. Remorse extinguished every hope. I had been the author of unalterable evils; and I lived in daily fear, lest the monster whom I had created should perpetrate some new wickedness. I had an obscure feeling that all was not over, and that he would still commit some signal crime, which by its enormity should almost efface the recollection of the past. There was always scope for fear, so long as any thing I loved remained behind. My abhorrence of this fiend cannot be conceived. When I thought of him, I gnashed my teeth, my eyes became inflamed, and I ardently wished to extinguish that life which I had so thoughtlessly bestowed. When I reflected on his crimes and malice, my hatred and revenge burst all bounds of moderation. I would have made a pilgrimage to the highest peak of the Andes, could I, when there, have precipitated him to their base. I wished to see him again, that I might wreak the utmost extent of anger on his head, and avenge the deaths of William and Justine.

Dracula

Read the extract, Text 16V. Examine how Stoker presents Dracula in this extract.

Text 16V

Within, stood a tall old man, clean-shaven save for a long white moustache, and clad in black from head to foot, without a single speck of colour about him anywhere. He held in his hand an antique silver lamp, in which the flame burned without chimney or globe of any kind, throwing long, quivering shadows as it flickered in the draught of the open door. The old man motioned me in with his right hand with a courtly gesture, saying in excellent English, but with a strange intonation:-

'Welcome to my house! Enter freely and of your own will!' He made no motion of stepping to meet me, but stood like a statue, as though his gesture of welcome had fixed him into stone. The instant, however, that I had stepped over the threshold, he moved impulsively forward, and holding out his hand grasped mine with a strength which made me wince, an effect which was not lessened by the fact that it seemed as cold as ice- more like the hand of a dead than a living man. Again he said:-

'Welcome to my house. Come freely. Go safely. And leave something of the happiness you bring!' The strength of the handshake was so much akin to that which I had noticed in the driver, whose face I had not seen, that for a moment I doubted if it were not the same person to whom I was speaking; so, to make sure, I said interrogatively:-

'Count Dracula?' He bowed in a courtly way as he replied:

'I am Dracula. And I bid you welcome, Mr Harker, to my house. Come in; the night air is chill, and you must need to eat and rest.' As he was speaking he put the lamp on a bracket on the wall, and stepping out, took my luggage; he had carried it in before I could forestall him. I protested, but he insisted:-

'Nay, sir, you are my guest. It is late, and my people are not available. Let me see to your comfort myself.' He insisted on carrying my traps along the passage, and then up a great winding stair, and along another great passage, on whose stone floor our steps rang heavily. At the end of this he threw open a heavy door, and I rejoiced to see within a well-lit room in which a table was spread for supper, and on whose mighty hearth a great fire of logs flamed and flared.

The Count halted, putting down my bags, closed the door, and crossing the room, opened another door, which led into a small octagonal room lit by a single lamp, and seemingly without a window of any sort. Passing through this, he opened another door, and motioned me to enter. It was a welcome sight; for here was a great bedroom well lighted and warmed with another log fire, which sent a hollow roar up the wide chimney. The Count himself left my luggage inside and withdrew, saying, before he closed the door:-

'You will need, after your journey, to refresh yourself by making your toilet. I trust you will find all you wish. When you are ready come into the other room, where you will find your supper prepared.'

The Handmaid's Tale

Read the extract, Text 16W. Examine how Atwood presents the Commander's house in this extract.

Text 16W

A chair, a table, a lamp. Above, on the white ceiling, a relief ornament in the shape of a wreath, and in the centre of it a blank space, plastered over, like the place in a face where the eye has been taken out. There must have been a chandelier, once. They've removed anything you could tie a rope to.

A window, two white curtains. Under the window, a window seat with a little cushion. When the window is partly open- it only opens partly- the air can come in and make the curtains move. I can sit in the chair, or on the window seat, hands folded, and watch this. Sunlight comes in through the window too, and falls on the floor, which is made of wood, in narrow strips, highly polished. I can smell the polish. There's a rug on the floor, oval, of braided rags. This is the kind of touch they like: folk art, archaic, made by women, in their spare time, from things that have no further use. A return to traditional values. Waste not want not. I am not being wasted. Why do I want?

On the wall above the chair, a picture, framed but with no glass: a print of flowers, blue irises, watercolour. Flowers are still allowed. Does each of us have the same print, the same chair, the same white curtain, I wonder? Government issue?

Think of it as being in the army, said Aunt Lydia.

A bed. Single, mattress medium-hard, covered with a flocked white spread. Nothing takes place in the bed but sleep; or no sleep. I try not to think too much. Like other things now, thought must be rationed. There's a lot that doesn't bear thinking about. Thinking can hurt your chances, and I intend to last. I know why there is no glass, in front of the watercolour picture of blue irises, and why the window only opens partly and why the glass in it is shatterproof. It isn't running away they're afraid of. We wouldn't get far. It's those other escapes, the ones you can open in yourself, given a cutting edge.

So. Apart from these details, this could be a college guest room, for the less distinguished visitors; or a room in a rooming house, of former times, for ladies in reduced circumstances. That is what we are now. The circumstances have been reduced; for those of us who still have circumstances. But a chair, sunlight, flowers: these are not to be dismissed. I am alive, I live, I breathe, I put my hand out, unfolded, into the sunlight. Where I am is not a prison but a privilege, as Aunt Lydia said, who was in love with either/or.

The Lovely Bones

Read the extract, Text 16X. Examine how Sebold presents the interaction between George Harvey and Jack Salmon in this extract.

Text 16X

But through the snow I noticed this: my father was looking toward the green house in a new way. He had begun to wonder.

Inside, Mr. Harvey had donned a heavy flannel shirt, but what my father noticed first was what he carried in his arms: a stack of white cotton sheets.

"What are those for?" my father asked. Suddenly he could not stop seeing my face.

"Tarps," said Mr. Harvey. When he handed a stack to my father, the back of his hand touched my father's fingers. It was like an electric shock.

"You know something," my father said.

He met my father's eyes, held them, but did not speak.

They worked together, the snow falling, almost wafting, down. And as my father moved, his adrenaline raced. He checked what he knew. Had anyone asked this man where he was the day I disappeared? Had anyone seen this man in the cornfield? He knew his neighbors had been questioned. Methodically, the police had gone from door to door.

My father and Mr. Harvey spread the sheets over the domed arch, anchoring them along the square formed by the crossbars that linked the forked posts. Then they hung the remaining sheets straight down from these crossbars so that the bottoms of the sheets brushed the ground.

By the time they had finished, the snow sat gingerly on the covered arches. It filled in the hollows of my father's shirt and lay in a line across the top of his belt. I ached. I realized I would never rush out into the snow with Holiday again, would never push Lindsey on a sled, would never teach, against my better judgment, my little brother how to compact snow by shaping it against the base of his palm. I stood alone in a sea of bright petals. On Earth the snowflakes fell soft and blameless, a curtain descending.

Standing inside the tent, Mr. Harvey thought of how the virgin bride would be brought to a member of the Imezzureg on a camel. When my father made a move toward him, Mr. Harvey put his palm up.

"That's enough now," he said. "Why don't you go on home?"

The time had come for my father to think of something to say. But all he could think of was this: "Susie," he whispered, the second syllable whipped like a snake.

"We've just built a tent," Mr. Harvey said. "The neighbors saw us. We're friends now."

"You know something," my father said.

"Go home. I can't help you."

Mr. Harvey did not smile or step forward. He retreated into the bridal tent and let the final monogrammed white cotton sheet fall down.

16.7 Bringing it all together: A Level

16.7.1 Self-assessment: check your learning

For each of the following statements, evaluate your confidence in each topic area:

Topic area	Very confident	Some knowledge	Need to revise
I understand how fictional worlds are constructed by novelists			
I can identify and comment on narrative structures that are used in the novel I am studying			
I can explain the significance of places in the novel I am studying			
I am able to explore the processes by which novelists shape and present characters			
I can explore the effects of the various ways of presenting time – and time switches – points of view, and speech and thought in the novel I am studying			
I can explore the effects of using specific types of narration in the novel I am studying			
I am confident in exploring the key conventions of the fantasy genre (and associated sub-genres) and can comment on how the novel I am studying both makes use of and develops these in interesting ways			
I can comment on the other significant aspects of context (for example historical, literary or biographical) on the production and possible interpretations of the novel I am studying			

16.7.2 The examination

Imagined worlds is assessed on Paper 1 of the A Level examination.

On this question you will need to analyse a key focus of the novel that you are studying, using a short extract as a springboard to exploring the whole novel. The questions will always be on one aspect of the following:

- Point of view
- Characterisation
- The presentation of time and place/space
- Narrative structure

The question will follow the same format as detailed here in the example from *The Lovely Bones*.

This identifies the place in the novel from where the extract has been taken

Read the extract [printed below]. This is from the section of the novel where Samuel and Lindsey discover an abandoned house.

Explore the **significance of the abandoned house** in the novel. You should consider:

This is the focus for the question, here highlighted in bold (location)

- the presentation of the house in the extract below and at different points of the novel
- the use of fantasy elements in constructing a fictional world.

These guide you to both draw on the extract in your answer and consider the importance of genre and other contexts on the writing of the novel and possible interpretations of it

Explaining the assessment objectives

There are three assessment objectives tested on this question and these carry different weightings.

- **AO1** (10 marks): Apply concepts and methods from integrated linguistic and literary study as appropriate, using associated terminology and coherent written expression

> Here you need to:
> - Express your ideas clearly
> - Use terminology associated with this topic and the question focuses accurately
> - Make reference to and use the various levels of language analysis as you explain your ideas and comment on effects of particular choices and narrative strategies that the novelist has used
> - Be able to comment in significant detail and with expertise on important aspects of narrative
> - Undertake a good stylistic analysis (read Unit 12.2 again to remind you of the principles behind how you should respond to texts on this specification).

- **AO2** (10 marks): Analyse the ways that meanings are shaped in texts

> Here you need to:
> - Address the focus of the question carefully and in a sustained way
> - Comment in detail on the interpretative effects caused by specific lexical, grammatical, phonological and discourse patterns used by the novelist
> - Select with care both from the extract and more widely from the novel and make focused and sustained comments on these to support the points you are making.

- **AO3** (15 marks): Demonstrate understanding of the significance and influence of the contexts in which texts are produced and received

> Here you need to:
> - Explore how the style and features of your chosen novel have elements of fantasy/gothic/magic realism/allegory and so on about them
> - Analyse other relevant contextual factors (social, historical, biographical, literary) influencing the writing and possible interpretations of the novel.

You can plan for this by thinking carefully about the following key questions.

Questions on narrative style

- How are fictional worlds set up and maintained throughout the novel?
- What narrative structures are used?
- How are places presented?
- How do novelists characterise? What techniques do they use to establish and develop aspects of characters?
- How are different points of view set up? How are perspectives presented in the novel?
- How are speech and thought controlled in the novel?
- What types of narrating voices dominate? Are there shifts in style?

Questions on interpretative effects

- What effects are created by specific choices that have been made by the novelist?
- How do these effects help to develop themes, characterisation, narrative structure and the importance of locations?

Questions on genre and context

- How does the novel fit into the fantasy genre?
- What specific elements of the fantasy genre does it subvert?
- How important are other biographical, literary, social and historical contexts to your chosen novel? (see 16.1.4)

ACTIVITY 29

Practice questions

You can practise and prepare for this paper by looking at the following questions on the novel that you are studying.

Frankenstein

Read the extract printed below (Text 16Y). This is from the section of the novel where the Creature tells Frankenstein about his feelings when he first experiences the world.

Explore the significance of the Creature's speech and thought in the novel. You should consider:

- the presentation of the Creature's speaking and thinking in the extract below and at different points of the novel
- the use of fantasy elements in constructing a fictional world.

Text 16Y

It is with considerable difficulty that I remember the original era of my being: all the events of that period appear confused and indistinct. A strange multiplicity of sensations seized me, and I saw, felt, heard, and smelt at the same time; and it was, indeed, a long time before I learned to distinguish between the operations of my various senses. By degrees, I remember, a stronger light pressed upon my nerves, so that I was obliged to shut my eyes. Darkness then came over me, and troubled me; but hardly had I felt this when, by opening my eyes, as I now suppose, the light poured in upon me again. I walked and, I believe, descended; but I presently found a great alteration in my sensations. Before, dark and opaque bodies had surrounded me, impervious to my touch or sight; but I now found that I could wander on at liberty, with no obstacles which I could not either surmount or avoid. The light became more and more oppressive to me; and the heat wearying me as I walked, I sought a place where I could receive shade. This was the forest near Ingolstadt; and here I lay by the side of a brook resting from my fatigue, until I felt tormented by hunger and thirst.

Dracula

Read the extract printed below (Text 16Z). This is from the section of the novel where Mina describes how she is worried about Lucy's deteriorating health.

Explore the significance of Lucy's physical state in the novel. You should consider:

- the presentation of Lucy's ill health in the extract below and at different points of the novel
- the use of fantasy elements in constructing a fictional world.

Text 16Z

When coming home – it was then bright moonlight, so bright that, though the front of our part of the Crescent was in shadow, everything could be well seen – I threw a glance up at our window, and saw Lucy's head leaning out. I thought that perhaps she was looking out for me, so I opened my handkerchief and waved it. She did not notice or make any movement whatever. Just then, the moonlight crept round an angle of the building, and the light fell on the window. There distinctly was Lucy with her head lying up against the side of the window-sill and her eyes shut. She was fast asleep, and by her, seated on the window-sill, was something that looked like a good-sized bird. I was afraid she might get a chill, so I ran upstairs, but as I came into the room she was moving back to her bed, fast asleep, and breathing heavily; she was holding her hand to her throat, as though to protect it from cold.

I did not wake her, but tucked her up warmly; I have taken care that the door is locked and the window securely fastened.

She looks so sweet as she sleeps; but she is paler than is her wont, and there is a drawn, haggard look under her eyes which I do not like. I fear she is fretting about something. I wish I could find out what it is.

The Handmaid's Tale

Read the extract printed below (Text 16AA). This is from the section of the novel where Offred remembers being with her daughter and Luke.

Explore the significance of Offred's memories of her family in the novel. You should consider:

- the presentation of Offred's memories in the extract below and at different points of the novel
- the use of fantasy elements in constructing a fictional world.

Text 16AA

I went to pick my daughter up from school. I drove with exaggerated care. By the time Luke got home I was sitting at the kitchen table. She was drawing with felt pens at her own little table in the comer, where her paintings were taped up next to the refrigerator.

Luke knelt beside me and put his arms around me. I heard, he said, on the car radio, driving home. Don't worry, I'm sure it's temporary.

Did they say why? I said.

He didn't answer that. We'll get through it, he said, hugging me.

You don't know what it's like, I said. I feel as if somebody cut off my feet. I wasn't crying. Also, I couldn't put my arms around him.

It's only a job, he said, trying to soothe me.

I guess you get all my money, I said. And I'm not even dead. I was trying for a joke, but it came out sounding macabre.

Hush, he said. He was still kneeling on the floor. You know I'll always take care of you.

I thought, already he's starting to patronize me. Then I thought, already you're starting to get paranoid.

I know, I said. I love you.

Later, after she was in bed and we were having supper, and I wasn't feeling so shaky, I told him about the afternoon. I described the director coming in, blurting out his announcement. It would have been funny if it wasn't so awful, I said. I thought he was drunk. Maybe he was. The army was there, and everything.

Then I remembered something I'd seen and hadn't noticed, at the time. It wasn't the army. It was some other army.

The Lovely Bones

Read the extract printed below (Text 16BB). This is from the section of the novel where Samuel and Lindsey discover an abandoned house.

Explore the significance of the abandoned house in the novel. You should consider:

- the presentation of the house in the extract below and at different points of the novel
- the use of fantasy elements in constructing a fictional world.

Text 16BB

"Do you think there's someone inside?" Lindsey asked.

"It's dark."

"It's spooky."

They looked at each other, and my sister said what they both were thinking. "It's dry!"

They held hands in the heavy rain and ran toward the house as fast as they could, trying not to trip or slide in the increasing mud.

As they drew closer, Samuel could make out the steep pitch of the roof and the small wooden cross work that hung down from the gables. Most of the windows on the bottom floor had been covered over with wood, but the front door swung back and forth on its hinges, banging against the plaster wall on the inside. Though part of him wanted to stand outside in the rain and stare up at the eaves and cornices, he rushed into the house with Lindsey. They stood a few feet inside the doorway, shivering and staring out into the pre-suburban forest that surrounded them. Quickly I scanned the rooms of the old house. They were alone. No scary monsters lurked in corners, no wandering men had taken root.

DEVELOPING

17 Poetic voices

In this unit, you will:

- develop your understanding of what poetry is and how it is distinctive as a form
- develop your understanding of the nature and function of poetic voice and how this has changed over time
- develop your understanding of how poetic voice can be seen as a representation and projection of identity
- develop your understanding of how poets use language to present time, place, people and events
- explore how best to prepare for assessment on this unit.

This relates to 'Views and voices' in the AS Level specification and to 'Telling stories' in the specification for A Level

17.1 Introduction

In Unit 3 you were introduced to the three main literary genres of prose, poetry and drama. In this unit, you will explore poetry in more detail, developing your understanding of its voices, forms, language and importance in literary studies.

Poetry is language in its raw and unrestricted form, and in this unit the emphasis will be on how the language of poetry is shaped to create meaning. When writing poetry, poets may exploit, manipulate, mould and bend language beyond the usual 'restrictions' that are often adhered to in other literary genres. Poetry breaks and bends rules, and the breaking and bending of these rules is what makes this literary genre so interesting and engaging. Studying poetry with a firm linguistic focus allows us to examine and investigate just how writers manage to do this. In Text 17A, journalist John Carey and poet Seamus Heaney give appropriately poetic descriptions of poetry itself.

Text 17A

The language is like lava, its molten turmoils hardening into jagged shapes, still hot from the earth's core … to read [poetry] is to experience the psychic equivalent of 'the bends'. It takes you down to levels of pressure where the under-truths of sadness and endurance leave you gasping.

Source: John Carey and Seamus Heaney describing Ted Hughes' 1998 poetry collection *Birthday Letters*

Watch tutorial video, Poetic Voice, on Cambridge Elevate

ACTIVITY 1

Expected shared conventions of poetry

In Section 3.2, 'genre' is defined as 'a way of grouping texts based on expected shared conventions'. Poetry can sometimes be difficult to define as a literary genre.

- What do you think the expected shared conventions of poetry are?
- What kinds of things do poems talk about?
- How are they set out and what are their different forms?
- Do they use certain language to create meaning?

17.1.1 What is poetic voice?

A useful starting point for defining **poetic voice** is to think of the variety of ways that the word 'voice' can be used. Consider these sentences:

1 She voiced her opinion.
2 He has a good voice.
3 I've finally found my voice.
4 I've lost my voice.
5 The proud voice of the working class.
6 Don't use that tone of voice with me.

Sentences (1) and (3) relate to the *content* of voice – how well an intended message is being conveyed to an audience, correlating voice with the language a **speaker** chooses to use. Sentences (2) and (4) relate to the *physical, acoustic properties* of the human voice. Sentence (5) suggests that voice can be used in a **metonymical** sense, representative of a group of people, ideology, company or institution. Sentence (6) relates to the *quality* of voice – the prosodic features a speaker chooses to use to further support and express meaning. We will see how each one of these meanings can be applied to poetry.

Poetic voice includes all of these elements – the content, phonology, persona and attitudes adopted by a writer in order to represent a particular person, place, group or object. All poets use poetic voices in slightly different ways, just like the way you use your own voice. Your own voice is unique to you – a vocal 'fingerprint' that forms a large part of your identity. Considering poetic voice is an important way of comparing similarities and differences across poems.

Key terms

poetic voice: the way in which a poet's sense of identity is projected through language choices so as to give the impression of a distinct *persona* with a personal history and a set of beliefs and values

speaker: the 'I' of a poem – sometimes synonymous with 'narrator'

metonymy: when a word or phrase is referred to by one of its characteristics rather than its name

ACTIVITY 2

Constructing poetic voice

Read Text 17B and describe the poetic voice being used. Think carefully about the idiolect of the speaker and how this contributes to the meaning created.

See 16.3.4 for an explanation of idiolect in literature

Text 17B

And the railings.
All around, the railings.
Are they to keep out wolves and monsters?
Things that carry off and eat children?
Things you don't take sweets from?
Perhaps they're to stop us getting out
Running away from the lessins. Lessin.
What does a lessin look like?
Sounds small and slimy.
They keep them in the glassrooms.
Whole rooms made out of glass. Imagine.

Source: Roger McGough, 'First Day at School'

Check your responses in the Ideas section on Cambridge Elevate

ACTIVITY 3

Voice in poems you already know

Look at a selection of poems from different poets from your previous studies at school, or poetry you might have read for pleasure. Try to classify their poetic voice. Are there any overlaps? Similarities? What kind of poetic voice do you prefer, and why?

ACTIVITY 4

Constructing voice in poem openings

The openings of poems are especially important when it comes to constructing voice. Read through the opening lines of the poems in Text 17C, all of which are taken from the poetry anthology.

Ask yourself the following questions which focus on the voice of the poem, making sure to explain *how* or *why* you have come to your answers.

1 What kind of identity does each speaker appear to be projecting?
2 Who, or what, is foregrounded in the poem?
3 What are the speaker's attitudes about the foregrounded entity?
4 Compare the poetic voice expressed in two (or more) of Texts 17C(a)–(d). What kind of differences and similarities can you find?

Text 17C

(a)

That's my last Duchess painted on the wall,
Looking as if she were alive. I call
That piece a wonder, now: Fra Pandolf's hands
Worked busily a day, and there she stands.

Source: Robert Browning, 'My Last Duchess'

(b)

Between my finger and my thumb
The squat pen rests; snug as a gun.
Under my window, a clean rasping sound
When the spade sinks into gravelly ground:
My father, digging. I look down

Source: Seamus Heaney, 'Digging'

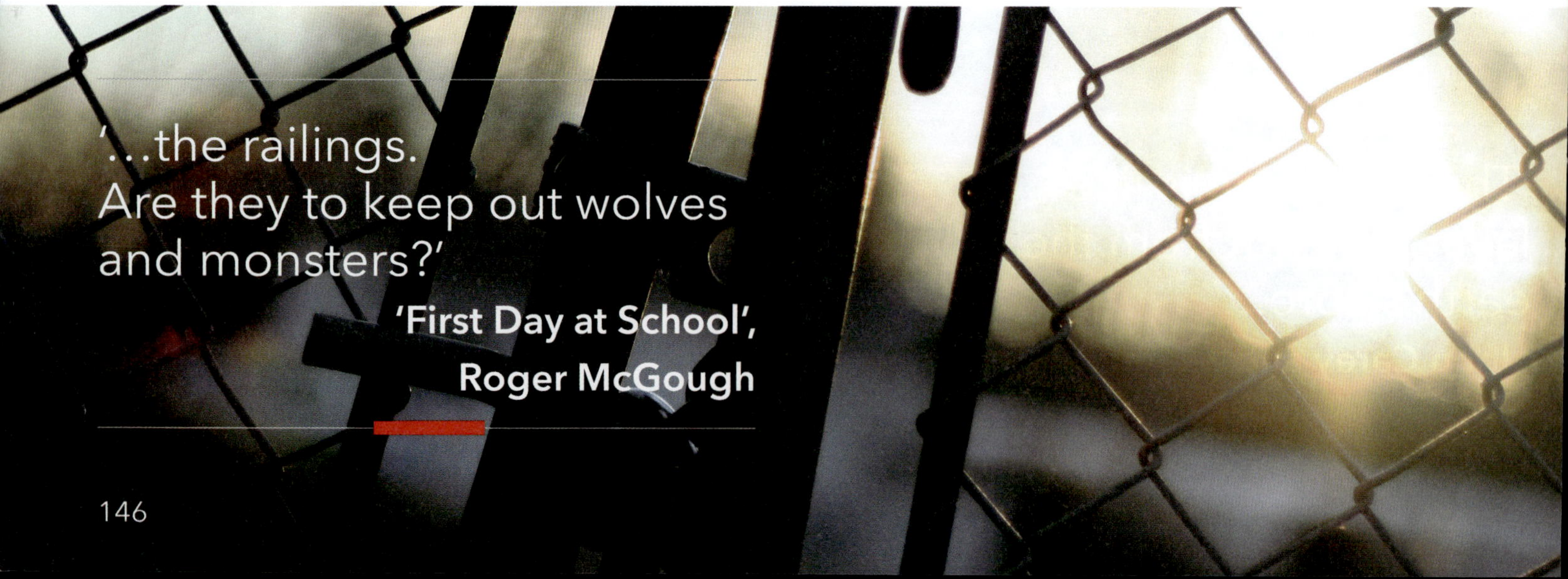

(c)

Busy old fool, unruly Sun,
Why dost thou thus,
Through windows and through curtains call on us?

Source: John Donne, 'The Sun Rising'

(d)

The clocks slid back an hour
and stole light from my life
as I walked through the wrong part of town,
mourning our love

Source: Carol Ann Duffy, 'Mean Time'

17.1.2 The position of poetry in literary tradition

Poetry has a long-standing and important place in **literary tradition** and world history. The earliest poetry is believed to have been spoken or sung in order to entertain, tell stories, recount history and law, or for religious purposes. Written in 350 BCE, Aristotle's *Poetics* is widely believed to be the earliest surviving work of literary theory, in which the author gives a definition of 'poetry' - the creative and purposeful use of language, rhythm and harmony.

Table 17A lists the poetic eras since the beginning of Old English. These divisions are useful for characterising general trends, but you should be aware that a poet from one era might well have characteristics in common with a number of others.

Table 17A: Poetic eras

Period	Years
Old English	449-1066
Middle English	1066-1485
Renaissance	1485-1603
17th century	1603-1667
Augustans	1667-1780
Romantics	1780-1830
Victorians	1833-1903
Georgians	1903-1920
Moderns	1920-1960
The Beat Generation	1950-1970
The Movement	1960-1980
Postmoderns	1980-2000
Early 21st century	2000-present day

Key terms

literary tradition: works of literature that may share connections such as historical and geographical roots, structures and style. Literary tradition is often encapsulated on a timeline

ACTIVITY 5

Researching literary periods

A detailed timeline of the position of poetry in the English literary tradition can be found online. Focusing on your set poet, undertake some research on the historical and social context of the appropriate era. What events, changes and trends can you find that might have influenced literature?

- John Donne - Renaissance
- Robert Browning - Victorians
- Carol Ann Duffy and Seamus Heaney - late 20th century

View the detailed timeline of the position of poetry in the English literary tradition via Cambridge Elevate

In Text 17D, contemporary poet Simon Armitage gives a well-rounded view of the nature of poetry and its 'difficulties'.

Text 17D

There's something about poetry which is oppositional and it's a form of dissent. I mean, even in its physical form, it doesn't reach the right-hand margin, it doesn't reach the bottom of the page. There's something a little bit obstinate about it ... Poetry's always had a complex relationship with language. It's alternative. It's independent. It simply cannot be a mainstream art form.

Source: Simon Armitage, 'Poetry is a form of dissent', *The Guardian*, 2011.

ACTIVITY 6

Attitudes to poetry

Watch the YouTube video, 'Simon Armitage: poetry is a form of dissent'. What are many people's attitudes towards poetry, and why do you think this is? Do you think poetry is 'obstinate', as Simon Armitage claims? Can you find any evidence from a poem from your set poet that supports this claim?

17.1.3 Approaching poetry

Perhaps the most empathetic exploration of the nature of studying (and teaching) poetry is found in Billy Collins' 1988 poem 'Introduction to Poetry'. In this poem, Collins adopts the narrative voice of a teacher, increasingly frustrated with his students trying to 'torture' the meaning out of poems by 'tying them to a chair with rope and forcing a confession' and 'trying to find out what it really means' by 'beating it with a hose'. Instead of this rather prescriptive approach, Collins wants his students to enjoy and experience poetry by 'holding it up to the light like a colour slide' or 'dropping a mouse into a poem, and seeing it work its way out'.

You should try and adopt this philosophy when approaching poetry – although you may be asked to write about meaning, do not be tempted to see this as a search for 'absolute' meaning. In other words, do no treat a poem like a maths question with a definitive 'answer'. Yes, all poets have an *intended* meaning (or in many cases, meanings), but use the language as a springboard for open-minded discussions and explanations, rather than a rulebook for the 'correct' reading. You will see how this approach works throughout this unit and especially in Section 17.7.

ACTIVITY 7

Poetic metaphor

Read Text 17E twice – out loud, and then in silence.

Text 17E

Don't be polite
Bite in.
Pick it up with your fingers and lick the juice that
may run down your chin.
It is ready and ripe now, whenever you are.
You do not need a knife or a fork or a spoon
or plate or napkin or tablecloth.
For there is no core
or stem
or rind
or pit
or seed
or skin
to throw away.

Source: Eve Merriam, 'How to Eat a Poem'

Now consider the metaphor the poet is using to suggest a way of approaching poetry. Do you agree? Are you convinced? Why? Can you devise your own metaphor or simile for approaching poetry; perhaps you can think of one that says something different about poetic interpretation?

See 15.6 for more on metaphor

17.1.4 Poetic devices

You will be familiar with some technical terminology associated with (and sometimes specific to) poetry. Many of these terms will be explored in more detail later on, so rather than simply listing and giving definitions of terms, let us consider why knowledge of poetic terminology is important. A good vocabulary of poetic devices will enable to you discuss the set texts in more accurate detail, something you will be rewarded for in the assessment for this unit.

See 17.3–17.6 for more on the technical terminology

See 17.7 for more about the assessment criteria for this part of the course

However, bear in mind that simple feature spotting of poetic devices is not the aim here. As emphasised throughout this book, good stylistics means balancing identifying features with providing an interpretation of those features. Always remember to:

- use precise language and relevant terminology where appropriate
- avoid impressionistic analyses; adopt an interpretative approach
- use evidence from the poems to support your interpretations.

ACTIVITY 8

A dictionary of poetic devices

Knowledge and application of technical **poetic devices** is an important part of this course - and chances are you already have a good 'poetic devices dictionary' in your memory. Start to write such a dictionary, giving definitions and examples of every poetic device you can think of. Add to this dictionary as you work through this textbook and your course.

ACTIVITY 9

Language features in 'Small Female Skull'

Read Text 17F to identify the language features in the list below and try to explain their effect. Also see if you can identify any additional ones of your own. Refer back to Units 6 -10 on language levels if you are unsure of the terminology, and remember what you have learnt about an interpretative approach.

- Noun phrases
- Semantic fields
- Possessive determiners
- **Isolated lines**
- Interrogatives (questions)
- Adverbials
- **Lexical ambiguity**

Text 17F

With some surprise, I balance my small female skull in my hands.

What is it like? An ocarina? Blow in its eye.

It cannot cry, holds my breath only as long as I exhale,

mildly alarmed now, into the hole where the nose was, press my ear against its grin.

Source: Carol Ann Duffy, 'Small Female Skull'

Check your responses in the Ideas section on Cambridge Elevate

Key terms

poetic device: a specific linguistic technique (such as enjambment or caesura) used in poetry to help shape meaning and effect. The analysis of poetic devices is an important part of poetry stylistics

isolated line: a line in poetry that stands by itself, usually intended to create prominence

lexical ambiguity: an individual word that has multiple meanings, such as 'She can't bear children', where 'bear' could mean either 'tolerate' or 'give birth to'. The context of a sentence usually solves the ambiguity

17.2 The set texts and approaching the poetry anthology

To prepare for the assessment for this unit, you will study a selection of poems from *one* of four poets, taken from the *AQA Anthology: Poetic voices*:

- John Donne
- Robert Browning
- Carol Ann Duffy (selected from *Mean Time*)
- Seamus Heaney (selected from *New Selected Poems 1966–1987*)

The poets have been chosen for their variety and representation of major periods of British poetry. In Section 17.5 you will discover more about the distinctive linguistic style that identifies each poet, and the following sections will outline some biographical details.

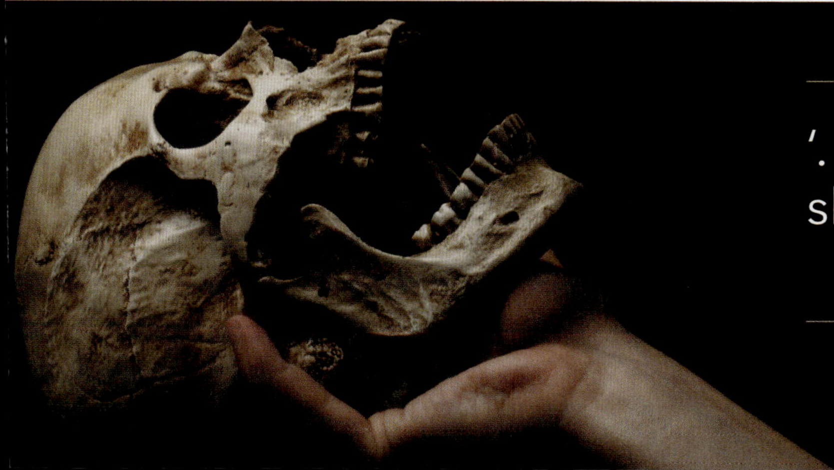

'... I balance my small female skull in my hands.'

'Small Female Skull', Carol Ann Duffy

17.2.1 The set texts

John Donne

John Donne was born in London in 1572 and died in 1631. He is recognised as a leading writer of **metaphysical poetry**. The poems from *Songs and Sonnets* deal with amorous themes, with a heavy reliance on conceit, forcing readers to combine objects and ideas in new and unconventional ways. His poems speak to readers with a sense of urgency and directness, many of them showing men's desire for women.

John Donne in his own words:

> To know and feel all this and not have the words to express it makes a human a grave of his own thoughts.

Robert Browning

Robert Browning was born in London in 1812 and died in 1889. He is known for his mastery of the **dramatic monologue**, creating and adopting a range of characters in his writing. Many of his poems are concerned with different aspects of human identity, seen by some as 'inaccessible' and overly dense. But this is what makes his poetry so appealing - its rich complexities, imaginative storytelling and ability to describe human experience with profound accuracy and authenticity.

Robert Browning in his own words:

> I never designed to puzzle people, as some of my critics have supposed. On the other hand, I never pretended to offer such literature as should be a substitute for a cigar or a game of dominoes to an idle man.

Key terms

metaphysical poetry: a type of poetry that typically uses unconventional and bold comparisons and conceits

dramatic monologue: a type of poetry that holds a theatrical quality, often narrated through an assumed voice, character or persona

Carol Ann Duffy

Carol Ann Duffy was born in Glasgow in 1955. Many of her poems deal with sadness and explore emotions from a female perspective. The poems in *Mean Time* focus on the plight of the self. Consider the pun and word play in the title, creating ambiguity: (1) *mean* as an adjective: how time can be mean in the sense of creating 'bad times', (2) *mean time* as a noun phrase: the mathematical sense of 'mean' (the average of something) suggesting that over one's lifetime there are ups and downs, and (3) *mean time* as the connection between time and mean(ing) - how does our understanding and reading of ourselves, others and the world change over time?

Carol Ann Duffy in her own words:

> Poetry, above all, is a series of intense moments – its power is not in narrative. I'm not dealing with facts, I'm dealing with emotion.

Seamus Heaney

Seamus Heaney was born in County Derry, Northern Ireland, in 1939 and died in 2013. Many of his poems are heavily influenced by his rural upbringing, and his writings in *New Selected Poems 1966–1987* deal with themes such as family, death, youth and conflict. The appeal of his poetry lies in its graceful and meticulous nature - the attention to sound and syntax, as well as the familiar, accessible and personal topics that he chose to write about.

Seamus Heaney in his own words:

> I can't think of a case where poems changed the world, but what they do is they change people's understanding of what's going on in the world.

17.2.2 Approaching a poetry anthology

An anthology is a collection of poems grouped together purposefully, not in an arbitrary, random way. Try not to see the poems in your chosen section as discrete, individual texts but as ones that complement each other and add to the overall voice, mood and ideas the poet is trying to create. Before studying the poems in detail, as you will do in class, read each individual poem and begin thinking about the kind of poetic voice expressed.

ACTIVITY 10

Writing a blurb

Read through a selection of poems from your chosen poet. Write a 100-word blurb of your chosen anthology section, imagining it were to appear on the back of the original book. Try to indicate the overall sense of what the poet is trying to achieve in the poems, and make reference to poetic voice. You may want to ask:

- what kinds of identities are projected?
- what kind of things does your poet write about?
- can you summarise the mood and style of language?

ACTIVITY 11

Exploring your chosen poet

Explore some other poetry collections by your chosen poet. Is there a different or similar poetic voice to the ones found in the set texts? How might you describe the poet's linguistic style? Some suggested readings are as follows:

- **Robert Browning**: *Men and Women* (1855); *The Ring and the Book* (1868); *Asolando* (1890)
- **John Donne**: *Biathanatos* (1608); *An Anatomy of the World* (1612); *Holy Sonnets* (1635)
- **Carol Ann Duffy**: *Standing Female Nude* (1985); *The World's Wife* (1999); *Rapture* (2005)
- **Seamus Heaney**: *Death of a Naturalist* (1966); *District and Circle* (2006); *Human Chain* (2010).

ACTIVITY 12

Exploring your chosen era

Explore some work by other poets from a similar era to your chosen poet. Wider reading is an important part of the course, especially if you are studying the non-exam assessment for the two-year A Level. You might like to read some of the suggested poets in Table 17B as a starting point.

Table 17B: Suggested wider reading

Era	Set poet	Suggested poets
Metaphysical poetry	John Donne	George Herbert Henry Vaughan Andrew Marvell
Victorian dramatic monologue	Robert Browning	Alfred Tennyson Dante Gabriel Rossetti Christina Rossetti
Late 20th-century verse	Carol Ann Duffy Seamus Heaney	Sylvia Plath Ted Hughes Billy Collins Maya Angelou Simon Armitage

17.3 Analysing poetry from a language perspective

A poet (or any writer, for that matter) sees language like putty or clay, in the same way that a sculptor sees their material as a malleable, dynamic and shapeable entity. As an analytical reader of poetry, your job is to try to unpick the writer's thoughts and to examine why language is crafted in certain ways and how this contributes to the overall meaning. Just as poets manipulate language in a self-conscious way, you should take the same approach in your reading.

In Section 1.3 you were introduced to stylistics: the way of looking at literature 'through' language (also sometimes called 'literary linguistics'), concerned with the application of formal linguistic tools to the analysis of literature. Stylistics integrates approaches from both linguistic and literary study, allowing for a level of understanding that can be rigorous and objective, yet theoretical and subjective at the same time. In this unit you will be introduced to how taking a descriptive linguistic approach to poetry can lead to a much better appreciation of how literature works.

ACTIVITY 13

Being a self-conscious writer

Read Text 17G. The underlined words and phrases have been modified from the original text. Focusing on these, which words or phrases would you choose to change or insert? Justify your reasons, thinking self-consciously about language and using specific linguistic terminology where appropriate. For example, what happens if you change the indefinite article 'a' underlined in the first line to the definite article 'the'?

Text 17G

Here is a girl's head like a dug up vegetable.

Round-faced, wrinkly skinned, dry stones for teeth.

Source: Seamus Heaney, 'Strange Fruit'

Now go to the original version and compare your ideas. Why do you think Heaney chose to use the words and phrases he did?

17.3.1 A stylistic approach

Before you begin any analysis, make sure you feel you understand the overall meaning of the poem, and that you could make some general references to language to support these early ideas. Assume that the author chose the language consciously, but be prepared to abandon any preconceptions you may have about 'why' a certain linguistic choice is 'usually' made in poetry. Be systematic in your approach, focusing on one level of language at a time, as you will see done in the following section. And remember that more practice at stylistics will lead to a greater confidence and expertise when reading any kind of literature.

17.3.2 A stylistic analysis of poetry

In Units 6–11 you were introduced to different language levels. These are the formal tools with which you can begin to unpick the language of poetry. A brief recap of these units may be useful here before continuing. Poetry is a tightly knit network of linguistic elements which constantly reinforce each other in meaning, and, to illustrate how stylistics is a useful and powerful way of approaching this network, it is useful to apply the methods to a poem and see the results. We will start here by looking at lexis, semantics, grammar, phonetics and phonology. The poem in Text 17H is told by a male speaker, travelling on the sea by boat at night-time to reach his lover's house. From the first line of the first **stanza** it is clear that we share the same **deictic centre** as the speaker.

Key terms

stanza: a verse or section of a poem, usually defined from other stanzas by a line break or indentation

deictic centre: the point of origin of an utterance, which establishes a reference point for participants

Text 17H

I

The grey sea and the long black land;
And the yellow half-moon large and low;
And the startled little waves that leap
In fiery ringlets from their sleep,
As I gain the cove with pushing prow,
And quench its speed i' the slushy sand.

II

Then a mile of warm sea-scented beach;
Three fields to cross till a farm appears;
A tap at the pane, the quick sharp scratch
And blue spurt of a lighted match,
And a voice less loud, thro' its joys and fears,
Than the two hearts beating each to each!

Source: Robert Browning. 'Meeting at Night'

Lexis and semantics

Remind yourself of what you learnt in Unit 6 if you need to.

- Colour adjectives and pre-modifying nouns play a significant role in describing the time and space in which this poem is set. The fact that the sea is 'grey', the land is 'black' and the moon is 'yellow' makes the reader infer that this poem takes place at night time, at the coast. The language used by Browning plunges us straight into the same temporal and spatial context as the speaker, creating a sense of shared viewpoint and feeling (known as *deictic centre*).

- A semantic field of 'coast/beach' further helps to create the setting: 'sea', 'land', 'waves', 'cove', 'sand', 'beach'.
- The absence of a word or phrase can be just as important as its presence. Notice that there is no main verb until the end of line 3: 'leap'. The absence of verbs creates a strong sense of timelessness and stillness. Thus, the dynamism, and indeed 'leaping' of the waves becomes further heightened. We notice things at the same time that the speaker does.
- The heavy use of material verbs in the second stanza ('cross', 'tap', 'scratch', 'spurt', 'beating') further adds to the sense of movement, as the speaker approaches his destination and lover.

Grammar

Remind yourself of what you learnt in Unit 7 if you need to.

- The morphological structure of every word in the first two lines is free from inflection or derivation, enhancing the idea of the static and simple scene to which we are introduced.
- The noun phrases and the lack of co-ordinating conjunctions (and) in the second stanza create a sense of urgency, as the speaker (and the reader) travel across the beach at speed.
- The grammar and meaning of the entire poem is in the declarative mood, suggesting the factual nature of the meeting.
- The placement of the noun 'tap' at the front of the clause 'a tap at the pane' and the beginning of the line foregrounds its importance and prominence.

Phonetics and phonology

- Remind yourself of what you learnt in Unit 8 if you need to. You will learn more about phonetics and phonology and their importance to poetic voice in Section 17.4.
- The open, long vowel /aː/ in 'large' and the diphthong /əʊ/ in 'low', both working in the modification of the 'moon', help to emphasise its sheer size and presence in the night sky.
- Two uses of lexical onomatopoeia ('quench' and 'slushy') mimic the sound of the boat hitting the sand. Loud plosives and fricatives such as /k/ and /s/ contrast with the quiet, still setting described up until this point in the poem, marking a change in the narrative.
- The phonetic structure of 'quick' also matches the meaning of the word. Two short stops, an approximant and short vowel – /kwɪk/.

Overall impact of language levels

Notice how each 'level' of stylistic analysis is linked to furthering our understanding of the poem's meaning. The overall impact of the language levels working together creates a poem that is rich in tension, secrecy and urgency. The vividness of the description is such that we share the same spatial and temporal setting as the speaker. The lexis, morphology and grammar add to the stillness of the setting and the immediacy of the events; the phonology adds to the sounds of the action and the overall secretive nature of the lovers' meeting. When you conduct your own stylistic analysis of poetry, take a holistic approach that synthesises the different language levels into a coherent reading.

Remember that analysing poetry from a language perspective is not just a case of simple feature spotting – explaining *why* linguistic elements are present or absent is the most important part of any analysis.

ACTIVITY 14

Your own stylistic analysis

Take a poem from your anthology and focus on (1) lexis and semantics, (2) grammar and (3) phonetics and phonology using Table 17C. Conduct an analysis of the poem and at each of these language levels. Remember to think about what is missing, or what the reader has to *infer* as well as the linguistic elements that are present. Aim for a text-based, interpretative analysis rather than an impressionistic approach. Before you start, read again about structuring your analytical writing.

Table 17C

Language level	Examples from the poem	Thoughts about interpretive effect
Lexis and semantics		
Grammar		
Phonetics and phonology		
Overall impact of the use of these techniques		

17.4 Voice

In Section 3.1 you learnt about mode, and the differences between speech and writing. Poetry is a literary genre that does not fit neatly into the oppositional distinction of either 'speech' or 'writing'. Although in modern times poems may primarily exist on the printed page as writing, poetry is traditionally an oral art form. Poems are of course still read aloud today - places such as classrooms, public readings and during rap battles. Knowing this, poets exploit speech sounds and craft their language consciously to take advantage of a language's sound inventory. This process is known as sound iconicity, and will be covered in more detail later in this unit. When reading a poem then, try to read it in the way the poet intended - out loud. Hearing it will allow you to pick up on the nuances and subtleties of sounds, and you will be surprised at the things you notice that you might not have done from the purely written form.

ACTIVITY 15

Voices from words

Read the original layout of the poem 'Sonny's Lettah' by Linton Kwesi Johnson and then listen to the poet reading his poem on The Poetry Archive website.

- How close were you with your interpretations of poetic voice?
- What can you infer about the voice of the poet and his situation?
- How do the sounds contribute to your understanding of the meaning?

See Linton Kwesi Johnson reading his poem 'Sonny's Lettah' via Cambridge Elevate

17.4.1 Voice and identity

Our voices contribute enormously to our identity, and we often change our voices (either consciously or sub-consciously) according to context - where we are speaking, when we are speaking and who we are speaking to. **Accent**, **dialect** and **sociolect** (the influence of geography and social groups on language use) are three more important factors that create variation in language.

Every person has a unique voice, known as an **idiolect** - though we may either **converge** or **diverge** towards other voices in order to adhere to or differ from other people or groups. Our voices can be thought of as simply a projection of our own identity, and poets often convey these identities through their writing. Text 17I explores this: in particular, the self-awareness of converging the poet's speech to 'fit in'.

See 16.3.4 for more about idiolect

Text 17I

I remember my tongue

shedding its skin like a snake, my voice
in a classroom, sounding just like the rest.

Source: Carol Ann Duffy, 'Originally'

Text 17J is an anonymous poem written in Yorkshire dialect and accent. Read it aloud, thinking about how the poet creates a sense of voice through the words and sounds used.

Text 17J

We're down in't coyle 'oyle
Where't muck slarts on't winders
We've used all us coyle up
And we're rait down't t'cinders,
But if bum bailiff comes
Ee'll nivver findus
Cos we'll be down in't coyle 'oyle
Where't muck slarts on't winders

Source: Anonymous, 'The Yorkshire Poem'

Reading this poem gives us a strong sense of a traditional Yorkshire idiolect, through the marked use of accent and dialect. The poet plays on the stereotypical view of 'it's grim up north', with a reliance upon coal ('coyle') as a fuel, and the voice of this poem telling the reader they are 'down in the coal hole' – a shed or cellar for storing coal. In a Yorkshire accent 'coal' would be pronounced as /kɔɪəl/. In this phonetic transcription, the superscript **schwa** vowel /ə/ indicates the clear audible distinction between the diphthong and the schwa. The poet also makes extensive use of another feature of Yorkshire accent – the pronunciation of 'the' / ðə/ and 'to' /tuː/ being reduced to a single plosive /t/. Use of dialect also helps to strengthen the Yorkshire setting and voice, with phrases such as 'muck slarts' (meaning 'a place where dirt collects'), helping to build the image of a grimy, coal-cloaked window. Dialect forms are often grammatical as opposed to simply lexical, and the use of 'us' as a possessive determiner in 'we've used all us coyle up' rather than the **standard English** form 'our' is an example of this in the poem.

Key terms

accent: a variation in language at the phonological level, often created and influenced by geography

dialect: a variation in language at the lexical and grammatical level, often created and influenced by geography

sociolect: the language used by a particular social group, e.g. teenage school children, adults in a book club

idiolect: idiosyncratic language use and choices specific to an individual

convergence: when an individual changes their language choices (usually temporarily) to become more *similar* to another individual or group

divergence: when an individual changes their language choices (usually temporarily) to become more *dissimilar* to another individual or group

standard English: a variety of English (among many), normally: (1) used in formal contexts, (2) often associated with 'educated' people, (3) taught to non-native speakers

schwa: the short vowel sound such as at the end of 'banan<u>a</u>', represented by /ə/

ACTIVITY 16

Exploring idiolect in the anthology

Each of the poets in the anthology has a particular writing style (idiolect) that can be thought of as a representation and projection of identity.

- Looking at the extract in Text 17K from your own choice of set poet, consider how idiolect is constructed. Focus on *accent and prosody* (how the words might be pronounced), *attitudes* (feelings projected in the poem, perhaps towards a particular object or person; what kind of character is constructed) and *dialect and sociolect* (the language choices representative of a particular group).

Text 17K

(a)

He is with her; and they know that I know
Where they are, what they do: they believe my tears flow
While they laughing, laugh at me, at me fled to the drear
Empty church, to pray God in, for them! – I am here.

Source: Robert Browning, 'The Laboratory'

(b)

When by thy scorn, O murd'ress, I am dead,
And that thou thinkst thee free
From all solicitation from me,
Then shall my ghost come to thy bed.

Source: John Donne, 'The Apparition'

(c)

Not a cute card or a kissogram.
I give you an onion.
Its fierce kiss will stay on your lips,
possessive and faithful
as we are,
for as long as we are.

Source: Carol Ann Duffy, 'Valentine'

(d)

I can see her drowned
body in the bog,
the weighing stone,
the floating rods and boughs.

Under which at first
she was a barked sapling
that is dug up
oak-bone, brain-firkin:

her shaved head
like a stubble of black corn.

Source: Seamus Heaney, 'Punishment'

Watch tutorial video, Sounds and Aesthetics, on Cambridge Elevate

17.4.2 Sounds in poetry

Literary texts often make use of sounds to create effect. Poetry is the ideal literary form for looking at this, as it is so often read and heard aloud. Reading aloud poems written in English is particularly important due to the complex nature of the language's **sound-spelling correspondence system**. English, for the most part, is not a phonetic language, meaning that there are often mis-matches in the relationships between the spelling and pronunciation of a word. For example, take the phoneme /f/ and the four ways its pronunciation is represented in English spelling: *<u>f</u>amous*, *<u>ph</u>one*, *mi<u>ff</u>ed* and *tou<u>gh</u>*. Consider the two pronunciations of the letters 'ng' in Text 17L(a), which is suggestive of the relationship between the 'you' (a swimmer) and the refracted light in the water.

Text 17L(a)

When you plunged

The light of Tuscany wavered

And swung ...

Seamus Heaney, 'The Otter'

You should be aware that differences in speech sounds are often subtle, making use of **voiced** sounds (those with vocal fold vibration) and **voiceless** sounds (those without vocal fold vibration) in order to achieve particular effects. For example, take the word 'tap' in the line 'a tap at the pane' in Text 17H. 'Tap' consists of two voiceless plosives /t/ and /p/ and a short vowel, which ensures a relatively low volume, much like the action of a 'tap' actually is.

Key terms

voiced: a phoneme that includes vibration of the vocal folds in its production, creating acoustic energy. For example, as in /m/, /b/, /g/, /z/, /ð/ and all vowel sounds

voiceless: a phoneme that is produced without vibration of the vocal folds. For example, as in /s/, /θ/, /ʃ/

As the action in the poem 'speeds up', voiced consonants are gradually introduced to indicate an increase in volume in Text 17L(b), as the speaker gets closer to his destination:

Text 17L(b)

'Then a mile of warm scented beach;
three fields to cross till a small farm appears'

Seamus Heaney, 'The Otter'

In Text 17L(c), heavy use of alliteration is employed to add meaning. The short bursts of voiceless plosives such as /t/ and /k/ could mimic the small, erratic movements of a flea; the longer, sometimes sibilant alliteration of fricatives such as /s/ and /ð/ could represent the blood-sucking nature of the insect.

Text 17L(c)

Mark but this flea, and mark in this,
How little that which thou deniest me is;
It sucked me first, and now sucks thee,
And in this flea our two bloods mingled be.

Source: John Donne, 'The Flea'

When analysing phonetics and phonology, try to see 'beyond' the spelling and focus on the sounds. Reading poems aloud will help you to do this - try doing this with Text 17L.

17.4.2.1 Phonetics and phonology

In Unit 8 you were introduced to the main human speech sounds, how to represent them in writing using the International Phonetic Alphabet and their classifications based on articulatory movements. This knowledge becomes especially important for the following sections.

ACTIVITY 17

An x-ray of the vocal tract

Watch the *YouTube* clip showing a real-time x-ray of an opera singer and a beatboxer performing. Pay close attention to the complexities involved in producing speech. Pause the video at certain points and refer back to the diagram of the vocal tract in Figure 8B to help consolidate your knowledge of the articulators involved in articulating different speech sounds.

Watch the *YouTube* clip of the real-time x-ray via Cambridge Elevate

'And in this flea our two bloods mingled be'

'The Flea', John Donne

Phonoaesthetics

An interesting and often-asked question in linguistics is 'what is the most beautiful sounding word?' We mean 'beautiful' in terms of sounds rather than semantics here, and we can expand this question to include the most beautiful sounds to both hear and produce. Why is it that certain words sound pleasant and are pleasant to say (**euphony**)? Similarly, why are some words deemed to be unpleasant sounding (**cacophony**)?

The study of the inherent beauty, or 'pleasantness' of sounds is called **phonoaesthetics**. The idea of the self-conscious writer is especially applicable to phonoaesthetics in poetry: poets are aware of how pleasant and unpleasant sounds can contribute to meaning. Poets see sound as simply another level of language that they can use to their advantage, along with lexis, grammar, semantics and pragmatics.

See 17.3 for more on the idea of the self-conscious writer

Perhaps the most appropriate way to demonstrate phonoaesthetics in action is to look at the poem in Text 17M.

Text 17M

Some words have such a lovely sound
It's pleasant to roll them round and round
And savor their syllables on the tongue, –
Words like oriole, melody, young.
Other words, though, of ungraceful letter,
Harsh, abrasive ... sound even better!
These are words of intrinsic beauty, –
Service, conscience, kindliness, duty.

Source: Alma Denny

There are many things at work here on a phonoaesthetic level, beyond the 'typical' phonological observations of rhyme and syllabic structure, which you will explore in Activity 18.

ACTIVITY 18

Phonoaesthetic patterns

Looking at the words judged to be either pleasant or unpleasant from Text 17M can you spot any phonological patterns that create a sense of 'pleasantness'?

Check your responses in the Ideas section on Cambridge Elevate

Key terms

euphony: a speech sound that is pleasing to the ear; deemed to be 'pleasant' by human perception

cacophony: a speech sound that is unpleasing to the ear; deemed to be 'unpleasant' by human perception

phonoaesthetics: the acoustic aesthetics of speech sounds based on human perception: how sounds are judged to be 'pleasant' (see **euphony**) or 'unpleasant' (see **cacophony**)

A phonoaesthetic scale

Rather than a simple oppositional view of pleasant vs. unpleasant, we can think of different sounds on a ranking scale. Such a scale is built out of perceptive, subjective judgments and is likely to be different for every individual. However, we would expect some trends in how sounds are ranked, so try Activity 19 by yourself and then compare your decisions with others and note any patterns that emerge.

ACTIVITY 19

Phonoaesthetic judgements

Rate the sounds of these words on the scale of pleasantness given in Figure 17A. Focus on the sound rather than the meaning.

jewel, violin, gripe, throw, rasp, gravel, heart, jazz, mellow, peril, chinchilla, rasp, thicken, phlegmatic, whispers

Figure 17A

unpleasant ⟷ **pleasant**

In 1995, the linguist David Crystal collected a corpus of pleasant sounding words suggested by poets, lexicographers and novelists. He then created a phonological profile of the corpus, analysing the frequency of phonemes within each word. His findings are shown in Table 17D. The higher the frequency of each phoneme, the more it was present in words judged to be pleasant sounding. Phonemes that have a low frequency suggest unpleasant sounds. Refer back to the International Phonetic Alphabet if you are unsure of which speech sounds the symbols represent.

Table 17D

Consonants	Frequency (%)	Vowels	Frequency (%)
l	15.65	ə	24.60
m	10.61	ɪ	19.76
s	9.28	æ	9.68
n	8.75	e	5.65
r	7.69	iː	5.65
k	7.43	aɪ	5.24
t	6.90	əʊ	5.24
d	6.37	ʌ	4.84
f	3.18	ɒ	4.03
b	2.92	eɪ	3.23
v	2.12	uː	2.82
ŋ	2.12	ɔː	2.82
w	2.12	aː	2.82
g	1.86	ɜː	1.61
z	1.86	ɪə	0.81
ʃ	1.86	aɪə	0.40
h	1.59	aʊ	0.40
tʃ	1.33	ʊə	0.40
dʒ	1.33		
j	1.33		
θ	0.80		
ʒ	0.26		
ð	0		

Source: David Crystal (1995), *English Today* 42, Volume 11 (2), Cambridge University Press.

As well as phonemic frequency in the corpus, Crystal also looked at the number of **syllables** (the higher the number, the higher the phonoaesthetic rating), where the **stressed syllable** fell (the earlier in the word, the higher the rating), the manners of articulation involved (the more, the higher the rating) allowing him to build a detailed matrix of phonoaesthetic criteria. His findings are shown in Table 17E.

The matrix of criteria suggests that phonoaesthetic judgements are multidimensional: for example, simply stating that '/l/ is a pleasant sounding phoneme' is inaccurate without considering the syllabic structure, stress pattern and the meaning of the word in which it appears, as well as the position of the word within a line of poetry. Avoid such single-dimensional judgments in poetic analysis, as this is akin to simple feature spotting. As an example, consider the following line from 'The Otter' by Seamus Heaney, in which the speaker reflects on the stillness and peacefulness of his setting:

The mellowed clarities; the grape-deep air

Words such as 'mellowed' and 'clarities' have inherent phonoaesthetic pleasantness here: they are **polysyllabic**; they use many of the phonemes deemed to be 'pleasant'; they have stress on the first syllable, and are being used to describe a pleasing setting.

Key terms

syllable: a unit of speech that consists of one vowel sound, with or without consonants. For example, there are two syllables in 'monkey': /'mʊnki:/

stressed syllable: the syllable in a word that carries the most emphasis, either due to loudness or vowel length. The stressed syllable in 'monkey' falls on the first syllable. Note the phonetic transcription of stressed syllables: /'mʊnki:/

polysyllabic: words that are built up of more than one syllable

ACTIVITY 20

Creating nonsense phonoaesthetic words

Based on your observations from Activities 18 and 19, and the data given in Tables 17D and 17E, create some nonsense words that are either pleasant or unpleasant sounding. For example, we would expect a nonsense form such as /æləmiːst/ to be judged as pleasant. Ask somebody else to judge them. Were the results in line with your hypothesis? What are the advantages and disadvantages of doing such an experiment with nonsense words rather than real ones?

Phonoaesthetics in poetry

Seamus Heaney is well known for his careful and deliberate phonetic choices, bringing landscapes evocatively to life through sounds, smells and sights. Read Text 17N, which describes a man digging potatoes using a spade.

Text 17N

Under my window, a clean rasping sound
When the spade sinks into gravelly ground
The cold smell of potato mould, the squelch and slap
Of soggy peat, the curt cuts of an edge

Source: Seamus Heaney, 'Digging'

Heaney uses onomatopoeia and **maintainable** sounds to great effect in these lines, in words such as 'rasping', 'gravelly', 'squelch' and 'slap'. We can pick apart some of these onomatopoeias in further detail here, with reference to phonoaesthetics.

- The high level of consonant clusters in 'gravelly ground' and 'squelch' / 'slap' represents the sound of the metal spade sinking into the earth, hitting a mixture of small stones, mud and water as it does so. The complexity and intricacies of the sounds, especially the range of modes of articulation,

Table 17E

Word	3+ syllables	Stress on first syllable	Uses /m/	Uses /l/	Uses other high-frequency cons.	No use of low-frequency cons.	3+ diff manner of artic
tremulous	✓	✓	✓	✓	✓	✓	✓
alyssum	✓	✓	✓	✓	✓	✓	✓
alumnus	✓	✗	✓	✓	✓	✓	✓
ramelon	✓	✓	✓	✓	✓	✓	✓
drematol	✓	✓	✓	✓	✓	✓	✓
Pimlico	✓	✓	✓	✓	✓	✗	✓
Wapping	✗	✓	✗	✗	✗	✗	✓
phlegmatic	✓	✗	✓	✓	✓	✗	✓
flatulent	✓	✓	✗	✓	✓	✗	✓
gripe	✗	n.a.	✗	✗	✓	✗	✗
jazz	✗	n.a.	✗	✗	✗	✗	✗
tart	✗	n.a.	✗	✗	✓	✓	✗
zoo	✗	n.a.	✗	✗	✗	✗	✗

mirrors the randomness of the rural earth. Note the high number of consonant clusters in the phonetic transcription: /grævəliː graʊnd skweltʃ slæp/. The vocal articulators move in complex and difficult and ways, just as the spade might have to do as it tackles the secret earth. According to Table 17C, 'slap' is deemed to be a particularly pleasant sound, its phonemes /slæp/ all appearing towards the top of the phonoaesthetic scale.

- Just as the bog squelches and slaps, the 'curt cuts' of the spade are highly representative. The short plosive sounds /k/ and /t/ mimic the accuracy, precision and sharpness of the spade, with the repeating consonance of /k/ indicating the repeating, relentless movement of the spade cutting into the earth.
- The smooth sounding sibilance used in 'spade sinks' mirrors the manner and ease in which the digger appears to be cutting into the earth. The /s/ fricative is a maintainable sound, meaning that the speaker can elongate the sound as long as they wish, further emphasising the movement of the spade.

The sheer noise Heaney manages to make out of English vowels here is remarkable – a dissonant cacophony that forces the mouth to work overtime if the reader speaks the lines aloud.

Neil Corcoran (1986), *A Student's Guide to Seamus Heaney*

ACTIVITY 21

Transcribing poetry and the stylistics of sound

Choose a poem from the anthology from your set poet that you think is interesting in terms of its sound patterns. Using the International Phonetic Alphabet (refer to Figure 8A), transcribe some lines from that poem to create some data that can be used to support your initial impressions of sound usage and effects. What can you say about the phonetic choices in the poem? Refer back to Tables 17D and E and discuss your findings in terms of phonoaesthetics and other sound devices.

Key terms

maintainable: a sound that can be continued for as long as a speaker's breath will allow, such as vowels and fricatives

17.4.3 A continuum of poetic voice

Blended-mode texts have elements of both speech and writing. Poetry is essentially a blended mode genre as it is generally written down yet designed to be read aloud. The poems you are studying for this section all exist on the printed page of course, but many of them still contain elements of speech.

ACTIVITY 22

Placing poems on a continuum

Read the extracts of poems in Text 17O (a)–(d), all of which are taken from the anthology. Thinking about how the poets have created a voice and a representation of speech, place them on a blended-mode continuum, with speech at one end and writing at the other. Justify each placement, using relevant terminology where appropriate. Complete your exploration of Text 17O by writing a comparison of the way the poets use language to create a voice.

Text 17O

(a)

That's my last Duchess painted on the wall,
Looking as if she were alive. I call that piece a wonder, now.

Source: Robert Browning, 'My Last Duchess'

(b)

As virtuous men pass mildly away,
And whisper to their souls to go,
Whilst some of their sad friends do say,
'Now his breath goes,' and some say, 'No.'

Source: John Donne, 'A Valediction: Forbidding Mourning'

(c)

How close can I get
To the sound of your voice
Which Emma Elizabeth Hibbert described –
lively, eager and lightly-pitched
with none of the later, bitter edge.
Cockney, a little.

Source: Carol Ann Duffy, 'The Biographer'

(d)

A combine groaning its way late
Bled seeds across its work-light.
A forest fire smouldered out.
One by one small cafés shut.

Source: Seamus Heaney, 'Night Drive'

17.5 Voice in poetry through time

Just as languages change over time, so do literary styles, forms and genres. Looking back in time through literature offers an interesting insight into the time of writing – what kinds of things were writers influenced by, and how is this reflected in the content and language of literature? Literary eras often move in 'waves', with writers influencing and being influenced by other writers of the same era. These waves can be described and summarised in terms of their 'typical' linguistic style. This unit will explore the typical styles of the genres the poems from the anthology are taken from: metaphysical poetry, the Victorian dramatic monologue and late 20th-century verse.

'... a dissonant cacophony that forces the mouth to work overtime if the reader speaks the lines aloud.'

Neil Corcoran,
A Student's Guide to Seamus Heaney

17.5.1 Metaphysical verse

Known for their provocative, intricate, highly metaphorical and speculative style of writing, many metaphysical poets were writing in reaction to the primarily religious focus that had typified Elizabethan poetry. Metaphysical poetry challenges its readers in emotional and intellectual ways, producing a vision of human behaviour. Many of the scientific and religious references may seem challenging to a modern-day audience, but these challenges are part of the appeal, and many of the ideas found in metaphysical poetry are highly applicable today. Much of the **figurative language** is seen to be far-fetched or unusual. Consider the following metaphors and similes in Table 17F, all taken from examples of metaphysical verse.

In addition to such metaphors and similes, metaphysical poetry often makes use of **paradox**, **hyperbole** and **word play**. Noted for its use of paradox, 'The Canonisation' by Donne compares profane love as if it were divine love. Poet T.S. Eliot describes metaphysical poetry as a 'constant inspection and criticism of experience'. Metaphysical poets observe human experience from many different angles, with all of these angles informing one another. The act of bringing together these different angles is often the source of wit.

Donne often refers to love as the supreme and ultimate human experience, believing that everything in the world can be used as a basis for comparison to love. The registers he employs range from the vulgar to the exalted, from the mundane to the absurd.

Table 17F: Figurative language in metaphysical poetry

Poet	Poem	Extract	Comparison
John Donne	A Valediction: Forbidding Mourning	If they be two, they are two so As stiff twin compasses are two; Thy soul, the fixed root, makes no show To move, but doth, if the other do.	Lovers compared to opposite ends of a compass point; no matter how far the lovers move away from each other, they are still connected through the soul.
John Donne	The Broken Heart	He is the tyrant pike, our hearts the fry.	Love devours and consumes men as a carnivorous pike (a fish) swallows other small fish
Andrew Marvell	To His Coy Mistress	Then worms shall try that long preserved virginity	Worms in the ground take the virginity of a deceased woman

Key terms

figurative language: Abstract language that uses words or expressions with a meaning that differs from the literal reading, such as metaphor or simile

paradox: the juxtaposition of odd and rarely paired ideas for striking and arresting effect

hyperbole: use of language to exaggerate and emphasise a particular point

word play: exploitation of the sounds and (multiple) meanings of words, often for humorous effect

17.5.2 Victorian dramatic monologue

Victorian dramatic monologues are characterised by the use of the first-person pronoun 'I', used by real or fictitious characters and voices. One way to think of a dramatic monologue would be as the events of a play that have been condensed into a single speech spoken by a single character from one point of view. Readers of this literary genre are faced with a number of ambiguities and questions to solve. Who is the true voice and speaker of the poem? What is the relationship between the poet and the 'I', and do they agree with each other? What level of insight do dramatic monologues give us into the possible intentions of the poet? Is the reader asked to take the literal or implied meaning as the most important? Such questions are impossible to answer when applied to the literary genre as a whole, but they all point to the central idea of multiple voices and perspectives. Reading Text 17P, we are faced with such questions.

Text 17P

Now that I, tying thy glass mask tightly,
May gaze thro' these faint smokes curling whitely,
As thou pliest thy trade in this devil's-smithy –
Which is the poison to poison her, prithee?

Source: Robert Browning, 'The Laboratory'

The genre is defined by literary scholar M. H. Abrams in Text 17Q.

Text 17Q

A dramatic monologue is … a type of lyric poem that was perfected by Robert Browning. In its fullest form, as represented in Browning's 'My Last Duchess' and many other poems, the dramatic monologue has the following features: (1) a single person, who is patently *not* the poet, utters the entire poem in a specific situation at a critical moment. (2) This person addresses and interacts with one or more other people; but we know of the auditors' presence and what they say and do only from clues in the discourse of the single speaker. (3) The main principle controlling the poet's choice and organization of what the lyric speaker says is to reveal to the reader, in a way that enhances its interest, the speaker's temperament and character.

Source: Meyer Howard Abrams (1993), *A Glossary of Literary Terms*, 6th edition, New York: Harcourt Brace College Publishers

The complexities of the poet-voice-audience relationship, coupled with the considerable amount of linguistic experimentation prevalent in this genre can often lead to dizzying levels of interpretation by readers.

The voices in Browning's poems are often characters experiencing psychological trauma or stress, in a particular setting or event. Take the male speaker of 'Porphyria's Lover' who strangles his lover with her own hair in wanting to stop time to preserve a perfect moment - seemingly ignorant of the pain it causes her ('no pain felt she; I am quite sure she felt no pain'). In 'My Last Duchess', the speaker is a Duke who describes a painting of a recently deceased beautiful girl, the title character of the poem. As the poem continues, it becomes increasingly clear that the speaker himself killed the Duchess.

17.5.3 Late twentieth-century verse

Late twentieth century (sometimes referred to as postmodernist) poetry began in reaction to the apparent norms in early twentieth-century literature. Although it is a wide-ranging term, **postmodernism** tends to reject hierarchy and objectivity, instead embracing subjectivity, contradiction and diversity. Postmodern poetry often examines states of consciousness as a means to reaching the inner self, often written in everyday, conversational language - which can create a deceptively simple art form and style. Seamus Heaney and Carol Ann Duffy write poems with acuity, clarity and truth, evoking vivid descriptions that are often grounded in real-life locations and times, inspired by memories. Indeed, much of their work has been said to be autobiographical and the transition from childhood to adulthood is a recurring theme in their work. Many modern poets explore **metafiction** in their work (such as 'Digging' by Heaney), investigating how language works, and the confines and limits of language to express human thoughts and behaviour.

Much of Duffy's work is written in the form of the dramatic monologue, giving voices to previously marginalised or silenced figures. By using a voice other than her own, she shows sympathy (sometimes empathy) with the speaker, and gives authority to a voice that we may never have heard from before. Female characters dominate her work - typically under-represented in this form of poetry. Her writing is frequently concerned with the confines and limits of language, and its inability to express human emotions - often love. In 'First Love', the speaker gets close ('waking, with a dream of first love forming real words, as close to my lips as lipstick'), but ultimately the imperfect 'stammering' nature of the speaker's voice holds back her desired expression ('tonight, a love letter out of a dream stammers itself in my heart').

Heaney's writing style and voice is characterised by evocative images through a precise manipulating of language. Strong sounds, sights and smells of the world are conveyed through heavy use of phonological effects and patterns. Heaney draws on his upbringing in rural Northern Ireland in his work, connoting memories of the life and landscape of the farming community he grew up in - provincial and local issues described in painstaking detail to render images with remarkable clarity. However, his poems are more than linguistically painted descriptions - they are springboards to wider political issues and human relationships. In 'Strange Fruit', the vivid description of a murdered corpse - and a stark reminder of ancient violence - is compared to nature through an extended metaphor ('prune skinned'; 'broken nose [as] dark as a turf clod').

Key terms

postmodernism: late twentieth-century movement applied to literature, art, philosophy and architecture

metafiction: writing that self-consciously draws attention to the writing process or the writer's work

17.6 Language and poetic voice

In this section you will look more closely at the set poems from the anthology, thinking about the nature and function of poetic voice in the telling of events and the presentation of people. In particular, you will study how language helps to shape meaning from the following aspects: perspective, time, location, sense of self, sense of others and memories. In each sub-section you will look at a selection of set poems and corresponding analytical, linguistic commentaries. The activities in this section will ask you to apply and build on ideas you have learnt throughout the book. Try to see this section holistically, as the ideas and approaches from each sub-section will often be relevant to others.

17.6.1 Constructing perspective

Perspective links neatly with poetic voice, and the variety of different narrative perspectives 'on offer' to poets allow them to achieve a number of different things when telling a story. We might ask a number of questions when thinking about perspective: from whose perspective is a poem told? The author? The speaker? A real or fictitious character? How do we know? Are these subjective or objective perspectives?

Key terms

perspective: the point of view or character from which a poem is told

Poets can adopt different perspectives in order to achieve different things. The two types of narration most important to poetry are homodiegetic narratives (told from a first-person perspective: 'I'; 'we') and heterodiegetic narratives (told from a third-person perspective ('he', 'she', 'they').

See 16.4.1 for more on types of narration

The speaker of a poem can speak directly to the reader, with a variety of different voices, or as an inward-looking observer. The point of view of the perspective is also important - the attitudes, beliefs and ideas expressed, and who or what these attitudes are directed towards. Identifying perspective in poetry can be problematic because as readers, we can never be certain whether the poem conveys the perspective of the poet, or the speaker within the poem. Nancy Sullivan sums up this idea well:

> Every poem, like the mind from which it springs, views life from a particular point of view.
>
> Source: Nancy Sullivan (1965), 'Perspective and the Poetic Process', *Wisconsin Studies in Contemporary Literature* 6(1): 114–131

17.6.1.1 Pronouns and perspective

The poems in the anthology make for a rich source of data when it comes to identifying and analysing perspective, as they are all told through a homodiegetic perspective. Remind yourself of the definition of dramatic monologue in Section 17.5 and then read Text 17R. In this poem, the speaker tells us of his dislike for a woman (presumably the Cristina in the title) and her 'disloyal' tendencies.

Text 17R

She should never have looked at me
If she meant I should not love her!
There are plenty … men, you call such,
I suppose … she may discover
All her soul to, if she pleases,
And yet leave much as she found them:
But I'm not so, and she knew it
When she fixed me, glancing round them.

Source: Robert Browning, 'Cristina (1)'

We can infer a significant amount of information about the character's perspective focusing on the choice of pronouns.

Browning makes extensive use of person deixis in Text 17R, specifically through the use of pronouns. He introduces three characters (or groups of characters): 'she', 'me' and 'them'. No names or physical descriptions (apart from gender) are given, meaning we focus on the relationships between our three characters rather than who they are as individuals. Usually a pronoun is used as an **anaphora**, to refer back to someone or thing already specified – the absence of this specification creates intrigue as to who are the 'she', the 'I' and the 'them'.

There is the use of **parallelism** in the phrases 'she should never' and 'I should not'. Both these phrases follow the same syntactical structure: PRONOUN + MODAL VERB + NEGATION, further implying there is some form of relationship between the 'she' and the 'I' (in that the syntactic structure is identical), but that all is not perfect in this relationship (in that the words and the meaning are different).

ACTIVITY 23

Rewriting perspective

All of the poems in the anthology are told from a homodiegetic perspective. Take a poem from the anthology by your set poet and rewrite a section of it as told from a different narrative perspective. So, you might choose to write from an external or internal heterodiegetic perspective.

See 16.4.1 for more on external and internal heterodiegetic perspective

ACTIVITY 24

Constructing perspective

Look at the poem from your set poet, given below. Focusing on the use of narrative perspective, pronouns, possessive determiners, anaphora, deixis and anything else of interest that you find, analyse the perspective constructed.

Think about the speaker's perspective, voice and point of view. What is your impression of her/him? What do they think of the other characters/objects/events? How do they behave towards them? How can you tell? Make sure to support your interpretations with evidence from the poem and relevant linguistic terminology.

- Robert Browning: 'The Laboratory'
- John Donne: 'The Canonisation'
- Carol Ann Duffy: 'The Biographer'
- Seamus Heaney: 'Punishment'.

Check your responses in the Ideas section on Cambridge Elevate

17.6.2 Location

In this section you will look at how poets use language to construct spatial locations - through deixis, lexical intensity and syntax. In most texts - not just poetry - the text producer and the text receiver do not share the same context, and therefore constructing location is important as it allows the audience to visualise the story being told. For our discussion on location, it is useful to call the text producer and the text receiver **participants**. In face-to-face conversation, participants share the same location and time, but in many written texts such as poems, these elements are not shared. How does a poet give an impression of place, if the participants are not in the same 'here and now'? Or, how do they synthesise shared deictic centres?

Key terms

anaphora: a word or phrase that refers back to someone or thing already specified. For example, in the sentence *Ian entered the poetry competition, but he didn't win*, 'he' is the anaphora, as it refers back to 'Ian'

parallelism: use of linguistic elements in a sentence that are similar or the same, in terms of grammar, lexis, semantics or phonology

participants: people involved in a discourse of communication, usually the text-producer(s) and text-receiver(s)

17.6.2.1 Deixis

You have learnt about spatial deixis, such as the use of the demonstrative 'that' in the opening line of 'My Last Duchess' by Robert Browning:

That's my last Duchess painted on the wall

The spatial deixis used in this phrase immediately gives us a significant amount of useful information about location. First of all, we share the same deictic centre as the speaker, and may even infer the preciseness and nature of the location - a room with a wall, most likely inside, possibly a room of grandeur due to the connotations of *duchess*. Secondly, our attention is immediately fixed upon the painting, and we feel we are being spoken to directly due to the typically shared and intimate activity of viewing a painting - creating a sense of proximal deixis. Incidentally, it might also be argued that this is an example of person deixis - is the speaker referring to a painting, or a person? The answer to that question is one you may want to explore in your deeper reading of the poem.

Consider another use of spatial deixis in the opening lines of 'Stafford Afternoons' by Carol Ann Duffy:

Only there, the afternoons could suddenly pause

Upon reading the adverb 'there', we are immediately drawn into thinking two things: (1) where is 'there', and (2) why is it 'only' there that gives it a unique quality? This is an example of distal deixis to show contrast between the poem's speaker in the present and the past. The title of course, gives us a clue as to where the poem takes place - Stafford is a town in the West Midlands, where Duffy lived as a child.

Both these examples of spatial deixis in poetry illustrate the importance of absence and withholding information from a reader - to evoke inference, curiosity and ambiguity. Note how proximal and distal spatial deixis can be used to achieve different effects, in terms of focusing our attention on a particular person, object or event.

ACTIVITY 25

Creating location through deixis

Read the poem given here by your choice of poet. Look at deictic patterns you can find in the poem, thinking about how the poets use proximal and/or distal spatial deixis to construct location. Prepare an analysis, using relevant linguistic terminology and examples from the text.

- John Donne, 'Twicknam Garden'
- Robert Browning, 'Home Thoughts, From Abroad'
- Carol Ann Duffy, 'Never Go Back'
- Seamus Heaney, 'Night Drive'

17.6.2.2 Lexical intensity

The levels of description and choices of individual words and phrases all help to construct a sense of location in poetry. This is known as **lexical intensity**: how, and to what extent, words are modified; the use of semantic fields and collocates; the use of sensory language and foregrounding.

Seamus Heaney has a distinctive ability to create a sense of shared place through his language choices. In Text 17S(a), we are plunged into his world of rural Northern Ireland. Heaney creates a vivid picture of the rural countryside, through lexical intensity. Heaney describes his horror at the sight of a flax-dam (a muddy patch of earth intentionally soaked with water to moisten the flax plant), a scene that opens the poem:

Text 17S(a)

All year the flax-dam festered in the heart

Of the townland; green and heavy headed

Flax had rotted there, weighted down by huge sods.

Daily it sweltered in the punishing sun.

Bubbles gargled delicately, bluebottles

Wove a strong gauze of sound around the smell.

Source: Seamus Heaney, 'Death of a Naturalist'

The muddy, watery dam location of the poem is immediately constructed through a semantic field and foregrounding of nature: word choices such as 'flax-dam', 'green', 'sods', 'sun' and 'bluebottles'. Pre- and post-modification of nouns is another important aspect of description. The bubbles gargling 'delicately' suggest bubbles rising to the surface of the water slowly, indicating the viscosity and uncleanliness of the water. The sun 'punishing' the flax suggests an unrelenting natural force, almost torturing the plants without mercy. Furthermore, the abstract noun 'smell' becomes a physical entity in itself, so strong and rank that it can almost be seen, taking on a quality that we associate with concrete nouns. To further illustrate, replace 'smell' with a concrete noun such as 'food' in the line:

Bluebottles wove a strong gauze of sound around the <u>food</u>

We can find similar linguistic features in Text 17S(b).

Text 17S(b)

The rain set early in tonight,

The sullen wind was soon awake,

It tore the elm-tops down for spite,

And did its worst to vex the lake.

Source: Robert Browning, 'Porphryia's Lover'

A semantic field and foregrounding of weather (and specifically a storm by a lake) is constructed through choices such as 'rain', 'wind', 'elm-tops' and 'lake'. The marked use of material verb processes – 'set', 'awake', 'tore, 'vex' – indicate a strong sense of movement and violence, furthering the idea of the weather as a powerful entity. **Pathetic fallacy** and personification, through choices such as 'sullen' and 'awake', imply the weather has human intentionality and purposefulness in its actions.

In both Text 17S(a) and (b), the absence of personal pronouns affects the framing of the poem – as readers we focus on physical description rather than worrying about who is talking. Instead of choosing to say 'I saw the flax-dam festering in the heart of the townland', where the I is somebody observing the events of the poem, the lack of pronouns means we regard Heaney's poem as a picture, seen through our own eyes rather than anyone else's. The same is true of 'Porphryia's Lover', where the absence of personal pronouns foregrounds the role of nature and its power.

ACTIVITY 26

Creating location through lexical intensity

Choose a poem from the poet you are studying and analyse how location is constructed, focusing on the use of semantic fields, collocates, sensory language, modification and foregrounding.

Key terms

lexical intensity: how language is used to create a strong sense of vividness, typically through the use of semantic fields, collocates, sensory language and foregrounding

pathetic fallacy: a kind of personification, where the weather creates a certain mood, through taking on human emotions or characteristics

17.6.2.3 Syntax

The syntactic structure of lines and phrases in poetry is another linguistic feature that can help to construct a sense of location. Read the extracts in Text 17S(a) and (b) again before continuing.

In Texts 17S(a) and (b), the careful and deliberate use of material verbs conveys a strong sense of location. Note how the poets choose to use verbs to create description, rather than adjectives or nouns, which in turn gives agency to non-human objects such as the flax, the wind and the rain - which remain in subject position throughout. This personification of nature serves to heighten the power that both poets consider nature to have, highlighting their respect and high regard for it. In 'Porphryia's Lover', the weather plays an active role remaining in a consistent syntactical position as the subject: 'rain', 'wind', 'it', suggesting it is in absolute control over the verb and the object. Other features of nature appear in the object position ('elm-tops', 'lake'), suggesting conflict between nature itself.

Subject	Verb	Object/location
flax-dam	festered	townland
flax	rotted	townland
sods	weighted	flax
flax	sweltered	sun
bubbles	gargled	flax-dam
bluebottles	wove	flax-dam
rain	set	tonight
wind	tore	elm-tops
wind	vex	lake

ACTIVITY 27

Creating location through syntax

Consider how syntax is used to construct location in Texts 17T(a) to (d). Look carefully for (1) objects or people that appear in subject and object position, (2) verb processes to create description and (3) absence or presence of pronouns.

Text 17T

(a)

Fear death? – to feel the fog in my throat,
The mist in my face,
When the snows begin, and the blasts denote
I am nearing the place,
The power of the night, the press of the storm,

Source: Robert Browning, 'Prospice'

(b)

'Twere wholesomer for me that winter did
Benight the glory of this place,
And that a grave frost did forbid
These trees to laugh and mock me to my face;

Source: John Donne, 'Twicknam Garden'

(c)

The way the trees
drew sly faces from light and shade, the wood
let out its sticky breath on the back of my neck,
and flowering nettles gathered spit in their throats.

Source: Carol Ann Duffy, 'Stafford Afternoons'

(d)

Others had echoes, gave back your own call
With a clean new music in it. And one
Was scaresome, for there, out of ferns and tall
Foxgloves, a rat slapped across my reflection.

Source: Seamus Heaney, 'Personal Helicon'

Check your responses in the Ideas section on Cambridge Elevate

17.6.3 Constructing time

Poets have always been fascinated by time. In 'The Sun Rising', John Donne tells us that his love is beyond time, that 'hours, days [and] months [are the] rags of time'. Carol Ann Duffy regularly uses time to explore emotions and memories, often experimenting with temporal perspectives, such as in the opening line from 'Before You Were Mine': 'I'm ten years away from the corner you laugh on with your pals'. Indeed, it is almost impossible to use language and not to make some reference to time (try it!) – almost all sentences we use contain verbs that indicate whether we are referring to the past, present or future. For centuries, poets have been using time as a source of inspiration for their writing.

Just as we have just seen, participants in poetry do not usually share the same time frame. How then, do poets give an impression of time through their language? How is the distant or recent past, the present, or the distant or near future conveyed through poetry? And how are changes and shifts in time brought about through language? You have learnt about the processes of analepsis and prolepsis, and in this subsection we will look at how these are used in poetry.

See 16.2.4 for more on analepsis and prolepsis

17.6.3.1 Reconstructing the past and imagining the future

Shifts in time references allow poets to reconstruct previous events and imagine ones that are yet to happen. In Text 17U, the poet speaks from the past – 10 years before she was born – directly to her mother (the 'you' in the title), constructing time in a strange way. Thus the poem is set in the present moment but is spoken by a voice that is yet to exist, imagining the future. This peculiar way of constructing time is surprising and absconds from what we might 'expect' a poem exploring such a mother-daughter relationship to be. We can explore how the poet is using specific linguistic features to achieve this.

Text 17U

I'm ten years away from the corner you laugh on
with your pals, Maggie McGeeney and Jean Duff.
The three of you bend from the waist, holding
each other, or your knees, and shriek at the pavement.
Your polka-dot dress blows round your legs. Marilyn.
I'm not here yet.

Source: Carol Ann Duffy, 'Before You Were Mine'

17.6.3.2 Temporal deixis

The opening sentence immediately frames the construction of time ('I'm ten years away from the corner you laugh on'). The temporal deictic reference of 'years' is the element that plays the trick here: as we read this line, we might expect a spatial deictic reference; something such as 'I'm ten miles/streets/yards away…'. In addition, the adverb 'away' can be used as a temporal or spatial marker, creating a sense of ambiguity. This ambiguity is only truly solved at the beginning of the second stanza, with the declarative 'I'm not here yet', asserting that the voice comes from before birth.

Text 17V is another poem in the anthology that constructs time through extensive use of temporal deixis. Read the lines from this poem, which are selected specifically for their references to time.

Text 17V

I sat all morning in the college sick bay
At two o'clock our neighbours drove me home
At ten o'clock the ambulance arrived
Next morning I went up into the room
I saw him for the first time in six weeks
A four foot box, a foot for every year

Source: Seamus Heaney, 'Mid-Term Break'

In Text 17V, 'all morning' indicates the speaker has been waiting for a number of hours in the sick bay – analepsis is constructed through the deliberate lack of precise time phrases, suggesting that the speaker is feeling dazed, with indistinct memories. Use of the precise time expressions 'two o'clock' and 'ten o'clock' indicate a vivid and clear sense of the past, alerting the reader to the seriousness of the (as of yet unknown) incident that has taken place, further heightened by the use of 'ambulance'. We are left to guess why the speaker is seeing 'him' (the corpse) for 'the first time in six weeks'. Six weeks may indicate the length of a boarding school half-term, linking to the poem's title; it may indicate the length of time the victim has been in hospital, or a number of other reasons. This is the longest length of time referred to in the poem - we would expect a family reunion after six-weeks to be a happy occasion, but not in this case. It is only until the parallelism in the final line 'a four foot box, a foot for every year' that we truly understand what has happened. Note how we are not directly told the boy was four years old, it is only through the comparison of spatial (four foot) and temporal (every year) deixis that we know the truth, almost as if the speaker cannot bring himself to say the words himself.

Shifts in tense

In Text 17U, Duffy frequently refers to the past through present tense markers, such as in 'I'm not here yet'. 'Here' is post-modified by 'yet', indicating inevitably of the child's birth. The mother at this point in time is blissfully unaware of her future - enjoying her youth dancing in ballrooms, wearing polka-dot dresses and high-heeled red shoes, enjoying 'fizzy' movies that suggest a love and appetite for youthful life.

In 'Home Thoughts, From Abroad' by Robert Browning, the story is told in the present tense (marked morphologically in 'to be' and by the temporal adverb 'now') and it is clear from the opening two lines that the speaker is lustful for April in England:

Oh, to be in England

Now that April's there

Yet, in a similar way to how Duffy imagines the future, the speaker imagines life in England after April has passed:

And after April, when May follows,

and the whitethroat builds, and all the swallows!

The speaker clearly desires two things, constructed through temporal and spatial deixis: (1) to be in the future, specifically April, and (2) to be in England. In turn, this raises two questions: (1) when was the poem written and (2) where was the poet?

ACTIVITY 28

Constructing time

Focusing on your set poet, look at the poem listed below. Underline each reference to time and then consider how they work together to contribute to the overall meaning of the poem. Think about the precision and scale of time references, the shifts in temporal deixis and shifts in tenses in particular. Refresh your knowledge of analepsis and prolepsis if you need to.

See 16.2.4 for more on analepsis and prolepsis

- John Donne, 'The Anniversary'
- Robert Browning, 'Porphyria's Lover'
- Carol Ann Duffy, 'First Love'
- Seamus Heaney, 'Blackberry Picking'

'A four foot box, a foot for every year'

'Mid-Term Break', Seamus Heaney

17.6.4 Sense of self

You have seen how voices and idiolect in poetry can contribute to identity. Many of the poems in the anthology deal with the projection of a specific persona, either as an assertive declaration, a conflict of identity or as a speaker's struggle to identify with or describe themselves. How do poets treat and describe the identities of their speakers? The poet Jackie Kay places identity and self at the heart of society:

Nothing matters more than who we are in the world,
where we have been and where we are going.

See 17.4 for more on voices and idiolect in poetry

17.6.4.1 Inference

You have learnt about how inference and gap-filling help to build identity and character. The way that poets construct a sense of self in their writing varies hugely, and also relies on a large amount of inference and gap-filling from the reader. This is an intentional, self-conscious way of using language – withholding information is often more powerful than simply spelling it out.

See 16.3 for more on inference and gap-filling

John Donne's poetry often deals with the individuality of oneself and the search for an identity, yet the voices he adopts are notoriously vague. Read Text 17W(a), from 'The Good Morrow', a poem in which the speaker explores love as an intense experience that is beyond the normal realms of reality.

Text 17W(a)

I wonder by my troth, what thou, and I
Did, till we loved? were we not weaned till then,
But sucked on country pleasures, childishly?
Or snorted we in the seven sleepers' den?
'Twas so; but this, all pleasures fancies be.
If ever any beauty I did see,
Which I desired, and got, 'twas but a dream of thee.

Source: John Donne, 'The Good Morrow'

Here Donne's speaker explores his own identity before and after meeting his lover, claiming he is a new person with new beliefs about the nature of love. He rejects his life previous to meeting his lover, describing it as immature through a semantic field of childhood ('were we not *weaned*'; '*childishly*'). In doing this, he questions and discards his own identity and understanding of love. He uses metaphor to compare his previous life to one of a deep sleep, unaware and naïve of the world and the possibilities of love ('or snorted we in the seven sleepers' den?'), and that if he did indeed ever see beauty, then it was simply a dream-like premonition of his new lover ('If ever any beauty I did see … 'twas but a dream of thee'). The marked use of interrogatives implies he is interested in finding answers to his own thoughts – but we are left to infer the answer, which we would not have to do if the declarative mood had been used, in which his own thoughts would be more assertively conveyed.

'Mid-Term Break' by Seamus Heaney is another poem that requires the audience to infer and fill gaps. As you read Text 17W(b), which is taken from the beginning of the poem, think about what kind of self is constructed – what do we learn about the speaker that is not explicitly spelt out?

Text 17W(b)

I sat all morning in the college sick bay
Counting bells knelling classes to a close.
At two o'clock our neighbors drove me home.

In the porch I met my father crying –
He had always taken funerals in his stride –
And Big Jim Evans saying it was a hard blow.

Source: Seamus Heaney, 'Mid-Term Break'

Heaney constructs a speaker that is clearly young: they are at 'college', and have some dependence upon adults: they need to be driven home and adult behaviour is foregrounded ('father crying'; 'Big Jim Evans saying it was a hard blow'). We infer some details about what has happened: references to 'funerals', about which we hold schematic knowledge; the fact that the child is leaving school early; the 'father crying' and the subtle reference to 'bells knelling'. Furthermore, the fact that the father is crying yet had previously 'always taken funerals in his stride' suggests the funeral in the poem is somehow different to past experiences.

ACTIVITY 29

Inferring self

Taking the poem by your set poet listed here, what information about the projected sense of self can you infer?

- Robert Browning, 'Johannes Agricola in Meditation'
- John Donne, 'The Sun Rising'
- Carol Ann Duffy, 'Mean Time'
- Seamus Heaney, 'Night Drive'

Check your responses in the Ideas section on Cambridge Elevate

17.6.4.2 Changing self

Projections of self in poetry often do not remain static – they can shift, develop and change over the course of a poem, and readers need to be able to track these changes as the poem develops. Some of the poems in the anthology take place over a short period of time, often highlighting a moment of sudden revelation, insight or change (such as in 'The Good Morrow' by John Donne and 'Porphyria's Lover' by Robert Browning), whereas some of the poems take place over a long period of time, highlighting the development from childhood to adulthood, in the manner of a *bildungsroman* (such as in 'Follower' and 'Personal Helicon' by Seamus Heaney and 'The Captain of the 1964 *Top Of The Form* Team' by Carol Ann Duffy). For example, in the beginning of 'Personal Helicon', the speaker sets out his child curiosities, how 'as a child, they could not keep me from wells'. The final stanza signifies the change in self from childhood to adulthood through a temporal adverb 'now': 'now, to pry into roots ... is beneath all adult dignity'.

See 16.3.1 for more on bildungsroman

ACTIVITY 30

Tracking a change in self

Take a poem by your set poet (such as those listed in Activity 29) that involves a change or development in self, either over a short or long period of time. What changes in self happen, and what are the reasons for this change? What changes in language help to construct the change?

17.6.4.3 Constructing characters

Some of the poems in the anthology, notably those that use the dramatic monologue form, use characters to project a sense of self. Before continuing, remind yourself of characters and characterisation if you need to.

See 16.3 for more on characters and characterisation

The sense of self in Robert Browning and Carol Ann Duffy's poetry has been long discussed in literary circles. Due to these authors often writing in the form of the dramatic monologue, how can we tell the relationship between the author and the speaker? Are the poets revealing their true voice through the speaker of the poem? As with all analyses, you should consider each language level and how they work together to construct character. The following structure and prompt questions are a useful starting point to doing so:

- **Lexis and semantics:** what kind of words does the speaker use to describe himself or herself, other participants and events? What kinds of verbs are used to describe the action, thoughts and speech in the poem? What kind of pronouns and possessive determiners are used in a deictic sense, and why?
- **Grammar:** look at the level and detail of description and modification. What kinds of phrases and clauses are used and why? Think about agency. Which characters are placed in subject/object position, and why? What sentence functions are used, and why?
- **Phonetics and phonology:** are words chosen deliberately for their phonoaesthetic appeal? How might prosodic variation add to the speaker's sense of self?

- **Pragmatics:** what might you infer about the psychological state of the speaker? What is suggested, hinted at or left out which forces the audience to arrive at their own conclusions? How 'tellable' is the poem?
- **Discourse:** to what extent can you apply Labov's narrative categories or Goodwin's story structure to the poem?

Table 17G takes a selection of poems from the anthology and uses the language levels and prompt questions to explore how different kinds of characters and projections of self are constructed. Read the poems before reading the analyses.

ACTIVITY 31

Constructing characters

Choose a poem by your set poet where a strong sense of character is constructed. Conduct your own analysis, focusing on how this is achieved. Use the language levels you have been introduced to and try to analyse the poem in a similar level of detail as is done in Table 17G. Some suggested poems are:

- Robert Browning, 'Porphyria's Lover'
- John Donne, 'The Apparition'
- Carol Ann Duffy, 'The Biographer'
- Seamus Heaney, 'The Skunk'.

17.6.5 Sense of others

What words do we choose to talk about other people? What are our perceptions of other people? Are poems about other people simply observational and descriptive, or can they be sympathetic and empathetic too? You have looked at constructing perspective, and it is often useful to associate this with the construction of others. Other individuals or groups are often constructed through the perspective of a particular individual and you should take this into account in your analysis of the sense of others. Can we truly trust the voice of a poem, or are we presented with a biased view?

See 17.6.1 for more on constructing perspective

17.6.5.1 Verb processes to construct others

Read 'Follower' by Seamus Heaney and think about how the two characters, the father and the son, are represented in the poem. The poem is told from the voice of a son, reminiscing about how his father used to work on the family farm. Much of the poem is given to physical descriptions of the father – his strength, efficiency and skill at handling horses, and how the son is a mere shadow in his father's footsteps – small, weak and inadequate. However, the poem ends with a shift in time to when the father has grown into an old man; a shadow of his former self. The use of verbal and material verbs to describe the two characters creates a strong sense of others. They are listed here:

Father	Son
worked	stumbled
globed	fell
sweating	follow
mapping	tripping
stumbling	falling
	yapping

The list of verbs associated with the father are all suggestive of strength and power: qualities that the son admires in his father. In this way the father is seen as an object of desire, as a symbol of everything the son wants to become. Contrast these with the verbs associated with the son: weakness, immaturity and irritation. It is not until the final verb to describe the father, 'stumbling', that the shift in sense of others happens – and because this same verb was the first one used to describe the son, the mapping of description is transferred from one character to another. Through the verb choices, the speaker eventually finds his and his father's roles reversed, an indication of generational conflict. The speaker is positioned between a sense of himself as a child (dependent upon his father), and his current self (struggling to establish his own independence).

Table 17G

Language level	Analyses from anthology poems
Lexis and semantics	**'Valentine' by Carol Ann Duffy** A semantic field of 'romance' is built through words such as 'red rose', 'lover' and 'kiss', but this is contrasted with words which we would not normally associate with this topic: 'onion', 'knife' and 'lethal'. This indicates the speaker has a 'different', somewhat cynical, view of love and avoids clichés, strengthened by the choice of negation in phrases such as '*not* a red rose or a satin heart' and '*not* a cute card or a kissogram'.
Grammar	**'Prospice' by Robert Browning** In this poem, Browning looks forward to fighting death, creating a sense of self that is strong willed and resolute. He uses interrogatives 'fear death?'; a conceit of war and violence ('foe'; 'fighter'; 'battle'); imperatives to demand a full and noble death ('let me taste the whole of it'); and verb phrases that include modal verbs such as 'shall' and 'will' to reinforce his determinism and belief.
Syntax	**'Close' by Carol Ann Duffy** In the lines 'you have me like a drawing, erased, coloured in, untitled, signed by your tongue', Duffy places the deictic 'you' in subject position implying the speaker ('me') is under control, in object position, an idea further emphasised by the metaphorical reference to the drawing - a self being shaped and constructed by another person and controlled through language: 'signed by your tongue'.
Phonetics and phonology	**'Hailstones' by Seamus Heaney** The physical force of the hailstones, suggesting the speaker is at their mercy, is evoked through short bursts of monosyllabic words such as 'hit' and 'hard'. Heaney makes extensive use of plosive sounds in verbs such as 'pelted', 'bounced', 'rattling' to evoke the speaker's helplessness and allow the audience to hear the sounds of the hailstone storm.
Pragmatics	**'My Last Duchess' by Robert Browning** Lines such as 'looking as if she were alive' imply the Duchess is now dead, an implication that soon becomes more factual as the poem progresses, through the use of past tense markers such as 'she had a heart'. The tellability of this poem is high; we infer that the speaker *wants* to tell this story. He addresses us directly from the opening line; the poet and the speaker want their audience to be entertained.
Discourse	**'Tollund Man' by Seamus Heaney** To an extent, Labov's narrative categories can be applied here, suggesting a sense of self that wants to tell stories, to transmit information from one person to another. Abstract: 'some day I will go to Aarhus' Orientation: 'to see his peat brown head… skin cap' Complicating action: 'In the flat country… for miles along the lines' Resolution: 'something of his last freedom… parishes' Coda: 'I will feel lost, unhappy and at home'

ACTIVITY 32

Verb processes

Take a poem from your anthology and conduct an analysis focusing on verb choices and processes and their construction of identity. Some suggestions are given here. What sense of others is created, and how?

Robert Browning

- 'Johannes Agricola in Meditation'; 'Porphyria's Lover'

John Donne

- 'The Good Morrow'; 'The Relic'

Seamus Heaney

- 'Strange Fruit'; 'The Otter'

Carol Ann Duffy

- 'Before You Were Mine'; 'Mean Time'

ACTIVITY 33

Closing lines

Remind yourself of the closing lines of 'Follower':

But today it is my father who keeps stumbling behind me, and will not go away

Many poems, such as this one, end with a particularly poignant or evocative line. Look at the closing lines from your choice of poet from the anthology. What is the lasting impact of the final lines? Does it affirm or change the meaning of the poem in any way, and how?

17.6.5.2 Person deixis to construct others

Read Text 17X from 'Woman's Constancy' by John Donne, in which the speaker, presumed to be male, addresses his female lover and asks her directly about what she will do tomorrow when she leaves - will she make a new vow of constancy (faithfulness) to a new man, substituting the one she had already made with the speaker? In this poem, we hear the voice of a man who believes infidelity and promiscuity are inevitable - he speaks before the woman has left him, in anticipation. But, who is the voice of the poem talking to, and what is its purpose? The positioning of the audience has an impact upon its reading. Is he addressing and giving 'advice' to men? Or is he aiming an insult at a particular woman, perhaps with sarcasm and spite?

Text 17X

Now thou has loved me one whole day,

To-morrow when thou leavest, what wilt thou say?

Wilt thou then antedate some new-made vow?

Or say that now
We are not just those persons which we were?

Source: John Donne, 'Woman's Constancy'

Donne uses the second-person pronoun to address his lover directly, all of which are examples of unspecified person deixis, suggesting this is a private conversation which the reader now witnesses – or, the poem is written directly to a woman that the poet has in mind. Words such as 'antedate' and 'vow' suggest the speaker sees love as a contract, and that the woman is going to make a new 'vow' with her next lover - is he being sarcastic and spiteful towards his short-term lover? The repeated use of interrogatives makes us see the speaker as desperate to understand in his relentless questioning of the woman, who we never hear from. The use of the first-person plural pronoun 'we' at the end of the stanza brings the speaker and the 'you' together, suggesting that the two people made some kind of faithfulness vow together in the past.

ACTIVITY 34

Deixis to create a sense of others

Person deixis can be used to create a sense of others. Look at Text 17Y(a) to (d), taken from the poetry anthology. Look specifically at the poet that you are studying, and try to write a description of the characters that are referred to through the deictic expressions. What words might you use to describe them, and why? Why do you think the poet decided to use a deictic reference as opposed to a name?

Text 17Y

(a)

Just for a handful of silver he left us,

Just for a riband to stick in his coat –

Found the one gift of which fortune bereft us

Source: Robert Browning, 'The Lost Leader'

(b)

Twice or thrice had I loved thee,

Before I knew thy face or name

Source: John Donne, 'Air and Angels'

(c)

Waking, with a dream of first love forming real words,

as to my lips as lipstick, I speak your name,

after a silence of years, into the pillow, and the power

of your name brings me here to the window, naked,

to say it again to a garden shaking with light.

Source: Carol Ann Duffy, 'First Love'

(d)

I can feel the tug
of the halter at the nape
of her neck, the wind
on her naked front.

Source: Seamus Heaney, 'Punishment'

Check your responses in the Ideas section on Cambridge Elevate

17.6.6 Memories

The ability to recall, picture and describe memories is a source of joy as much as of frustration. As we saw in Unit 15, memories can evoke emotions, reactions and behaviours in ourselves and others.

17.6.6.1 Nostalgia

In *Mean Time*, Duffy uses memory as a respite or 'safe place' from the melancholy atmosphere of many of the poems. The characters in her poems often use nostalgic memories to escape the realities of the present, such as in 'Before You Were Mine', where **synesthesia** is employed ('I see you, clear as scent'), combing the senses of sight and smell to create a rich sense of memory and time for the reader.

Key terms

synesthesia: the description of a sense in terms of another sense. For example: 'a loud perfume' (sound + smell) and 'a soft light' (touch + sight)

Read 'The Captain of the 1964 *Top Of The Form* Team', a dramatic monologue by Carol Ann Duffy and think about how the poet creates a sense of memory. In this poem, we hear the voice of a man who is disillusioned by adulthood and all that it brings. Instead, he longs for a time in the 1960s (1964, to be precise) when he was a schoolboy - top of his class, and captain of a quiz team. The speaker looks back on his youth with fond memories and a clear sense of nostalgic longing, all of which serve to contrast with the unhappiness he feels in his adult life.

- The reference to popular songs and musicians such as 'Baby Love' and 'Supremes' sets this poem firmly in the year that the title gives. The specific months of record release dates are even given, suggesting the speaker has a vivid and fixed memory of his childhood. Music is often associated with memory; we all associate certain songs with personal, often long-term memories.
- Use of erratic and varied sentence lengths marked by ellipsis ('The blazer. The badge. The tie.'; 'And the photograph') suggest that as he grows older, the speaker's memory is failing him, as he struggles to retrace and recount his thoughts. The elliptical constructions (indicating missing elements) match the idea of the memory being patchy and fragmented. Thus, his memory is increasingly a misrecognition of his self, shreds of memories that he is losing against his will - all encoded through syntax.
- Pre-modification of objects in his present being through negative adjectives increase the idea that he is unfulfilled and disappointed with his adult life ('my *stale* wife'; 'my *thick* kids'). Having kids and a wife are typically seen as a badge of adulthood pride; a clear indicator of being a 'grown-up', and a state that our speaker now rejects.

ACTIVITY 35

Nostalgia

Choose a poem in the anthology by your set poet that includes nostalgic memories. What is the effect of presenting memories in this way, and what kind of poetic voice does it create?

17.6.6.2 Childhood

Many of the poems in the anthology by Seamus Heaney use childhood memories, focusing on the cost and losses of the (sometimes difficult) transition from childhood to adulthood. Memories of childhood innocence are explored in 'Blackberry Picking', in which the poetic voice describes the gluttonous pleasure of hoarding fresh wild blackberries, only to find that they rot before there is a chance to eat them. Read the poem and think about how the poet sets up a simple image of a happy memory before diminishing it towards the end.

- The structure of the poem highlights the contrast between childhood and maturity. The first stanza is filled with deliberate, colourful description of the sheer joy of picking ('lust for picking') and eating ('its flesh was sweet'; 'stains upon the tongue') fruit. The second stanza shifts the mood to the realisation that the harvest is useless ('a rat grey fungus'; 'sweet flesh would turn sour'; 'smelt of rot').
- Phonology and onomatopoeia are used to great effect, suggesting Heaney's speaker has a vivid and film-like memory of his youth (plosive alliteration in 'until the tinkling bottom [of the cans] had been covered'; affricates and fricatives in 'briars scratched our boots').
- The final line underlines the loss of childhood innocence and **idealism** and the shift towards adulthood and **realism**. The past tense morpheme '-ed' in 'hoped' confirms this is merely a memory; the parallelism of the epistemic modal 'would', coupled with the mental verb processes 'hope' and 'knew', signifies two different views. Essentially, Heaney speaks to us in two different voices in the same line, as a child and as an adult:

Child: I **hope** [the blackberries] will keep.

Adult: I **know** [the blackberries] will not.

ACTIVITY 36

Constructing memories

Choose a poem from the anthology that includes an element of memories. Prepare an analysis of this poem, remembering to consider different language levels and then how these work together to create an overall sense of meaning. Discuss how the poet creates memory through his or her language choices, the contrast (if any) between childhood and adulthood, and the nature of poetic voice in the poem.

Key terms

idealism: regarding things as they should be, or as one would wish them to be

realism: regarding things as they are, regardless of how one wants them to be

17.7 Bringing it all together: AS Level

17.7.1 Self-assessment: check your learning

For each of the statements in Table 17H, evaluate your confidence in each topic area.

Topic area	Very confident	Some knowledge	Need to revise
I understand the concept of poetic voice			
I can comment on poetry as a literary genre and talk about some of its features and conventions			
I can explore how poetic techniques are used for interpretative effects			
I am able to use the different language levels to examine and analyse the poems I am studying			
I am able to explore in detail how poets and their speakers present themselves and their relationships to others, and the importance of time, places and memories in their poems			

Poetic voices is assessed on Paper 1 of the AS Level examination.

In this question you will need to compare and contrast two poems that you are studying. These poems will be printed on the paper for you. The questions will always focus on one aspect of the following:

- How speakers in the poems project an identity/identities
- The presentation of time and memories, and places and the people and events associated with them
- The presentation of relationships between speakers and others
- How narrative events are shaped through the use of particular narrative frames or techniques.

All exam questions follow the same format and are presented in two parts. Look at the practice question from Carol Ann Duffy.

These are the poems you need to read about

Read 'Beachcomber' and 'Stafford Afternoons', printed below.

Compare and contrast how Duffy presents **time** in these poems.

This instruction reminds you that you need to compare and contrast. It also contains the focus for the question, here highlighted in bold (time)

Explaining the assessment objectives

There are three assessment objectives tested here and they all carry different weightings as shown here.

- **AO1** (15 marks): Apply concepts and methods from integrated linguistic and literary study as appropriate, using associated terminology and coherent written expression

The key elements are your:

- clear expression of ideas
- accurate use of terminology associated with this topic
- reference to and use of various levels of language analysis to explain your ideas and comment on effects of particular language choices that the poet has made
- good stylistic analysis.

- **AO2** (15 marks): Analyse the ways that meanings are shaped in texts

Here you need to:
- interpret the question carefully and in a sustained way
- comment in detail on the interpretative effects caused by specific lexical, grammatical, phonological and discourse patterns used by the poet
- select parts of the poems carefully and comment on these in detail to support the points you are making.

- **AO4** (10 marks): Explore connections across texts, informed by linguistic and literary concepts and methods

You need to think about:
- similarities – how the poems are similar in the ways that they present the focus of the question
- differences – how the poems are different in the ways that they present the focus of the question
- narrative connections – how the poems can be connected in terms of how the poets shape the experiences of their speakers and make use of narrative conventions.

17.7.2 Exploring possible questions

You can plan for this by thinking carefully about the following key questions.

Questions on poetic style

- How are poetic voices set up and maintained throughout poems?
- What poetic techniques are used?
- How do the poets use and manipulate lexical, grammatical and phonological features?
- How might the poems be analysed using insights from semantics and pragmatics?
- How do speakers present others and their relationships to them? What techniques do they use to establish and develop aspects of characters?
- How are different points of view set up? How are perspectives presented in the poems?
- How are time and space presented as significant?

Questions on interpretative effects

- What effects are created by specific choices that have been made by the poet?
- How do these effects help to develop themes, characterisation, and emphasise the importance of specific times, the memories associated with them and locations?

Questions on connections

- What similarities or differences are there between the two poems in terms of the question focus?
- What connections can be made between the two texts in terms of how the poets and their speakers shape and present their narratives?

ACTIVITY 37

Practice questions

You can practise and prepare for this paper by looking at the following question on the poet that you are studying.

John Donne

- Read 'The Good Morrow' and 'The Anniversary'.
- Compare and contrast how Donne presents the relationships between the people in these poems.

Robert Browning

- Read 'Porphyria's Lover' and 'My Last Duchess'.
- Compare and contrast how Browning presents places in these poems.

Carol Ann Duffy

- Read 'Beachcomber' and 'Stafford Afternoons'.
- Compare and contrast how Duffy presents time in these poems.

Seamus Heaney

- Read 'Follower' and 'Mid-Term Break'.
- Compare and contrast how Heaney presents childhood in these poems.

17.8 Bringing it all together: A Level

17.8.1 Self-assessment: check your learning

For each of the statements in Table 17I, evaluate your confidence in each topic area.

Topic area	Very confident	Some knowledge	Need to revise
I understand the concept of poetic voice			
I can comment on poetry as a literary genre and talk about some of its features and conventions			
I can explore how poetic techniques are used for interpretative effects			
I am able to use the different language levels to examine and analyse the poems I am studying			
I am able to explore in detail how poets and their speakers present themselves and their relationships to others, and the importance of time, places and memories in their poems			

Poetic voices is assessed on Paper 1 of the A Level examination.

In this question you will be given a poem and a focus to write about and asked to explore this focus using that poem and another one of your choice by the poet that you have been studying. You will therefore need to think very carefully about what might make a good second poem to choose.

Although for the A Level question there is no explicit need to make comparisons and contrasts *between* the two poems, you will need to concentrate on both poems equally and draw attention to the specific ways that each poem represents ideas about the set focus.

The questions will always focus on one aspect of the following:

- how speakers in the poems project an identity/identities
- the presentation of time and memories, and places and the people and events associated with them
- the presentation of relationships between speakers and others
- how narrative events are shaped through the use of particular narrative frames or techniques.

The question will follow the same format as detailed below. The example here is from Carol Ann Duffy.

This is the named poem that you will need to use in your answer. This instruction reminds you that you need to choose another poem to explore. It also contains the focus for the question, here highlighted in bold (connections with places)

Examine how Duffy presents speakers' **connections with places** in 'Never Go Back' and one other poem of your choice.

Explaining the assessment objectives

There are two assessment objectives tested on this question and these carry different weightings as shown here.

- **AO1** (15 marks): Apply concepts and methods from integrated linguistic and literary study as appropriate, using associated terminology and coherent written expression

The key elements are your:

- clear expression of ideas
- accurate use of terminology associated with this topic
- reference to and use of various levels of language analysis to explain your ideas and comment on effects of particular language choices that the poet has made
- good stylistic analysis.

- **AO2** (10 marks): Analyse the ways that meanings are shaped in texts

Here you need to:

- focus on the question carefully and in a sustained way
- comment in detail on the interpretative effects caused by specific lexical, grammatical, phonological and discourse patterns used by the poet
- select parts of the poems carefully and comment on these in detail to support the points you are making.

You can plan for this by thinking carefully about the following key questions.

Questions on poetic style

- How are poetic voices set up and maintained throughout poems?
- What poetic techniques are used?
- How do the poets use and manipulate lexical, grammatical and phonological features?
- How might the poems be analysed using insights from semantics and pragmatics?
- How do speakers present others and their relationships to them? What techniques do they use to establish and develop aspects of characters?
- How are different points of view set up? How are perspectives presented in the poems?
- How are time and space presented as significant?

Questions on interpretative effects

- What effects are created by specific choices that have been made by the poet?
- How do these effects help to develop themes, characterisation, and emphasise the importance of specific times, the memories associated with them, and locations?

ACTIVITY 38

Practice questions

You can practise and prepare for this paper by looking at the following question on the poet that you are studying.

John Donne

Examine how Donne presents views about relationships between lovers in 'The Sun Rising' and **one** other poem of your choice.

Robert Browning

Examine how Browning presents speakers' attitudes towards others in 'The Lost Leader' and **one** other poem of your choice.

Carol Ann Duffy

Examine how Duffy presents speakers' connections with places in 'Never Go Back' and **one** other poem of your choice.

Seamus Heaney

Examine how Heaney presents the importance of remembering in 'Punishment' and **one** other poem of your choice.

DEVELOPING

Introduction to *Exploring conflict*

What will you study?

What might occur to you first when you see that the title of this section of the course contains the word 'conflict' is that you are going to be studying 'war'. However, here it's more about the ongoing conflicts that occur between people in their daily interactions with others – and the ways that writers present these in either literary prose or non-fiction texts, as well as in the dramatic genre. Each text you will study presents a relationship between characters, or sometimes partly fictionalised representations of real people, depicting the small and large conflicts that occur regularly between individuals and groups who have contrasting viewpoints, different values and diverse wants and needs. We start in Activity 1 by defining *conflict*.

ACTIVITY 1

Defining conflict

- Use dictionaries to note synonyms for the word 'conflict'.
- Put the synonyms you have found into a continuum from what you think are the mildest to the strongest meanings of the word conflict.
- Now try to match the definitions with an example you can think of, perhaps by using your own experiences. Identify the people, their relationships to each other and the topics of conflict that may be involved in your examples.

If you start by considering the synonyms for the word 'conflict', then you will already be thinking about what this particular topic is about and why drama is such a good genre for exploring it. Conflict in its most extreme sense, and one that might be familiar to you from global news reports, is a word used to describe a long drawn-out war. However, its other meanings – disagreement, squabble, falling-out, clash, and so on – might make you see that it can have more immediate connections to people in personal relationships and exchanges with others. If you relate it to your own daily interactions with other people, 'conflict' might range from a brief Twitter exchange in which you disagree with someone else's opinion, a difference with a friend about a group you plan to meet at lunch in a series of text messages, or a face-to-face argument with a parent over where or how you want to spend your free time. From this you can see that conflicts (large or small) are a feature of people's lives on an ongoing basis.

If you have watched any popular reality TV programmes, you will appreciate how these too are built explicitly around conflict; perhaps because it would not be an entertaining experience for the audience if everyone got along and agreed with each other. Likewise, soap operas have to have more than their fair share of arguments, marital breakdowns and tragic or dramatic deaths in order to sustain their existence over many decades. These two types of programme also indicate the blurred boundaries between fiction and non-fiction, although in contrasting ways. Soap operas present a fictionalised version of possible real-life events and human experiences, whereas reality shows present real people seeking to present themselves in a certain way and build alliances with others in a false, set-up environment. So, before focusing on your set texts, explore conflicts through the TV programmes that you watch, to show you the 'conflict' that continually surrounds us and how such interactions are fictionalised.

ACTIVITY 2

Exploring conflict

Watch either an episode of a reality TV show (for example, *Come Dine with Me*) or an episode of any TV soap opera. As you watch, note the following points.

- **The types of characters or people involved** – What can you interpret about their personalities and their beliefs from their language, interactions and non-verbal communication? Do they change in different interactions?
- **The settings used for their interactions** – These could be places or times of the day.
- **The relationships between the characters/people** – Are they with friends or family?
- **The ways their 'stories' are told** – For example, do the scenes cut between different interactions?
- **The topics of their interactions** – How are the 'conflicts' between them shown? You might consider their language use as well as their non-verbal communication.

For further debate, it would be really interesting to compare these with other students to establish common themes and findings and also to consider the similarities and differences between the scripted drama of soap operas and the more spontaneous talk of reality shows. Another interesting extension to this activity would be to look at conflict in online texts to see how you can apply the bullet points to social media sites such as Twitter. You could explore how aspects of character, relationships and conflict are enacted in this hybrid mode where we experience relationships in a virtual world of 'friends' and in larger, possibly global, networks of people we might have never met.

With a broader definition of conflict, you might now see how this surrounds us in our everyday lives as people build and negotiate relationships or position themselves and their views against other people's. So, before you focus your study on the set texts you should already see how universal the nature of the conflict you will be exploring is, and how essential it is to our human experience.

Section A: *Writing about society* (Unit 18)

There are three elements to your study in Unit 18, although this will be assessed by two tasks in the final examination. Firstly, you will study the writer's presentation of conflict in one of the following novels:

- Jon Krakauer, *Into the Wild*
- Kate Summerscale, *The Suspicions of Mr Whicher: or the Murder at Road Hill House*
- F. Scott Fitzgerald, *The Great Gatsby*
- Khaled Hosseini, *The Kite Runner*.

Then, in the examination, a creative intervention task allows you to demonstrate your understanding of the original text, as well as your understanding of how to create characters, how to indicate point of view and how to control a narrative. Finally, producing a critical commentary to support your own writing enables you to reflect on the process of reshaping the writer's original material into a new text.

Section B: *Dramatic encounters* (Unit 19)

In Unit 19 you will study the kinds of dramatic encounters portrayed in plays, specifically the conflicts between characters within the dramatic worlds the playwrights create. You will have the opportunity to explore one play with a choice from:

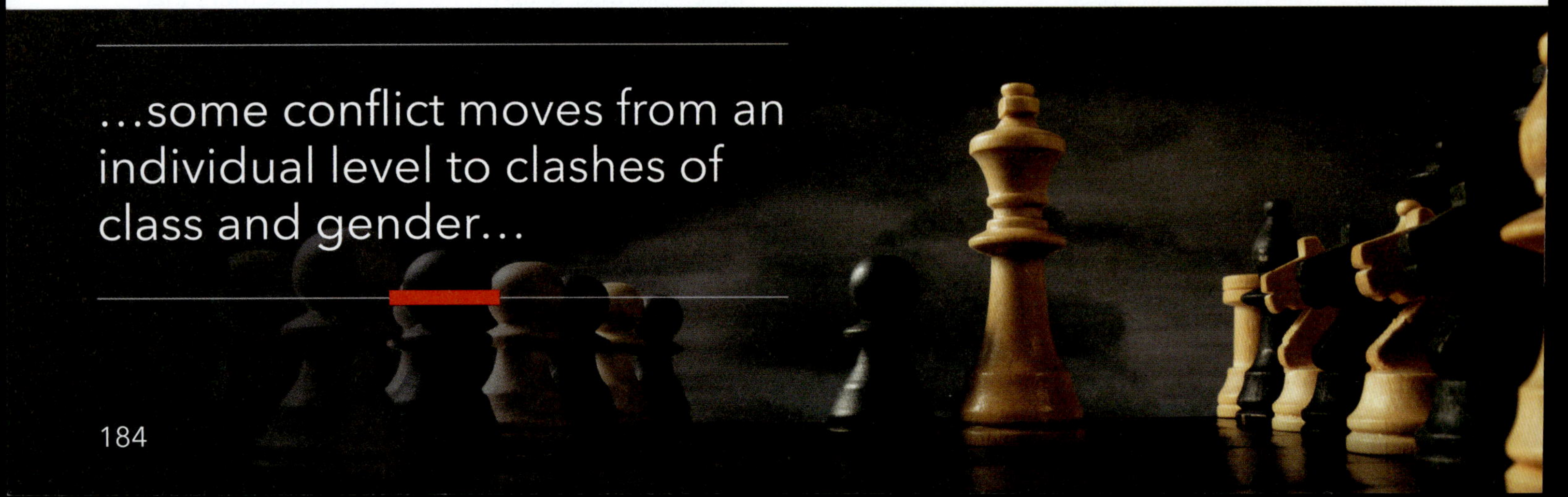

...some conflict moves from an individual level to clashes of class and gender...

- William Shakespeare, *Othello*
- Arthur Miller, *All My Sons*
- Tennessee Williams, *A Streetcar Named Desire*
- Rory Kinnear, *The Herd*.

What knowledge and skills will you develop?

Whichever texts you study for Units 18 and 19, you will get a rich interpretation of conflict, building on what you've learnt from your understanding of the key concepts you have already studied on this course. The links to *Telling stories* are evident in that both the dramatic genre and literary and non-literary texts tell stories and are shaped into narrative discourse. Links to the non-exam assessment, *Making connections*, are found in the connections you will be building constantly with the source text you study and use as the basis for your own creativity in Unit 18.

What types of conflict do the set texts present?

The texts for both Unit 18 (*Writing about society*) and Unit 19 (*Dramatic encounters*) have been carefully selected because they all present strong views about how things are or should be, interactions where people are in opposition or conflict and sometimes because they enable different groups or individuals to be 'heard'. At one level it can simply be a conflict of contrasting points of view about a particular topic or interpretation of an event. However, some conflict moves from an individual level to clashes of class and gender, to conflict at the level of society with potentially political consequences.

Surveying the texts you might study introduces you to these different types of conflict. To illustrate these contrasting presentations of conflict, some of the texts explore individuals in conflict with people around them. In *Into the Wild*, the protagonist (the main character around whom the action revolves) is a young man who wants to escape the demands of the modern, materialistic world and the pressures of family. Equally, *The Herd* explores the modern dilemmas of family breakdown, the ensuing bitterness between the family and the struggles created by coping with caring for others.

The Kite Runner presents a complex conflict, between outsiders and insiders within the 1970s Afghani society depicted, from illegitimate and legitimate family members to the larger political and social world of Afghanistan and exploring the ideologies and values underpinning these. Similarly, in *Othello*, the conflict focuses on an outsider, whose racial difference conflicts with a Venetian society that needs his militaristic skills but struggles to accept his intermarriage within it. Set in the post-Second World War era, *All My Sons* highlights the conflict between family, neighbours and the larger society based on human greed and guilt. This type of conflict within a close-knit community is reflected in *The Suspicions of Mr Whicher*, which presents the murder of a child and the resulting police investigation.

The Great Gatsby depicts an elite society with 'old' and 'new' money in conflict. *A Streetcar Named Desire* is also about conflicts between different parts of society – pitting the old money and French cultural heritage of the southern American states against members of a newer immigrant background. However, it is also a domestic conflict between siblings, and an exploration of the effects of gender and sexual politics, showing that conflict is also about the exercise of power in personal relationships – a common theme in all the texts you might study.

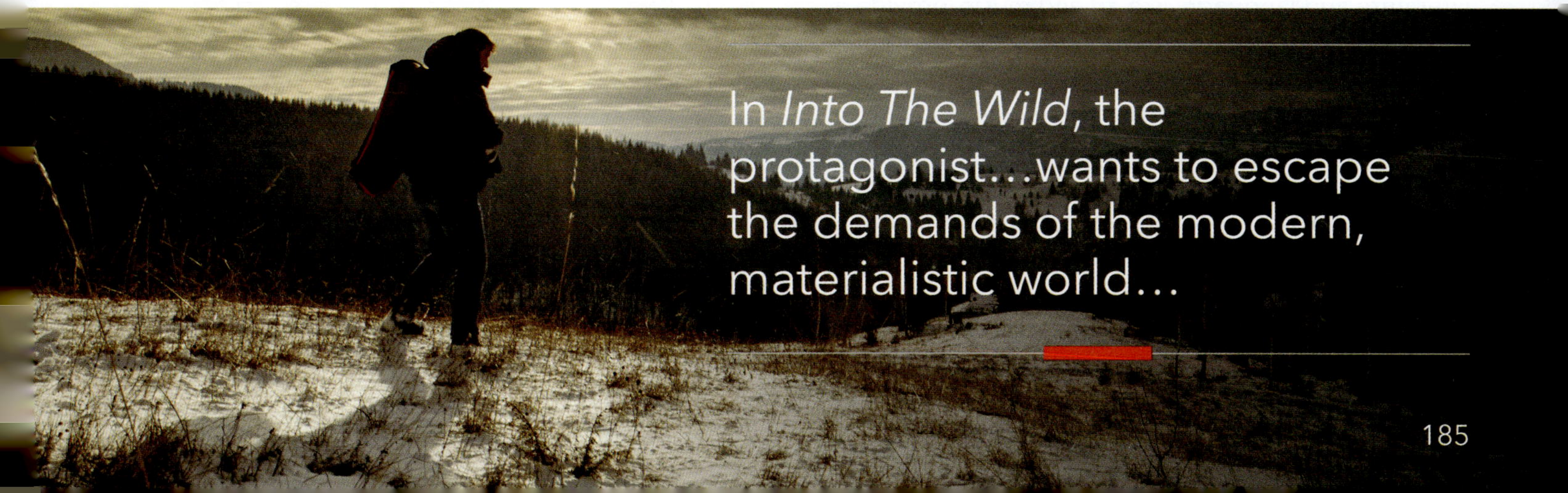

18 Writing about society

In this unit, you will:

- use appropriate stylistic and linguistic terminology, concepts and methods to analyse genre, narrative, point of view and characterisation
- explore how interpretations are influenced by writers' choices and by contexts
- craft creative and controlled interventions in texts
- communicate stylistic analysis of your own creative interventions through clear, well-structured commentaries.

This relates to 'Exploring conflict' in the specification for A Level.

18.1 Literature, society and re-creative writing

18.1.1 Why explore writing about society?

Literature and language, like art and music, provide a reflection of, and a window upon, society. One of the most enjoyable and fascinating aspects of reading a novel is the way in which it provides a view of the world – or, perhaps, deconstructs or reconstructs the world – through a new perspective. Reading literature offers a perpetual means of seeing the world anew, and of exploring different life experiences, across the globe, across time and across realities. Novels are born out of societal moments and contexts.

Authors' ideas grow out of their own experiences of environments, communities and relationships. An author's motivations and themes can't help but be informed by (and are often written in reaction to) the social movements and ideas with which they are surrounded, including scientific and technological progress, and political and religious ideologies. Whether or not a novel overtly engages with society through its themes, it is fundamentally embedded in the social context of its writing, just as readers' interpretations are informed by the social contexts of their readings.

ACTIVITY 1

Exploring society

1 Think about what you understand by the term 'society'. Write down some of the different contexts in which you have encountered the term 'society' (e.g. perhaps to define a community – how small or large? – or perhaps part of the name of a group who share an interest or political stance).
2 Research definitions of society in dictionaries and on the internet. What defining characteristics are mentioned most often? What language does it originally come from? Have its forms and meanings evolved at all over time?
3 How is a concept of society constructed? Think of a particular society: what gives people within that society an impression of community, a bond, a 'togetherness'?

Check your responses in the Ideas section on Cambridge Elevate

18.1.2 Literature and themes of society

This unit will discuss and investigate a range of texts which, through many different means, are thematically concerned with some of the following:

- the individual and their relationship to society
- society and culture
- dominant people, forces and ideas in society
- society, space and place
- society and the family
- how different forms of power influence societal changes
- different kinds of, and feelings about, kinship, community and belonging.

Thinking about how the novel you read explores these themes will enable you to develop a deeper appreciation of different perspectives on society, the influence of society upon the individual, and the role of society in everyday life. Reflecting on these themes will also help you to understand some of the ways in which so much literature resonates so powerfully with the experiences and concerns of readers across time.

ACTIVITY 2

Society in fiction

1. Think of a fictional text you have recently read (other than the set texts for your course!), or a film or TV programme you have recently watched - it could be a novel, short story, comic, a reality TV show, a documentary, an action thriller, etc. What kinds of society were involved?
2. Think of some literary texts you're familiar with that were written in different periods and places. How far and in what ways do you think concepts and types of society have influenced the kinds of literature (e.g. different genres, forms and dominant themes) that have arisen in different eras and across different cultures?

Every act of creative writing is individually and socio-culturally situated - it always comes from an individual and social context. In this way, and others, creative writing thus inevitably *is* writing about society. A literary work also meets and engages with a new and different individual and socio-cultural context in every different instance it is read and interpreted. Just like authors, readers bring to the novel their own experiences, assumptions, beliefs, etc., influenced by the society and culture in which they live, and these interact with the literary work to shape interpretation. Creative writing is fundamentally **interpersonal** and intertextual. The socio-cultural contexts of writing infuse its meanings, just as the socio-cultural contexts of reading shape interpretation of those meanings.

Key terms

interpersonal: between people; existing in the site/relationship between an individual and others

The kinds of approaches and exercises illustrated in this unit are valuable study tools for any novel, whether or not re-creative writing is a means of formally assessing your understanding of that novel. For this reason, some of the extracts used in examples and activities in this unit will be drawn from different sections of the specification, while others will be extracts that you are not expected to have read before.

However, the four novels which will be referred to repeatedly, and used in some of the activities and examples, are Jon Krakauer's *Into the Wild*, Kate Summerscale's *The Suspicions of Mr. Whicher: Or the Murder at Road Hill House*, F. Scott Fitzgerald's *The Great Gatsby* and Khaled Hosseini's *The Kite Runner*. As some of the activities will make reference to some of these key novels that you have not read and studied (you are only likely to be studying one of the four), here is a brief summary of all four of them.

Jon Krakauer's *Into the Wild* tells the story of Chris McCandless, a young American who hiked into the hostile wilderness of Alaska, and whose body was found four months after he set out. The narrative is fairly journalistic. It is based on Krakauer's magazine article on McCandless. The expanded story in the book includes interviews with those who knew or encountered Chris, extracts from Chris's journal, annotations he made in books, and newspaper reports. The book explores, in a lot of depth, what might have happened to him, and how the news of his story, and his end, was taken amongst his family, and amongst American and Alaskan society more widely. The structure of the tale is itself rather rambling, moving backwards (through analepsis) and forwards (through prolepsis) in time, and presenting an array of points of view, as the narrator reports different people's experiences of Chris, and different aspects of his past, his travels and his Alaskan hiking adventure. The story is intertwined with the tales of other travellers, in a broader rumination on the ambitions of solitude, the romantic ideal of living in the wild or escaping from the contemporary world, and other possible motives for Chris's journey – his motives, and the cause of his death, ultimately remaining a mystery.

See 16.2.4 for more on analepsis and prolepsis

Kate Summerscale's *The Suspicions of Mr. Whicher: or the Murder at Road Hill House* is in some ways similar to Krakauer's book, in that it draws upon and cites a lot of historical documentary evidence (including photographs) in telling the tale of a real-life mystery, ultimately unsolved. This mystery, though, is of a murder, in the mid-nineteenth century, of a very young child in his family home. The novel focuses on the investigations of Detective-Inspector Whicher, on his process and evidence, and on the impact the case has on his reputation and on the reputation of the new detective force more generally over the course of half a century. It also explores the broader social and cultural significance of the murder mystery – its influence on literature of the time, and the furore it created around issues such as the sanctity of the family home, and the relationships between the wealthy landowners and their servants.

F. Scott Fitzgerald's *The Great Gatsby* is narrated from the perspective of Nick Carraway. It is set in 1920s America, in what is known as the Jazz Era. The novel explores the moral crisis of post-war America, particularly the fascination with wealth, power, status and pleasure, all of which Jay Gatsby seems to epitomise. The novel traces Nick's initial enchantment with Gatsby and his experiences of Gatsby's mysterious past and frivolous lifestyle, through to his disillusionment with Gatsby and all he stands for – or, to be more precise, with the fact that Gatsby and his society don't seem to stand for anything.

Khaled Hosseini's *The Kite Runner* tells the story of two boys growing up in Kabul, Afghanistan, and explores the impact of brutal racial oppression, war, shame and betrayal on friendships, families and societies. The narrator is Amir, one of the two boys, whose journey we follow from childhood in Kabul, into adulthood and respite in America, before he journeys back into war-ravaged Afghanistan to face his past and the hidden truths that have torn his family and his life apart. It is in some ways a *bildungsroman*, but one with social concerns that run deeper than the life of one boy. Religion and tradition, hierarchy and power, and honour, as a matter of family status and as a matter of personal integrity, lie at the heart of this novel.

See 16.3.1 for more on the bildungsroman

With this basic introduction to all four novels in mind, you should be able to use the full range of texts in this chapter to develop your practice of re-creative writing. If you'd like to learn more about the other three novels you aren't studying, you could also do your own research using material available

'Society exists only as a mental concept; in the real world there are only individuals.'

Oscar Wilde

online (reader reviews are available on the Amazon and Goodreads websites, publishers' marketing descriptions, etc.).

ACTIVITY 3

Themes of society

1 Using the concept of society you developed in Activity 1, write down some notes to describe the different kinds of societies and social contexts that feature in the novel you are studying for this unit. You might start by thinking about the period(s) and location(s) of the novel's settings.

2 Look back at the bullet point list of different themes related to society. Identify which of these themes is explored in the novel you are studying, and try to identify other themes related to society in that novel (which you can then add to the list).

3 Consider the three quotations about society in Texts 18A(a), (b) and (c), voiced from different social contexts and from different political and ideological stances. Then reflect back on the ways in which society is portrayed in the novel you are studying.
   - Which of these quotations most closely corresponds to the views presented in the novel, and how?
   - Which of the three quotations in Text 18A do you believe to be true?

Text 18A

(a)

Society exists only as a mental concept; in the real world there are only individuals.

Oscar Wilde

(b)

He who is unable to live in society, or who has no need because he is sufficient for himself, must be either a beast or a god.

Aristotle, *Politics*, Book 1

(c)

Society does not consist of individuals but expresses the sum of interrelations, the relations within which these individuals stand.

Karl Marx, *Das Capital*

4 Text 18B is from Jane Austen's *Northanger Abbey*, portraying a conversation between the characters Henry Tilney and Miss Morland. How does Tilney view his own society? For example:
   - What does he believe to be his society's core principles and determining principles?
   - What holds society together, in his view?
   - What does he imply is positive and negative about his society?
   - How does his expression convey his evaluation of his society?

Text 18B

Dear Miss Morland, consider the dreadful nature of the suspicions you have entertained. What have you been judging from? Remember the country and the age in which we live. Remember that we are English: that we are Christians. Consult your own understanding, your own sense of the probable, your own observation of what is passing around you. Does our education prepare us for such atrocities? Do our laws connive at them? Could they be perpetrated without being known in a country like this, where social and literary intercourse is on such a footing, where every man is surrounded by a neighbourhood of voluntary spies, and where roads and newspapers lay everything open? Dearest Miss Morland, what ideas have you been admitting?

They had reached the end of the gallery; and with tears of shame she ran off to her own room.

Jane Austen, *Northanger Abbey*

5 Text 18B is used as an **epigraph** at the start of Ian McEwan's *Atonement*, published in 2001. Epigraphs are an example of explicit intertextuality, through which an author calls upon - and positions his/her work in relation to - other texts. If you know *Atonement* and *Northanger Abbey* at all, consider what the use of this epigraph contributes to the themes of the novel. If you don't know the novel(s), think about the implications of lifting these words, penned in around 1803, into a novel published 200 years later. What do you think McEwan might be trying to suggest about society in doing so?

Check your responses in the Ideas section on Cambridge Elevate

18.1.3 What is re-creative writing?

Re-creative writing is a form of creative writing which responds to and intervenes in a text. It alters the original text (called the base text), by changing it or adding to it in some way to evoke new meanings. You can intervene in a text in many different ways: playing with its title, its structure, its genre and audience, its metaphors, the voice of the narrator, and much more. All of this play can be enacted by simple and strategic manipulation of language at different levels – phonology, morphology, graphology, lexis, syntax, semantics and discourse. With a good understanding of language and how it works – how interpretative effects are achieved – you can take an original work and build on it, alter it, complement it or challenge it in ways which reflect your understanding of its themes and your analytical appreciation of the linguistic, stylistic and **narratological** techniques employed which communicate those themes. The process of changing the text, and creating new meanings, entails investigation and understanding of both the ways in which the meanings of the original text are created and the ways in which new meanings can be developed.

Re-creative writing can be experimental and exploratory, playing with the text in an uncontrolled way, or can be targeted and strategic, changing or adding to particular elements of the original text with the intention of evoking specific new interpretative effects. Either approach (experimental or targeted) can complement and elaborate on the meanings of the base text, or can undermine and problematise it. The experimental and targeted approaches can perhaps be best thought of at either end of a line, with lots of approaches falling somewhere in between, exploring the text either through *additive* or *alternative* creative acts. The fun lies in the intervening act itself – the playful collaboration with the original author, and the creativity involved – and in what that process reveals about the workings of texts and the creation of meanings.

As well as a line of interventionist approaches, from 'targeted' to 'experimental', we can perhaps think of a scale of intervention acts, from 'subtle', perhaps only changing one small aspect of a text, such as the title, or the kinds of adjectives used, to more 'radical' interventions, perhaps recasting the entire text in a different genre or form.

Key terms

epigraph: in literature, a text or extract from a text used at the beginning of a different literary text or at the beginning of a section of that text

narratological: relating to narrative, its characteristics, features, functions, etc. (e.g. plot, character, narration, tellability)

See 24.4.1 for more on fanfiction

The effects of re-creative interventions are of course yet another dimension, but one which doesn't have a simple relationship to either of the scales in Figure 18A. Changes made in any of the quadrants of Figure 18A can have either subtle or radical effects, depending on the nature of the original and re-cast text, and the writer's and reader's context.

Figure 18A

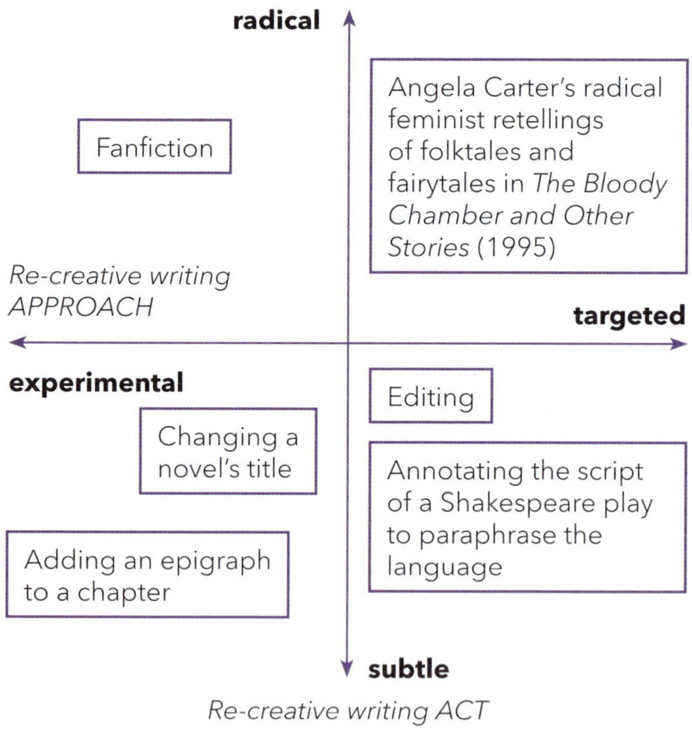

Source: private data

ACTIVITY 4

Kinds of re-creativity

1 Let's start by thinking about ways of describing the process and relationship between a re-creative act and the base text. Can a re-creative act be something which is *done to* the base text, *done with* it, *made with* it, or *performed upon* it? Can you think of any other appropriate verbs and prepositions? Try to think through the connotations of different verbs and prepositions, using different contexts (e.g. compare 'a surgical act is *performed upon* a body', and 'a religious blessing is *performed upon* a congregation'). What does each suggest about the nature of the process?

2 Now let's think about the effects different kinds of re-creative acts can have upon the base text. Consider and compare the connotations of the following verbs, which can be used to express these effects:

- change
- intervene
- transform
- counter
- complement
- supplement
- augment
- elaborate
- distort.

How do the terms relate to each other? Which are positive and which are negative? Which overlap in their meaning? Are any directly opposed?

Check your responses in the Ideas section on Cambridge Elevate

The act of reflection upon these terms ties into a key part of what re-creative writing involves - exploration of the ways in which linguistic choices evoke interpretations of **presuppositions**, preferences, orientations, arguments, rationales and beliefs about the subject. For example, thinking about re-creative writing as something which is enacted upon a text entails perception of the base text as an object, probably in a fixed state, and available to be passively subjected to active processes by other agents (editors editing, readers reading and interpreting, writers rewriting), while the notion of re-creative writing as something which is performed suggests an act which is deliberate, motivated, considered and artful.

One way of re-creatively intervening in a text is to add to it in some way. For example, you can create an additional description of a key event in the plot, perhaps a description in the voice of a particular character whose perspective wasn't provided in the original. You can provide a fuller narration of a scene which was only briefly mentioned, in summary form, in the original. You can construct a character's response to an event or revelation where none was given. There are many options, and many opportunities, for writing into a text - for inserting, supplementing and embellishing the original. This unit will help you to explore the different kinds of gaps and affordances in a text, sections left un- (or under-) developed by the author, which can provide fruitful opportunities for your own re-creative writing.

18.1.4 Exploring the relationship between creativity, analysis and critical commentary

A re-creative intervention in a text is a productive, interpretative and analytical act all in one. A commentary on the re-creative piece holds a mirror up to that act. A commentary presents an explicit analysis of the stylistic choices made in the process of creative composition of re-writing, and discusses the new meanings and interpretations evoked by those choices. It is an opportunity to clearly communicate what re-creative decisions have been made and why - what insights about the base text informed the re-creative strategies, and what interpretative effects are intended - thereby reflecting on the relationships between genre, context, language and meaning in both the base text and the new writing. The re-creative writing is the 'doing', and the commentary is the explanation of 'what you did' and 'why', but both parts involve in-depth analysis and understanding of text and meaning.

Key terms

presupposition: an implied precondition or assumption

Watch tutorial video, Recreative Writing, on Cambridge Elevate

18.2 Re-creative writing, from the exploratory and experimental to the targeted and strategic

This section will discuss how to do different kinds of re-creative writing, introducing a range of (more) subtle and (more) radical additive and alternative re-creative writing acts as a means of gaining a deeper understanding of a novel, and as a means of demonstrating that understanding. We will begin with some more experimental and exploratory activities – the kind of re-creative writing acts that can be plotted on the left-hand side of Figure 18A. Though experimental re-creative writings tasks are rarely the kinds of exercises that are used for formally assessing your understanding of texts, these kinds of re-creative acts offer interesting, fun and fruitful ways of exploring texts, and enable you to gain deeper and richer understanding of their themes and workings. As this section progresses, it will focus more and more on targeted and strategic kinds of re-creative writing (the kind of acts that can be plotted on the right side of the chart), which are supported by more experimental interventions and the kinds of knowledge and understanding you can gain from them. All of these acts involve play with language at different levels – from the minutiae of punctuation up to discourse types and genres. Practising these acts of intervention will help you to think about literature in new ways. It will help you to develop your skills in analysing the relationships between linguistic expression and interpretative effect. This analytical understanding will, in turn, enable you to manage those relationships between language and interpretation tactically and strategically, and to manipulate meaning yourself, in your own re-creative compositions and critical commentary.

18.2.1 Re-framing texts: beginning re-creative writing through creatively rewriting beginnings

ACTIVITY 5

En-/re-titling *Frankenstein*

In Unit 16, you explored some of the titles of the key texts for that section. In this exercise, we are going to pick up on some of that work, and extend it, through re-creative writing. Let's start by thinking about the connotations and associations of the parts and whole of the original full title of Mary Shelley's novel, *Frankenstein; or the Modern Prometheus*.

a Did you have to research who Prometheus was? What does Shelley's re-creative use of the myth of Prometheus here suggest to you about the character of Frankenstein, and about the likely plot or themes of the novel?

b What subtle changes in effect are created if we cut the conjunction 'or' and alter the order of the title to *The Modern Prometheus: Frankenstein*?

c Consider what is evoked by Shelley's use of the adjective 'modern' in this context. Compare what is suggested by the title with and without this word. What other adjectives could you replace it with, and what might these alternatives suggest about the character and the story?

d A fairly common mistake made by those discussing this novel – even those who are very familiar with it – is to refer to the creature as Frankenstein, when Frankenstein is actually the name of his creator.
  - How far do you think the choice of title propels this confusion?
  - How far do you think the nature of the name Frankenstein contributes to this, and why?
  - How would the implications of the title, and of the novel, be changed if the title was *Frankenstein's Creature*, or just *The Creature* (which is how the character is most often referred to)?

Check your responses in the Ideas section on Cambridge Elevate

There are many other ways of intervening in and altering this title such as:

- What happens to its available interpretative impressions if, for example, none of the words are capitalised?
- What if we changed the myth referred to here, and cast Frankenstein in the light of a different Greek legend (Icarus, for example)? Or what if we changed the intertextual reference altogether, and used a figure from a different cultural background?
- Consider what would be 'done to' the novel if it was titled with the name of a different character, perhaps *Elizabeth* (Frankenstein's love interest), or *Walton* (the sea-faring person

to whom Frankenstein tells his story, and the over-arching narrator).

- What if the title was entirely different – not the name of the protagonist, or any character, but a place mentioned in the novel, or an abstract concept?

You can probably think of other ways of changing the title, too. Any change in a title will have an effect, subtle or radical, in shaping the reader's expectations, and altering the balance of what is foregrounded and backgrounded in the novel.

We have now laboured over and reworked this title extensively (though nowhere near exhaustively), playing with grammatical and semantic aspects like adjectives and word order, and discourse features such as intertextual choices (e.g. the myth of Prometheus). We have been thinking about the linguistic means by which a title is made meaningful, and re-creatively playing with some of those means. This intervention process can change and enhance your understanding of a title and novel – and of the relationship between the two – in terms of foregrounded themes and the generation of meaning. It also illustrates how even subtle and seemingly small linguistic choices can have a significant impact upon interpretation.

ACTIVITY 6

Texts and titles

a Apply some of the questions in Activity 5 to the titles of the texts by Summerscale and Fitzgerald. For example, does the 'or' in Shelley's title function in the same way as the 'or' in *The Suspicions of Mr. Whicher: or the Murder at Road Hill House*? What is evoked by the adjective 'Great' in Fitzgerald's title? Reflect on what the interventions you make reveal to you about the workings of the original titles. Here are all four titles again, for reference:

- Jon Krakauer, *Into the Wild*
- Kate Summerscale, *The Suspicions of Mr. Whicher: or the Murder at Road Hill House*
- F. Scott Fitzgerald, *The Great Gatsby*
- Khaled Hosseini, *The Kite Runner.*

b Kate Summerscale's novel has a different title for its American edition: *The Suspicions of Mr. Whicher: A Shocking Murder and the Undoing of a Great Victorian Detective*. The jacket is quite different too – you can see it if you search for this title online. How does this alternative title frame the text differently, and why do you think the title might have been altered in this way for the American market?

Titles are **paratextual features** – textual matter, additional to the body of the text itself, which can serve a variety of functions, from categorising and marketing the text (in the case of paratextual features such as book jackets and blurbs, designed to entice a particular audience, a subset of readers), to opening and introducing or closing and concluding it (performed by introductions, forewords, prologues, prefaces and author's notes, afterwords and other means), to structuring it and in some way guiding or assisting readers through it (as in the case of chapter numbering, titles and epigraphs, footnotes and so on). All of these devices frame the text in some way.

Key terms

paratextual features: textual matter additional to the body of the text which serves to make that text accessible, name and structure the text and its parts, and/or guide the reader

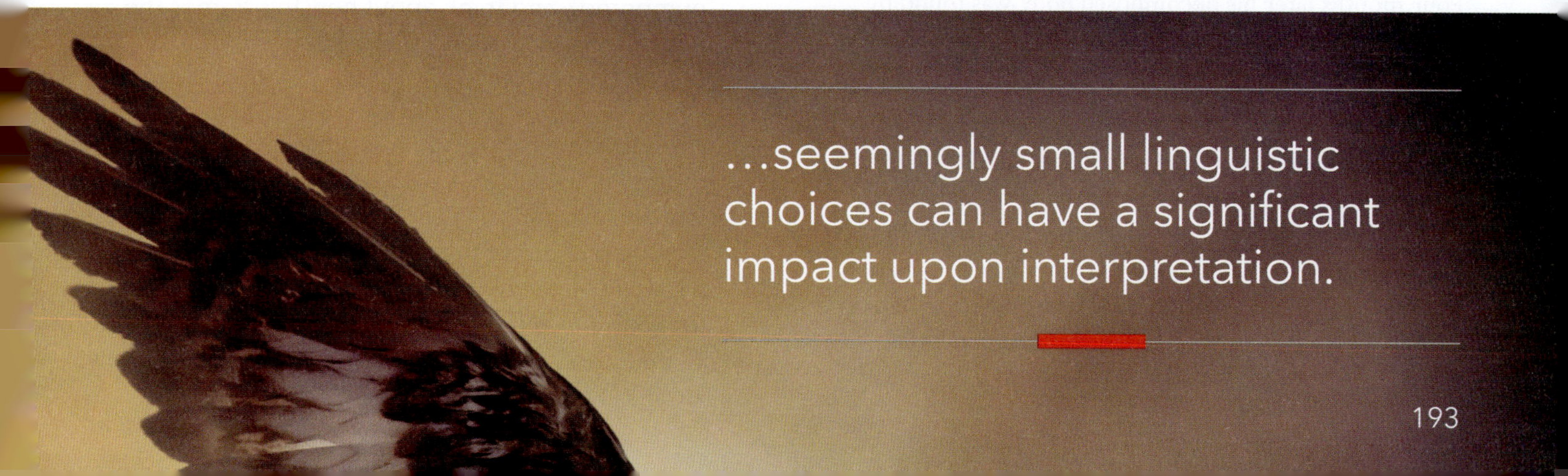

You might recall Rabinowitz's argument that openings (titles, first lines, etc.) occupy a privileged position with respect to their guiding and foregrounding functions. Here we are going to explore the openings of novels in more depth, through some re-creative gestures, and with that foregrounding in mind. Framing texts raise some tricky and intriguing questions for debate. For example, where do we draw the line between the opening paratextual material and the beginning of the novel – at what point does the novel begin? Is the voice in the opening framing sections that of the author, or the narrator? Are the author and the narrator distinct in these kinds of texts? Indeed, could the narrator in a text such as Krakauer's even be considered to be close to a character in some ways? Playing with the various ways in which a text is framed can highlight the interesting discourse relationships between author and reader, author and implied author, implied author and reader, narrator and reader, and so on, and can reveal a lot about a novel's workings, its themes and the foregrounded and backgrounded layers of meanings the novel offers to the reader.

See 16.2.8 for more on Rabinowitz's argument

See 16.2.2 for more on discourse relationships

Text 18C contains extracts from the 'Author's note' of Krakauer's *Into the Wild*. This 'Author's note' is surprising in that it reveals the death of the main 'character' in the first paragraph, quashing a lot of the book's capacity for suspense.

Text 18C

In April 1992, a young man ... hitchhiked to Alaska and walked alone into the wilderness north of Mt. McKinley. Four months later his decomposed body was found by ... moose hunters ... His name [was] Christopher Johnson McCandless ...

I spent more than a year retracing the convoluted path that led to his death in the Alaska taiga, chasing down details of his peregrinations ... In trying to understand McCandless, I ... came to reflect on other, larger subjects ... the grip wilderness has on the American imagination, the allure high-risk activities hold for young men of a certain mind, the complicated, highly charged bond that exists between fathers and sons. The result of this meandering inquiry is the book now before you.

... My convictions should be apparent soon enough, but I will leave it to the reader to form his or her own opinion of Chris McCandless.

Source: Jon Krakauer, *Into the Wild*, Author's note

Part of Krakauer's intention here seems to be to suggest that this will not be a conventional narrative along the lines of a hero's journey, with the climax being a tragic death, but rather a 'meandering' report of an investigation into this death, and into the aspects of Chris's existence that led up to it. In framing the book in this way, Krakauer is managing the reader's expectations regarding the slightly unconventional structure and status of the text.

Krakauer also situates McCandless' fate within a broader social context. By associating McCandless' choices with escapist dreams and familial relationships that are common to society at large, Krakauer offers up a possible personal connection between the reader and McCandless. By explicitly inviting the reader to form his or her own opinion of McCandless, Krakauer implicitly asks the reader to approach the book with a questioning and reflective reading strategy. At the same time, this framing will most likely already have evoked not only curiosity about, but also some empathy with, McCandless, and so has already made some effort to shape the reader's opinion, despite claiming to 'leave it to' the reader.

ACTIVITY 7

Analysing authors' introductions

Now read the extracts from the 'Introduction' of Summerscale's novel in Text 18D (with sentences numbered), and think about how this frames the ensuing book, working through questions a–d.

Text 18D

(1) This is the story of a murder committed in an English country house in 1860, perhaps the most disturbing murder of its time. (2) The search for the killer threatened the career of one of the first and greatest detectives, inspired a 'detective-fever' throughout England, and set the course of detective fiction. (3) For the family of the victim, it was a murder of unusual horror, which threw

suspicion on almost everyone within the house. (4) For the country as a whole, [it] became a kind of myth – a dark fable about the Victorian family and the dangers of detection … (5) The officer who investigated the murder [was] Detective-Inspector Jonathan Whicher … (6) For as long as the crime went unsolved, the inhabitants of Road Hill House were cast variously as suspects, conspirators, victims. (7) The whole of the secret that Whicher guessed at did not emerge until many years after all of them had died.

Source: Kate Summerscale, *The Suspicions of Mr. Whicher: or the Murder at Road Hill House*, Introduction

a What are your interpretative impressions of Text 18D? What is it about, and what do you think the author thinks and feels about the subject?

b What impact does the opening of Text 18D have on your expectations of the following content of the book (in terms of themes, context and style)? Note down any words and associations that come to mind.

c What information does Summerscale communicate in Text 18D? There are often two or three facts presented within each sentence. Try to create a bullet point list all of these facts, starting with:

- a murder took place
- it took place in an English country house
- it took place in 1860
- this murder is the main subject of the story.

d What do you observe about Summerscale's style of expression in Text 18D? Write some notes on the different language features you see and, crucially, think about how each feature contributes to your interpretative impressions. You might like to think about the following questions (which engage with various levels of language - see if you can identify which questions relate to which levels).

- How are the sentences structured? Are there any common patterns? If there are, can you describe the grammatical structures involved? How do these patterns (and deviations from these patterns) contribute to the effect of Text 18D?
- What kind of evaluative language is used to express opinion (such as evaluative adjectives, modality, etc.)?
- What verbs are used? What do these verbs suggest?
- What kinds of processes are portrayed?
- Are there any overt or covert metaphors in Text 18D?
- Are there any other patterns in Text 18D? Are words or phrases repeated? Is there any alliteration? What words or concepts are linked and associated by this repetition?
- Is it the author who is 'speaking' here, or a narrator, distinct from the author?

Now for your first wholesale stylistic intervention in a short stretch of text. Using your responses to Activity 7 to guide you, try out the simple (and simplifying) transformation in Activity 8.

Check your responses in the Ideas section on Cambridge Elevate

ACTIVITY 8

Changing authors' introductions

a Re-creatively adapt Text 18D from Summerscale's 'Introduction', transforming it and reducing it into a more objective summary of the details you identified in Activity 7c. Aim to present only the bare facts in a simple, unbiased way, and without sensationalising or dramatising them.

b Review your rewritten paragraph, and compare it to the original. In doing so, do you notice anything more about what details and what stylistics features are present in the base text, and how the language of the paragraph is functioning to evoke particular interpretative effects? Make a note of anything your comparison reveals.

c What impact do your changes have on the ways in which the 'Introduction' shapes the framing of the book if it replaced the base text, Text 18D? How would your expectations be different from those you noted in Activity 7b?

Check your responses in the Ideas section on Cambridge Elevate

Working with the text as it stands, we can make alternative moves by switching around the sections of the text, changing the order of narration and the order in which the events of the plot are revealed, and we can make additive moves, adding sections into the structure of the text, perhaps bridging two events, or adding a different beginning or ending. All of these moves involve a consideration of the relationship between the story and the narrative discourse, and what the author has chosen to present as central events and as secondary events. As with all textual intervention, the effects can be subtle or radical. We'll come back to these textual intervention strategies, but for now let's briefly explore some of the effects of alternative beginnings.

See 18.2.3 for more on textual intervention strategies

ACTIVITY 9

Changing chapter openings

The Kite Runner opens with the date 'December 2001', and begins with the words shown in Text 18E.

Text 18E

I became what I am today at the age of twelve, on a frigid overcast day in the winter of 1975. I remember the precise moment, crouching behind a crumbling mud wall, peeking into the alley near the frozen creek. That was a long time ago, but it's wrong what they say about the past, I've learned, about how you can bury it. Because the past claws its way out. Looking back now, I realize I have been peeking into that deserted alley for the last twenty-six years.

Source: Khaled Hosseini, *The Kite Runner*, Chapter 1

Consider the following questions.

1 What is the function of the opening of a novel? What might be the author's priorities?
2 On the basis of this opening, do you expect the event in the alley that day in 1975 to be the main 'complicating action' of the narrative (in Labov's terms)?
3 Which of Labov's narrative categories do you feel are present in this chapter opening, and to what extent?
4 What impact do you think this opening has/had on your expectations of the rest of the novel (in terms of its historical context, tone, the narrator's character, themes, genre, style, etc.)?
5 Intervene in Text 18E to cancel out this opening: the novel now begins with Chapter 2. Chapter 2 opens with 'When we were children, Hassan and I used to climb the poplar trees in the driveway of my father's house and annoy the neighbours by reflecting sunlight into their homes with a shard of mirror' (Hosseini, *The Kite Runner*, p.3). It goes on to describe some of the shared childhood experiences of Amir and Hassan, but also to begin to reveal their very different statuses in society and in their shared household due to their racial differences. The novel then predominantly follows events chronologically, from this point onwards to the moment in the alleyway in 1975, and then on beyond this. How would your expectations of the novel be different without the ominous opening of the original Chapter 1 and its reference to these future events, and with Chapter 2 instead being the first chapter you encounter?

This novel could be said to begin ***in medias res***, in that the narrative begins at a point much later than the first plot event of the novel. This opening is particularly interesting in that it starts from a deictic centre in 2001, then analeptically reflects back on a moment in 1975, in relation to that moment in 2001, and all of this is through **retrospective narration** (narration of events from some point in their future), though we don't know from what point. The events referred to in 1975 and 2001 are both significant turning points in Amir's life, and start new phases of the narrative: they are both beginnings, in some ways, and are brought together to form the beginning of the narration, but neither is the beginning of the story.

Key terms

in medias res: a Latin phrase meaning 'in the midst of things', used in narratology to describe a story which starts somewhere in the middle of the chronological plot sequence, then moves back to the beginning and progresses through the starting point to the later plot points

retrospective narration: telling the story in the past tense from a point after the events have happened

So far, you have looked in a lot of detail at the framings and openings of texts. In doing so, you have begun to play with some of the language used in titles, prologues and chapter openings. You have investigated how meaning is made across all of the language levels within these kinds of structural framing devices. In doing the activities, you have experimented with a wide range of ways you can creatively recast even the smallest of phrases to help expose and analyse its workings.

These activities have been experimental and exploratory, testing out textual changes to see what effects would be created, without particular strategies and priorities in mind. They have furthered your understanding of aspects of the key texts, and of others. Now that you've had some playful practice with these kinds of re-creative intervention, Section 18.2.2 will introduce more strategic and targeted kinds (though still incorporating the experimental and exploratory). As well as some of the terms and concepts introduced in the previous Part 2 units, we will be engaging, quite systematically, with all of the elements of language use discussed in Units 6 to 11 of Part 1 of this book (all 6 levels) and so if you need to, now would be a good time to revise those Part 1 units.

18.2.2 Reviewing characters and narrators: developing re-creative writing through strategic and targeted responses

Rewriting tasks on this specification require you to transform a base text (a small section from a novel) through re-creatively writing a different (and shorter) version of that section through the eyes of a particular character. This kind of task is much more targeted than the experimental kinds of re-creative writing we have predominantly practised so far, in that it requires you to be able to demonstrate a good understanding of the events and relationships in the novel, and to have a sensitive appreciation of characterisation. Though the task may focus you on a specific section, sometimes just a few paragraphs or pages, you will need to draw on your insights and awareness of many other sections of the novel, and your interpretation of the novel as a whole, if you want to create a really good piece of re-creative writing.

You will also need to draw on many of the linguistic, stylistic and narratological tools and concepts you have studied in previous units, including:

- point of view and types of narration
- verb processes
- modality
- narratorial reliability
- tellability
- narrative structures
- perceptual dimensions and deixis
- focus, themes and motifs
- characterisation.

See 16.4 for more on point of view and types of narration

See 16.4.2 for more on modality

See 16.4.3 for more on narratorial reliability

See 16.2.3 for more on narrative structures

See 16.2.3 and 16.4 for more on perceptual dimensions and deixis

See 16.2.6 for more on focus, themes and motifs

See 16.3.1 for more on characterisation

In this section, we will bring these tools and concepts together, and expand this toolkit, to explore characterisation and narration through rewriting.

The intervention task requires you to demonstrate both stylistic expertise and creative flair in your ability to recast a base text. You need to stay within the parameters of the base text (so need to recognise and adhere to the scope of the narrative moment); write in an appropriate style for the task, and do so consistently; and show creativity and originality in your approach to the recasting.

In order to be able to perform this kind of re-creative writing task well, you have to develop some careful strategies for studying the text and for your process of re-creative composition. There are three key areas you need to focus on, each of which can be broken down into two sub-points, as shown in Figure 18B.

Figure 18B

CHARACTERISATION	attitude and behaviour
	style of expression
NARRATIVE	the narrative moment
	themes and motifs
DISCOURSE	the genre/discourse type
	audience

These key areas are explained in more detail in section 18.2.3.

18.2.3 Re-creative writing and characterisation

The re-creative writing task will ask you to write something from the perspective of a particular character. To do this, you need to understand who that character is, and how she/he is constructed in the novel. A character is developed through the details and clues in the text and the assumptions we, as readers, add to these details to fill in gaps. A character's attitudes to others and to their context - her/his hopes, beliefs, likes and dislikes, fears and desires - are a central aspect of what brings him or her to life. Characters' behaviour also contributes significantly to their characterisation, from their manner of moving around (e.g. body language), to their responses to other people, to the kinds of actions and activities they are most often represented as doing. In a way, a character's behaviour is actually an expression of his or her attitude (let's go with 'her', for the moment), though the more complex a character is, the more likely that she will not have one single manner of thinking or being: psychologically realistic characters are paradoxical in the way that most humans are, and grow and change over time. A reader's impressions of a character are also contributed to by other characters' attitudes and behaviour towards that character, as well as descriptions of her. Though these descriptions should not always be assumed to be reliable even when from a narrator, they do help us build up an impression of the character.

See Figure 16C for more on the process of characterisation

See 16.3.5 for more on body language

We draw a lot of inferences about characters based on the way their speech and behaviour is portrayed. This involves empathy, deduction, extrapolation and any knowledge or assumptions we have about human psychology (and this is part of what makes literary study so interesting and valuable). It's important to keep in mind that in the real world, with respect to the people we interact with, we actually aren't as presumptuous about what deeper things certain behaviours or utterances might signify, or as confident in our psychological analysis and insight, as we are with fictional characters. Our interpretation of characters works through a kind of simplified version of reality because of the discourse relationship between the author and reader that exists behind the character's behaviour. We assume that the text is designed to guide our interpretation - that the author is trying to communicate to us things about the character - and we make assumptions based on our schema (or what we expect the author expects our schema to be).

Characters express their attitudes through their style of language use. One character may tend to interrupt others, and use long, complex sentences with long, Latinate words. Is she highly educated? Does she naturally talk in a very articulate and elevated style, or is this a style she performs to impress or intimidate people, or to fit in with others around her? She may refer to herself quite a lot, and the topics she chooses to discuss may be self-centred. She might talk a lot about her own actions and behaviour. She might use a lot of modal language to complain about her situation or to express her desires or opinions.

Alternatively, she might express her opinions as facts, in categorical assertions without any modal qualification. She may tend to use adjectives from a particular semantic field such as nature, or may often use metaphors relating to the sea, or the military, and so on. A character's manner of expression may be fairly consistent, or it may change subtly or dramatically depending on their situation and who they are interacting with. All of these aspects of expression, and more, contribute to characterisation.

See 16.3.4 for more on personal vocabulary

There are three important points to remember in terms of characterisation:

1 Some re-creative writing tasks merely require you to recast the episode in question through the perspective of a different character, without specifying a particular discourse type, genre or audience. In such circumstances, the manner of description should be prose narration (as in the case of the base text) as if this were to be an insert in the novel, with the same general readership in mind.

2 Re-creative writing tasks will ask you to transform the text by recasting it either through the perspective of a character that is explicitly mentioned in the base text (an **included participant**) or through the perspective of a character not explicitly mentioned but assumed or inferred to be there (an **excluded participant**). For example, in text 18D, we can say that Mr Whicher is an included participant whilst the butler, servants and other staff at Road Hill House are excluded, as they are not explicitly mentioned but their presence in the fictional world can be assumed. Sometimes included participants are major characters and appear throughout the novel; other included participants have little presence in the novel, for example, they may only appear for a few pages, and not interact much with other characters. Moutot in *The Suspicions of Mr Whicher* is one of these latter types, as are Assef's childhood friends Wali and Kamal in *The Kite Runner*, and Mr Sloane and Mr Wilson in *The Great Gatsby*, and as are many of Krakauer's interviewees in his book. Intervention tasks involving more marginal characters or excluded participants require more original creativity from you than ones with major included participants. There is less material in the base text from which to flesh out marginalised or excluded participants, and so you will have to do more 'gap-filling'. On the other hand, this also gives you a little more freedom!

3 Less commonly, a re-creative writing task might ask you to transform a base text from the perspective of first-person homodiegetic character-narrator to the perspective of a third-person heterodiegetic narrator, or vice versa. This presents slightly different challenges, as you have no character to provide you with a voice. You'll often be given no restriction or guidance as to whether, if you are to relocate the narration from a homodiegetic to a heterodiegetic position, the new narration is internal (e.g. omniscient) or external – this might be left up to you to choose. However, changing the point of view from a first-person homodiegetic narration to a third-person heterodiegetic narration, for example, isn't simply a matter of changing all first-person pronouns to third-person pronouns. The deictic centre of the text needs to be shifted entirely, so all language directly related to that point of view, including temporal and spatial deixis, needs to be re-anchored to the new deictic centre. Similarly, all evaluative language needs to be expressed at one remove. We'll explore some of these issues in Activities 10–12.

Key terms

included participant: a character who is explicitly mentioned in the text and speaks or is spoken to, or about

excluded participant: a character who is not explicitly mentioned in a text and must be constructed through inference

Re-creative writing tasks test your ability to create an imaginative response, carefully managing the dual aims of drawing on the base text but also developing something original. The response needs to be stylistically consistent – that is, a character's or narrator's voice should be coherent throughout your composition. The response must also have a clear and direct relationship to the base text: it should demonstrate thorough engagement with the base text's content and style. Each of these aspects of the task involves developing a good understanding of your novel's characters, themes and style, and developing your own stylistic skill through practice in carefully controlled creative compositions.

ACTIVITY 10

From character studies to re-creative characterisation

This activity is a step-by-step character study. Start by choosing a fairly prominent character from the key text that you're studying for this unit.

See 16.3.1 for more on characterisation and tracking characters

1. One of the first steps in studying a character is to locate them in the novel - identify all of the sections of text in which they appear or are referred to by the narrator or other characters. Do this now for your chosen character; make a list.
2. Read through the sections in your list (or perhaps just a few representative sections), and make some notes about the impressions you get of the character in those sections.
3. Map out of some details about your character's relationships with others: create a 'relationship tree' - like a family tree, but involving everyone that character socially interacts with. For every interconnecting branch you draw between your character and another, try to add a few details about the relationship or social interaction.
4. If you were being interviewed by a journalist about the character, could you respond to the following questions? If so, what would you say?
   - What does he/she believe in?
   - What are his/her priorities?
   - What are his/her strengths?
   - What are his/her weaknesses?
5. There are lots of activities you can do to develop your understanding of a character. Here are three fairly straightforward and popular methods:
   - Create a Facebook profile for the character
   - Write the character's CV and personal statement
   - Put together a few pages of a scrapbook of memories for the character - what kinds of things would go in there?

   Choose one of these activities and complete it for your character.

The 'Prologue' opening Kate Summerscale's *The Suspicions of Mr. Whicher* describes Paddington Station, and Mr Whicher's arrest there, in the second class carriage of a train, of a criminal called Louisa Moutot. Text 18F contains extracts from this 'Prologue'.

Text 18F

At this terminus … he apprehended a stout, blotchy woman of about forty [on] a Great Western train, with the words: 'Your name, I think, is Moutot.' … When Whicher captured Moutot … he noticed that she was busying her arms beneath her cloak. He seized her wrists and turned up the stolen bracelet …

Whicher, at forty-five, was the doyen of the Metropolitan force – 'the prince of detectives', said a colleague. He was a stout, scuffed man with a delicate manner, 'shorter and thicker-set' than his fellow officers, Dickens observed, and possessed of 'a reserved and thoughtful air, as if he were engaged in deep arithmetical calculations'. His face was pitted with smallpox scars. William Henry Wills, Dickens' deputy at his magazine *Household Words*, saw Whicher in action in 1850. His account of what he witnessed was the first published description of Whicher, indeed of any English detective.

Kate Summerscale, *The Suspicions of Mr Whicher: or the Murder at Road Hill House*, Prologue

Imagine you are given the re-creative writing task in Figure 18C.

Figure 18C

Recast the details into the account of the detective that Louisa Moutot gives to a fellow prisoner while in prison following her conviction for fraud. In your transformation you should consider:

- Louisa Moutot's impressions of Mr Whicher
- her attitudes to 'the detective force'.

The base text needs investigating in two ways: firstly, looking for useful and relevant information from which you can build an impression of Moutot; and secondly, looking for useful and relevant details about Whicher and the detective force which you might want to incorporate into your re-creative composition. If this is the novel you are studying for this unit, you can read the 'Prologue' as a whole. If not, you are not actually at a disadvantage in this task, as the 'Prologue' doesn't give you a great deal to go on with respect to the character of Moutot, and she is never mentioned again in the book. You are given a few details about her exploits (her tactics in gaining others' trust by pretending to be wealthy and upper class, exactly where she was caught, etc.), but you aren't given so much as a word from Moutot's mouth or a thought from her mind to work with. You would therefore have quite a bit of work to do 'fleshing out' Moutot into a 'rounded' character drawing on minimal textual cues, and thus have some creative freedom in doing so. The 'Prologue' also provides little information about Whicher – only that quoted in Text 18F.

See 16.3.2 for more on characterisation

With respect to Louisa Moutot's impressions of Mr Whicher, we can infer some details about Moutot on the basis of Text 18F. She is described as 'a stout, blotchy woman of about forty'. Her appearance would probably be more likely to be incorporated into a narration from a perspective other than her own, or, at least, if she was to describe her own appearance in this context (to prisoners who could probably see what she looked like for themselves), there would be some other communicative purpose (e.g. conveying how she thought she must have appeared to Whicher). Whicher's appearance, as described in the final paragraph of Text 18F, is more likely to be the focus than hers, given the brief of the task.

Moutot is also described in the full base text of the Prologue as a 'notorious fraudster'. We might assume, based on crude stereotypes of jewellery thieves, that she is not upper class. It would seem obvious that she does not have a strong sense of justice or respect for the law. The further description of Moutot as an 'up-to-the-minute urban criminal' and as 'a mistress of … twisty deceits' suggests she is intelligent, that she quickly adapts her methods to the changing opportunities in her environment, and that she is skilful in exploiting the context of the busy city for her crimes. She must know London and its workings well. However, what makes this task particularly difficult is that Moutot is a woman of multiple identities. She is capable of impersonating someone with a good education and manners (hence her successful swindling of the jewellers), and she is adept with lots of other disguises (including disguising herself as a man). Her choice to travel in a second class carriage may suggest a degree of cautious prudence in managing her stolen money, or perhaps a desire not to draw attention to herself, and/or remain in a context where she can be more natural (e.g. not impersonating someone wealthy and, probably, upper class). The composure, discretion and control she needs for her fraudulent escapades is not consistent, however: she was apparently caught partially due to her 'busying her arms beneath her cloak', perhaps trying to secure or keep concealed her jewels, maybe relishing wearing them, or perhaps merely reassuring herself of their presence.

With some of this in mind, we could perhaps conjecture that Moutot would quickly adapt herself to her environment in prison, and try to work its opportunities to her advantage. She would want to befriend her fellow prisoners, and in doing so she would want to convey that they have a lot in common and are on the same side. Using expressions similar to that of the other criminals would help her cause so, stereotyping again, perhaps using a schema that draws on Dickens' Victorian urban criminals, we could assume a cockney accent and dialect might work well, but you may want to consider how far the name 'Moutot' suggests French origins, and possibly a French accent. Moutot might want to impress them, perhaps through boasting about her crimes, or perhaps through being able to brag about detective Whicher, who was becoming quite notorious himself, it seems, given what the passage tells us about Dickens' writing of him. Also, we mustn't lose sight of the focus of the task: Moutot giving a description of Whicher to a fellow prisoner, and so the second stage of investigating the base text should explore the portrayal of the detective.

There are many other aspects we could discuss here, such as the options with regard to narration. It could be a written account, or an oral account – the task doesn't stipulate this. Logically, access to writing materials would be limited in prison, and the lower classes of that era were less likely to be able to read, so an oral account might be more fitting, but you can choose, as long as you acknowledge and explain your choice in your commentary. Let's assume for now that you choose to represent an oral account. What does this leave you to consider?

Say, for example, you want to represent Moutot's voice using a cockney accent (and assuming you can mimic phonetic spelling a little to do this, with enough familiarity with the region's accents). Are you going to narrate from Moutot's perspective through direct speech alone? Could the passage be narrated through a first-person homodiegetic narration from her viewpoint, with a mix of direct speech and other narrative elements (including, for example, report of her fellow prisoners' reactions, her own thoughts, etc.)? Might a heterodiegetic internal narration work, in the third person but with access to her thoughts and still presenting her speech directly? These are just a few things to think about, and some suggestions about how to start going about a task like this. More often, you will have a fuller character to work with (or no character at all), avoiding some of these complexities, but tasks like this one on Moutot require both inventiveness and a deep consideration of narratological and stylistic issues.

One avenue for further research, if you are interested, might be to investigate the ways in which Dickens re-creatively cast Whicher in at least two of his works of fiction, as Inspector Bucket in *Bleak House*, and as Sergeant Witchem in 'The Detective Police', a short story (which can be found in full online). You could compare the re-creative versions of Whicher to the real-life observations he reported in his article 'On Duty with Inspector Field', in the journal he edited, *Household Words*.

For further information access the Dickens Journals Online via Cambridge Elevate

ACTIVITY 11

Re-creative voicing

Using the guidance and suggestions above for support, carry out the re-creative writing task on Moutot in Figure 18C. Write 300 words of Moutot describing Whicher to a fellow prisoner while in prison following her conviction for fraud, giving consideration to her impressions of Mr Whicher and her attitudes to 'the detective force'.

Check your responses in the Ideas section on Cambridge Elevate

In Activity 11 you re-creatively constructed a transformed text from the perspective of a character who did not have a voice in the base text. In Activity 7 you investigated Summerscale's point of view on her material, and her style of expression, in Text 18D from her 'Introduction'. In Activity 12 you are going to combine and develop these practices, writing from the perspective of a character – one with a voice in the base text – and paying attention to their style of expression a little more systematically.

ACTIVITY 12

Researching and re-voicing characters

To do this activity, you need to choose a character in the novel you're studying, and then find three sections (of just a few pages each) in which your chosen character speaks or narrates (or as many sections as possible, if there are fewer than three).

a Using the sections you have picked out, study the character's language use in close detail, and write down any noticeable features of her or his style of expression in relation to each of the levels of language. Look back at the brief summary of Summerscale's expression in the Ideas on Activity 7, on Cambridge Elevate, to give you an indication of some of the kinds of features you could explore. Use Table 18A to help you. If you need to, look back at Units 6–11, where these levels are outlined in detail, to refresh your memory.

b Now you've identified some aspects of the way in which the character speaks – the 'how' – you need to come back to the kinds of things she or he might say – the 'what' – which depends on all the things discussed earlier: behaviour, beliefs, priorities, desires, etc. Note down these kinds of details about the character – see just how much you can glean from the sections you've picked out.

c Find a paragraph in one of the sections you have selected in which the character is speaking or narrating. Add a few sentences in that character's voice to the original text (embedded between two of that character's sentences, or continuing on at a point where, in the original, she or he stops). Try to maintain the character's style of expression.

Table 18A

	Notable features of the character's style of expression
lexis and semantics (e.g. word classes, semantic fields, metaphor)	
grammar (e.g. morphology and syntax)	
phonetics, phonology and prosodics (e.g. alliteration, accent)	
graphology (e.g. multimodal features)	
pragmatics (e.g. co-operation, politeness, deixis)	
discourse (e.g. medium-specific features, layout)	

d Now try out using the character's voice to create a longer stretch of text – a paragraph or two. Planning what you are going to say first, perhaps with a bullet point list of the key details of each paragraph, describe something going on in one of the sections you selected from her or his perspective, which she or he doesn't describe in the base text. This is an 'additive' form of text transformation (though obviously 'alternative' too, in that the new version, with the addition included, is different from the original).

Check your responses in the Ideas section on Cambridge Elevate

Understanding and re-creating the expressive style of a character is one of the most challenging kinds of strategic re-creative writing. This requires careful study, with very close attention to language. On this specification, the re-creative task only requires you to write 300 words of re-creative composition: think carefully about how you use them. Try to make every word count. Thorough and extensive character studies and lots of practice is the best way to develop your skills.

18.2.4 Re-creative writing and narrative

Re-creative writing tasks focus you on a particular narrative moment in a novel – a stretch of narrative that lasts a few pages and narrates an event, or a few events. The event(s) will not necessarily be the most important event(s) in the narrative, but a lot of seemingly insignificant events can have a big impact on characters and on relationships between them, can contribute to the development of the novel's major themes, and can also be crucial catalysts for other more significant or dramatic events. It is important that you are very familiar with the events of the novel and that you have a deep appreciation of how they relate to each other and to the text as a whole. You will need to be aware of these extended implications of an event – that is, its implications for characters, themes and other events – if you are to transform a base text around it. Thinking through the event from the perspective of characters other than the narrator, or the main character through whom the event is portrayed, helps you to develop insight into its significance to the meanings of the story.

The themes and motifs that feature in the base text – the section the task refers to – are also worth thinking about. If you are recasting the base text from a particular character's perspective, you might want to consider how those themes relate to her (or how she relates to those themes) and what significance the motifs in the passage may or may not have for her and why. What would this character be likely to focus on, in describing this episode? Which aspects of the event would she focus on, and which characters (and which aspects of those characters)? You should use this thinking to decide, in describing the moment from her point of view, why and how she may or may not talk about particular characters, themes and motifs.

ACTIVITY 13

Themes and motifs in recasting

a One or more of the following four themes features in each of the texts in this unit in different ways:
- inscription
- evidence
- trails
- concealed identity.

Which of these themes is at work in the text you are studying, and at what points in the plot is each of these themes most prominent?

b Consider the text you are studying for this unit: how far and in what ways would you agree that the corresponding concrete object in the list below figures as a motif? Describe its significance to the text.
- Kites in *The Kite Runner*
- The breast flannel in *The Suspicions of Mr Whicher*
- Automobiles in *The Great Gatsby*
- Maps in *Into the Wild*

c Identify a section in the text you are studying in which one of the themes in Activity 13a or the relevant motif in Activity 13b is present. Think about how that section might be represented differently from the perspective of a character other than the character or narrator through whom it is represented in the original. Would the theme(s) and/or motif be approached differently by that character, and represented differently from their perspective? If so, how? For example, would the motif be of less significance to that character than to the protagonist? Might that character be associated with very different motifs that are backgrounded in the original text?

The narratologist Gerard Genette (1980, 1988) distinguished between four subtypes of narrative movement, or 'duration' (the speed at which the narrative narration progresses in relation to the story):

- **summary**, in which a lengthy event (with respect to the chronological progression of time in the storyworld) is presented via a brief summary in the narration
- **scene**, in which the temporal duration of an event and the amount of text devoted to representing that event are reasonably equivalent (dialogue being a good example of this)
- **ellipsis**, in which an event in the story is entirely absent from the narration
- **descriptive pause**, in which an event of short duration with respect to the temporal progression of the story is described in great detail and at length in the narration.

ACTIVITY 14

Exploring the duration of events

Find an event in the text you are studying which has been only briefly summarised, or has been elided from the narration altogether. What does the minimal treatment of this event in the narrative discourse suggest to you? What does the fact that this event is summarised or elided contribute to your interpretation and understanding of the novel?

In the re-creative writing task, you will be working with a base text of only a few pages, and will be asked to recast this into something that is only 300 words long. This is going to require you to be strategically selective so as to focus on aspects of that base text that are the most appropriate to the representation of your character's point of view. You might want to also consider, in that selection process, what she or he may prioritise in communicating to the designated reader/hearer of the transformed text, if, that is, a particular addressee is specified (the reader, or a fellow character). Sometimes the question itself will give you a focus – make sure you pay close attention to the details of the question and any bullet points providing further direction. If you are not restricted in this way or by the parameters of a particular character's voice and/or addressee, there is less to guide or limit your options in terms of what, from the base text, you choose to focus on. But whether you are given a character or not, a sensitive appreciation of what has been focused on, and what has not, in the base text, and why, will help you to craft something controlled in its differences from the original.

18.2.5 Re-creative writing and discourse

Re-creative writing tasks will often require that, in transforming the base text, your writing takes a different discourse type or genre form from that of the novel: you may be asked to portray an instance of oral storytelling (if, for example, you are asked to recast a base text as an account one character might give to another later that day), or a letter, etc. You therefore need to have a good idea of the nature of a range of discourse types, in terms of form, structure and any other features, including pragmatic aspects such as relative formality, likely levels of detail and so on. For example, an oral account is likely to be more structurally incoherent and disorganised (possibly even within the grammatical structures of phrases), more informal and more focused on feelings and thoughts than a letter (though bear in mind that the difference may be less stark if the letter writer is very open with, and honest and close to, the recipient).

This leads us on to consideration of the kind of audience the genre or discourse type is conventionally written for. Unlike most letters, a diary is usually written for the writer's eyes only, chiefly as an avenue for expression of emotions and reflections, sometimes as a way of 'thinking things through' via writing, and a means of recording experiences and events. A re-creative writing task may explicitly state a specific person that the rewritten piece should be crafted for, such as a character's friend, a partner, a parent, an interviewer or the police. The type of audience might influence what the character would choose to reveal or not, and deliberately draw attention to, or background, how personal they might be, how far they might feel the need to explain certain things (and what they can expect the reader/hearer to understand without them needing to explain), and how they might express themselves (in terms of register, politeness, how far they might moderate their personal vocabulary and so on).

See Unit 15 for more on memoir, travel writing and blogs

Here is a list of twelve discourse types and genres, some of which appear in the set novels. Note that this list is not exhaustive and neither is it a 'list' of genres you would be expected to write in for the examination. Rather it is designed to allow you to practise the skills of re-creative writing.

1 blog
2 memoir
3 script for a TV news item
4 email
5 travel writing
6 hotel website
7 diary entry
8 letter
9 song
10 postcard
11 newspaper article
12 account of an interview

ACTIVITY 15

Recasting across genres and discourse types

a Go through the list of twelve discourse types and genres. Choose two, use each as a subheading and underneath each subheading write down everything you can think of regarding:
- the prototypical form and structure of the genre or discourse type
- the kinds of language use you expect to find in the discourse type or genre.

Look back at the left-hand column of Table 18A if it helps to refresh your memory about the range of language features which you might want to consider.

b Identify two genres or discourse types for which you would find task 15a most difficult, and do some independent research into those text types - look for examples (on the internet, within other texts, around your home, etc.) and study these closely to familiarise yourself with the common features of these genres or discourse types a little better.

c Read Text 18G(a) and (b). How would you define the genre or discourse type of the books discussed, and why?

Text 18G

(a)

I was asked by the editor of *Outside* magazine to report on the puzzling circumstances of the boy's death ... I wrote a nine-thousand-word article, which ran in the January 1993 issue of the magazine, but my fascination with McCandless remained ... I was haunted by the particulars of the boy's starvation and by vague, unsettling parallels between events in his life and those in my own ... I won't claim to be an impartial biographer: McCandless's strange tale struck a personal note that made a dispassionate rendering of the tragedy impossible. Through most of the book I have tried – and largely succeeded, I think – to minimize my authorial presence. But let the reader be warned: I interrupt McCandless's story with fragments of a narrative drawn from my own youth. I do so in the hope that my experiences will throw some oblique light on the enigma of Chris McCandless.

Source: Jon Krakauer, *Into the Wild*, Author's note

(b)

This book is modelled on the country-house murder mystery, the form that the Road Hill case inspired, and uses some of the devices of detective fictions. The content, though, aims to be factual. The main sources are the government and police files on the murder, which are held in the National Archives at Kew, south-west London, and the books, pamphlets, essays and newspaper pieces published about the case in the 1860s, which can be found in the British Library. Other sources include maps, railway timetables, medical textbooks, social histories and police memoirs. Some descriptions of buildings and landscapes are from personal observation. Accounts of the weather conditions are from press reports, and the dialogue is from testimony given in court.

Source: Kate Summerscale, *The Suspicions of Mr. Whicher: or The Murder at Road Hill House*, Introduction

Check your responses in the Ideas section on Cambridge Elevate

Preparing and planning re-creative transformation

Here are some useful steps to take and questions to think about in preparing and planning a cross-genre/discourse type re-creative transformation:

- Some aspects of the discourse situation may not be determined by the question. What decisions do you need to make to provide yourself with workable parameters for the transformation? For example, Text 18G(a) describes the disappearance of the main character of the book, Christopher McCandless, and provides some details about his background and about his actions before his disappearance. Imagine you were asked to transform Text 18G(a) into a missing person's appeal, but that is all that the task states. Where might the appeal be publicised? Using what medium? Now imagine you were asked to transform the same base text into an obituary, but again, that's all the direction you are given. Where is the obituary to be published? Is it for a national or local newspaper, or on a college alumni page? Who is the audience? Where details like these aren't stated and are not obvious given the text type, you have some freedom. Bear in mind, though, that you would normally need to clarify your choices in your commentary.
- 300 words equates to about two short paragraphs in a novel, but different genres and discourse types are structured differently. How do you think you should structure your text?
- What key points and details from the base text are you going to use, and in what ways do they need recasting to alter aspects of the focus and foregrounding?

ACTIVITY 16

Moutot in the media

Look back at the base text, Text 18F, and the re-creative writing task in Figure 18C, on the character Moutot from *The Suspicions of Mr. Whicher*. Now choose either task a or task b, and use the guidance in the section entitled 'Preparing and planning re-creative transformation' to help you complete it.

a Recast Text 18F into a 'Wanted' notice placed by Detective Whicher, to appear in a daily newspaper in London in the 1850s, appealing for information or the capture of Moutot. In your transformation you should consider:

- Mr Whicher's impressions of Moutot
- how Mr Whicher might appeal to the public for action.

You should write about 300 words.

or,

b Recast the details into a newspaper report of the arrest written by a journalist for a daily newspaper in London in 1859. In your transformation you should consider:

- the journalist's impressions of and attitude towards Louisa Moutot and Mr Whicher
- the journalist's presentation of the event as a news story.

You should write about 300 words.

Here are some questions to use to reflect on your re-creative writing planning, process and result:

- Did you consider the parameters of the task carefully in planning your re-creative writing?
- Did you think about your interpretative impressions of the base text, and which aspects of stylistic expression were helping to create those interpretative effects?
- Did you analyse the base text closely for relevant and useful content and stylistic features?
- Did you pay attention to characterisation, narrative and discourse?
- Did you make every word count?
- Does your recast text create the interpretative impressions you intended it to?
- Did you write about 300 words?

Use Activities 10 to 16, and any others you can generate yourself, and keep all of the levels of language in mind throughout all stages of your re-creative writing process. Doing so will give you all the tools and knowledge you need to be able to craft a strong re-creative composition, which, in summary are:

- techniques for in-depth research into characters and an understanding of how characterisation is constructed
- an appreciation of narrative events, themes and motifs, and the ability to selectively focus on and retell part of a story on the basis of what is relevant to a particular character and/or addressee
- the ability to structure a text, and use language and shape meaning, according to the conventions of particular genre or discourse type
- skills in analytical comparative commentary.

It is this last and very important aspect of re-creative writing tasks that we will move on to now.

18.3 Commentary: analytical explanations of re-creative writing

The commentary task will be phrased like this:

Write a commentary explaining the decisions you have made in transforming the base text for this new account and the effects of reshaping the original description. You should write about 400 words. In your commentary you should:

- consider how you have used language to shape your intended meaning
- demonstrate the connections between the base text and your transformed text
- structure your commentary clearly to express your ideas.

Let's think about this task in a bit more detail and break these points down a little. The purpose of a commentary on a re-creative writing composition is for you to explain the decisions you made in transforming the base text into the recast version, and also to discuss the intended effects of altering the original text – the impact of the changes upon the text's meaning(s). You only need to write about 400 words. You can do quite a lot in that space, but you will, as with the recasting, need to be selective. Good commentaries offer a clearly expressed, descriptively precise and analytically insightful account of how you've expressed the content – the stylistic and narratological choices you've made – and directly relate these choices to the interpretative effects you were aiming for. You can give less attention to precisely *what* content you've chosen to present, though the details of your focus still need to be acknowledged and justified to some extent, especially if the focus is not stipulated in the question.

The commentary must involve description of your use of language, and must use appropriate and accurate linguistic terminology in doing so. You should be able to use the correct terms to talk about the grammatical class of words you've used, the structure of your sentences, phonetic representation of accent, pragmatic aspects of politeness, or whatever other features are present in your composition. This is why a clear and detailed understanding of kinds of features of language use at each of the language levels is important.

You must not stop at the point of mere description of the language of your composition, however. A commentary should present an analysis of the stylistic features of your text in relation to interpretative effects. In fact, it is only worth describing an aspect of your use of language if you are then going to talk about *and relate it to* its interpretative effects. What features of language did you use, why and what interpretative effects did you intend that they should create? These are the questions your commentary should answer. Again, you have to be selective in what you discuss, prioritising the features which are interpretatively significant, and those which perhaps need explaining more than other more obvious choices.

The commentary is also inherently comparative, in that it discusses the transformative relationship between the base text and the new text. In explaining the particular stylistic choices you have made, you should discuss the related features of the original text (i.e. the original author's stylistic and narratological choices, and the interpretative impact of these choices), and how these features shaped your creative decisions in constructing your rewrite. Make explicit connections between the two texts.

You must not forget, also, that your commentary is fundamentally communicative - it should be clearly and sensibly structured, using appropriate lexis and correct grammar, and should convey your main points in a logical order. As always, planning is essential in producing clear, effective writing, as much in your re-creative text as in your commentary. Activities 17 and 18 look at some different commentaries, and explore the planning and process involved.

See Unit 15 for more on essay writing

ACTIVITY 17

Strengths and weaknesses

Text 18H is an example of a commentary on the re-creative writing provided in the Ideas on Activity 11 (Text 18I - take a quick look at this again now). What do you think are the strengths and weaknesses of the commentary in Text 18H?

Text 18H

Commentary on Text 18I (a recasting of Text 18F)

The description of Moutot in the base text as a 'notorious fraudster', an 'up-to-the-minute urban criminal' and 'a mistress of … twisty deceits' suggests she is extremely intelligent, able to assess (and usually avoid) threats and dangers, and good at adapting her appearance and manner to blend into different environments. Such a character would want and need allies in prison, and so would benefit from presenting herself as similar to the other prisoners. In the recast text she is portrayed as using a lower class accent, with aspects of a cockney accent in particular, such as the elided initial 'h' and 'th' in words like 'he', 'here' and 'them,' and final consonants such as 't', 'th', 'd' and 'g' in words like 'different', 'with', 'and' and 'doing', respectively. Phonetic spelling is also used to mimic cockney pronunciation of the word 'who' (as 'oo') and 'ordinary' (as 'ordin'ry'). She also uses simple language, and lexis common to a cockney dialect, such as 'fella' (fellow). Her deviant grammar, occasionally moving the subject and verb to the end of a phrase (or repeating them there as in 'he knew what was what, he did'), and in missing 'ly' off the adverb 'clearly' are further markers of dialect, as are phrases like 'he knew what was what' and 'you mark my words'.

Use of third-person narration allows for an objective description of the setting, and comment on her appearance, whilst still being able to include her speech in reported form. Moutot's self-assuredness is shown in the phrases 'she still held her head high, with [an] air of … confidence', and in her manner of speaking, with declaratives without any modal shading. The inclusion of an argumentative interjection by another prisoner suggests how Moutot interacts with others, responding to the face threatening act with confident re-assertion.

Moutot's description of Whicher and the detective force creates a slight mysticism around him, saying he appeared from nowhere and could achieve what many before him could not. She adds to his growing celebrity status, but possibly to be deliberately sensationalist, to keep her audience and impress them with her previous consistent outsmarting of the police. Her warning to the other prisoners about the threat detectives pose to criminals helps her to create the impression of her being one of them, referring to the detectives as 'them' and to the prisoners and fellow criminals with 'we' and 'us'.

Source: private data

Check your responses in the Ideas section on Cambridge Elevate

Keeping the strengths and weaknesses of this commentary in mind, let's now look at some ways of going back over the process and improving upon this attempt.

ACTIVITY 18

Developing a commmentary on Text 18F

This activity will take you through a step-by-step process of planning and drafting a stronger commentary on Text 18I than Text 18H.

Look back again at the base text, Text 18F, in Activity 11 and the sample re-creative Text 18I (within the Ideas on Activity 11). The latter includes some details from the 'Prologue' further to those quoted in Text 18F. To recap, the requirements of the transformation task were to write 300 words of Moutot describing Whicher to a fellow prisoner while in prison following her conviction for fraud, communicating her impressions of Mr Whicher and her attitudes to 'the detective force' and to her life as a criminal.

a Identify points of connection between Texts 18F and 18I. You could start by simply annotating the texts, underlining and labelling points of connection. From this, try to break the points down into two columns alongside each other. The first column, down the left-hand side of the page, should list the features of the base text, and the second, down the right-hand side of the page and in parallel, should list the features of the re-creative writing which connect with the first. Make sure you leave a large gap in between the columns. The start of your lists might look something like Table 18B.

b Now review the two columns in Table 18B, and think about the relationships between connected points – try to draw out the rationale behind the stylistic choices made in adapting, transforming and rewriting the features in the first column into the features of the second column. Use the space in between the two columns to write down the nature of the relationships, rationales and choices. Note: if you need a little help, you could look back at the passage in this unit just before Activity 11 which provides guidance on the re-creative writing task. This passage presents an analytical investigation of the base text, and suggests some features to consider including in the re-creative writing in response to features identified in the original.

c Try to group the connections together into two or three groups, perhaps by the aspects of Moutot's character they relate to, or by the narrative content they express.
In other kinds of re-creative writing – less additive and more alternative – these groupings could be organised by the degree of change between the two connecting points (subtle or radical). Other ways of subdividing kinds of connections between the base text and re-creative writing are possible, too.

Table 18B

Feature in base text		Connected feature in rewritten text
description of appearance of Moutot as 'a stout, blotchy woman of about forty'		a mirroring description of appearance of Moutot as 'A woman of about 40, thick-set and blotchy'
description of nature of Moutot as a 'notorious fraudster', an 'up-to-the-minute urban criminal' and 'a mistress of ... twisty deceits'		presentation of Moutot as skilled in adapting to different social situations, wary of the police and detectives and as identifying with convicted criminals

d Your task now is to draft your own version of a commentary on this re-creative writing, a commentary structured around the points of connection you've identified: dedicate a paragraph to each group. You won't be able to talk about all of the connecting features – you'll need to select the most significant and interesting connecting features in each group to discuss. Keep your reflection on the strengths and weaknesses of the commentary Text 18H in Activity 17 in mind, and try to construct a different and better commentary.

There are a great many ways you can go about writing and structuring a commentary. As noted earlier, the commentary Text 18H was loosely structured around discussion of characterisation of Moutot first (with attention to her style of expression, then other aspects), and then discussion of her views on Whicher and the detective force (the points of focus specified by the re-creative writing task). The version of the commentary you constructed in Activity 18 was constructed around points of connection between the base text and the re-creative writing. Different structures can push your writing towards particular strengths or away from particular weaknesses (for example, in the re-creative text you constructed, you would have been likely to strongly satisfy the requirement of the commentary task to draw connections between the two texts). Some commentary structures can suit different transformative tasks (more additive or more alternative) in different ways. Likewise, different commentary structures can suit your own individual thinking patterns and analytical and writing processes and skills in different ways. The best way to explore is to practise.

The comparative nature of the commentary task explicitly requires you to draw connections between the base text and the re-creative writing. In doing so, and as part of this, it may be valuable to talk about the points of disconnection too – that is, differences between the two texts. For example, talking about something you have elaborated on (and why), which was present or suggested in some minor way in the base text, would be drawing a connection, whereas highlighting what you have added (and why), which was absent in the base text, would be discussing a point of disconnection. Points of disconnection are the other side of the coin to points of connection. Though the emphasis should be on points of connection, depending on the nature of the transformative relationship between the base text and your re-creative writing, points of disconnection can be a valuable part of your commentary too.

The process of creating a commentary outlined in Activity 18 was in some ways artificial due to the fact that you didn't create the transformative text yourself. If you had, you would have thought through some of the connections already: indeed, you would have generated the features of the re-creative text yourself in relation to the base text – that is, you would have created the connections, based on your own analytical and interpretative reasoning (hence Activity 18b pointing you towards the earlier partial description of that analytical process). Though the three texts involved in these processes can be thought of sequentially – the base text is transformed into the re-creative text, on which the commentary then reflects, as illustrated by Figure 18D – the actual processes of creating the transformative text and commentary, and the stages of thinking involved, are not so simply sequential. In fact, they might be better represented by loops of analytical reflection, comparison and creation circling through and around the three texts, or analytical attention oscillating between the three.

Figure 18D

base text → re-creative text → commentary

ACTIVITY 19

Commentaries on re-creative writing

a Look back at the re-creative writing composition you created in Activity 16, using Text 18F as the base text. Plan and write a commentary on what you did and why – that is, to create what interpretative effects.

b Now recast Text 18F differently, doing whichever of the tasks in Activity 16 you chose not to do the first time around. This time, plan your commentary while you re-create the base text – keep the commentary in mind, and start making notes on what you might want to say in it, while you're preparing, planning and writing your re-creative text.

c Which process did you find easier - beginning to think about your corresponding commentary only after (albeit in this case, unusually, quite some time after) completing your recasting (as in Activity 18a), or intertwining the planning processes of the two written pieces (as in Activity 18b), and why?

Check your responses in the Ideas section on Cambridge Elevate

You have 100 more words to write the commentary than you do to write the re-creative composition: again, make every word count. Each task requires quite different skills, but both are based on a good understanding of language and the relationship between expression and meaning.

Here are some further questions to help you reflect on, and assess, your commentary.

- Have you drawn connections between the base text and your re-creative writing?
- Have you explained the reasons for your transformative choices?
- Have you used appropriate terminology to describe features of language?
- Have you gone beyond description to analysis of interpretative effects?
- Is the commentary clearly structured?
- Have you discussed the ways in which your re-creative writing addresses the points required by the transformation task?
- Have you written about 400 words?

If we step back from the re-creative writing and commentary processes a little, we can see that they are closely interlinked and that the strength of the commentary greatly depends on the earlier processes of, firstly, the analytical understanding of the base text you develop in initially studying it, and, secondly, the act of generating your responsive and transformative re-creative writing.

18.4 Bringing it all together

18.4.1 Revise and prepare

ACTIVITY 20

Reflecting and revising

a Look back at Figure 18A. Can you plot some of the re-creative writing acts you have 'done' or 'performed' in the course of this unit on the graph, according to the nature of the approach (more experimental or more targeted), and the interventionist act (more subtle or more radical)?

b Here is the beginning of a list of some strategies to help you revise and prepare for your exam on this unit. Use these ideas, and see how many you can add.
   - Create a 'bank' of character profiles for your novel.
   - Draw a relationship tree for all of the characters in your novel.
   - Which two characters in your novel never or rarely meet? Imagine an encounter between them; what would they say to each other? How would they interact?

18.4.2 Self-assessment: check your learning

For each of the following statements, evaluate your confidence in each topic area by completing the table:

- use appropriate stylistic and linguistic terminology, concepts and methods to analyse genre, narrative, point of view and characterisation
- explore how interpretations are influenced by writers' choices and by contexts
- craft creative and controlled interventions in texts
- communicate stylistic analysis of your own creative interventions through clear, well-structured commentaries.

For Paper 2 of the A Level examination, Section A offers a choice of eight possible questions - two questions per text. You must answer two questions in relation to one text. The first of your two questions will be a transformative writing task, and the second question will ask for a commentary on that transformative writing.

18.4.3 Explaining the assessment objectives

When answering the questions, you should be aware of the assessment objectives that are being tested. There are three assessment objectives tested in Section A of Paper 2 and they all carry different weightings. For the intervention task, the assessment objectives and weightings are as follows:

- **AO5** (25 marks): Demonstrate expertise and creativity in the use of English to communicate in different ways

For the commentary, the assessment objectives and weightings are as follows:

- **AO2** (15 marks): Analyse ways in which meanings are shaped in texts
- **AO4** (10 marks): Explore connections across texts, informed by linguistic and literary concepts and methods
- **AO5** (5 marks): Demonstrate expertise and creativity in the use of English to communicate in different ways

Intervention task

- **AO5**: Demonstrate expertise and creativity in the use of English to communicate in different ways

In this you are assessed on your ability to create a new and original piece of writing, recasting the base text. The assessment of your expertise and creativity is based on the following criteria:

- creation of a new and original piece of writing
- control of any chosen style(s)
- use of the base text by staying within feasible parameters of the narrative.

This means you need to understand the relationships between textual features and interpretative effects; construct controlled and effective prose; recognise and work within the narrative scope of the base text; and demonstrate creative flair.

Commentary

- **AO2**: Analyse ways in which meanings are shaped in texts

In this you are assessed on your ability to identify, describe and analyse the linguistic, stylistic and narrative features you have used. This means you need to:

- describe significant linguistic, stylistic and narrative features of your recast text, across the language levels, in relation to the base text
- explain how these features may contribute to meanings.

You need to be selective in what you describe and analyse; use appropriate terminology in demonstrating your understanding of the relationship between language and meaning; explain the rationale behind your stylistic choices; and evaluate the effectiveness of those choices.

Area	Very confident	Some knowledge	Need to revise
I can use appropriate stylistic and linguistic terminology, concepts and methods to analyse aspects of genre, narrative, point of view and characterisation			
I can explain relationships between stylistic and linguistic features and interpretative effects			
I can create targeted and controlled transformative writing			
I can draw connections between base texts and re-creative writing			
I can explain my choices in crafting re-creative writing			
I can construct coherent and convincing commentaries			
I understand the requirements of transformative writing tasks and commentary tasks.			

- **AO4**: Explore connections across texts, informed by linguistic and literary concepts and methods

> In this you are assessed on your ability to draw connections between the base text and your re-creative writing. This means you need to:
> - compare the stylistic choices and interpretative effects in the base text to the related stylistic choices you have made and their intended interpretative effects in the recast text
>
> Drawing connections between the base text and recast text is the fundamental priority here.

- **AO5**: Demonstrate expertise and creativity in the use of English to communicate in different ways

> In this you are assessed on your ability to communicate a commentary on your re-creative writing. This means you need to:
> - demonstrate expertise in the use of English to express your ideas effectively
> - use linguistic and stylistic terminology and concepts accurately
> - structure your commentary clearly and logically.

Though this assessment objective is the same objective assessed in the intervention task, here it is assessed in slightly different ways.

You have been developing and practising these skills throughout this unit. Now it's time to test them out with a practice question.

18.4.4 Exploring questions

In this section, you have the opportunity to run through a complete re-creative writing and commentary exercise.

ACTIVITY 21

Re-creative writing and commentary combined

a Design a re-creative task of your own, exploring an aspect of your set text, modelled on the way in which this would be structured in the exam. Use the following template to guide you. (You can look also back at 18.2.5, Activity 15 and 18.3, for models of the task format.)

b Now either swap your task design with a partner and do theirs, or do your own. You could try doing the task under timed conditions, to practice what it would be like in the exam. Don't forget to plan your answers!

> Read pages ....
> [specify an extract of three pages or so] from
> '............'
> [quote the words at the start of the extract] to
> '............'
> [quote the words with which the extract ends].
>
> Here the writer describes ....
> ....
> [give a one-sentence summary of the context of the extract you've selected].
>
> Recast this description into ....
> ....
> [state the nature of the re-write, including the character it is focussed on or narrated by, the genre/discourse type, and perhaps the audience]. You should write about 300 words.
>
> In your transformation you should consider:
>
> - ....
>   ....
> - ....
>   ....
>
> [here, provide two bullet points listing two things that the transformation should consider –perhaps part of the focus of the extract, or someone's particular perspective or attitude, or the audience type]
>
> And...
>
> Write a commentary explaining the decisions you have made in transforming the base text for this new account and the effects of reshaping the author's original description.
>
> You should write about 400 words.
>
> In your commentary you should:
>
> - consider how you have used language to shape your intended meaning
> - structure your commentary clearly to express your ideas.

DEVELOPING

19

Dramatic encounters

In this unit, you will:

- develop your expertise in analysing the meanings created by the playwright's crafting of characters, themes and use of the stage
- learn to apply terminology, concepts and methods accurately and relevantly to the play that you are studying
- build on your ability to evaluate the importance of contextual factors and broader historical and social issues
- explore how best to prepare for assessment on this unit.

This relates to 'Exploring conflict' in the specification for A Level.

19.1 Exploring conflict

You have explored the spoken mode in different forms, engaging with its complexities. You have analysed naturally occurring speech, speech that had been planned and written first, blended modes from internet sources and its representation in dialogue from memoirs and travel experiences. You have also engaged with the presentation of speech in the literary genres of prose fiction and poetry. It seems obvious that the dramatic genre lends itself to further exploration of spoken interaction as a play relies on the spoken word and the interplay between the characters to express the writer's intentions. It's also the genre that depends not only on the actual words spoken but on the other non-verbal parts we associate with spoken interaction that add so much to the meanings that others infer from what we say.

See Unit 15 for more on the different forms of the spoken mode

See Units 16 and 17 for more on prose fiction and poetry

What drama does is fictionalise interaction into a world of characters and stories for us to observe and interpret as an audience. The stylistician Mick Short (1996) identifies the prototypical structure of drama as having at least two discourse levels: firstly at the level of the playwright addressing the audience/reader; and secondly at the level of character to character. What this highlights is that drama has an additional complexity in what Short calls a 'doubled' structure, since audiences can listen in to characters talk, a device allowing the audience knowledge and understanding to which not all characters have access. He presents this as the model shown in Figure 19A.

Figure 19A: Short's model of the prototypical dramatic discourse structure

Addresser 1 (Playwright)	Message	Addressee 1 (Audience / Reader)
Addresser 2 (Character A)	Message	Addressee 2 (Character B)

However, it's not just about simply seeing drama as representing real-world interaction, or simply as performance. You have the very specific focus of conflict as a way of framing your approach to the play. In the introduction to *Exploring conflict* you began thinking about broad notions of conflict based on your own communications with others. This definition of conflict highlights that relationships are built and maintained through negotiation, compromise and resolution (or not) of differences between people's wants, needs and intentions. So, drama is the genre that delves into aspects of how we interact with others, assert ourselves, express our identity and use strategies to cause (or resolve) conflict with others.

At one level, the dramatic conflict may be a family or domestic one, presenting arguments and disagreements between parents and children, siblings and friends. At another level, the conflict depicted may have wider significance at a larger, society level by presenting arguments between characters from different backgrounds, of different genders and between those in either a public or a private context. This link between the individual and society, combined with the immediacy of seeing this played out in front of us as an audience, is what makes studying the dramatic genre so exciting and why we can relate to it so easily.

So, how can you explore ideas about conflict through drama? Well, one way is to think about what you know about speech. Reflecting on this will allow you to begin confidently with your study of drama and conflict by focusing on what you already know about spoken interaction and from this you'll be able to select the language levels you need to focus on in analysing dramatic discourse.

Here's a list to remind you of the language levels and ways that these can relate specifically to the dramatic genre.

- **Phonetics, phonology and prosodics:** how aspects of spoken language such as pitch, intonation and volume are represented.
- **Lexis and semantics:** how the different associations of terms of address and characters' lexical choices can present characters' identities.
- **Grammar:** how sentence types express characters' attitudes and feelings and how lines are structured.
- **Pragmatics:** how assumptions and inferences can be made by characters and by audiences through the writer's language choices.
- **Discourse:** how playwrights use the conventions of the dramatic genre to structure their play and use typical features of naturally occurring speech to represent character's interactions.

ACTIVITY 1

Revising speech

Use the language levels and examples above as a prompt to revise the specific terminology you need to analyse spoken interaction, so that you can explore how playwrights use these features of real speech and interaction to create their dramatic dialogue.

a Revise pragmatics and spoken discourse.
b Create a glossary for the key terms used and their definitions.

19.1.1 Creating dramatic speech

Before you study dramatic dialogue, it's really helpful to think about the extent to which it is similar to real speech. Indeed, it's the literary genre that most resembles naturally occurring interactions between people. Playwrights tell their stories through speech, creating individual characters that have their own recognisable speech styles and building tension.

In order to explore some of the similarities and differences between naturally occurring speech and scripted dialogue, it's useful to put yourself into the position of a playwright.

ACTIVITY 2

Turning natural speech into scripted speech

a Record yourself recalling a brief but vivid childhood memory (it could be a happy or sad one). Limit yourself to one to two minutes of talk.
b Transcribe it, using the transcription conventions.
c Imagine that an actor will be presenting this memory to an audience and write the script from your transcript.

d Give directions to the actor playing you, both about the staging and delivery of your speech.

e List the features you removed from your written version and those you had to add.

19.1.2 Creating monologue

In Activity 1 you created a **monologue**, a particular convention of drama when one character gives a long uninterrupted speech. In naturally occurring spontaneous speech, a monologue might resemble Text 19A where Tom describes a funny story from his trip to New York.

Text 19A

er (1) I was in a hotel in New York (1) u::m (.) right at the very near Times Square (.) and (.) I had (.) my heelies on (.) u::m which are huge big wheels on at the at the back (.) um (.) I came out of the hotel and (.) um (.) there was (.) there was (.) it was a marble floor and there was a big slope at the bottom to leading to a road (.) and we were going out for dinner that night an (.) erm (.) we got er got a taxi to go out to a restaurant and were going out with some friends that we were picking up (1) and um ((*chuckles*)) I had only bought these heelies that day ((*chuckles*)) so um I I didn't know really what to do with them (2) so anyway I (1) um ((*chuckles*)) came out of the hotel and um slipped and um I weh slipped I slipped and fell over but sort of er managed to landed on my feet but (.) also on my wheels so I I landed on my wheels and went shooting down the slope ((*laughs*)) and and our friend that we brought was talking to my dad um but er he'd opened he's also opened (.) he'd managed to open the door to the taxi and wasn't paying attention (.) I uh anyway I ((*chuckles*)) came whizzing down the slope and (.) er (.) crashing into the taxi with in my heelies and um I ((*laughs*)) banged my shins on the doorframe and went er um headfirst flying ((*chuckles*)) into the seats

Source: private data

What you may have noticed when you scripted your speech is that each individual word matters more because it has to keep the interest of an audience. Like Tom, if you were telling a friend the same anecdote, then the non-fluency of **filled pauses** does not generally matter but in front of an audience it's the dramatic elements contained within the dialogue, along with the staging and presentation of this that need to be foregrounded, so that they can see why they are being told the story. Above all, scripted speech needs to entertain and sustain interest, perhaps even provoking some kind of reaction in the audience's emotions. The play that you will study contains monologues, mainly because they are a good way to present particular characters' feelings and for the playwright to raise or develop important themes. Although you will explore these further as a key dramatic genre convention later, here we're thinking about the types of one-speaker talk that happen quite naturally in our spoken interactions with others – we can then start to make links to how dramatists use such typical features of speech to create characters and present themes.

Key terms

monologue: a long uninterrupted speech by one speaker

filled pause: a spoken sound or word used to fill gaps in speech, such as 'er' or 'um'

ACTIVITY 3

Exploring monologues

Read Text 19B, from Blanche's first monologue in Scene 1 of *A Streetcar Named Desire*, where she tells her sister Stella about the loss of their family home.

Compare this to Tom's spontaneous monologue in Text 19A.

a What features does it share? You could consider spoken discourse features, as well as those from other language levels (lexis/semantics and phonology).

b In what ways does it differ? You could consider features from language levels (grammar and rhetorical devices).

c How does it sustain the audience's interest?

Text 19B

I, I, *I* took the blows in my face and my body! All of those deaths! The long parade to the graveyard! Father, Mother! Margaret, that dreadful way! So big with it, couldn't be put in a coffin! But had to be burned like rubbish!

Tennessee Williams, *A Streetcar Named Desire*, Scene 1

Find and watch Scene 1 of Tennessee Williams' *A Streetcar Named Desire* via Cambridge Elevate

Check your responses in the Ideas section on Cambridge Elevate

19.1.3 Creating interaction

It's also important to consider how playwrights create dialogue to represent interactions between their characters and how this both resembles and differs from speech. The first key question posed earlier was how do people interact? By returning to this, it's possible to list some of the features from the language levels that writers need to decide how to present in their scripted dialogue. People in naturally occurring interactions usually:

1 take turns
2 give feedback
3 are non-fluent
4 use their voice and body language to signal feelings
5 show their identity and their personality in their language choices.

Playwrights either recreate these features in their own way, choosing their own method to present such aspects of interaction as overlapping speech, or sometimes using the particular conventions of the time they were writing. Certainly you might see a contrast in the seemingly very stylised way that Shakespeare writes his dialogue to more modern playwrights who appear more naturalistic in their approach. To demonstrate that all playwrights strive to convey elements of natural speech, Text 19C(a) and (b) are extracts from the beginnings of *Othello* and *All My Sons*.

Text 19C

(a)

Enter RODERIGO *and* IAGO

RODERIGO Tush, never tell me, I take it much unkindly
That thou, Iago, who hast had my purse
As if the strings were thine shouldst know of this.
IAGO 'Sblood, but you will not hear me.
If ever I did dream of such a matter,
Abhor me.
RODERIGO Thou told'st me thou didst hold him in thy hate.
IAGO Despise me if I do not: three great ones of the city,
In personal suit to make me his lieutenant,
Off-capped to him; and by the faith of man,
I know my price, I am worth no worse a place.
But he, as loving his own pride and purposes,
Evades them with a bombast circumstance,
Horribly stuffed with epithets of war,

William Shakespeare, *Othello*, 1.1.1–14

(b)

FRANK: Hya.
KELLER: Hello, Frank. What's doin'?
FRANK: Nothin'. Walking off my breakfast. [*Looks up at the sky*] That beautiful? Not a cloud.
KELLER: [*looks up*] Yeah, nice.
FRANK: Every Sunday ought to be like this.
KELLER: [*indicating the sections beside him*]: Want the paper?
FRANK: What's the difference, it's all bad news. What's today's calamity?
KELLER: I don't know, I don't read the news part any more. It's more interesting in the want ads.

Arthur Miller, *All My Sons*, Act 1

It's clear just from the layout that turn-taking is occurring in Text 19C through the adjacency pairs. In *All My Sons*, the turn-taking is based around greetings and the typical phatic talk about the weather, topics and conversational starters recognisable from natural speech and a question and answer structure. In contrast, Shakespeare places us *in medias res*. It is as if Roderigo and Iago have started their conversation off-stage and we, the audience, are just overhearing it - just like we do daily as we catch snippets of other people's conversations. Both characters are talking about someone else, not named, for whom they seem to share a common hatred, creating the ambiguity of overheard conversations.

See Unit 19.2.1 for more on adjacency pairs

In both Text 19C(a) and (b), the characters offer feedback to each other. In Shakespeare this is shown through Iago's acknowledgement of Roderigo's complaints and criticisms, displaying that he is listening to them. More typical of today's style of speech is Keller's colloquial response, 'yeah, nice' which suggests his agreement with Frank's statements about the weather.

Whilst neither Text 19C(a) nor (b) is particularly non-fluent, some of the stiltedness of the conversation between the neighbours in *All My Sons* is presented graphologically through the full-stops in Frank and Keller's longer utterances and the commas in Roderigo's opening line could suggest his speedy pace as he vents his annoyance at Iago. Although prosodic features aren't explicitly evident in Text 19C(b), this could be because of the context - these are just neighbours engaging in social chit-chat. Neither does Shakespeare signal prosody, although it could be supposed that an actor playing Iago would place emphasis or increase the volume on the expletive ''Sblood' to show frustration.

Clearly some aspects of individual characterisation are shown in the language. Miller's choice of 'hya' for Frank's greeting, along with the clipping of 'doin' and his elliptical sentences 'walking off my breakfast', suggests both his accent and also perhaps his laidback manner. In *Othello*, the characterisation and speech styles seem masked by the **iambic pentameter**, a common dramatic convention of the time, but Iago's apparent honesty to Roderigo is conveyed in his direct and declarative style, compared to Roderigo's complaining tone.

19.1.4 Representing speech features graphologically

Different writers choose varying methods to indicate such features as interruptions and overlaps, non-fluency features and prosodic features. Depending on the writer, you may have found that prosodic features are represented by italics and non-verbal communication by stage directions, whereas graphological choices represent some non-fluency and turn-taking features.

ACTIVITY 4

Exploring the presentation of dramatic dialogue

Take a short section of your play where dialogue occurs, perhaps up to ten lines, and note the devices that the writer uses. List the graphological devices - i.e. punctuation symbols like ellipses (…) - to represent the following features:

1. **turn-taking**: interruptions and overlaps
2. **non-fluency**: pauses, false starts, repairs
3. **prosody**: stress, pitch, volume, intonation.

One device you may have noticed used frequently by more contemporary playwrights is the ellipsis in its form of trailing dots. Depending on its placement within the lines, this seems to signal both aspects of non-fluency (false starts, thoughts unsaid, a pause, awkwardness) and interruptions and overlaps by other speakers. In Text 19D, a short extract from the opening dialogue between Keller and his neighbours, the ellipsis appears to be used differently. In the first example, Keller either interrupts Frank enthusiastically with the actor's name or fills in the answer to an unspoken question. In the second, Jim interrupts Frank sarcastically, perhaps responding to Frank's implied criticism of him.

Text 19D

FRANK: Why, I saw a movie a couple of weeks ago, reminded me of you. There was a doctor in that picture …

KELLER: Don Ameche!

FRANK: I think it was, yeah. And he worked in his basement discovering things. That's what you ought to do; you could help humanity, instead of …

JIM: I would love to help humanity on a Warner Brothers salary.

Arthur Miller, *All My Sons*, Act 1

Shakespeare also makes conscious choices to represent speech, despite the constraint of iambic pentameter which appears a more conventionally poetic form. However, if you read lines from a Shakespeare play aloud using the punctuation, rather than by treating each line as a piece of verse, you will hear how he replicates, to an extent, the natural rhythm patterns of speech. In Text 19E are Roderigo's first lines of dialogue. Try reading it line by line first and then read it using the punctuation and you'll hear the difference.

Text 19E

RODERIGO: 'Tush, never tell me, I take it much unkindly
That thou, Iago, who hast had my purse
As if the strings were thine shouldst know of this.

William Shakespeare, *Othello*, 1.1.1–3

Here, Roderigo's opening lines are actually one complex sentence. However, the first line runs on into the next, something you would recognise from poetry as **enjambment**. The commas also function to create pauses. What makes Shakespeare sometimes seem hard to understand is the different syntax from modern English. Sometimes this is a deliberate choice by Shakespeare as he conforms to the conventional patterns of five stressed and five alternate unstressed syllables per line, although he will also diverge from this pattern. You have already explored ideas about writer's internal deviation; once you're confident with the structure of iambic pentameter, you can explore the significance of those occasions when Shakespeare breaks this pattern. In addition, Shakespeare often splits a line of verse between speakers to simulate the pace of conversation or interruptions and overlaps and presents this graphologically, so it can be seen visually on the page.

What he does not do is use italics for prosodic features, as you saw in Blanche's monologue in Text 19B and will also see with other playwrights. Instead, the iambic pentameter often foregrounds the key words to be stressed. Read aloud Iago's lines in Text 19F creating a now-famous metaphor for jealousy, to see which words are stressed.

Key terms

iambic pentameter: verse form comprising five metric feet called iambs (two syllables with the stress on the second: da-DUM)

enjambment: the continuation of a sentence without a pause beyond the end of a line, couplet or stanza

Text 19F

IAGO: It **is** the **green**-eyed **mon**ster **which** doth **mock**
The **meat** it **feeds** on.

William Shakespeare, *Othello*, 3.3.168–169

ACTIVITY 5

Interpreting speech features in dialogue

Read Texts 19G(a), (b), (c) and (d). You can either complete the activity by choosing the play you are studying or look at all the Texts 19G(a)-(d) to examine the devices that different playwrights use.

- In Text 19G(a) two siblings, George and Ann, are discussing their estranged father who is in prison for supplying faulty engine parts to the American Airforce during World War Two.
- Text 19G(b) features three extracts where Carol is preparing for her son's twenty-first birthday party along with her daughter, Claire, who has arrived to help her.
- In Text 19G(c) Blanche tells her sister Stella about her feelings for Mitch, a new man she has been seeing and a friend of Stella's husband Stanley.
- Text 19G(d) shows Roderigo's attempts to tell Brabantio the unwelcome news that Brabantio's daughter, Desdemona, has eloped to marry Othello, a soldier. Roderigo and Brabantio are both Venetian noblemen and Roderigo had hoped to marry Desdemona himself.

a How do the ellipses, dashes, commas, full stops and empty space create speech-like effects?

b How do these contribute to meaning?

Text 19G

(a)

GEORGE: [*discovers hat in his hand*]: Today. From now on I decided to look like a lawyer, anyway. [*He holds it up to her*.] Don't you recognize it?
ANN: Why? Where … ?
GEORGE: Your father's … he asked me to wear it.
ANN: … How is he?

Arthur Miller, *All My Sons*, Act 1

(b)

(1)

Carol is on her home phone, perched on a living-room armchair, busily wrapping some presents.

CAROL: And is he in the bus?... He *is*? And you're in the bus with him? ... How? ... How are you in the bus with him?

(2)

CLAIRE: Fine. You. Are Going. To Calm. Down.

(3)

CLAIRE: Just ... he's called Mark.

A moment.

CAROL: Mark?

CLAIRE: Yes.

A moment.

CAROL: A new friend?

CLAIRE: No.

CAROL: A close friend?

CLAIRE: Yes, reasonably.

CAROL: An old friend, newly close?

CLAIRE: Stop it, Mum. He's a friend.

CAROL: Fine.

A special friend?

Rory Kinnear, *The Herd*

(c)

BLANCHE: Because of hard knocks my vanity's been given. What I mean is – he thinks I'm sort of prim and proper, you know! (*She laughs out sharply.*) I want to *deceive* him enough to make him – want me ...

STELLA: Blanche, do you want *him*?

Tennessee Williams, *A Streetcar Named Desire*, Scene 5

(d)

RODERIGO: Sir, sir, sir –

BRABANTIO: But thou must needs be sure
My spirit and my place have in them power
To make this bitter to thee.

RODERIGO: Patience, good sir.

William Shakespeare, *Othello*, 1.1.103–105

Check your responses in the Ideas section on Cambridge Elevate

19.2 Representing turn-taking

Dialogue is built upon turn-taking and our understanding of how that occurs in the real world and playwrights can use this knowledge to show relationships between characters. The difference is that the turn allocation is being decided by the writer, not the speaker, and so there is no self-selection. This is demonstrated by the allocation of dialogue to particular characters, as set out by the writers in the form of a script. Arguably, for reasons of clarity and for dramatic purposes, playwrights might choose to neaten some of the structures of conversations but they will still play with the exchange structure of conversations.

19.2.1 Structuring turns: adjacency pairs

Adjacency pairs have patterns and predictability, forming patterns of question/answer, greeting/response and so on. You have already analysed these in naturally occurring speech and explored the different nature of preferred and dispreferred responses. What's useful is to engage with the writer's intention in using these patterns and what characters' compliance or disregarding of conventions show about their feelings, attitudes or behaviour.

Text 19H(a) (the opening) establishes the relationships between neighbours and displays Miller's establishing of Frank and Keller's camaraderie through preferred responses of greeting/response and question/answer. In contrast, Texts 19H(b) and (c) show how writers can use dispreferred responses.

Text 19H

(a)

FRANK: Hya

KELLER: Hello, Frank. What's doin'?

FRANK: Nothin'. Walking off my breakfast.

Arthur Miller, *All My Sons*, Act 1

(b)

DESDEMONA: Will you come to bed, my lord?

OTHELLO: Have you prayed tonight, Desdemon?

William Shakespeare, *Othello*, 5.5.23–24

(c)

ANN: How is he?
GEORGE: He got smaller?
ANN: Smaller?
GEORGE: Yeah, little.

Arthur Miller, *All My Sons*, Act 2

In Text 19H(b), Othello's response seems irrelevant as a simple yes or no would be the preferred response to Desdemona's question. However, Shakespeare's purpose is for **dramatic irony** and to build tension as the audience are well aware by this stage that Othello proposes to kill Desdemona. Shakespeare's handling of this exchange foregrounds Othello's concern about the state of Desdemona's soul in the after-life. The significance of Desdemona saying prayers would have resonated with some members of Shakespeare's contemporary audiences. Text 19H(c) shows Ann asking her brother about their father, who she has not seen since he went to prison. Here, the dispreferred response is in the ambiguity of George's response as on the face of it he gives a preferred response by answering Ann's question. Ann queries this with 'smaller?', presumably trying to establish if the meaning of the comparative adjective is literal or metaphorical.

Key terms

dramatic irony: where the audience knows more than a character does at a particular point in the action

19.2.2 Structuring turns: insertion sequences

Just as playwrights can use adjacency pairs, they can also call upon other typical aspects of turn-taking such as insertion sequences. Text 19I, from *All My Sons*, occurs near the start of the play. Frank, Keller's neighbour, is telling him about a horoscope he is preparing for Larry, Keller's eldest son and a wartime airman who had been missing in action for three years.

Text 19I

FRANK: Well I'm working on his horoscope.
KELLER: How can you make him a horoscope? That's for the future, ain't it.
FRANK: Well, what I'm doing is this, see. Larry was reported missing on November 25th, right?
KELLER: Yeah?
FRANK: Well, then, we assume that if he was killed it was on November 25th. Now what Kate wants ...
KELLER: Oh, Kate asked you to make a horoscope?

Arthur Miller, *All My Sons*, Act 1

In fact, the topic of horoscopes continues for a further five exchanges between Frank and Keller. Indeed, Keller's initial question 'That's for the future, ain't it' is only answered by Frank at the end of this exchange when he says 'it's completely possible he's alive', implying a future for Larry. Frank signals this with the skip connector 'see, the point is', bring it back to Keller's question. Another typical speech-like feature is evident in Frank's repeated use of discourse markers 'well' and 'now' to highlight to Keller that he is keeping focus on the topic and attempting to hold the floor.

19.2.3 Structuring turns: overlaps, interruptions and simultaneous speech

You've already looked at how a specific feature such as an ellipsis, in its graphological form, can represent both turn-taking and non-fluency. In Text 19J, Kinnear offers a key to the text, indicating that a forward slash (/) is an overlap in speech. From Text 19J you can see that in this exchange Kinnear wishes to signal that Patricia and Carol ask questions of Mark simultaneously. You can also see from the stage directions that he attempts to complete the adjacency pairs with both speakers, illustrating his attempt to be polite and conform to social conventions.

Text 19J

PATRICIA: / And what is it you do, Mark?
CAROL: / Are you hungry, Mark?
MARK: (to CAROL) . I could be. (To PATRICIA.) Sorry?
PATRICIA: And what is it you do?
CAROL (SOTTO): Mum.
MARK: I'm er ... I'm a poet.

Rory Kinnear, *The Herd*

Although Shakespeare uses iambic pentameter, he often divides lines of these between characters to create a more natural effect. He also uses these to quicken the pace of the interaction, for comic effect and to suggest overlaps and interruptions. The exchanges in Text 19K(a) and (b) between Othello and Desdemona show Desdemona's quick denials of Othello's cruel accusations but also represent adjacency pairs within the split lines.

Text 19K

(a)

OTHELLO: Are you a strumpet?
DESDEMONA: No, as I am a Christian

William Shakespeare, *Othello*, 4.2.81–82

(b)

OTHELLO: What, not a whore?
DESDEMONA: No, as I shall be saved.

William Shakespeare, *Othello*, 4.2.84–85

ACTIVITY 6

Exploring turn-taking

Take the opening of your play and select about ten lines of dialogue. Examine the turn-taking patterns.

a What types of adjacency pairs are used? For example, are they structured as question/answer or in other patterns? Do the characters offer preferred or dispreferred responses? What does the choice of responses suggest about the characters' feelings?
b What evidence is there for overlaps and interruptions? What do these suggest? If there aren't any, why not?

19.2.4 Showing feedback

In naturally occurring interactions, as hearers, we tend to show the speaker that we are paying attention and listening to what they have to say. Sometimes we do this non-verbally (nodding, smiling, etc.) and verbally, often doing enough to demonstrate our interest but not to take the turn from them. This kind of speaker activity can be called back-channelling or minimal responses, terms that signal both the supportive nature and the desire not to take a turn from the speaker and are often characterised by words that act as back-channelling behaviour ('mm', 'really') or **affirmatives** ('yeah') or the mirroring of the speaker's language. In scripted dialogue there may be less need for such feedback and every line needs to count. It would be very unappealing for an audience to listen to these continually as they add little to the action.

Key terms

affirmative: a word that shows agreement

Playwrights will, of course, call upon feedback as a realistic conversational feature for a specific, more subtle effect.

ACTIVITY 7

Exploring feedback

Read Text 19L(a) and (b). In Text 19L(a), Mitch and Blanche are returning from an apparently unsuccessful date. In Text 19L(b) Iago is hinting to Othello that Cassio, who Othello has recently promoted, is untrustworthy. What types of feedback can you identify? What meaning can you interpret from these features?

Text 19L

(a)

MITCH: They call that stuff alpaca.
BLANCHE: Oh. Alpaca.
MITCH: It's very light weight alpaca.
BLANCHE: Oh. Light weight Alpaca.
MITCH: I don't like to wear a wash-coat even in summer because I sweat through it.
BLANCHE: Oh.

Tennessee Williams, *A Streetcar Named Desire*, Scene 6

(b)

OTHELLO: Indeed? Ay, indeed. Discern'st thou aught in that? Is he honest?
IAGO: Honest, my lord?
OTHELLO: Honest? Ay honest.
IAGO: My lord, for aught I know.
OTHELLO: What doest thou think?
IAGO: Think, my lord?
OTHELLO: Think, my lord! By heaven, he echoes me

William Shakespeare, *Othello*, 3.3.101–107

Check your responses in the Ideas section on Cambridge Elevate

19.3 Representing speech and meaning

So far, we have only considered the devices and features used to represent some of the mechanics of speech. We now need to focus on the words used and how these are placed together syntactically to make meaning in sentences. Playwrights can assign sentence types to characters to reflect aspects of their identity or personality. They use sentences that convey typical or conventional features of interaction. We will also look at how sentences contribute to the structure of dialogue. Considering the functions of the sentences characters use at various stages of the play helps us to interpret meaning.

To illustrate how playwrights use sentences, here's an example from *The Herd*. Kinnear uses Carol's sentences to indicate both her attitudes about characters at certain points of the play, as well as to reveal her own feelings and allow the audience to make their own judgements about her motivations and character. To Ian, her ex-husband who she feels deserted her and their children, her imperative, 'Don't you dare patronise me' shows her anger. Later in the play, she asks her family to allow Ian to stay at Andy's party and the declaratives state her reasons matter of factly:

'This isn't an act of forgiveness. Or generosity. He is here. He has said he wants to see Andy.'

To her daughter, in the heat of a debate about motherhood, her interrogatives are not only sarcastic but reveal her own frustrations with her life and maternal role: 'Am I, Claire? Am I? I've been so lucky, haven't I, so blessed? A son with a mental age of ten months / and a daughter with an emotional age of a nine-year old'.

Playwrights also call upon pragmatics, using contextual factors to influence meaning. One notable idea was of schemas, where we call upon our own experiences in the world to interpret what we see presented on stage and playwrights can use this knowledge to shape our interpretation. For example, although we may have no cultural experience of 1940s New Orleans and may not be able to identify any of the American town settings of *A Streetcar Named Desire* and *All My Sons*, we can use our family schema to relate to the events and relationships presented. Likewise, in *The Herd*, the family party schema is the entire setting for the play, the reason the action takes place. In *Othello*, while we may not have a war or battle schema, we might have a work or relationship schema that allows us to decode what we see on stage.

19.3.1 Speech acts

Speech acts can take many forms. Amongst others, they can be suggestions, apologies, threats, compliments, warnings, invitations and advice. The sentence functions that you already know from Unit 7 seem to link naturally to speech acts: declaratives are often assertions or statements, imperatives are commands and interrogatives are questions or requests but clearly these, along with exclamatives, have to be read carefully for more subtle and distinct forms of speech acts.

Speech acts can be explored at three levels:

- **locutionary act:** the utterance itself
- **illocutionary act:** the significance and pragmatic force of the utterance
- **perlocutionary act:** the actual effect of the utterance on the hearer.

The philosopher John Searle (1975) classified locutionary acts into the following five groups:

1. **Directives**: speech acts that trigger the hearer to take a particular action, such as commands or requests. For example, 'Don't forget to hand in the essay next lesson.'
2. **Commissives**: speech acts that pledge the speaker to a future action, such as promises. For example, 'I promise that I won't forget my essay.'

3 **Declarations**: speech acts that make a pronouncement that change the reality of the situation, such as speech acts in the marriage service. For example, 'I now pronounce you man and wife.'
4 **Assertives**: speech acts that commit the speaker to the truth of what they are saying, such as a statement. For example, 'It is going to rain today.'
5 **Expressives**: speech acts that express the speaker's feelings and attitudes towards the proposition. For example, an apology like, 'I am really sorry that I can't attend your party.'

Speech acts depend on **felicity conditions**, where the participants can determine how appropriate the speech act is in the actual context. Text 19M from *All My Sons* exemplifies these ideas. Firstly, here's the context for you. In Act 2, George arrives to confront the Kellers after visiting his father, Steve, in prison and hearing his side of the story. Steve has been imprisoned for deliberately selling faulty parts for aircraft to the American Airforce during the Second World War. His business partner and ex-neighbour, Joe Keller, was jailed too for this, but was released on appeal. George and his sister Ann had not seen their father since his court case and Ann, who wishes to marry Chris Keller, is still unwilling to listen to her brother and father's version of events.

Key terms

directive: a speech act that triggers the hearer to take a particular action

commissive: a speech act that pledges the speaker to a future action

declaration: a speech act that makes a pronouncement that changes the reality of the situation

assertive: a speech act that commits the speaker to the truth of what they are saying

expressives: a speech act that expresses the speaker's feelings and attitudes towards the proposition

felicity condition: the conditions needed for a speech act to achieve its purpose, such as the authority of the speaker and the situation of the utterance

Text 19M

CHRIS: What's the matter, George, what's the trouble?
GEORGE: The trouble? The trouble is when you make suckers out of people once, you shouldn't try to do it twice?
CHRIS: What does that mean?
GEORGE [to ANN]: You're not married yet, are you?
ANN: George, will you sit down and stop ...?
GEORGE: Are you married yet?
ANN: No, I'm not married yet.
GEORGE: You're not going to marry him.
ANN: Why am I not going to marry him?

Arthur Miller, *All My Sons*, Act 2

Here, the felicity conditions are complex. It may depend on whether it is acceptable for a brother to issue a directive to his sister about whom she can marry and legally this is not enforceable, especially as Ann is an adult. There is also the physical context to consider and the implications of George and Ann being visitors in the Kellers' house. However, there are deeper issues also about beliefs and values and about the moral correctness of Ann aligning herself to the family potentially responsible for her father's unfair imprisonment. George's repeated directives in the forms of interrogatives and declaratives are all intended to control Ann's decision making but the perlocutionary force is not the desired one for George as she does not agree. In contrast, Ann's speech acts are a mixture of assertives and directives as she attempts to calm her brother down and request him to give her reasons for her not to marry Chris Keller.

ACTIVITY 8

Examining speech acts

Take 5–10 lines of dialogue between characters in the play you are studying and carry out tasks a–e.

a Summarise the context of the interaction within the play.
b Identify the sentence functions (declarative, interrogative, etc.).
c Assign a type of speech act to each character's sentences or lines of dialogue.
d Within the interaction, identify the illocutionary and perlocutionary force of the lines of dialogue you think are key in your extract.

e To finish, write a paragraph developing your analysis, linking context to the features you are exploring.

19.3.2 Conversational maxims

When you were first introduced to the co-operative principle of our communication with others, you were introduced to the idea that, in general, people work together to communicate. Now you can apply it when exploring conflict between speakers in dramatic situations, as co-operation (or a lack of co-operation) may be significant in resolving or creating conflict in plays. Exploring the four conversational maxims of quantity (how much is said), quality (the truth of what is said), relevance (the appropriateness of what is said to the topic) and manner (the way it is said) can all add to your interpretation of the relationship dynamics writers are presenting.

If we look at Text 19N, focusing on its pragmatic qualities, we can see how Claire breaks the maxim of quantity. Carol is being an inquisitive mother and the implicature is that Claire doesn't want to reveal too much about this man, Mark, to her. Carol, in her silence, offers Claire the chance to continue her turn, which is rejected and Carol has to delve further with a series of questions. To each, Claire offers minimal responses too, continually breaking the maxim of quantity (from Carol's perspective) and Carol substitutes different adjectives 'new', 'close', 'old' and 'special' to prompt a more detailed response from her daughter. Carol knows these have different nuances and is trying to establish the nature of the relationship between Claire and Mark, the man Carol is about to meet for the first time at Andy's birthday party – a significant family event. We cannot judge whether Carol breaks the maxim of quality, as she responds with the affirmative 'yes' and negative 'no' in answer to her mother's question. However, we later find out that Claire and Mark are expecting a baby together and so the modifying adverb in 'reasonably close' is arguably less than truthful.

Text 19N

CLAIRE: Just … he's called Mark.
A moment.
CAROL: Mark?
CLAIRE: Yes.
A moment.
CAROL: A new friend?
CLAIRE: No.
CAROL: A close friend?
CLAIRE: Yes, reasonably.
CAROL: An old friend, newly close?
CLAIRE: Stop it, Mum. He's a friend.
CAROL: Fine.
A special friend?

Rory Kinnear, *The Herd*

ACTIVITY 9

Exploring conversational maxims

Take a section of the play you are studying where dialogue occurs.

1 How do characters conform to conversational maxims? Find examples and identify the maxims.
2 Where do they break them? Which maxim(s) are broken? What are the implicatures for these breaches?

19.4 Exploring dramatic conventions

As plays are the dramatic genre, playwrights follow or adapt certain conventions to suit. These may be in the structure and organisation of the play into acts and scenes or in the enacting of a sub-genre of drama, such as tragedy. Some of the playwrights' decisions may be based on the conventions of the time they were writing, or because they are highlighting a particular genre or to make a personal, individual statement. It's therefore important to look at the choices playwrights make and think about what they are trying to say with these.

19.4.1 Structuring plays

The convention of dividing the action in parts goes back to the Ancient Greek and Roman concepts of drama. The simplest idea that a narrative has a beginning, middle and an end emerged from the Greek philosopher Aristotle, resulting in a typical three-act structure of setup, conflict and resolution. The Roman poet Horace believed that there should be five acts, a division adopted in presenting Shakespeare's plays.

From these, later critics, such as the nineteenth-century German playwright Gustav Freytag, suggested that plays adhere to the following narrative structure:

- **exposition**: introducing the characters, the setting and a piece of significant action
- **complication**: a problem or dilemma arising
- **climax**: the actual crisis and a change to the fortunes of the main character
- **resolution**: the outcome of the decisions made to resolve the crisis
- **denouement**: the consequences and tying up of the remaining loose ends.

In addition to acts, which contribute to the overall dramatic structure, individual scenes can add another sub-layer of structure. Unlike acts, scenes focus on specific characters and events. Modern playwrights can take more of a free-form approach with no break of action or distinctions between scenes. However, the decisions playwrights make add meaning to the drama and have an effect on our responses to it as audiences and readers.

19.4.2 Tragic conventions

Tragedy originated in Greek drama. In Greek plays, human suffering was presented with some kind of healing (what Aristotle terms **catharsis**), gained at the end through the audience's response to witnessing this. For example, Joe Keller's suicide at the end of *All My Sons* illustrates this. Keller's actions show him taking responsibility and punishing himself for the deaths of twenty-one airmen and Miller presents Keller's wife and son's immediate acceptance of his death in the play's concluding dialogue. Through both the Kellers' actions and the dialogue confirming the family's willingness to move on with their lives, the audience gain closure and the healing process begins.

Tragedy can explore the downfall of an individual, or present this as a failing of society. As a result, the tragic hero may gain some self-knowledge and there are often moral aspects, reflecting the concerns and contexts of the time period in which they were written. Shakespeare is renowned for his main tragedies, mainly featuring noble heroes. *Othello* is one of these but the hero is not a nobleman but more the ordinary man that Arthur Miller presents in *All My Sons*. Arguably, Williams too presents a tragedy but with a focus on female experience. With its **stereotypes** of men and women, perhaps this is most aptly classified as a **melodrama**.

Not only does there have to be a tragic hero, there also needs to be a plot which really explores a single issue. Another Aristotelian tragic convention is the unity of time, where the events in the play occur within one day and combine with the unities of space and action.

Key terms

catharsis: a purifying of the emotions brought about in the audience of a tragic drama through the feelings of intense fear or pity created in response to the action

stereotype: characteristics given to groups of people in an oversimplified way

melodrama: a drama characterised by the use of stereotyped characters, exaggerated emotions and language, simplistic morality and conflict

19.4.3 Monologues, soliloquies and asides

At the beginning of this section you explored the differences between a planned monologue and a naturally occurring monologue in unplanned speech. In doing this, you saw that monologues are a part of human communication but now you need to reflect on their dramatic function. You have also explored monologues in the literary genre of poetry, which allow a speaker to present their thoughts and feelings either to the reader or to an imagined audience. Thus it has a similar function in drama, either being delivered to another character on stage or alone on stage directly to the audience. In contrast, a **soliloquy** – the conventional solo speech used by Shakespeare – is only addressed to the audience and is used to both reveal inner feelings and indicate future actions.

Monologues frequently have a narrative element, telling a story about past experiences, or they can be used to achieve a goal or reveal feelings at that specific moment in the action.

In *All My Sons*, this narrative element is made explicit by Miller when he presents Joe Keller's recollections in Act 1 to Ann, his son's girlfriend, of his return home after being exonerated for murder and released from prison. Keller asks Ann to 'picture it now' as he 'got out of his car' and walked 'down the street'. This monologue also reveals Keller's bravado and self-confidence at this time, as he describes walking 'slow' and 'with a smile' and in regaining his reputation with the neighbours as 'a respected man again; bigger than ever'.

Shakespeare also uses **asides** signalled in the stage directions, which are brief observations that are not meant to be overheard by other characters. In this way, the audience get a brief insight into a character's private views and thoughts that they do not wish to share with others. This stylised device allows one character to include the audience in what in real conversation would be left as private thoughts.

Key terms

soliloquy: a dramatic device in which a character is presented alone on stage and offers their thoughts and feelings to the audience

aside: a dramatic device where a character briefly addresses the audience but is conventionally unheard by the other characters on stage

19.4.4 Shakespearian conventions of verse and prose

Shakespeare uses Elizabethan dramatic conventions in mixing prose and verse. In many plays, these can signify social status – characters of lower social rank speak in prose and those more highly ranked use verse, partly because of the associations of verse with an elevated register. However, Shakespeare doesn't stick with these conventions rigidly, often adapting his characters' speech from prose to verse because of contextual factors linked to the particular interactions being presented. When reading *Othello*, ask yourself some questions if there are changes between verse and prose within scenes, from scene to scene or shifts in characters' speech styles: who is speaking? What is their rank in the social world? To whom are they speaking? What are they speaking about? The examples in Table 19A demonstrate some of these subtleties.

Most of Iago's interactions with Roderigo are conducted in prose, signifying their private plotting and Iago's continued manipulation and defrauding of Roderigo. However, Iago is able to shift his register to use verse when addressing either the audience in his soliloquies or other characters when he wants to exert influence over them, highlighting his skilful use of language. Likewise, Othello's use of verse is also indicative of his persuasion of a potentially hostile audience of Venetian Senators, who may feel the dishonour of his presumption in marrying one of their own citizens. Later in the play, Othello's prose signifies his loss of control as his jealousy takes hold.

Although Shakespeare is utilising conventions, he also is exploiting the speakers' **accommodation** of other speakers, either converging to their speech styles or diverging from them. Indeed this **upwards convergence** and **downwards convergence** characterises his language use.

Playwrights' manipulation of a speaker's speech styles is not unique to Shakespeare. Look at Text 19O, where Stanley and his male friends are playing poker while the women are at the theatre.

Table 19A

Character	Act/scene	Prose/verse	Context and/or topic
Iago with Roderigo	Act 1, Scenes 1 and 3 Act 2, Scene 1	prose	plotting against Othello
Othello speaking to the Senate	Act 1, Scene 3	verse	defending his marriage to Desdemona
Cassio and Iago	Act 2, Scene 3	prose	celebrating their military victory
Iago's soliloquies	Act 1, Scene 3 Act 2, Scene 3 Act 3, Scene 3	verse	revealing his plans and motivations to the audience

Key terms

accommodation: how people adjust their speech behaviours to match others. This can be aspects of accent, grammar, vocabulary and even the style of speech delivery

upwards convergence: a speaker's emphasis on the standard aspects of their speech emphasising the prestige of standard forms

downwards convergence: a speaker's emphasis on the non-standard aspects of their speech in order to match another speaker's style

Text 19O

MITCH: Kind of on your high horse, ain't you?
STANLEY: How many?
STEVE: Give me three.
STANLEY: One.
MITCH: I'm out again. I oughta go home pretty soon.
STANLEY: Shut up.

Tennessee Williams, *A Streetcar Named Desire*, Scene 2

The men's language is elliptical and non-standard, as they mutually **converge** downwards. However, when speaking to Blanche at other points in the play, both Stanley and Mitch upwardly converge. In Text 19P(a), Stanley interrogates Blanche about the loss of the Dubois family home, Belle Reve. Note how he uses full sentences and more polysyllabic lexical choices in his apparent attempts to intimidate her. Mitch also adopts more standard prestige forms of speaking when he first meets Blanche. You can see this in Text 19P(b), one of the first exchanges between them.

Text 19P

(a)

STANLEY: There is such a thing in this state of Louisiana as the Napoleonic code, according to which whatever belongs to my wife is also mine – and vice versa.

(b)

BLANCHE: I'm an old maid schoolteacher!
MITCH: You may teach school, but you're certainly not an old maid.
BLANCHE: Thank you, sir! I appreciate your gallantry!
MITCH: So you are in the teaching profession?

Tennessee Williams, *A Streetcar Named Desire*, Scene 2

Key terms

converge: move speech styles and patterns to more closely match those of other speakers

19.5 Psychological and social drama: Williams, Miller and Kinnear

All My Sons, *A Streetcar Named Desire* and *The Herd* all demonstrate the desire by audiences and playwrights to engage with ordinary lives and experiences in more recent times.

The psychological style of drama evolved from the nineteenth-century Norwegian playwright Ibsen, who pioneered an approach where characters have more psychological depth and where dialogue sounded like real conversation, characters were more believable and stage sets were more realistic. Miller, in particular, admired Ibsen's focus of 'bringing the past into the present' (as he explained in his own Introduction to his 1957 *Collected Plays*), as well as the concept of the delayed revelation. Miller also wanted to connect psychological and social drama, by following the Greek tradition of linking the individual character to notions of the character as a social actor responsible to more than just himself. You can see how Williams' play fits into ideas about psychological drama as he charts Blanche's downfall through her emotional and mental deterioration and descent into madness. However, Williams is also responsible for coining the term 'plastic theatre' to encompass his experimental use of stagecraft (sets, lighting, music, etc.) to construct the dramatic world of *A Streetcar Named Desire*.

Kinnear's play, *The Herd*, follows on from these ideas of realism and social drama with the presentation of a suburban modern lower to middle class, intergenerational family dealing with the powerful emotions resulting from caring for a severely disabled child. It is not a tragedy in the traditional sense, as the tragedy is Andy's, the disabled son who never appears on stage and who is not the hero of the play.

ACTIVITY 10

Exploring conventions

Survey the play you are studying to explore its structure and the dramatic conventions it demonstrates.

a Consider the dramatic conventions used in the play. Before you do this, you might want to further research the conventions, as well as using the ideas in the section above.
  - How is it divided?
  - Why do you think the dramatist has separated the action in these ways?
  - How does the structure link to conventions of tragedy?
  - What conventions of realistic and naturalistic theatre does it use?

b Identify which characters have monologues or soliloquies.
  - Chart when these occur in the play.
  - What are they about?
  - Are they delivered to the audience or another character?
  - What's the dramatic function of each one when it occurs?

19.5.1 Stagecraft

The choices a playwright makes about the staging of the play is key to how we as an audience engage with it, interpret it and make meaning from it. So, although we have been focusing on the playwrights' language choices in representing speech, the technical elements of stagecraft (the set, the lighting, the props, etc.) cannot be overlooked. Not all playwrights offer the same level of detail in terms of stage directions to advise directors and actors how they want lines performed or characters interpreted. Some, like Williams, give very detailed instructions while others, like Shakespeare, offer few precise instructions.

However, directors and actors still have scope to interpret the directions playwrights give them. You only have to watch different stage or film versions of *Othello* and *A Streetcar Named Desire* to see how a play, despite its crafting, is not a static form.

For the play you are studying, ask the following questions.

- What set is chosen?
- What do the characters wear?
- What props are used?
- What sound effects are there?
- How does the lighting change?
- What music is used?
- Where do characters enter and exit the stage?
- How are monologues/soliloquies and asides used?
- What stage directions are there?

The next question to ask once you have listed what staging resources the playwright calls upon, is what symbolic meanings you think these have.

ACTIVITY 11

The set: first impressions

Read Text 19Q(a), (b) and (c). This comprises a description from the opening of the three plays, although in Text 19Q(c) the lengthy opening stage directions introduce the larger setting of New Orleans rather than the stage set.

a What do we learn about the setting?

b What clues are there about the possible themes or significance of the setting? You might consider how each playwright modifies the noun phrases. Consider the effect of the determiners and their specificity, as well as the choice of adjectives and adverbs. What effect do these have on our first responses to the setting?

c Draw the set from the information given. What else does this add to your interpretation?

The Herd follows on from these ideas of realism and social drama…

Text 19Q

(a)

The front room of a suburban house. An adjoining kitchen and living/dining room. Stairs leading to an unseen second floor. A corridor to the bathroom. A downstairs bedroom off the living room. The room is cursorily decorated for a birthday party.

Rory Kinnear, *The Herd*

(b)

The back yard of the Keller home in the outskirts of an American town. August of our era.

The stage is hedged on R. and L. by tall, closely planted poplar which lend the yard a secluded atmosphere. Upstage is filled with the back of the house and its open, unroofed porch which extends into the yard some six feet. The house is two stories high and has seven rooms.

Arthur Miller, *All My Sons*, Act 1

(c)

Two rooms can be seen, not too clearly defined. The first one entered is primarily a kitchen but contains a folding bed to be used by Blanche. The room beyond this is a bedroom. Off this room is a narrow door to a bathroom.

Tennessee Williams, *A Streetcar Named Desire*, Scene 1

Check your responses in the Ideas section on Cambridge Elevate

In contrast, Shakespeare's set does not change from play to play. The stages on which his plays were originally performed were non-localised, with no specific scenery for each one. Everything is evoked from the atmosphere created through the language, from castle battlements in *Hamlet,* woods containing fairies in *A Midsummer's Night Dream* and two settings in *Othello* - Venice and Cyprus. Shakespeare's simple stage had a canopy, a balcony, columns and doors at the back of the stage, as seen in Figure 19B.

To explore how Shakespeare used a non-localised set, the dialogue and stage directions in Text 19R(a) give an orientation towards the location of the action and the setting the stage depicts at this juncture of the play. Iago and Roderigo have been talking outside Brabantio's house and it is obviously night. Yet almost immediately afterwards, the stage becomes the Venetian Senate's meeting room.
Text 19R(b) is the opening of Act 2 after some of the Venetian military have arrived in Cyprus following their victory at sea. From the dialogue, it appears that the first Gentleman must be at the front of the stage looking out over the audience and we imagine this is where the sea lies. Behind would be the stage, ready to be the next setting as various locations in Cyprus.

Figure 19B

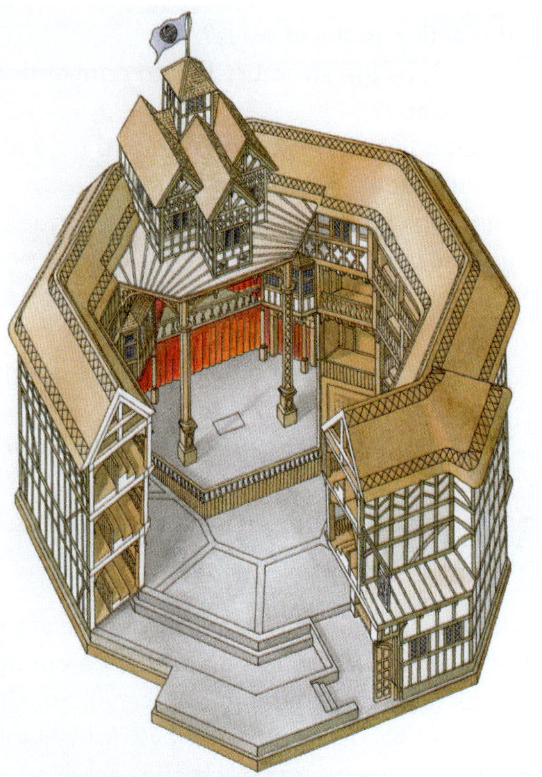

Text 19R

(a)

RODERIGO: Here is her father's house (75)

Brabantio [appears] above at a window (after 82)

Enter Brabantio in his nightgown and Servants with torches (after 158)

William Shakespeare, *Othello*, 1.1.

(b)

MONTANO: What from the cape can you discern at sea?

I GENTLEMAN: Nothing at all; it is a high-wrought flood.
I cannot 'twixt the heaven and the main
Descry a sail

William Shakespeare, *Othello*, 2.1.1–4

ACTIVITY 12

Exploring stagecraft

For your play, create a list of the props, sound effects, music and lighting used. Identify where they are used in the play (by act and/or scene or section).

Explore the symbolism these have. How do they link to the play's action, individual characters or themes?

Check your responses in the Ideas section on Cambridge Elevate

19.6 Creating characters

The characters themselves are crucial in any play as it is the characterisation of these that both sustains our interest and helps us as an audience engage with their story. Characters can be categorised as major or minor ones but each individual character has a dramatic function, otherwise there would be no point in their appearing on the stage. For example, *A Streetcar Named Desire* opens with a minor character (who Williams terms in the language of the time he was writing as 'Negro Woman') *in medias res* telling a gossipy story. Although she has only a few more lines in the scene, her function is to establish the racial diversity and harmony of a vibrant 1940s New Orleans. In contrast, the major characters of the play are given a significant amount of dialogue, fleshed out with personalities, and contribute to the plot and action.

In drama, where conflict is being foregrounded there is usually a **protagonist** (the main character) and an **antagonist** (a competitor and a threat to the protagonist, although it can also be a group of characters).

Key terms

protagonist: the central character around which the plot revolves

antagonist: the character in conflict or in opposition to the main character

ACTIVITY 13

Exploring characters

a Use the list of all the characters in the play you are studying printed before the text of the play starts. This will help you understand the roles and functions of characters and the relationships the playwrights are drawing between the characters (i.e. family, friendship, social hierarchies, etc.) in order to build conflict for dramatic purposes. Divide them into major and minor characters.

b Identify the protagonist and antagonist(s). What function does each minor character have? Look at where they appear in the play - what do they do? What's significant about the point in the action when they appear?

c Draw a relationship chart between characters - for example, family, friends, etc. This will give you an idea of the social connections that the playwrights are drawing between characters - for example, parents and children, wife and husband. How might these roles and relationships add to the characters' identities or the potential for conflict between them?

19.6.1 Constructing identity

If we reflect on our own identity, we might think of all the things that contribute to it - our gender, age, ethnicity, cultural heritage, the region we come from, our family values and beliefs, the roles we have at work and within families, as well as the experiences that we have through our lives that continue to mould us. How we demonstrate our identity can be in the way we dress, what we buy and own, the leisure and career choices we make, the food we eat and the language we use. It can even be in the name we have. Think about what your name shows about you - your ethnicity (first and surnames can show where your family come from, even if from a long time ago), your age (different names can be popular at different times), your gender, class and even your parents' marital status (whether you have your mother or father's surname or a combination of both).

ACTIVITY 14

Surveying character's names

Use the list of the characters' names before the play text. For each name, see what connotations or ideas about the characters' identities you gain from the writer's choices of the following:

a age
b gender
c class
d ethnicity
e relationships to other characters
f setting
g links to possible themes.

Check your responses in the Ideas section on Cambridge Elevate

19.6.2 Constructing and conveying identity through dramatic techniques

Writers call upon this understanding of identity in order to create characters. For the purposes of dramatic study we can group these into four areas:

1 **appearance** – what information is given about the way the character looks and how they dress?
2 **background** – what do we learn of their experiences or lives before the play's action?
3 **behaviour** – what do they do?
4 **speech style** – what characterises their language? Are there patterns in the words they use or in the grammatical structures to their lines that indicate accent or their social background?

So how do playwrights show these? They present these through a combination of three aspects:

1 **stage directions**: tell us about appearance, background, behaviours
2 **the character's own dialogue**: tells us how they speak – and possibly their behaviour and background
3 **other characters' observations:** can tell us about their appearance, behaviour and background.

These can be built up through the course of the play but an audience's first impressions of characters allow for judgements to be formed. Take Williams' introduction of Stanley in Text 19S. Stanley briefly returns home to his flat in a culturally diverse area of New Orleans after work on his way to bowling with his friend, Mitch. Stanley's neighbours are talking outside the flats and watch this exchange with Stella, who is inside their top-floor flat.

Text 19S

Stage directions

Twenty-eight or thirty roughly dressed in blue denim work clothes. Stanley carries his bowling jacket and a red-stained package from a butcher's.

He heaves the package at her.

Tennessee Williams, *A Streetcar Named Desire*, Scene 1

The character's own dialogue

1 Naw, we gotta have odds!
2 Stanley (*bellowing*): Hey, there! Stella, Baby!
3 Stanley: Catch!
Stella: What?
Stanley: Meat!

Other characters' observations

- Negro Woman: What was that package he th'ew at 'er?
- She rises from steps, laughing louder.

Williams wants us to see that Stanley is an ordinary working man, possibly a manual worker from his clothes. We learn a little about Stanley's leisure interest, bowling, which was very popular in 1940s America and suggests Stanley's interest in competitive sport and his camaraderie with men. The package of meat seems symbolic. Think what this could represent. Firstly, it could be Stanley as a provider for Stella, typical of a 1940s world where married women were less likely to work. Secondly, this could have sexual connotations and that seems to be what the neighbour responds to in her laughter. We also get a sense of Stanley's character from his tone of voice, 'bellowing', and his actions 'heaving'. Additionally, his dialogue is elliptical, exclamative and non-standard. These verbal and non-verbal clues create the first impression that he is working class and dominating of others, especially women.

Some characters may seem like stereotypes and playwrights use these in order to explore their themes. For example, in *A Streetcar Named Desire*, Williams creates Stanley to represent a stereotypical **hegemonic masculinity** and Blanche, the equivalent **hegemonic femininity.** Other characters, such as Mitch and Stella, present other stereotypes of men and women such as the doting son and the dutiful wife.

Key terms

hegemonic masculinity: the prevalent view of society about what it is to be masculine, i.e. behaviours, appearance, interests, etc. that keep men in a dominant position over women

hegemonic femininity: the prevalent view of society about what it is to be feminine, i.e. behaviours, appearance, interests, etc. that keep women subordinate to men

ACTIVITY 15

Exploring stereotypes

1 Consider the stereotypes evident in your play's characters. Do they fall into any of the following categories? If not, suggest others.
   - Gender
   - Class
   - Occupations
   - Ethnicity
   - Age
2 How are these stereotypes presented? Identify language, behaviours, quotations that support your conclusions.
3 Why do you think the playwright is using these stereotypes? How are they used for dramatic effect?

19.6.3 Representing characters' speech styles

Playwrights create an **idiolect** for their characters to give them distinct voices, just as we ourselves have a distinct speaking style made up from our regional background and influences like our peers, family, education and media that can also suggest a **sociolect**. It's likely that people would recognise you even if you weren't identified just from your style of speech in the phrases and fillers you use regularly in conversation and your written posts and texts with their conversational traits.

Likewise playwrights create their characters' voices by calling upon features from the different language levels. Some of these can be illustrated from the following list, although there are many others that you may think of as you examine how each character speaks.

- **Phonetics, phonology and prosodics:** the devices writers use to present a character's way of saying words that express their feelings and pronouncing words that may convey an accent – for example, the stress placed on words or the end clipping of words.
- **Lexis and semantics**: the individual words or phrases that characters use – for example, formal or informal choices such as idioms or lexical choices that depict a dialect.
- **Grammar**: the types of sentences a character uses and the construction of these in standard or non-standard ways – for example, the use of imperatives or non-standard elliptical constructions where words are omitted.

Key terms

idiolect: the variety or form of a language used by an individual

sociolect: a distinct speaking style made up from our regional background and influences like our peers, family, education and media

Look at Text 19T, a selection from some of Joe Keller's first lines, where he is having a conversation with his neighbours, Jim and Frank, and reading the wanted advertisements in the Sunday newspaper.

Text 19T

What's doin'?

Want the paper?

To see what people want, y'know. For instance, here's a guy is looking for two Newfoundland dogs?

Ain't that awful?

All the kind of business goin' on.

Arthur Miller, *All My Sons*

Miller presents Joe's dropping of the final 'g' on words with the use of the apostrophe to show the omission. The apostrophe is also used to show assimilation 'y'know' and the contractions are typical of American non-standard speech, 'ain't'. You might notice Joe's elliptical style of speech: this could either be characteristic of his speech style or because of the context of a comfortable, casual chat between neighbours that opens the play. Certainly, there seem to be many interrogatives used either to be neighbourly or offer his opinion but you might also see the non-standard aspects of his speech in some sentences. Clearly, because this comes from the opening there will be further features used to present Joe Keller's character but we, the audience, are already starting to form judgements about him from his speech style.

ACTIVITY 16

Exploring identity

Investigate the characteristics in Table 19B and use this table to create an A3 sheet or poster for all four aspects of identity. Skim through the text, writing down quotations and stage directions as you find them. Finally, think about what meanings and interpretations these might have after you have completed your poster and can see it in front of you.

Table 19B

Appearance	Behaviours
Background	Speech style

Choose the character in the list from your play. (You can repeat this activity until you have a character checklist for each character in your play.)

a Desdemona (*Othello*)

b Mitch (*A Streetcar Named Desire*)

c George (*All My Sons*)

d Carol (*The Herd*)

19.7 Power and positioning

It's probably not surprising if we link 'conflict' to ideas about power, as claiming and exerting power over other people is a key way to get what we want. Firstly, let's explore some different kinds of power by relating it to you personally. Power can be categorised in many ways but the following list will offer you some starting points for reflection.

- **Positional**: where issues of hierarchy, status, relationships and roles (occupational or social) are significant – for example, the power of a school principal over both pupils and staff.
- **Knowledge**: where others' expertise and ideas afford power – for example, a doctor's medical knowledge over a patient.
- **Personal**: where others can have an influence over us based on such things as charisma, admiration and fear – for example, a school bully or a political leader.

ACTIVITY 17

Exploring power in interactions

Note down all the people you interact with regularly from thinking about your daily routines and activities. Now separate your list to reflect who holds power over you and who you hold power over. Identify the types of power using the categories suggested, or create others that you think are important. What did you notice about your two lists? Are the people listed completely different?

Check your responses in the Ideas section on Cambridge Elevate

In reality, power is complex and constantly negotiated, rather than something that is fixed and unchanging and, in plays, this complexity is vital for creating interest and plots often hinge on power shifts – especially in the tragic genre where the downfall of one character is often signalled by a loss of power.

19.7.1 Presenting power on stage

Now think about how you might perceive power on stage. Playwrights can encode power through aspects of stagecraft as well as language. Playwrights can signal these in the stage directions, or they can be interpreted by the actors and/or directors from the inferences of the dialogue. Some playwrights choose to be very explicit by indicating what the character is doing and how they are expressing themselves, but others like Shakespeare leave it to the language itself to suggest instructions for performance.

In terms of staging and its links to power, the following three areas are significant and pose a number of questions that you can examine in the play.

1 **Stage setting and location of the action**
Where is the play set? What is the actual set on the stage? What's the significance of the set? Does the location (or parts of it) belong to any of the characters? Is the setting private or public? Does the setting change? Does the change affect the characters' power?

2 **Proxemics and body language**
Who shows ownership of the space on stage? What does the physical positioning of one character to another suggest? What do characters do non-verbally with their bodies - facial expressions, gestures, movements?

3 **Action/events**
What occurs on stage? In what order do events happen? What meaning do the actions have to characters and their relationships?

In *A Streetcar Named Desire,* the first proper interaction between Stanley and his sister-in-law Blanche, after her arrival in New Orleans, occurs in Scene 2. Blanche has come to stay with her sister, Stella, and Stella's husband, Stanley, who Blanche has not yet met. Blanche is getting dressed after a bath but the small apartment setting offers little privacy and all her belongings are in the main shared living area. Stanley wants to talk to Blanche alone about the loss of his wife's inheritance - a historic plantation house from the days of slavery and prosperity in the southern states of America - which Stella has only just revealed to Stanley. In Text 19U are some of the stage directions within the scene, in the order they occur, which suggest the way that Williams shows the shifting of power between them.

Text 19U

She closes the drapes between the rooms.
He crosses through the drapes with a smouldering look.
She smiles at him radiantly.
She pauses with an indefinite gesture.
[Blanche] (pressing her hands to her ears)
He crosses to the trunk, shoves it roughly open and begins to open compartments.
He indicates another sheaf of papers.
He snatches them up. She speaks fiercely.
He rips off the ribbons and starts to examine them.
Blanche snatches them from him and they cascade to the floor.
She now seems faint with exhaustion and she sits down.
She hands him the entire box.
She removes her glasses with an exhausted laugh.
She leans back and closes her eyes.

Tennessee Williams, *A Streetcar Named Desire*, Scene 2

Watch tutorial video, Power on Stage, on Cambridge Elevate

It seems that the setting, a rather intimate one in a confined space, establishes a rather flirtatious atmosphere between them. However, this changes with Stanley's actions of touching Blanche's case containing her belongings, their subsequent tussle over the private love letters he finds and her capitulation to his intention to read all her papers - shown through her body language and physical response to his actions.

An audience cannot see the written stage directions but interprets the relationships between characters from the ways the playwright's suggestions are presented. By looking at Figure 19C, which contains images from performances of *A Streetcar Named Desire*, you can interpret the power dynamics from the characters' proxemics and body language and the setting.

Figure 19C

ACTIVITY 18

Exploring power on stage

a Take the stage directions from a section of the play you are studying.

b Find images from stage or film versions (for *Othello*, use these as your primary source, although try to match these with specific scenes).

c Write a paragraph of around 300 words analysing how power is shown through the setting and the characters' non-verbal communication and actions.

19.7.2 Presenting power in language

Clearly, writers can also show power relations between characters in the language they use and their conversational behaviour, both in interactions with other characters and when addressing the audience in monologues and soliloquies. And, of course, exerting power in language is a valuable tool in gaining an advantage over other characters, particularly in situations of conflict.

ACTIVITY 19

Examining power in dialogue

Pick a short section of dialogue from your play and explore the conversational behaviour of the characters using the questions below. Highlight quotations to illustrate these behaviours. You could break these down further by examining turn-taking, topics, interruptions and fluency together first, then focus on speech acts and finally follow this by exploring lexical features and address terms together.

What are your conclusions about power from your findings? For example, which features most closely associate with powerful and powerless behaviours in your extracts? Which characters show most power in the interaction you have selected and which the least? What contextual reasons can you give for these?

a Turn-taking
- Who has the most turns?
- Whose turns are the longest?
- Who initiates the turns?
- Who decides whose turn it is to speak?
- Who responds?

b Topics
- Who introduces the topics or topic shifts?

c Interruptions
- Who interrupts?
- Who is interrupted?

d Fluency
- Who uses full utterances?
- Who uses incomplete utterances?
- Who is fluent?
- Who uses fillers and false starts?

e Speech acts
- Who uses the speech acts: questioning, demanding, complaining, threatening and commanding?
- Who uses the speech acts: answering, agreeing, apologising and giving in?
- Who uses interrogatives?
- Who uses imperatives?
- Who uses declaratives?

f Terms of address
- Who uses first name address terms?
- Who uses titles or more formal address terms?

g Lexis
- Who uses formal or informal lexis?
- Who uses technical and field specific lexis?
- Who uses euphemism or dysphemism?
- Who uses metaphor?
- Who uses rhetorical devices?

Check your responses in the Ideas section on Cambridge Elevate

19.7.3 Exploring power through terms of address

We can all be addressed in very different ways and these convey much about our roles and our relationships with others, as well as being determined by the situations we are in. Who calls you by your first name, your nickname or your full name? Who would you use a nickname for, or their full name or a name that denotes their role and relationship to you? Writers make use of **social deixis** (where the words a speaker uses encodes their attitudes to another person) to explore characters' roles, identities and relationships to each other. This may not be fixed throughout the play and changes to the ways that characters address each other can symbolise their shifting feelings as the action progresses. Look at the exchanges in Text 19V between Othello and

Desdemona. Text 19V(a) is when they are reunited in Cyprus, soon after their marriage. Text 19V(b) is after Othello has been persuaded of Desdemona's infidelity. Both are delivered publicly, in front of many other characters.

Text 19V

(a)

OTHELLO: O, my fair warrior!

DESDEMONA: My dear Othello!

William Shakespeare, *Othello*, 2.2.173–174

(b)

DESDEMONA: Why, sweet Othello

OTHELLO: Devil!

William Shakespeare, *Othello*, 4.1.229–230

Desdemona's choice of vocative is unchanging, showing her constant feelings and she premodifies these with affectionate adjectives. In contrast, Othello's fond address and flattery in the noun 'warrior' which gives both of them equal status is replaced by a harsh and insulting address of 'Devil', which at a period of strong religious beliefs would have held very emotive power.

Looking at one of the more modern plays, we can see how **asymmetry** is not at different points of the play but signalled by different characters in their interactions. Take Ann's first entrance on to the stage in Act 1 of *All My Sons*. Ann is a former neighbour of the Kellers and childhood sweetheart of Larry, their eldest son who went missing in action during the war. She has come to visit at the request of Chris, the Kellers' other son, who wishes to marry her. In this interaction, the Kellers call her 'Annie', a newly introduced neighbour calls her 'Ann' and her fiancée calls her 'kid'. In return, she calls the Kellers 'Kate' and 'Joe', the neighbour she is introduced to by Chris, 'Jim … Doctor Bayliss' and she does not refer to Chris by any address term. All these show asymmetry as Ann is addressed by the Kellers in the **diminutive**, placing her back in her childhood self and Chris's fond address seems to be infantilising her also. The introduction to Jim appears more symmetrical, but Chris's modification of the introduction gives Jim his medical title, elevating his status to Ann.

With Shakespeare, because he was writing many centuries ago, grammatical forms also contribute to the social deixis. In older forms of English there were options to choose 'you' or 'thou' as second-person pronouns, whereas today we just use 'you' no matter how many people we are addressing and what our relationship is with them. In Shakespeare's time, the singular subject pronoun 'thou' – and its object form 'thee' – indicates a familiarity and a **solidarity** between speakers. In contrast, the pronoun 'you' connotes a social distance when addressed to one person, as well as signifying social status. In **unequal encounters**, 'sir' could be used as an **honorific**, 'you' would be used to address a person of perceived higher status in society so as to show respect and to be polite and social superiors might use 'thou' to their inferiors. So, Shakespeare can mark characters claiming or exerting power very subtly, showing solidarity and demonstrating politeness between characters. Look at Iago's use of pronouns in his interactions with other characters and you'll see how Shakespeare uses this grammatical deixis to full effect.

Key terms

social deixis: a category for words and expressions that encode a speaker's attitude towards another person

asymmetry: a power imbalance between speakers shown by the unequal way they address each other

diminutive: the informal form of a name, often characterised by the addition of a suffix

solidarity: words chosen to strengthen social ties between speakers

unequal encounters: where one person has more power than another in a social situation or communication exchange

honorific: a word, title or grammatical form that signals social deference such as 'Dame'

ACTIVITY 20

Interpreting social deixis

Either look at the following selection for your play, or see what you can infer from looking at all of them from the contextual information given. Identify the lexical choices (pronouns, nouns, etc.) and grammatical choices (possession, determiners, etc.).

What are the connotations of the address choices? What relationship or attitudes do these express?

1. *Othello:* Iago is speaking about Othello. He has just been passed over for promotion by Othello, general of the Venetian armed forces although not a citizen of the state:
   'him'/ 'he', 'His Moorship', 'the Moor', 'an old black ram'
2. *A Streetcar Named Desire:* Stanley is speaking to his wife, Stella, about her sister Blanche who has been living with them for a few months:
   'Her Majesty', 'that girl', 'Sister Blanche', 'Dame Blanche'
3. *The Herd:* Carol is speaking about her ex-husband, Ian, to her parents and daughter:
   'your father', 'Ian', 'him', 'Claire's father', 'Ghandi', 'the martyr'
4. *All My Sons:* Chris is speaking about his father, Joe Keller:
   'Joe Mcguts', 'great guy', 'dad', 'my father'.

Check your responses in the Ideas section on Cambridge Elevate

19.7.4 Exploring power shifts

The downfall of the hero in the plays that are tragedies is often presented through their loss of power and one way that playwrights can demonstrate this is through changes to a character's language. Compare Texts 19W(a) and (b) from *Othello*. In Text 19W(a), from the beginning of the play, Shakespeare presents Othello's public defence to the Venetian Senators of his secret marriage to Desdemona. Text 19W(b) from Act 3 depicts his changed language as Iago's plan to discredit Desdemona by suggesting that she has been unfaithful starts to take effect.

Text 19W

(a)

It is most true; true I have married her;
The very head and front of my offending
Hath this extent, no more. Rude am I in my speech
And little blessed with the soft phrase of peace,
For since these arms of mine had seven year's pith
Till now some nine moons wasted, they have used
Their dearest action in the tented field.

William Shakespeare, *Othello*, 1.2.78–85

(b)

Lie with her? Lie on her? We say lie on her when they belie her. Lie with her! Zounds, that's fulsome! Handkerchief – confessions – handkerchief! To confess and be hanged for his labour. First to be hanged and then to confess. I tremble at it. Nature would not invest herself in such a shadowing passion without some instruction. It is not words that shakes me thus. Pish! Noses, ears and lips.

William Shakespeare, *Othello*, 4.1.35–41

The contextual factors that make Othello powerful at the beginning are his military success and value to the Venetian state. His later powerlessness is due to his seeming lack of personal power in his relationship with Desdemona or in the reflection of her alleged infidelity on his reputation, thereby lessening his positional power in the sight of others. In Text 19W(a) you can see his confidence presented in the verse as he first reminds the Senate of his soldierly qualities. His loss of power in Text 19W(b) is reflected in the shift to prose. Notice too the elliptical sentences in contrast with the syntactical variation and complexity shown in Text 19W(a). Likewise, there is a change in the formal lexis of Text 19W(b) with the references from the semantic field of war to his cruder wordplay with 'lie' and his taboo exclamation 'zounds'.

ACTIVITY 21

Examining power shifts

Focus on the power of individual characters. Use the language levels to examine the ways that their power or powerlessness is shown in their lexis, grammar, discourse, phonology and prosodics and through pragmatics.

- *All My Sons*: compare Joe Keller's language in Act 1 when talking to Chris and Ann about his return from prison to the end of Act 2 when he admits to Chris his involvement in the shipping of faulty aeroplane parts.
- *A Streetcar Named Desire:* compare Blanche's interactions with Stanley in Scene 2 and Scene 10.
- *Othello:* compare Cassio's language in Act 2, Scene 1 with Act 3, Scene 1.
- *The Herd:* compare Carol's telephone conversation in the opening to her interaction with Ian when they are alone on stage together discussing Ian's reasons for visiting.

19.8 The importance of politeness

Politeness is a social norm that has been ingrained in our behaviours, both verbally and non-verbally, since we were young. It has its own routines (think of all the phatic talk at the beginnings and ends of conversations where we ask how people are and tell people that we look forward to seeing them soon) and lexical markers ('please' and 'thank you'). Politeness does depend on context. You might get away with ending a conversation abruptly with a close friend but with others, such as your grandparents, this would appear rude and impolite. Politeness, an aspect of pragmatics, is about maintaining social harmony but its use, the manner of its use or even not using it, all indicate much about ourselves and our relationships with others. Writers can use this shared understanding of politeness strategies to good effect to highlight where conflict happens, showing either how it is maintained and escalated or diffused and resolved.

You have already seen how important politeness is in our spoken interactions. The sociologist Goffman's concept of face, the image that we present of ourselves to others is also relevant to the study of the dramatic genre and exploring conflict. The idea of '**face-work**' (Goffman's term for the behaviours used in presenting or protecting our face to others, as well as those that show our respect of other speakers' 'faces') is important when examining drama. In the plays you are studying conflict is being foregrounded and either the preservation or the threats to face are important to both characterisation and action.

According to the linguists Brown and Levinson (1987), decisions about politeness strategies can depend on the *social distance* and *relative power* of the speakers/hearers and the *ranking* of the imposition accordingly. For example, to apply these ideas to a real-life situation, you could imagine the difference in the amount of face threat between a request from a new class mate asking you to lend them your lesson notes and a school friend that you've known for a long time making the same request. Here, the social distance means that you might see a new class mate as more face threatening. If the same new student asks the teacher directly for their lesson notes then the power variable between teacher and students makes this potentially even more face threatening.

However, if the class mate asks the teacher (or even you) to lend them a pen, in ranking terms this is less threatening than asking for the lesson notes. So, to transport this to a dramatic situation, it might be interesting to explore how dramatists both play with our preconceived notions of impositions and face threats in the ways that they present these and sometimes overturn these expectations for dramatic effect.

Key terms

face-work: Goffman's term for the behaviours used in presenting or protecting our face to others, as well as those that show our respect of other speakers' 'faces'

In *A Streetcar Named Desire*, there is a very awkward moment for the audience and the Young Man, a minor character who appears only in Scene 5. He is a paperboy and has come to collect money. Blanche is the only person at home and she tries to keep him with her for company by asking him questions and giving him compliments. As they have never met before, the social distance is quite large between them, but Blanche has power over him as an older adult and the Young Man politely answers her questions. The shock for the audience is in the ranking of her imposition when Blanche says 'I want to kiss you' and does not get his agreement before moving to do this on stage. Her following words that she's got to be 'good' and keep her 'hands off children' not only foreground her imposition and highlight her threat to the Young Man's face but also remind the audience that Blanche is abusing her power and status as a teacher.

Try asking the following questions of your play and its characters.

a Who needs to be admired and liked: i.e. have their positive face needs been met?
b Who meets their positive face needs? What politeness strategies are used to minimise the loss of positive face?
c Who threatens their positive face? What face threatening act (FTA) strategies are used?
d Who needs to be unimpeded by others: i.e. have their negative face needs been met?

e Who meets their negative face needs? What politeness strategies are used to minimise the loss of negative face?
f Who threatens their negative face needs? What FTA strategies are used?

19.8.1 Exploring positive and negative politeness

You have learned that positive politeness is about ensuring that others feel appreciated and valued and is a strategy that speakers adopt to preserve face in the light of an FTA. There may be times in the action and in exploring relationships that the representation of positive politeness is crucial. In Text 19X(a), Cassio is signalling overtly his gratitude to Iago for his offers to help Cassio regain his reputation, although the audience is aware of the dramatic irony of Cassio's statement. We know that Iago has caused this to happen to gain his revenge on Cassio for taking the promotion he believed was rightly his. In Text 19X(b) he is expressing his gratitude to Emilia for her help in trying to restore his reputation by placing it on record.

Text 19X

(a)

[to IAGO]
CASSIO: I humbly thank you for't

Exit [IAGO]

I never knew a Florentine more kind and honest.

William Shakespeare, *Othello*, 3.1.37–38

(b)

[to EMILIA]
CASSIO: I am much bound to you.

William Shakespeare, *Othello*, 3.1.53

In Act 2 of *All My Sons*, George uses positive politeness about Kate Keller when he first arrives at their house when he says '[with forced appreciation] Good old Kate, remembered my grape juice'. Kate is presented in the nurturing role of a mother throughout and so her reliving of his childhood tastes is demonstrative of both hospitality and a shared history. His reluctance to do so reflects his awareness of positive politeness as good manners.

In *A Streetcar Named Desire*, Stella is desperate to preserve Blanche's positive face, aware that her sister is worried about aging and losing her attractiveness to men. Throughout the play she compliments Blanche on her appearance and asks others to do so. In Scene 1, when they are reunited after a long time apart, Stella says to Blanche that she looks 'just fine' and 'it's just incredible, Blanche, how well you're looking' – although Williams signals with the stage direction that Stella says this 'a little wearily' that this positive politeness strategy is a ritual and a means to keep Blanche happy. Even at the end of the play when she agrees to having Blanche sent away to an institution, she wants Blanche's positive face to still feel rewarded, asking Eunice, her neighbour, to tell Blanche 'how well she's looking'.

Negative politeness is a strategy concerned with protecting the speaker from a FTA by ensuring that others are not imposed upon. You can see a negative politeness strategy being used by Cassio in Text 19Y. Here he is asking for Emilia's help in arranging a meeting with Desdemona, who he hopes will persuade Othello to reinstate him to his job. He is addressing Emilia's negative face needs to be unimpeded through his use of modality, shown in the auxiliary verb 'may' and the conditional 'if'.

Text 19Y

CASSIO: Yet I beseech you
If you think fit, or that it may be done,
Give me an advantage of some brief discourse
With Desdemon alone

William Shakespeare, *Othello*, 3.1.48–51

In *The Herd*, Ian (Carol's ex-husband) is presented using negative politeness strategies in many of his lines, using 'sorry' as a discourse maker almost to his contributions to the interaction, as in 'Sorry, do you know where the lemons are'. This apologetic tone reflects his social distance from the other family members and his apparent inferiority to them based on his earlier desertion of his wife Carol, daughter Claire and disabled son Andy.

19.8.2 Exploring impoliteness

But, despite the fact that from being very young we are socialised to be polite, we also know how to be rude to others and attack their positive and negative face needs with FTAs. Sometimes this can be accidental and we might feel sorry that we have upset someone; however, sometimes we can be impolite deliberately.

ACTIVITY 22

Examining impoliteness strategies

Recall recent situations where you have been impolite. Who were these with? What linguistic and non-verbal strategies did you use to be impolite? How were these situations resolved, or not resolved?

Although each situation may be unique to you and your relationships with others, it is likely to have some common patterns, particularly in its linguistic and non-verbal components, as identified by the linguist Jonathan Culpeper (1996).

a conventional impolite expressions in the taboo vocatives used to address others, or taboo language used to describe a person
b personal evaluations marked with negatives: e.g. 'you're not'
c dismissals: e.g. 'get lost'
d silencers: e.g. 'shut up'
e threats: 'I'm going to…'
f condescension: 'that's stupid'
g insincere politeness: e.g. 'I'd like to thank you for breaking my phone'
h non-verbal gestures: e.g. not shaking someone's hand, staring at someone.

In addition to the list above, Culpeper adds bald on-record impoliteness, where the rudeness is explicit and directly face-threatening to the hearer. You can see this in Patricia's lines addressed to her ex-son-in-law, Ian, in Text 19Z. The declaratives - 'you are', 'I have imagined'- along with the adjectives she uses for him - 'hateful' and 'loathsome' - express the strength of her feelings.

Text 19Z

You are a hateful, hateful, loathsome man. I have imagined you in countless accidents over the years, not all of which have been fatal, but none of which have captured satisfactorily the ferocity of my antipathy towards you.

Rory Kinnear, *The Herd*

One way that speakers can be impolite is by refraining from using politeness strategies. Look at Text 19AA, where Stanley withholds a compliment that his sister-in-law Blanche requests from him. Here Stanley's 'okay', rather than a stronger adjective which holds positive connotations for female beauty, acts as a deliberate putdown to Blanche.

Text 19AA

BLANCHE: Would you think it possible that I was once considered to be – attractive?
STANLEY: Your looks are okay.
BLANCHE: I was fishing for a compliment.
STANLEY: I don't go in for that stuff.

Tennessee Williams, *A Streetcar Named Desire*, Scene 2

Elsewhere in the play, Stanley's FTAs to Blanche (and other characters) are in the form of speech acts such as orders, sarcasm and mimicry. However, it's not just Stanley who is impolite in *A Streetcar Named Desire*. Blanche and Stella also use speech acts like insults and criticism. Look at Text 19AB(a), Blanche's monologue - secretly overheard by Stanley. She has just discovered that her sister has been reconciled to Stanley, who had hit her violently the previous night. In Text 19AB(b), Blanche and Stella are watching Stanley eat while miserably celebrating Blanche's birthday.

Text 19AB

(a)

BLANCHE: He acts like an animal, has an animal's habits! Eats like one, moves like one, talks like one!

Tennessee Williams, *A Streetcar Named Desire*, Scene 4

(b)

BLANCHE: Apparently Mr Kowalski is not amused.
STELLA: Mr Kowalski is too busy making a pig of himself to think of anything else!
STANLEY: That's right, baby.
STELLA: Your face and your fingers are disgustingly greasy. Go and wash up and then help me clear the table.

Tennessee Williams, *A Streetcar Named Desire*, Scene 8

Although in Text 19AB(a) Blanche thinks she is just addressing Stella, it acts as a bald on-record FTA because the audience knows that Stanley is listening. She offers her personal evaluation of Stanley in the comparison to an animal that is emphasised through the repetition of this noun and the rhetorical tripling of verb phrases to extend the unfavourable comparison. In Text 19AB(b), the sisters act together to insult Stanley's table manners, although Stella is more explicit with the conventional metaphor of a 'pig' associated negatively with food and eating habits. Stella continues her insult with the possessive determiner 'your' to reinforce Stanley's physical unpleasantness to her, intensified further in the emotive and judgemental phrase 'disgustingly greasy'. Her final insult, to an audience who knows by now Stanley's sense of power in his own home and over Stella, is in her imperatives to him 'Go and wash up'.

ACTIVITY 23

Examining politeness and impoliteness in drama

Explore the playwright's use of politeness and impoliteness in your own play. Some suggestions for your focus are:

- *Othello* – compare Iago's soliloquies where he talks about Othello with his interactions with Othello (for example, 1.3.365–386 with 3.3.90–166)
- *A Streetcar Named Desire:* compare Mitch's and Stanley's interactions with Blanche (for example, Scene 3 and Scenes 9–10)
- *All My Sons:* George's interactions with the Kellers and his sister, Ann, in Act 2
- *The Herd*: characters' interactions with Ian and Ian's responses (for example, pages 44–58).

19.9 Exploring themes

As you read the play, build up a bank of the themes the playwright is exploring. Some may be highlighted in the name of the play giving you a beginning point, but often writers will reveal themes more subtly and it is only at the end of your reading, or watching as an audience, that you can reflect on the writer's themes and messages. These themes might be presented through:

- staging
- action/events/plot
- words and images (visual and verbal).

Indeed, it's the combination of what the writers give the characters to say and do and the signifiers created from what the audience can see and interpret from the staging that make themes evident. A brief discussion of *All My Sons* might demonstrate the ways playwrights can use dramatic devices together to illustrate key themes.

Staging

The apple tree acts as Kate's memorial to her son Larry, the Kellers' lost son. At the beginning of Act 1 the 'slender' tree has toppled over in a storm. At the beginning of Act 2 the surviving son, Chris, is cutting down the tree stump. The living and the fallen tree are symbols for Larry and the loss of him.

Action/events/plot

Larry never appears in the play as a character but he is much discussed. The play begins with the neighbour, Frank, preparing a horoscope about him for Kate, and Kate recalls a nightmare about Larry from the previous night. Ann's previous relationship with Larry looms over her current and future one with Chris Keller, his brother, and Kate will not accept that Larry is dead. The final plot revelation in Act 3 in Larry's letter that he committed suicide when hearing about his father's responsibility for the death of twenty-one airmen results in Keller's final action.

Words and images (verbal and visual)

The title, *All My Sons*, makes the link between Larry and the twenty-one airmen killed on planes with the faulty engine parts deliberately shipped by Keller's company.

Another approach is to focus closely on the language choices to see how the playwrights highlight themes. Table 19C consists of quotations from *Othello*. As you read these, look at the hexagons in Figure 19D to decide to which themes the lines link, or if you would suggest other themes. You might also consider the significance of the character delivering these lines; this will allow you to reflect on their possible motivations. If you are unfamiliar with the full plot of *Othello*, this synopsis may help you:

The play presents the story of Othello, who is not from Venice (an independent Italian state in the time this was set) and his secret marriage to Desdemona, daughter of Brabantio, a Venetian Senator. Iago, bitter from being passed over by Othello for promotion, reveals the marriage to Brabantio and plots against Othello. Iago convinces Othello that Cassio, who was promoted, and Desdemona have been conducting a secret affair.

Figure 19D:
Themes and characters from *Othello*

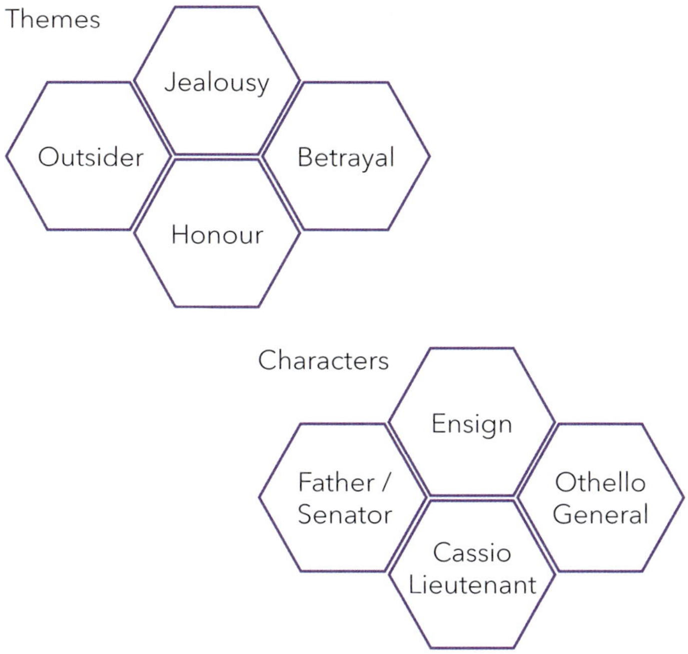

ACTIVITY 24

Examining themes

1. List as many of the themes as you can think of for your play. Some starting points for each play are:
   - *All My Sons*: money, reputation, deceit, fathers and sons, idealism
   - *A Streetcar Named Desire*: past and present, old and new American values, truth and lies, love, desire, loss
   - *The Herd:* bitterness, betrayal, resentment, disability, family.
2. List the characters and their roles and/or aspects of their identity you think are relevant, as modelled with *Othello* in Table 19C and Figure 19D.
3. There are different ways that you can present these creatively but a few ideas are:
   a. Make your own hexagons. You could cut out blank ones for writing key quotations on as you select these and the themes, characters and even aspects of staging (such as sound effects and props) that are relevant. Slot the hexagons together as you find links.

Table 19C

Iago: Even now, now, very now, an old black ram Is tupping your white ewe. (1.1.89–90)	Othello: She loved me for the dangers I had passed, And I loved her that she did pity them. This only is the witchcraft I have used. (1.3.166–169)
Brabantio: She is abused, stol'n from me, and corrupted (1.3.60)	Iago: I hate the Moor And it is thought abroad that 'twixt my sheets He's done my office. (1.3.367–369)
Brabantio: Look to her, Moor, if thou hast eyes to see: She has deceived her father and may thee. (1.3. 287-288)	Cassio: Reputation, reputation, reputation. O, I have lost my reputation! I have lost the immortal part of myself, and what remains is bestial. (2.3.242–244)
Othello: I had rather be a toad And live upon the vapour of a dungeon Than keep a corner in the thing I love For others' uses. (3.3.272–275)	Othello: I have done the state some service, and they know 't; No more of that. I pray you, in your letters When you shall these unlucky deeds relate, Speak of me as I am; (5.2.335–338)

b Design posters for each theme, using images and quotations.

c Devise a PowerPoint or Prezi presentation, using audio or visual clips, key quotations and visual images.

19.10 Bringing it all together

19.10.1 Self-assessment: check your learning

For each of the statements in the table, evaluate your confidence in each topic area.

For Paper 2 of the A Level examination, Section B constitutes 45 of the final marks and offers a choice between two possible questions for the play you have studied. Both questions will ask you to explore an aspect of conflict and will offer selected lines as a starting point for your analysis. It's an open book exam, so you can have a clean, unannotated copy of the play with you. The intention is that you use the text to help you structure your answer in addition to finding sections to analyse in detail that allow you to develop your argument.

All exam questions follow the same format and are presented in three parts. Look at Figure 19E for a practice question for *Othello*.

Explaining the assessment objectives

There are three assessment objectives tested here and they all carry different weightings as shown here.

- **AO1** (15 marks): Apply concepts and methods from integrated linguistic and literary study as appropriate, using associated terminology and coherent written expression

The key elements are your:
- expression of ideas
- use of terminology
- selection of language levels.

- **AO2** (20 marks): Analyse ways in which meanings are shaped in texts

Here you need to:
- interpret the question
- select appropriate sections from the play that will add to your interpretation
- explore aspects of characters' identities and relationships between them and the writer's use of stagecraft.

- **AO3** (10 marks): Demonstrate understanding of the significance and influence of the contexts in which texts are produced and received

Topic area	Very confident	Some knowledge	Need to revise
I know the events of the play in the order they occur			
I understand the genre conventions the playwright uses			
I can explain how features construct characters and relationships between characters			
I can identify contextual factors that relate to the play			
I can explore how language and stagecraft contribute to conflict			

Figure 19E: Practice question for *Othello*

Refer to Act 1 Scene 3 lines beginning from 'Wilt thou be fast to my hopes' and ending at 'must bring monstrous birth to the world's light'.

← *This indicates your starting point for the question, directing you to the section of the play you need to start from.*

This interaction occurs near the end of the scene. Iago is persuading Roderigo to follow him to Cyprus.

← *This gives you contextual information to help you locate the starting section.*

Referring to these lines and other parts of the play, **explore how and why Shakespeare presents manipulative behaviour** throughout the play.

← *This is the question itself, with instructions to (1) refer to the section specified and (2) find other sections of the play that you think examine the specific focus. Lastly, the question focus is given to you (here highlighted in bold).*

You need to consider the impact of the following:
- **mode**: the nature of a play as scripted dialogue and performed to an audience
- **genre**: associated conventions of the play; for example, if it is a tragedy
- **social and historical contexts**: relevant to the focus of the question.

19.10.2 Exploring possible questions

It's crucial that you identify the question focus, find the starting extract, note down how this links to the question and begin constructing your argument.

By starting with the question focus, you can read the extract you have been directed to for meaning. So, to continue with this practice question for *Othello*, the kinds of questions you might want to ask yourself are some larger ones like these about the play.
- What is manipulation?
- Who manipulates whom?
- What's the purpose of the manipulation?
- What does the manipulation add to the play?
- What forms does the manipulation take?
- How is the manipulation shown?

Then you would need to select sections of the play that would illustrate these such as Iago's (further) manipulations of Roderigo – as a tool for Iago's revenge and his plots – and Iago's manipulations of Othello – using jealousy, Othello's age, ethnicity and status.

ACTIVITY 25

Making selections

1 Choose your play and read the question carefully.
2 Identify the key words that are the focus of the question.
3 Read the starting extract.
4 Mind-map the different ways that you could approach these questions.
5 Note down other sections of the play that you could use for analysis.
   a *Othello*
      - Refer to Act 4 Scene 3 lines beginning from 'O these men, these men' and ending at 'The ills we do, their ills instruct us so'.
      - This interaction occurs near the end of the scene. Emilia is helping Desdemona to prepare for bed.
      - Referring to these lines and other parts of the play, examine how and why Shakespeare presents characters' contrasting views of marriage throughout the play.
   b *All My Sons*
      - Refer to Act 2 beginning from 'Then why'd you ship them out' and ending at 'My Chris'.
      - This interaction occurs near the end of Act 2. Keller's part in the decision to ship faulty parts to the American Air Force has just been revealed.
      - Referring to these lines and other parts of the play, examine how and why Miller presents conflicting ideas about responsibility throughout the play.
   c *A Streetcar Named Desire*
      - Refer to Scene 2 beginning from 'What's all this monkey doings?' and ending at 'Let's see the papers!'.
      - This interaction occurs at the beginning of the scene. Stanley is expressing his unhappiness to Stella about Blanche's arrival in Elysian Fields.
      - Referring to these lines and other parts of the play, examine how and why Williams uses marital conflict throughout the play.
   d *The Herd*
      - Refer to the section beginning 'And is he in the bus' and ending 'bye then'.
      - This telephone conversation occurs at the start of the play. Carol is arranging the details of her son's visit home with his carers.
      - Referring to these lines and other parts of the play, examine how and why Kinnear presents characters' lack of control throughout the play.

Next, you might want to refine your focus to look at the specifics and examine the directed lines. Ask yourself the same questions but also begin to drill down into how the manipulation is shown in the language and in the stagecraft. Making notes of these linked to quotations from the text is a good technique to use. For example, in the sample question for *Othello*, possible language features and aspects of stagecraft to explore in the interaction between Roderigo and Iago are:
- Roderigo's interrogatives
- status-marked pronoun choices and their use in stages of the interaction

- the vocatives used (e.g. 'Roderigo' / 'the Moor)'
- Iago's grammatical choices (e.g. imperatives)
- Iago's speech acts (e.g. promises)
- aspects of turn-taking
- contractions (e.g. 'I'll') and the pauses suggested by punctuation
- felicity conditions: Roderigo as willing to be led/ instructed – and Iago's appeals to Roderigo's positive face
- the significance of staging and setting as an interaction.

There are more features in Iago's soliloquy, such as:

- suggestions of thought processes and spontaneity in his plan: short rhetorical questions ('how?') and set phrases ('let me see now', 'let's see')
- modality and conditionals ('would', 'if') and Iago's declaratives acting as statements of intent
- Iago's impoliteness and FTAs
- the significance of the soliloquy.

19.10.3 Selecting contextual factors

Returning to our *Othello* question in Figure 19E, contextual factors you may consider are:

- scripted interaction as presenting plot development, characterisation and relationships
- the representation of a private conversation between Roderigo and Iago
- social hierarchies of the time
- political aspects and the importance of role and status
- the significance of this speech to Othello's personal tragedy and downfall and Iago's role.

ACTIVITY 26

Analysing language and meaning, stagecraft and context

Use the practice question in Activity 25 again for your play.

1. Read the passage given as the starting point for the question.
2. Apply your knowledge of language levels and select features you think are relevant.
3. Ask yourself how these features you have chosen shape the meaning.
4. Explore the aspects of stagecraft used in the extract cited in the Activity.
5. Consider the contextual factors that are relevant to the question.
6. Repeat these activities with the other extracts you will use in your essay.

The final stage is to write this up.

DEVELOPING

20 Making connections

In this unit, you will:

- consider what types of active connections you can make between literary and non-literary texts
- explore the requirements of the research project including research methods, academic conventions and the structure of the investigation
- understand how the project will be assessed through identifying the relevant assessment objectives to be awarded.

This relates to 'Making connections' in the specification for A Level.

20.1 What is *Making connections*?

Making connections is the non-exam assessment where you have the opportunity to bring together your learning in a research project of your choice. This will allow you to select and closely investigate aspects of your study of English Language and Literature that you have found interesting, while developing skills as an independent learner and researcher – powerful tools that introduce you to a particular style of academic writing that you will not have tackled elsewhere in your study.

The skills you will acquire by undertaking the research project are invaluable, either for further academic study or for roles within the workplace. These skills vary from those to do with critical thinking, such as being open-minded and not forcing conclusions to suit an initial hypothesis or prediction about your findings, to the skills required of being an independent learner – including the ability to judiciously select methodologies, create and refine research questions, as well as draw conclusions from close analysis.

In *Making connections* you will also demonstrate your understanding of language and literature as integrated. Although you may not do this right at the end of the course, it's the most synoptic element (bringing together all your learning throughout your study), combining texts and discourses from a variety of genres. By the time you complete your investigation, you will have produced a research project that combines literary and non-literary material containing the following sections:

- *introduction and aims*
- *review*
- *analysis*
- *conclusion*
- *appendix*
- *references.*

ACTIVITY 1

Self-assessing your current skills

Checking the research and writing skills you already have will give you confidence to begin your research. It will also show you what skills you need to develop or acquire to become an independent and inquisitive learner who can make 'active' connections between your choice of literary text and non-literary material.

At all stages of your investigation you will need to think, read, plan, draft and redraft.

a What methods have you used previously to research a topic (for example, interviews, questionnaires)?
b What sources have you used to research topics (for example, newspapers, books)?
c What styles of academic writing have you used (for example, essays, reports, investigations)?
d When have you planned to do your writing?
e When have you redrafted and rewritten your work to make improvements?
f Have you ever quoted from other people's work in your writing and referenced this?

20.2 Choosing connections

What's exciting about this part of the course is that you get to choose the links you make between a literary text and non-literary material, so it's centred on you and your own interests. You might want to ask yourself some key questions at this stage to help your decision-making, such as:

1 What types of literary and non-literary texts interest you?
2 What focus do you want to take for the links you make between the literary and non-literary material?

ACTIVITY 2

Self-assessing your personal interests

Reflecting on what you have both learned and enjoyed in your study is useful at this early stage of the process. You could do this by using earlier units of this book to remind you of the knowledge and skills you have acquired, as well as the types of texts you have studied closely.

a Which literary genres have you most enjoyed studying on the course?
b What concepts have interested you most?
c Survey the *AQA Anthology: Paris* for the types of sources: what ideas does this give you for non-literary material?
d Explore yourself: what kinds of experiences do you have that might offer ideas for non-literary material? Think about your use of social media, other online media sources, any forums/blogs you use, etc. Also think about your own interactions with other people - family, friends, hobbies, education, etc.

Check your responses in the Ideas section on Cambridge Elevate

One of your first crucial decisions is regarding the type of focus or connection you want to make. There are two potential avenues. You can investigate:

- *either* a particular theme as a connection
- *or* specific linguistic strategies and/or features that are common to both.

So, to get underway you need to decide broadly on what approach you want to take (thematic or strategy/feature driven) and within those areas what you specifically want to investigate so that you can think about the right literary text and non-literary material to select. Don't worry about committing yourself at the beginning: your first task is to consider and shortlist ideas before you come to any final decisions. As any researcher will tell you, this is often the most time-consuming element as you start to formulate your thoughts and make choices about texts, topics and research methods.

20.3 Thinking about texts

As it's essential that a literary text forms the basis of your research project, one option is to begin with the literary text you wish to use, then think of connections that you could make in order to select your non-literary material. You do need to know your literary text well, so however you go about starting this project, you do need to take the time to read your text carefully. The compulsory element of this project is that it includes a substantial literary text.

There is no particular literary text that you need to choose for your research project, but you cannot choose a text that has been prescribed for study elsewhere on the course - although you can choose another text by the same author. This means that even if you didn't study that particular text, you still can't choose it. For the purposes of this project, literary texts are defined as those from the three main literary genres - poetry, drama and prose fiction. However, within the category of prose fiction you might want to consider that these not only include novels but also short stories, diaries or epistolary forms, among others.

20.3.1 Mapping out ideas

Once you have thought of the literary text you would like to use, you can begin to map out some initial ideas about themes or significant language features that you could explore for connections to non-literary material. Figure 20A maps themes for Jane Austen's *Pride and Prejudice*, an early nineteenth-century novel about a family of five sisters who need to secure their places in society by marrying well. Firstly, you can consider the major themes as your initial level of mapping.

Figure 20A: Mapping themes in *Pride and Prejudice*

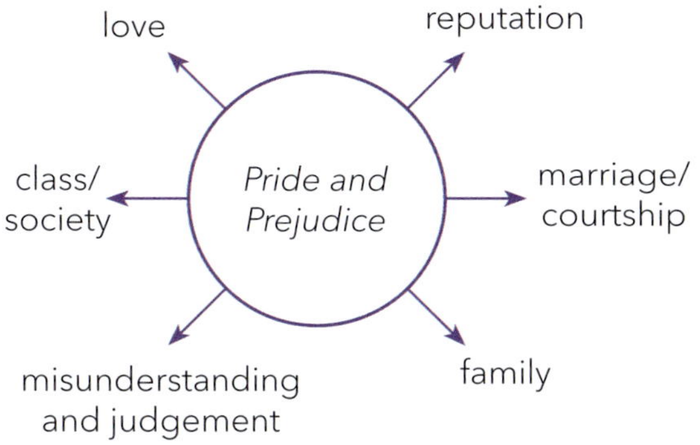

The next step is to map in more detail the types of representations or significant aspects of narrative choices that link to the themes that you have identified (see Figure 20B). This will help to tighten the focus and your selection of relevant extracts.

Figure 20B: Mapping investigations: ideas for *Pride and Prejudice*

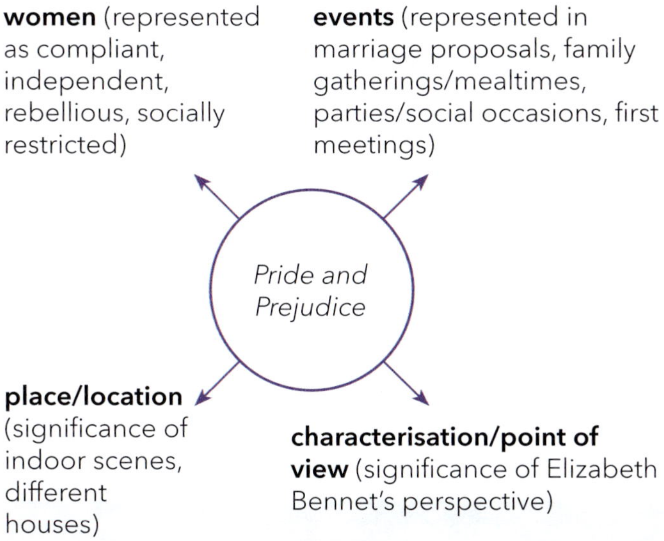

Finally, the third level of mapping is to think about the linguistic strategies/features that you might explore in the literary text (see Figure 20C). These could either form the basis of the connections you are making to non-literary material or they could suggest what you might analyse within the text.

Figure 20C: Mapping linguistic strategies in *Pride and Prejudice*

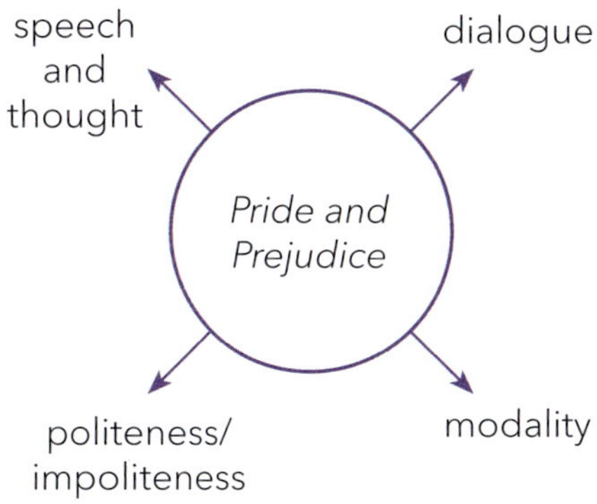

One way of presenting these different levels is in a table like Table 20A, showing also how they can be linked to extracts that might be suitable to choose for either making connections on a thematic basis or through specific linguistic strategies.

Whatever approach to mapping the connections you can find in your literary texts, it's really useful to make your own notes as you read. Thinking carefully about the choices you could make and the extracts you could use will make the transition to the next step of choosing the non-literary material much easier. And, although the discussion has focused on the genre of prose fiction, don't forget you can take exactly the same approach by starting with a collection of poems or a play.

ACTIVITY 3

Mapping project ideas

Read the opening of Angela Carter's novel, *Wise Children*. Using the levels suggested in Figures 20A–20C, map some suggestions for project ideas. If you are unfamiliar with the novel, you will need to research its themes. You could do this by using a search engine, such as Google. From here, you can search the web but you can also refine your search to Google books, which offers a selection of critical viewpoints. For linguistic concepts and features, analyse Text 20A for your first thoughts.

Table 20A: Mapping events and features

Theme	Representation of event	Linguistic concept features
marriage	marriage proposal	politeness (FTAs) speech acts modality speech and thought
Mr and Mrs Bennet Mr Collins and Charlotte Lucas	Darcy's proposal to Elizabeth Mr Collins' proposal to Elizabeth	politeness – Mr Darcy and Elizabeth at Netherfield Ball, the marriage proposal, Darcy's letter

Text 20A

Why is London like Budapest?

Because it is two cities divided by a river.

Good morning! Let me introduce myself. My name is Dora Chance. Welcome to the wrong side of the tracks.

Put it one way. If you're from the States, think of Manhattan. Then think of Brooklyn. See what I mean? Or, for a Parisian, it might be a question of rive gauche, rive droite. With London, it's the North and South divide. Me and Nora, that's my sister, we've always lived on the left-hand side, the side the tourist rarely sees, the bastard side of Old Father Thames.

Source: Angela Carter, *Wise Children*

Check your responses in the Ideas section on Cambridge Elevate

20.4 Thinking about non-literary connections

The main criterion for selecting your non-literary material is whether it's a good source of data to make connections with either your literary text or your topic focus. Surveying the sorts of things you read, watch and activities and/or interests you have might offer ideas for topics, themes or a linguistic focus you wish to pursue. It will also give you ideas for data collection methods.

ACTIVITY 4

Exploring non-literary material

Look at the selection of Emma's personal and social media communications from one day in Text 20B. Text 20B(a) contains Emma's tweets, Text 20B(b) her direct messages to her friend Shamila and Text 20B(c) is part of an email chain to her college tutor. What linguistic features or aspects of her communication would be interesting to explore?

Text 20B

(a) Emma's tweets

12.59 Ooooh guys it's the first day of December!
1.00 That means it's time to open my advent calendar!
1.06 Surely it should've started snowing by now?
1.11 Where is the 100 days of snow we're supposed to have?
1.12 Impatiently waiting here
1.14 Snow where are you?
1.50 Hunger pangs

(b) Emma's direct messages

@emma5798 Eastenders>>>>>>>>>Corrie
@shamila5555 na s'll about corrie more realistic blud
@emma5798 mate. Realistic? It bloody snowed in Corrie, it didn't even snow in Manchester this year! Pft realistic my a****
@shamila5555 but have you seen the men in Corrie? Mmm, give me a bit of Peter Barlow any day
@emma5798 shamila, you have some serious problems yano

(c) Emma's email

This is my final draft of my personal statement. I would like to put it on UCAS today, so could you please tell me if it is ok to put on today.
Thanks

Source: private data

Check your responses in the Ideas section on Cambridge Elevate

ACTIVITY 5

Collecting non-literary material

Compile initial thoughts on the types of non-literary material you could find from this list of potential sources:

- spoken language (for example, real speech from everyday life or speech in reality TV shows, news interviews)
- texts around us in our daily lives (for example, cards, text messages, letters and notes)
- non-fiction writing (for example, advice guides, information leaflets, books about science)
- written media texts (newspapers, magazines, advertising)
- personal media and online texts (Twitter, blogs, chat rooms).

Now you've begun to think about non-literary material more closely, you should be able to reflect on the connections you can make between the literary and non-literary texts. In Section 20.3 you looked at the mapping of research ideas using *Pride and Prejudice* as the chosen literary text. So, what kinds of active connections could you make using these? Let's take two of the large themes, marriage and events, to reflect on possible connections (see Table 20B).

ACTIVITY 6

Making active connections

Return to the ideas you suggested for *Wise Children* in Activity 3. Using the types of possible sources you looked at in Activity 5, suggest connections, or the non-literary material you could find for each one. Create a table similar to Table 20B to list your ideas on:

a spoken language
b texts around us
c non-fiction writing
d written media texts
e personal media and online texts.

Alternatively, return to Texts 20B(a) and 20B(b). What connections can you find between Emma's real communication and Dora's fictional one?

Check your responses in the Ideas section on Cambridge Elevate

20.5 Thinking about topics

The other option is to start with a specific focus in mind for a topic, theme or linguistic strategy you want to investigate. Here, imagine that you wanted to either investigate a particular genre, in this case letter writing, or you wanted to investigate how writers represent war. Now, consider the options for appropriate literary texts. You might choose a novel that is written entirely in letters (epistolary fiction) or a novel that uses letters at specific moments as a narrative technique. Some novels like A S Byatt's *Possession* incorporate fictional diary entries, letters and poetry that might offer lots of different ideas for connections! Equally, dramatists have focused on the horrors of war, such as J C Sherriff's presentation of officers in the trenches written from personal experience in *Journey's End* or Peter Whelan's reflective look at a northern town's loss of its young men in *The Accrington Pals*.

Watch tutorial video, Data Collection, on Cambridge Elevate

Table 20B: Matching literary with non-literary material

Marriage	Events
marriage rituals – the wedding ceremony planned written speeches – best man and bridegroom (or a transcript of the speeches) websites offering advice on marriage proposals articles about marriage in specialist magazines, or celebrity feature transcripts from TV shows like *Don't Tell the Bride*	transcripts of family interactions (mealtimes, arguments) transcripts of people recalling first meetings with friends and partners transcripts from *Come Dine With Me*

20.5.1 Keeping context in mind

What kinds of contextual factors are there? This is by no means an exhaustive list but some to consider are:

- time: a period that the texts are from, or set in, a time of life, a time of day
- place: the location of the texts and their worlds
- ideology: values and beliefs expressed by speakers, writers, characters. These may be related to society's views or individual beliefs
- mode: spoken, written, blended, multi-modal
- genre: the text type and the influences and uses they have
- purpose: broad categories of entertainment, persuasion, information and instruction, as well as more subtle distinctions such as to educate, to sell
- audience: age, gender, specialisms (for example, interests or expertise in areas), individual, global, etc.

Others could be the broader contexts of production and reception. Factors such as who the text producer is and the associated influences on them might need bearing in mind. The ways that different texts might be received or obtained by audiences affect interpretation of them. Think of the variation between your reactions depending on whether you have actively chosen to search and find out about things that interest you using the internet, or if you discover it at a talk at a school or college assembly, or in a flyer handed to you in the street.

ACTIVITY 7

Exploring connections

Read Texts 20C(a)-(c), which are from literary texts. Use these as the basis for making comparisons with non-literary material - the letter from the soldier in Text 20D.

Texts 20C(a) and 20C(c) are both from epistolary novels. Text 20C(a) presents a narrator writing to her husband about their troubled son, Kevin, who is in prison. Text 20C(b) charts fictional soldiers' experiences during the First World War, and Text 20C(c) is the opening of a poem by Wilfred Owen, who was killed in the final stages of the First World War.

a Use Texts 20C(a) and 20C(b) to explore connections based around genre. What connections could you make about the conventions of letter writing? What similarities and differences are there between the literary and non-literary? Think about the typical features of letters such as discourse structure, topics, as well as lexical and sentence choices to meet the informational and interactional purposes.

b Use Text 20C(c) to explore connections based on the representation of war. How does the writer represent war and soldiers? What linguistic strategies and devices do they use to present these?

Text 20C

(a)

November 15, 2000

Dear Franklin

You know, I try to be polite. So when my co-workers – that's right, I work, at a Nyack travel agency, believe it or not, and gratefully, too – when they start foaming at the mouth about the disproportionate number of votes for Pat Buchanan in Palm Beach, I wait so patiently for them to finish that in a way I have become a treasured commodity: I am the only one in the office who will allow them to finish a sentence.

Source: Lionel Shriver, *We Need to Talk About Kevin*

(b)

Lighting another cigarette beneath his tree, listening to the screech of a shell going over the British line about half a mile south, Jack Firebrace began to tremble.

He had thought himself immune to death; he thought he had hardened himself against it but it was not so. If they found him guilty they would take him alone at daybreak to some secluded place behind the lines – a glade in a forest, a yard behind a farm wall – and shoot him dead.

Source: Sebastian Faulks, *Birdsong*

(c)

Halted against the shade of a last hill,
They fed, and, lying easy, were at ease
And, finding comfortable chests and knees
Carelessly slept. But many there stood still
To face the stark, blank sky beyond the ridge,
Knowing their feet had come to the end of the world.

Marvelling they stood, and watched the long grass swirled
By the May breeze, murmurous with wasp and midge,
For though the summer oozed into their veins
Like the injected drug for their bones' pains,
Sharp on their souls hung the imminent line of grass,
Fearfully flashed the sky's mysterious glass.

Source: Wilfred Owen, 'Spring Offensive', lines 1–12

Text 20D is from a real soldier's letter to his family while he was fighting in France during the First World War. The letter was written as this soldier prepared to fight in what became one of the bloodiest of its battles, the Battle of the Somme, where over a million men died between July and November 1916.

If you don't have access to this kind of personal, family material, you can source similar letters about the First World War from The National Archives or from non-fiction books like *Letters from a Lost Generation, First World War Letters of Vera Brittain and Four Friends*, edited by Alan Bishop and Mark Bostridge. Alternatively, there are many other collections of letters written by a range of ordinary people and literary writers' private letters accessible from either online sources or as published books.

Text 20D

1916

June 30th. Resting much as possible in case of emergencies. Dinner time happened to say to May it was my birthday, 5 minutes afterwards small parcel handed to me containing lovely silver-plated cigarette case & note with birthday wishes from Billie – don't know how he managed to get such a splendid present just handy unless he knew before & asked dispatch rider to get one at Amiens. If weather keeps like this, boys will '**go over**' on the morning as we must '**stand to**' all night ready for anything. Have had 4 weeks without shells already.

It is now evening 8.30p.m. – the evening before the 'Great Event'. What peculiar atmospheric disturbances. Every body feels it. What will the next few hours bring? None of us yet know the exact time but all know it is tonight, before tomorrow really starts. I have just been out. There are 16 observation balloons & 18 aeroplanes all within sight. I have seen as many balloons up at one today. I have also just seen the boys English & French passing up the roads to the front trenches, company after company – 250 in each endless numbers – French at one side of our dugouts English at the other, all to take part in these stirring events & all eager & quite keen to be doing something. It is difficult to analyse feelings under strains of emotion such as these but as I close my eyes I seem to see two visions, just bits of the scene outside – first the clear outline of five trees standing out against the horizon with the red poppies & blue cornflowers. They have taken deeper root in my mind's eye than all else, surely we are all in a topsy turvy world.

go over (the top): to leave the trenches by climbing over the parapet of the trenches to attack the enemy head on

stand to: the order for all men in the trench to stand ready in the trench in readiness for a surprise attack, usually at dawn or sunset

Source: private data

Check your responses in the Ideas section on Cambridge Elevate

20.6 Choosing methodologies

By thinking about 'making connections' between literary texts and non-literary material, you have already been introduced to the types of data you can gather and you have even begun considering the methods you might choose to collect it. But in order to consider how you are going to gather your non-literary material, you really need to focus first on the following questions.

- Where am I going to get my non-literary data from?
- What collection method(s) am I going to use?
- What skills and knowledge do I need to acquire?
- What assistance do I need from others?
- What equipment do I need?

As you're answering these, you're really reflecting on both the *theoretical* and the *practical* aspects of undertaking a research project.

ACTIVITY 8

Data gathering exercises

Choosing the right data gathering method for your non-literary material is important, so it's worth investing some time practising the decision-making you'll do for your own data.

Use the ideas in Table 20C for possible research projects, assuming that you have already chosen your literary text (although you could also research novels, plays or poetry collections that could be used). For each project focus suggest what types of non-literary data you could get and where/how you would get the material. Be imaginative and think of as many options for data from the source category for each project as you can.

Check your responses in the Ideas section on Cambridge Elevate

ACTIVITY 9

Practising data collection methods (spoken)

Imagine that you are collecting data for an investigation into planned persuasive speeches. Search online for famous speeches and find examples of spoken and written versions.

Some famous speeches you could search for are Martin Luther King's 1963 'I have a dream' speech, Winston Churchill's 1940 'We shall fight them on the beaches' speech or Earl Spencer's eulogy to his sister, Diana, at her funeral in 1997.

a What is different about the speeches in each mode?

b What would you get from choosing the spoken version?

Check your responses in the Ideas section on Cambridge Elevate

20.7 Data collection methods

Linguistically focused projects can call on a variety of methods, including interviews, questionnaires and observational studies. But given the constraints of making connections between your literary text and non-literary material, it is likely that your main collection methods are going to centre on whether you choose spoken or written material.

20.7.1 Collecting spoken non-literary material

Collecting spoken data means audio or video recordings and these may originate from you in the sense that you record people in your environment – at school, at home, at work. Spoken data can also be collected using the internet, from archives of speech and TV and radio websites amongst others.

20.7.2 Collecting written non-literary material

For written data, you already appreciate how varied the sources can be. What might be time-consuming is finding the right kind of written material you are looking for, whether it is found on the internet or from your environment (i.e. texts that you can collect from around you in your daily life such as leaflets, family notes or mail sent to you, etc.).

ACTIVITY 10

Practising data collection methods (written)

Practise collecting data for an investigation into the representation of women, with media representation of sportswomen chosen for the non-literary material. How will you begin your search? Will it be a general

Table 20C

Project focus	Sources
• legal language • sports commentaries • travel writing • speech features in real-world communication • interviews	• spoken language (for example, real speech from everyday life or speech in reality TV shows, news interviews) • texts around us (for example, cards, text messages, letters and notes) • non-fiction writing (for example, advice guides, information leaflets, books about science) • written media texts (newspapers, magazines, advertising) • personal media and online texts (Twitter, blogs, chat rooms)

search or will you narrow it down to a particular media source, i.e. specific newspapers and their sport sections? Try both the general and narrow search. Which is more successful? Another way to focus your search would be to narrow it to look at women in particular sports, such as football or tennis, or by searching the names of players or teams.

Check your responses in the Ideas section on Cambridge Elevate

20.8 Ethical considerations

For some non-literary material that you select, there will be ethics around the methods you use to gather it. This is especially true if you are gathering spoken data. What is fundamental is that your participants give informed consent - people should know why you're collecting the data and what you'll be doing with it. If you have recorded people, you should give them the opportunity to listen to what has been recorded to check that they are happy for it to be used. It is unlikely that people will refuse but you can also reassure them about their anonymity. Participants need to be anonymised, so giving then alternative names or using letters in transcription for different speakers is one way of overcoming any potential concerns participants may have.

There may be some legal, copyright issues with other types of data, such as recording from TV, radio or downloading from the internet. Though some sources may be readily downloadable from organisations' websites, this does not always mean it is available for you to use as you wish. You should always check the information provided with the source you wish to use to find out about the terms for its use. However, some broadcast and internet material is copyright. If in doubt, it's worth checking. Your learning resource centre can offer advice on copyright but there are also specific guidelines for student researchers published by the British Association for Applied Linguistics (BAAL).

Find and read the BAAL good research practice guidelines via Cambridge Elevate

20.9 Working with spoken data

You have studied naturally occurring speech in *Remembered places*, representations of spoken interaction in plays in *Dramatic encounters*, as well as the presentation of speech in prose, poetry and non-literary texts. You may not, however, have transcribed your own. Transcription is not only a practical skill to acquire but also requires some theoretical understanding in order to make decisions about style and approaches.

Your previous experience of transcripts has centred on analysing them, rather than creating them and you now need to produce a transcript that makes sense to other readers. Transcription can be a lengthy process but it is worthwhile because not only will you get to know your data well, you will also have got some original material.

If you start by asking yourself what a transcript needs to record about real speech, your answer is likely to be that it needs to show the speakers and their turn-taking, the messy, non-fluent aspects of speech and the external things that add to the talk (like non-verbal communication or contextual aspects). But it's not only about what it needs to record, it's about its coherence when turned into writing on a page. To achieve this, your checklist of the ideal 'ingredients' of a transcript may be that it indicates:

- **turn-taking**: the organisation of talk by speakers, their turns, simultaneous speech, overlaps and interruptions
- **non-fluency**: the messy, unwritten-like qualities of pauses, fillers, repairs and false starts
- **non-verbal**: paralinguistic features and body language
- **non-standard pronunciations**: clipping and accent features
- **prosody**: pitch, emphasis, volume and speed
- **external contextual events**: other sounds in the environment such as people talking in the background or actions.

There are some theoretical approaches to analysing talk that may also impact some of your production decisions. So, having an idea about what you want to do with your spoken data might inform the level of detail you want to add into the transcription.

One of the earliest methods devised was **Conversational Analysis** (CA), which is a data-centred analysis of talk. Harvey Sacks, an American sociologist, pioneered the discipline in the 1960s, establishing the conventions of transcription as a way of organising talk. For followers of the CA approach, the patterns in the data are central and analysis foregrounds what occurs in the talk itself rather than any other factors such as the speaker's gender or age.

Another method is **Critical Discourse Analysis** (CDA), an approach that looks behind and beyond the text for the ideology and the social forces that might affect it. The recent focus on power in CDA has been spearheaded by the linguist Norman Fairclough. CDA can also be applied to written texts and promotes textual analysis by focusing on certain features such as modes of address, lexis and grammar in addition to traditional spoken discourse features.

The relevance of these to your project is in your choice of focus and the connections you make. For example, if you want to look specifically at turn-taking patterns and sequences in your literary text and non-literary material, then a CA approach would be advisable. However, if you wanted to look at aspects of power, using a CDA approach would be the best one. Furthermore, you may need to consider the approach you choose critically in your reading around your project focus, as well as the way that it informs both your methodology and your analysis of particular features.

Key terms

Conversational Analysis (CA): an approach to the study of conversation in everyday interactions

Critical Discourse Analysis (CDA): an approach to the study of both written and spoken language focusing on the ways that power is enacted

20.9.1 Transcription conventions

There are two main ways that you can transcribe speech:

1 **orthography**
2 **phonemic transcription**.

Key terms

orthography: the conventional spelling system of a particular language

phonemic transcription: a transcription method that uses the phonological properties of spoken language and maps phonemes (individual sounds) to written symbols

Always provide a key to your symbols, because there can be some variation. Number your data lines too, as this makes it easier to manage when you want to analyse it. You can use the transcription key at the front of this book to transcribe your data, although there are other versions that you might want to use. Whatever you do, ensure that you provide a key for your reader.

You will mainly transcribe orthographically. In literary texts, writers often represent dialect orthographically by spelling it in a manner that suggests its pronunciation for a reader. Look at the opening of Irvine Welsh's *Trainspotting* to see how he represents the Glaswegian accent orthographically:

> The sweat wis lashing oafay Sick Boy; he wis trembling. Ah wis jist sitting their, focusing oan the telly, tryin no tae notice
>
> Source: Irvine Welsh, *Trainspotting*

But, in certain circumstances, you might want to transcribe phonemically. This may be if you are looking at the language of young children or focusing on aspects of accent where you need to analyse how someone actually pronounced something.

In the following example, Aunty Jenni is playing with her niece, Isla, who is 10 months old:

AJ:((*holding Isla in the air*)) Isla go flying (.) ((*sing song voice*)) flying (.) w-ho w-ho

w-ho ((*Isla laughs*)) w-ho w-ho (.) w-ho ((Isla – a a a)) did you enjoy that (.) did you enjoy that

---

The transcription is currently orthographic but, in this situation, perhaps Aunty Jenni's sound-making and Isla's early sounds would be more usefully presented phonemically. For this, you need to use the International Phonetic Alphabet (IPA). The convention for the phonemic presentation of words is to place them in slanted brackets //. In this example, Aunty Jenni's 'w-ho' might then be /wəhu/.

ACTIVITY 11

Practising data collection methods (spoken)

a Record friends or family talking or download a radio podcast (sport, entertainment, interviews).

b Transcribe 1–2 minutes of each.

c Reflect on the process. Did you encounter any problems? How did you overcome these? What have you learned about transcription?

Check your responses in the Ideas section on Cambridge Elevate

20.10 How much literary and non-literary material?

Another question you might have at an early stage is how many extracts from the literary text and what length and how much non-literary material you need to get. There's no easy answer to this one as it depends on the following questions.

- What questions are you going to be asking of it?
- How much are you going to write about it?
- What are you going to do with it?

What's important is that the data is suitable, so you might initially collect too much and reduce the amount you need to use, keeping in mind the final length of your project. By returning to the example of *Pride and Prejudice* as the literary text from the beginning of this unit, you can see how extract choices can be made according to the project focus. If you are selecting the representation of marriage proposals, then Mr Darcy's proposal to Elizabeth Bennet might be the appropriate extract to use. If you are exploring mealtime rituals, then a series of shorter extracts where Austen depicts the mealtime rituals of the Bennet family might be the most salient to select.

ACTIVITY 12

Deciding data quantity

To develop your decision-making skills about the relevant amount of material to select, read Text 20E. Texts 20E(a)–(c) are transcripts from a series of team meetings between English teachers at a sixth form college and are their interactions before the meeting has officially started. The same letter is used for the same speaker in each of Texts 20E(a)–(c).

Imagine that you're investigating the genre of workplace meetings. The questions you might be asking of it are: What role does phatic talk have at the beginnings of meetings? Are the topics context-dependent on the job roles of speakers? How do the speakers convey their identities? What's the typical structure of meetings? The features that you're going to analyse are topic choices, topic control, topic shifts, turn-taking and speaker contributions.

Have you chosen:

- enough data to answer your research questions?
- the right data to address all strands of your research focus?
- appropriate features to analyse?

Text 20E

(a) Meeting 1

A: I can't get this one to work so I'm using two

B: yeah ((*replying to another colleague*))

C: you know what I'm like with technology ((*laughs*))

D: you can kind of hide it to a certain extent you can't really hide (.) although

A: technology you know why why do it with one when you can do it with two ((*referring to mobile phone also recording*))

E: I remember the time I tried that (.) er (.) yes

D: yeah (.) yeah (.) yeah

(b) Meeting 2

C: we're going to see the National Theatre's Hamlet

D: oh yeah yeah (.) yeah yeah we saw Hamlet last time we're in London

A: where's that on then

C: the Lowry

E: when's King Lear

D: it's March (.) well you can try but mind you the matinee (1.0) you must buy our tickets if we can swap and go in the week (.) if you're not going on the demo and wanna go Saturday we can perhaps do a swap

F: um

D: they're not cheap though (.) they're twenty five quid each

(c) Meeting 3

F: he was in West Side Story last night

D: yeah apparently yeah

G: ((*to JP*)) is this for me then

D: he'll get in though he's the kind of person

B: (*unintelligible*)

A: ((*to B*)) I wasn't ignoring you

E: (*unintelligible*) deadlines for re-marks

F: I'll have a look at the agenda ((*to H who has entered room*)) I volunteered for the minutes

B: ((*to A*))(*unintelligible*)

D: ((*to H*)) because I-'s not here

G: ((*to F*)) yes it's on the back

Source: private data

Check your responses in the Ideas section on Cambridge Elevate

20.11 Devising research questions

Once you have made your final selections of both the literary text extracts and non-literary material and your particular focus, your next action is to pose some research questions. In one way, your data is a problem to be solved and you can hone in on what aspects are the most interesting and significant to explore. By using the investigation idea you explored earlier when searching for newspaper articles about sportswomen, we can establish a main question: Is the representation of players of sports the same in a literary text and in media articles about players?

To illustrate how this can be broken down into further sub-questions, look at Text 20F.

- Text 20F(a) is the opening of an article from 2011 about the England women's football team.
- Text 20F(b) is the opening stanzas of a 2010 poem about football.
- Text 20F(c) is an extract from *A Prayer for Owen Meany* by John Irving. This novel depicts a childhood friendship between the narrator and his friend, Owen Meany, who is presented as a unique individual with strong religious beliefs about his purpose in life. In the novel, Owen Meany accidently kills the narrator's mother with a foul ball at a baseball match.

ACTIVITY 13

Choosing research questions

a Use Text 20F(a) as your non-literary material and Text 20F(b) as your literary source. (If you choose poetry for your own research project, you would need to consider a whole collection of poetry, not just one poem.)

b Read Texts 20F(a and b) carefully and identify up to three research questions that you could ask of these texts.

Text 20F

(a)

The group of leggy and enviably toned young women in acid-bright designer sportswear could be a bunch of yummy mummies about to do an aerobics class. The only clue to their real identity are the studs on the soles of their high-tech trainers.

These girls are no dilettante exercisers getting ready for a pre-skinny latte workout, but members of the England women's football team, nicknamed the Three Lionesses. Throw a ball at them and they are likely to juggle it on their toes before whacking it back with interest. Almost certainly you won't have heard of any of them, but (whisper it quietly) the girls' recent record is much more successful than that of England's toothless Lions. They reached the quarterfinals of the World Cup in 2007, were runners-up in the 2009 Women's Euros, being beaten in the final by Germany (some things never change), and this summer will compete in the World Cup finals in Germany, beginning in June.

Source: John Koski, 'A whole different ball game: Meet the women aiming to win the world cup', *The Daily Mail*, 11 March 2011

(b)

He was not a good baseball player, but he did have a very small strike zone and as a consequence he was often used as a **pinch hitter** – not because he ever hit the ball with any authority (in fact, he was instructed never to swing at the ball), but because he could be relied upon to earn a walk, a base on balls. In **Little League** games he resented this exploitation and once refused to come to bat unless he was allowed to swing at the pitches. But there was no bat small enough for him to swing that didn't hurl his tiny body after it – that didn't thump him on the back and knock him out of the batter's box and flat upon the ground. So, after the humiliation of swinging at a few pitches, and missing them, and whacking himself off his feet, Owen Meany selected that other humiliation of standing motionless and crouched at home plate while the pitcher aimed the ball at Owen's strike zone – and missed it, almost every time.

pinch hitter: a substitute batter for the person scheduled to bat next in order to try to score more runs

Little League: an organisation that runs local youth baseball

Source: John Irving, *A Prayer for Owen Meany*

Check your responses in the Ideas section on Cambridge Elevate

'These girls are no dilettante exercisers getting ready for a pre-skinny latte workout...'

20.12 Selecting language levels

Picking the right areas for analysis includes the selection of the appropriate levels of language for your investigation. Whatever you choose, you will need to adopt a close language focus in your analysis. You have been applying these language levels in all the topics you have studied so far.

In the investigation, you need to make a critical selection of the levels to analyse that best suit your own project. The application of these areas will of course depend on the specific topic chosen. For example, an investigation of how speech is represented may well focus in more detail on phonetics, phonology and prosodics, while an investigation of how storytelling works may focus in more detail on pragmatics and discourse.

- **Phonetics, phonology and prosodics**: the sounds of spoken language
- **Lexis and semantics**: the words and meanings of words
- **Grammar, including morphology**: the combinations of words to form phrases and sentences; the construction of words
- **Pragmatics**: the meaning of language in context
- **Discourse**: the features of different text types.

20.13 Analysis: structuring connections

Text 20G is from a Dickens' novel which criticises the social effects of nineteenth-century industrialisation on the poor in a fictitious northern town, where Mr Gradgrind runs the local school. In Text 20G Mr Gradgrind interrogates one of his pupils.

Text 20G

In such terms Mr. Gradgrind always mentally introduced himself, whether to his private circle of acquaintance, or to the public in general. In such terms, no doubt, substituting the words 'boys and girls', for 'sir', Thomas Gradgrind now presented Thomas Gradgrind to the little pitchers before him, who were to be filled so full of facts.

Indeed, as he eagerly sparkled at them from the cellarage before mentioned, he seemed a kind of cannon loaded to the muzzle with facts, and prepared to blow them clean out of the regions of childhood at one discharge. He seemed a galvanizing apparatus, too, charged with a grim mechanical substitute for the tender young imaginations that were to be stormed away.

'Girl number twenty,' said Mr. Gradgrind, squarely pointing with his square forefinger, 'I don't know that girl. Who is that girl?'

'Sissy Jupe, sir,' explained number twenty, blushing, standing up, and curtseying.

'Sissy is not a name,' said Mr. Gradgrind. 'Don't call yourself Sissy. Call yourself Cecilia.'

'It's father as calls me Sissy, sir,' returned the young girl in a trembling voice, and with another curtsey.

'Then he has no business to do it,' said Mr. Gradgrind. 'Tell him he mustn't. Cecilia Jupe. Let me see. What is your father?'

'He belongs to the horse-riding, if you please, sir.'

Mr. Gradgrind frowned, and waved off the objectionable calling with his hand.

'We don't want to know anything about that, here. You mustn't tell us about that, here. Your father breaks horses, does he?'

'If you please, sir, when they can get any to break, they do break horses in the ring, sir.'

'You mustn't tell us about the ring, here. Very well, then. Describe your father as a horsebreaker. He doctors sick horses, I dare say?'

'Oh yes, sir.'

'Very well, then. He is a veterinary surgeon, a **farrier** and horsebreaker. Give me your definition of a horse.'

(Sissy Jupe thrown into the greatest alarm by this demand.)

'Girl number twenty unable to define a horse!' said Mr. Gradgrind, for the general behoof of all the little pitchers.

farrier: a person who shoes horses

Source: Charles Dickens, *Hard Times*

This literary text might well provide a focus for the exploration of classroom discourse, or the representation of teachers and/or students, and be paired with some spoken language data that you have obtained from your lessons. Using the language levels, it might be clear that the key aspect to explore will be *discourse* (the representation of speech in the literary text and the features of naturally occurring speech). Other interesting aspects of the two kinds of texts may be to focus on *pragmatics* (politeness and formality) and *lexical/ semantic choices*. You might have noticed some of the metaphorical language Dickens uses to present Mr Gradgrind.

So your first ideas for structuring your *Analysis* could be:

- speech features: adjacency pairs / **IRF** patterns typical of teacher talk / topic control
- politeness: positive and negative politeness / face-threatening acts / address terms
- lexis: field-specific choices
- metaphor: individual metaphors / patterns
- sentence functions: declaratives / imperatives
- point of view / ideology: the presentation of Mr Gradgrind's beliefs.

Key terms

IRF: an abbreviation for initiation-response-feedback turn-taking exchanges, as in a question, answer then a feedback comment on the answer

ACTIVITY 14

Choosing language levels

a Return to the questions you chose for the representation of players and sport.

b Read Texts 20F(a)–(c) and analyse features that you think might be significant to address the questions.

c Consider each language level and decide which ones are the most relevant to use for your analysis.

20.14 Reading and writing critically

The kind of academic reading and writing you'll undertake here will probably be new for you but it will equip you with new skills that will be useful to you. One of the main demands of this research project is to take an academic focus and maintain this throughout your study in this part of the course. You have already seen that the early stages of a linguistically focused investigation are not about writing but about reading critically both your literary text and your non-literary material to help you make decisions about the focus you want to take, based on informed choices about what is possible given your texts. Added to this, you need to develop your skills in reading theories and ideas about language from an academic perspective. Finally, your academic focus is conveyed through your writing of the report, and in your ability to demonstrate in the report your understanding of key concepts, your interpretation of textual features and your reflection on your findings.

20.14.1 Reading critically

In order to understand your topic focus and apply this understanding in both your *Review* and your *Analysis*, you will need to read around the texts, concepts or strategies you are investigating. You will need to do this early on in your project, so that you can approach your data analysis and report writing effectively. For any researcher, the process is to find, understand, evaluate and finally use and synthesise the relevant information sources into the written investigation.

Finding and understanding sources

Once you know your focus you need to find the right sources. Your first research avenue is the Learning Resource Centre at your school or college. Search library catalogues, as it's likely that they will have chosen books and purchased other resources specifically for English language, literature, stylistics and narratology to help you with your study.

You can use internet search engines, which can be useful but are often too general. Refining your searches by using key words or narrowing the searches down to books or scholarly articles and journals is one way to overcome the problem of an overwhelming number of results – not all of which will be relevant or valid sources. Academics have their own pages (usually on their university sites), containing details of their work and often PDFs that you might find useful. If some of the sources seem too scholarly, then there are specialist English magazines (such as *emagazine* and *The English Review*) that feature articles aimed specifically at A Level students, which you may find helpful.

What you need to read depends on the focus of your project. Later in this chapter, suitable readings are suggested and exemplified for a concept-led project. However, if you wanted to approach connections between a literary text and non-literary material from a thematic or genre perspective then your choice of readings might differ and be more from literary-critical sources. For example, earlier you read Text 20C(a) from Lionel Shriver's *We Need to Talk About Kevin* and Text 20C(b) from Alice Walker's *The Color Purple*. If you were studying these novels then it might be useful to do some reading around the narrative structure and conventions of epistolary novels. In addition, readings around black-feminist writing for Walker's work would inform an understanding of the parameters from which she is working in her novel. Likewise, undertaking some reading around what literary critics have said about Shriver's novel could inform your own argument and support comments that you are making. It's important to remember that whilst your background reading can come from any established academic field, including both linguistics and the literary-critical tradition, it should always be appropriate to the focus of your project.

Evaluating sources

All researchers need to be aware of how reliable and credible a source is. Clearly this is more important in some types of research than others but you should still evaluate the sources you use as good academic practice. Some of the key elements to consider are *who has written it* (i.e. their level of expertise), *when was it written* (the research from a source from a long time ago may not still be valid) and *where it was published* (published works rather than information on a blog are likely to have more credibility). If in doubt, check with your supervising teacher.

Selecting from and synthesising sources

Obviously you're not going to be using everything you read, so make careful notes or highlight passages or quotations that you think you might want either to incorporate into your report or that help you understand and engage with the concepts and strategies.

You should try to find a range of different people's perspectives, arguments or theories relevant to your specific focus to demonstrate your wider reading. The way you'll synthesise your sources is in your writing of the report.

20.14.2 Writing reports: ordering your investigation

This may be the first report that you have written, but this kind of writing is a conventional form of academic writing and one that you are likely to have to adopt in any future studies in Higher Education.

The six required sections of your project are outlined for you in this section. For each section, the content is generally indicated, except for your *Analysis* where you will choose sub-headings suitable for your individual research investigation.

Introduction and aims (750 words)

This is the first section of your investigation and it is important because it:

- introduces your chosen literary text
- identifies the focus of your investigation
- justifies and contextualises the non-literary material you have selected.

Review (300–500 words)

In your *Review* you need to demonstrate that:

- you have read and understood secondary sources
- you can discuss the ideas clearly (either about the material itself or about ideas for analysis or both)
- you can accurately apply citations and references.

Analysis (1250 words)

This is the largest individual section of your investigation. You can choose to analyse the literary text and non-literary material separately or together but the *Analysis* should:

- have subheadings to shape your analysis
- focus on different aspects of language (identified as salient features in the earlier sections)
- be clear and readable.

Conclusions (200–500 words)

This section needs to give a summary of the main points revealed by your study. This should:

- be an overview of what has been revealed by bringing the textual sources together
- show how the understanding of each text has been enhanced by consideration of the other.

Appendix

This contains your literary extracts and non-literary data.

References

This is your recorded list of the work of others that you have read and used in your investigation.

20.14.3 Writing reports: adopting a suitable style

Reflect on your daily writing activities and you'll see how you shift your style of writing according to your medium, your audience and your purpose. A text to one friend might vary in style to a post on a blog seen by many, and both of these may be less formal than an email applying for a job.

Writing up a research project does not mean that you have to adopt an overly formal style, although neither is a chatty, anecdotal style appropriate either. Impressing the person who assesses your investigation is not achieved by using the longest, most complex synonyms you can find from a thesaurus. You are being asked to guide a reader through your project by shaping it effectively and writing your ideas clearly. So, you need to have your audience in mind. As your reader will know something about your topic and the associated terminology, you won't need to explain these to them but you need to convey your own understanding of these in the way you write.

ACTIVITY 15

Practising proof-reading and redrafting

Read Text 20H, an early draft of a student's analysis of the representation of the main character's death in *Death of a Salesman* by Arthur Miller. Miller presents the failure of an ordinary man, Willy Loman, both in his job and in his relationships with his sons. The play ends with his funeral.

a How does Text 20H need to be reshaped? What sub-headings could you suggest?

b Identify any spelling, punctuation and grammatical errors.

c What is good in this writing? List the positives you would offer as feedback.

Text 20H: Student draft

In *Death of a Salesman,* at the beginning of the final scene 'Requiem' the use of the Latin word 'requiem' meaning for souls of the dead gives greater effect and also reinforces the location of the scene. Although Miller doesn't give a clear location with stage directions it's obvious through the speech of the characters that it was Willy's funeral. 'it was a very nice funeral' Charley says, this clearly reinforces the location. Miller has Charley say 'he don't put a bolt to a nut' which appears like an everyday saying in America, so the metaphor is presenting Willy as an ordinary man, and also creating the personal relationship between Charley and Willy, showing how well he knew him. The other metaphor 'riding on a smile and a shoeshine' shows that Willy relied on the way he looked and presented himself to others, he wanted to look approachable which would help his job, being a salesman, and that he took pride in himself and others, This would make the audience feel empathy for Willy as Charley is the only one trying to defend his name.

Miller has a totally different approach to death as he presents some optimism and realisation from the passing of Willy. His son, Happy, claims 'I'm Gonna win it for him' and 'I'm staying right in this city and I'm gonna beat this racket'. The repetition of the informal lexis 'gonna' suggests his determination to change things, along with the repetition of the personal pronoun 'I' which shows that this is important to him and that's it is a personal achievement that he wants to accomplish from his father's death. Also Happy's declarative 'I'm gonna show you and everybody else that Willy Loman did not die in vain, he had a good dream,' this shows he's determined to make something of his father's name and make him proud. The reference to a 'dream' explicitly offers others hope in the connection to 'The American Dream' as a land of hope and opportunity, and suggests that although Willy was disappointed by not achieving this, his son will continue to strive for it.

Source: private data

Check your responses in the Ideas section on Cambridge Elevate

20.15 Academic conventions: *References*

It is important to reference your sources in order to:

- give others credit for their work
- avoid **plagiarism** (trying to present the work of others as your own)
- show the depth and range of your own reading
- show that you understand the concept you are writing about by selecting relevant sources.

Plagiarism is taken very seriously as malpractice. You must be confident when you submit your final investigation that the work is your own and that you haven't copied directly from books, the internet or other sources without acknowledgement of them. So what's crucial is that you become familiar with the conventions around referencing other people's ideas and words and apply these in your research report. In your investigation, your references will appear in two different forms in two separate places. Firstly, they will be used in your *Review* – in the form of either a quotation or what is known as a *citation* – and secondly, in the *References* section.

Because you are only producing a very short literature review, your number of secondary sources may be quite narrow. However, practising academic referencing is another really useful and practical skill that you may use again if you continue your studies at university. These days if you are using an online catalogue to search for sources relevant to your particular topic through a library or learning resource centre, you will find that references have been done for you and you can cut and paste these as they will be accurate. But this is not a substitute for having a broad understanding of the conventions of referencing. There are different methods of referencing used by some academic institutions and sometimes there are variations according to the subject, so you may need to adapt your style at a later stage.

In your investigation, it's better to keep it simple and straightforward, following the principle of being consistent and using the same method throughout. One of the most famous ways of referencing is the **Harvard Referencing System** which works on the premise that you refer to the author(s) and date in the text (i.e. in your *Review*) and full references to the whole work are included alphabetically at the end (your *Appendix* detailing your *References*). For an example of what this looks like, go to the back pages of an academic text you have read and you'll see the alphabetical list of references for that text.

Key terms

plagiarism: presenting the work of others as your own by citing their work but not adding a reference

Harvard Referencing System: a citation style used for referencing by many universities and academics, where the author and date are cited in the text and the full reference is listed in alphabetical order at the end

20.15.1 Referencing in your *Review*

Most importantly you need to understand the terminology for what you are doing in your *Review* when you use other people's theoretical views. Broadly, these can be placed into two categories:

- *quotations* – the actual words that appear in the original and are marked by inverted commas
- *citations* – references to a source but without direct quotations. These are often used when you have read someone else's comment about another's work and want to include it, although you haven't read the original yourself. (You'll be able to look at an example of this later in this section.)

The next stage is to think about how you can apply these in practice in your writing. The following example shows how you reference when you have read the secondary source and are quoting or referring to their ideas:

Author's name followed by date of publication and page numbers, for example, Jones (2012: 44)

20.15.2 Compiling references

The final section of your investigation is called *References* and is a list of all the writers, texts and sources you used in your project. There are conventions determining the presentation and layout of these according to the types of texts: for example, if they are from books, websites or journal articles. Yours should not be too complicated, or lengthy, given that the literature review is fairly brief. Should you have references that don't fit into the categories listed later, then an internet search should take you to university websites with instruction guides for referencing. There are even online tools that you can use to convert to references and on many library catalogues there are accurate references already formatted for you to use.

The golden rules are to:

- arrange references alphabetically
- order by the author's names (if more than one) according to the original source.

Here's an example of a straightforward reference to a single author book, where you can see that the author's name, the data of publication, the title (in italics), place of publishing and publisher need recording:

Cameron, D. (2001) *Working with Spoken Discourse*, London: Sage.

It is also common for books to be co-authored and both names need to linked by 'and':

Thornborrow, J., and Wareing, S. (1998) *Patterns in Language*, London: Routledge.

Sometimes the books you read will be collections of writings and have been brought together and edited, which needs acknowledgment:

Semino, E., and Culpeper, J. (eds) (2002) *Cognitive Stylistics,* Amsterdam: John Benjamins.

Referencing an internet source requires similar details to those of a book – the author's name or that of the organisation and the title. It also differs from the conventions of book referencing in that it also needs to contain the full web address and the date on which you accessed it:

Short, M. (2005). *Language & Style.* Available: http://www.lancaster.ac.uk/fass/projects/stylistics/introduction/start.htm. Last accessed 6 July 2014

You might have found a chapter of an edited book a helpful source and so the required elements for a reference are:

Myers, G. (2009). 'Language in advertisements', in: J. Culpeper *et al.* (eds) *English Language: Description, Variation and Context,* Basingstoke: Palgrave Macmillan, pp. 454–463.

What's different here is that you have to acknowledge the chapter author and the chapter title (but not in italics) and the book it came from. You might notice that initials are followed by surnames with 'ed.' or 'eds' after the last name. The title of the book needs to be in italics and the chapter number or first and last page numbers followed by a full stop.

As you may also have read articles in magazines or journals, the required elements for a reference are the author and year, the title of the article and the full title of the journal in italics. Also needed are the volume number (issue/part number) and page number(s):

Semino, E. (2011) 'The adaptation of metaphors across genres', *Review of Cognitive Linguistics*, 9 (1), 130–152.

20.16 Exploring connections

To illustrate how some aspects of conducting investigative work in preparation for *Making connections* that you have considered earlier come together, a 'mock' investigation is outlined for you in this section. This is not intended as a 'model' of the ideal or the only way that you could develop and structure your work. Rather, its purpose is to outline the contents of the investigation sections and offer an approach for you to discuss and critique. The intention is that this will help you make some of the key decisions right for you about your topic and text choices and your analytical approach.

See 20.17 for a mock investigation

The mock investigation focuses on a specific technique – in this case, metaphor. The literary text chosen for illustration is *Small Island* by Andrea Levy, a novel about the entwined lives and loves of four characters set against the issues of immigration and racial divide in post-Second World War England, and the non-literary material is a corpus of popular love song lyrics. These could be any that use metaphor as a way of exploring different aspects of love – from youthful love and attraction in a song such as the Arctic Monkeys' *I Bet You Look Good on the Dancefloor* to a more conventional ballad like Dolly Parton's song declaring eternal love, *I Will Always Love You*. Arguably, the 'active connection' being made is both thematic (about feelings of love) and a particular linguistic feature (the representation of love through metaphor), but it is not a required element for you to cover both the theme and the concept. Other suitable non-literary material could have been song lyrics more generally or advertisements that use metaphor – using these types of material mean that the study of metaphor as a device, rather than the metaphorical representation of love, would be the connection being made.

In Section 20.17, you don't need to be familiar with these texts as you are here acting both as a 'reader' being guided through the connections being drawn and as a 'student' thinking about how you can reflect and use the approach chosen to inform your own choices, investigative approach and crafting of your own writing. However, you could download the lyrics to these songs, as well as making some of your own selections of love song lyrics, to help you understand the connections being made.

20.17 Keeping context in mind

The contextual influences on literary and non-literary texts are important to consider at all stages of your research project and will need to be embedded in all sections where relevant to your discussion. So, to relate back to this investigation into metaphors exploring feelings of love, Table 20D shows some contextual influences of potential relevance. This could be an activity that you replicate with your own investigation, allowing you to highlight possible contextual influences to explore in your research and report.

20.17.1 *Introduction and aims*

Ultimately, what you need to show is that you understand the texts you have chosen and that you can

Table 20D

Contextual influence	*Small Island*	Song lyrics
time	Second World War 1948 contemporary novel – reflecting back	range from 1960s–present
place	London Jamaica wartime experiences	significant in some songs e.g. Arctic Monkeys – nightclub setting
ideology	of post-war Britain – Empire, racism, stereotyping audience ideology – multiculturalism, globalisation, acceptance of difference	social attitudes of different times audience ideology – different beliefs in love
mode	written	written, sung
genre	prose fiction narrative	song lyrics
purpose	entertain enlighten / challenge views	amuse / entertain create empathy / describe personal experiences
audience	anyone	Dolly Parton – country and pop enthusiasts Arctic Monkeys – rock/alternative listeners
text producer	Levy – Jamaican heritage	individual / groups Dolly Parton – American country singer Arctic Monkeys – UK indie group from Sheffield
text reception	book purchased individual / shared	listen / download shared / solitary experience repeated

demonstrate this understanding to a reader. So, firstly, you must give an account of the literary text which enables a reader to understand why you have arrived at the aim(s) of the study and why you have made your selection(s) from the literary text. You will need to confirm that you have read and understood the literary text as a whole in order to make your selection. One thing to be mindful of is that you are not simply describing your literary text. Secondly, you must justify your choice of non-literary material in order to demonstrate the connections between this and your literary choice. Your aim is to write about 750 words.

ACTIVITY 16

Critical reflection 1

Read Text 20I, which is a first draft of the *Introduction and aims* for an investigation which outlines the choice of literary text. Consider how far it fulfils the criteria of:

a giving an account of the literary text
b showing an understanding of the whole text
c not describing the literary text
d identifying the selections made for close focus
e outlining the aims of the study.

You could rank these: 1 (not at all), 2 (some evidence), 3 (fulfils completely). From this, decide what advice you would give to the student to improve and redraft their introduction.

Text 20I: First draft

I have chosen to look at the use of metaphor in *Small Island*, specifically the use of hurricanes as a metaphor. *Small Island* is set during and after the Second World War and presents four characters, two white English and two black Jamaicans. It follows the story of Hortense and Gilbert's arrival to live in London and their early experiences boarding with Queenie, while her husband is missing after the war. Their two women's lives are intertwined without them knowing through the character of Michael, who is a relation of Hortense's but who has an affair with Queenie during the war which results in her giving birth to a mixed-race child. Levy's themes are of attitudes to immigrants, racial bigotry and England's relationship with countries in its Empire at this time in history.

Source: private data

What you might have noticed in Text 20I is that it really only offers an outline of the plot and a brief overview of the characters and their relationships. Rather, in this opening section of your investigation, it is important that you offer an account of the text which says *why* you have arrived at the aim of your study and your selections of extracts from the literary text. So, it's vital to think about how demonstrating your understanding of the text you have chosen links to your specific focus. In this investigation, the important technique being explored is metaphor, so you might ask yourself the following questions as a way to decide how to structure your introduction.

- Why is metaphor important in this novel?
- What types of metaphors are used throughout the novel?
- Why have you selected to focus specifically on the metaphor of hurricanes?
- Where do references to this particular metaphor occur in the novel?
- What is the significance of the metaphor to the narrative, the development of characters or themes?

Once you have answered these questions, your revised introduction might now look something like Text 20J.

Text 20J: Revised *Introduction and aims*

I am exploring the use of metaphor in *Small Island* and in song lyrics to present love.

In *Small Island*, Levy presents four distinct narrative voices to present themes of immigration, prejudice and the conflict between romantic expectations and life's reality. The narratives are structured into Before and After, following the characters' individual and intertwined experiences of the Second World War and Hortense's and Gilbert's emigration from Jamaica for a new life in London. The two female narratives both explore the compromise between idealistic hopes and the acceptance of a future different from early ambitions. They are further linked by the character of Michael, who Levy gives no voice of his own in an individual narrative. Hortense's unrequited love for Michael causes her heartache and affects her acceptance of her relationship with her husband, Gilbert. Queenie's meeting with Michael during the Second World War proves a catalyst as embarking on a brief passionate affair with him both allows her to escape temporarily her unhappy and unsatisfactory marriage and her intense feelings of loneliness but also results in a baby – perhaps the symbol of the new post-war multicultural Britain. Interestingly, Levy chooses never to reveal the women's connection to Michael, allowing this to be a strange coincidence that only the readers know but implying that Michael's impact on both women's lives will be ongoing but unknown to them.

While there are many metaphors used to explore the inter-racial aspects of the relationships, I will focus on the metaphor of the hurricane which Levy uses as a motif through the novel to present the impact Michael has on the women's lives. The first extract I have chosen is from Hortense's narrative 'Before'. This offers an account of an actual hurricane during which she bitterly reveals Michael's affair with Mrs Ryder, a married white woman, that results in both their expulsion from the family home and foreshadows Michael's relationship with Queenie. Here the hurricane is both metaphorical in its association with Michael and literal in its destruction of the Jamaican landscape and human life.

The second extract is from Queenie's '1948' narrative which presents her brief relationship with Michael when he returns to see her after the war has ended before he emigrates to start a new life in Canada. Like a hurricane, Michael's visit is fleeting but destructive to Queenie, with the long-term effect being a baby who is the physical evidence of the betrayal of her marriage vows and whose life will also be affected by the prejudices of her country and her husband who returns to her unexpectedly.

Source: private data

ACTIVITY 17

Critical reflection 2

- Return to the ranking scale used in Activity 16. Has this revised version moved further towards the fulfilment of the criteria? What aspects could be improved?
- Highlight the revised *Introduction and aims* to see where it has answered the questions that were posed about the use of metaphor.

Check your responses in the Ideas section on Cambridge Elevate

20.17.2 *Introduction and aims*: non-literary material

The next part of the introduction requires you to justify and contextualise your choice of non-literary material, but this does not have to be the same length as your discussion of your literary text. So the kinds of questions that you need to address are as follows.

- Why have I chosen this particular non-literary material?
- How is it a good source of data?
- Where does it come from?
- How does it connect to the literary text?

Again, being a critical reader of other people's work will help you think about your own writing in the ways that you respond to these questions. Look at this first draft of this section of the introduction:

For my non-literary material I have chosen the lyrics of four popular songs connected by the theme of love; love is a universal human experience and a common theme of popular songs I have chosen songs that present different aspects of love from youthful attraction, to love as eternal and to the loss of love. I have also chosen individual pop songs by a variety of artists, rather than one particular period of time so my lyrics span from 1973 to 2005. This will allow me to discover if they are common representations of love.

My aim is to explore the metaphors used to present feelings of love. I am interested to see if, as in Small Island, there is also a particular metaphor that runs through each song, or if a range of metaphors are used by the lyricists to present their view of love.

ACTIVITY 18

Advising on redrafting

a Decide whether the extract from the introduction shown in this section answers the bullet pointed questions in section 20.17.2.

b Offer suggestions for improvements or expansions for any of the questions.

Check your responses in the Ideas section on Cambridge Elevate

20.17.3 *Review*

If your *Introduction and aims* serves to show that you understand your literary and non-literary material and the reasons for your choices and an outline of your focus, the *Review* shows that you understand the concepts you are investigating. A review is a very important element of academic writing as not only does it convey your conceptual understanding, it also indicates that you have read appropriately around the topic. Obviously the type of reading you need to do depends on the topic you have chosen, but you do need to demonstrate that you have the theoretical knowledge to proceed to your analysis and draw findings together from your own literary and non-literary material. Although word count guidance indicates that this should be between 300–500 words - potentially shorter than your *Introduction and aims* - you will need to spend time researching, note-taking and writing your *Review* to ensure that have brought together relevantly the main ideas.

Finding relevant sources

The first step is to find secondary sources relevant to your topic. In the examples of *Reviews* in Texts 20K–20M, notes have been taken from the following books:

Simpson, Paul. (2014) *Stylistics, A Resource Book for Students*, 2nd edition, London: Routledge.

Kövecses, Zoltán. (2002) *Metaphor: A Practical Introduction*, New York: Oxford University Press.

Burke, Michael. (ed) (2014) *The Routledge Handbook of Stylistics*, London: Routledge.

In this 'model' investigation, the underlying linguistic strategy being analysed is metaphor and whether the sorts of metaphors connected to the emotion of love used in literary and non-literary discourses differ. Firstly, it would seem sensible to define metaphor by showing your reading of secondary sources as in Text 20K.

Text 20K

Simpson's definition (2014: 41) is that 'a metaphor is a process of mapping between two different conceptual domains known as the target domain and the source domain'.

Discussing concepts

Perhaps what is then required is some further discussion of the ways that metaphor can be identified. In Text 20M it is presented using notes taken from readings rather than direct quotations and is linked to the specific focus of this investigation on love in literary and non-literary texts.

The target is the topic or concept that the metaphor aims to describe (in this example the concept of love) and the source refers to the concept being drawn upon. The connections between these domains are known as mappings. Common ones to do with love are LOVE IS A JOURNEY, LOVE IS A GAME and LOVE IS WAR. Some of these common ones were mapped by Lakoff and Johnson in their famous 1980 work, *Metaphors We Live By*.

There is also opportunity to link the concept of metaphor to ideas for analysis in your connected literary text and non-literary material and so you can make it specific to the concept of love and ways that metaphors conceptualise it as in Text 20L.

Text 20L

Building on their research, Kövecses (2002) also lists different common source domains used to explore human experiences and among these are 'forces'. Within these forces he lists 'wind' which is interesting in relation to the extracts from *Small Island*, suggesting that this is a common source from which writers can make different metaphorical conceptualisations. However, he also lists other common sources and it will be interesting to map the source and target domains in the song lyrics for either patterns or unconventional ones.

One of the key ideas in this investigation is the ways that love is presented metaphorically in a literary text and song lyrics, which although are not 'literary' in the definition for the non-exam assessment do exhibit literary qualities. So, it might also be good to include some discussion of 'literariness', to show an understanding of some of the debates and ideas surrounding 'metaphor' and its linguistic aspects.

ACTIVITY 19

Discussing theoretical interpretations

Read Text 20M, which contains three references that foreground this discussion of metaphors and literariness.

Text 20M

1 According to Kövecses (2002), in literature metaphors are typically more *novel* and typically *less clear*.

2 According to Simpson (2014: 42–43), 'writers consciously strive for novelty in literary expression' and this means exploring new conceptual mappings. He also says that it is 'not a special or exclusive feature of literary discourse but 'a natural part of conceptual thought'.

3 Lakoff and Turner express the view that conceptual metaphors are 'part of the common conceptual apparatus shared by members of a culture' and that literary writers call upon these to appeal to readers' shared understanding but use these in creative and imaginative ways (1989: 51).

Match the references in Text 20M to these interpretations.

a Everyone uses metaphor in their everyday lives but writers try to invent new ones to be creative.
b An understanding of metaphor is shared by communities, and writers exploit these so that readers can relate to them.
c Metaphors in literary texts differ from those in everyday use as writers deliberately try to be obscure.

Check your responses in the Ideas section on Cambridge Elevate

ACTIVITY 20

Writing cohesively

Take the three references in Text 20M and write a paragraph for the *Review* discussing the debates around the use of metaphor in literature and everyday life.

- Use connectives to link the ideas together.
- Check your writing by asking a peer for feedback on its clarity of expression and clarity of ideas.
- Redraft, if necessary, from the feedback given.

20.17.4 *Analysis*

Once you have researched the concepts that you are exploring, applying these to your own chosen literary text and non-literary material is the next stage of your research project. It is the *Analysis* section where you make the connection between theoretical perspectives and demonstrate your understanding of these in a practical way.

Texts 20N(a) and 20N(b) are two short extracts from *Small Island*, each part of a longer segment that would be used for full analysis in the actual investigation.

Text 20N

(a) Extract from Hortense's narrative

A hurricane can make cows fly. It can tear trees from the ground, toss them in the air and snap them like twigs. A house can be picked up, its four walls parted, its roof twisted, and everything scattered in a divine game of hide-and-seek. This savage wind could even make the 'rock of ages' take to the air and float off as light as a bird's wing.

But a hurricane does not come without warning. News of the gathering storm would sweep the island as swiftly as any breeze, scattering rumours of its speed, the position of its eyes, the measure of its breath.

Mrs Ryder told me, without concern. 'This will be my first hurricane and I don't mind telling you, Hortense, I find it quite exciting.' She skipped like a giddy girl bolting the shutters with a delighted laugh. She hummed a song as we stowed chairs and desks and locked cupboards. She looked in the mirror, combing her hair, before we secured the doors. And turning to me she said, 'Wouldn't it be something to stand in the hurricane, to feel the full force of God's power in all its might?'

(b) Extract from Queenie's narrative.

It was softly spoken and out of the blue when he said, 'I lost them all in a hurricane.' If I'd have asked more questions, I'm sure he would have wept.

But then he surprisingly bucked up – made me quite jump. Looking up at me his roving eyes started nibbling me all over. He placed his large hand on top of mine. 'Tell me, have you ever felt the force of a hurricane?' One by one he slipped his fingers between mine, forcing them apart while gently increasing the squeeze.

'No,' I said.

He put his lips against my ear his tongue lightly licking the lobe. 'Would you like to?' He bit me.

And I said, 'In Herefordshire, Hertfordshire and Hampshire hurricanes hardly ever happen.'

Source: Andrea Levy, *Small Island*

First *Analysis* of the literary text

In Queenie's narrative [Text 20N(a)], the hurricane is presented firstly in a seemingly literal way in its power to destroy people's habitats and belongings. Noticeably, the hurricane's force is conveyed through modality, with the repetition of the modal auxiliary 'can'. Levy's opening declarative makes the actual power of the hurricane explicit in its actual ability to make something impossible such as cows to fly possible. The dynamic verbs 'tear, 'toss' and 'snap' also foreground its physical power. Although the passive 'a house can be picked up' seemingly takes away the hurricane's agency, this grammatical construction further reinforce mankind's powerlessness, as the hurricane destroy human structures so effortlessly. Certain words seem to collocate, for example 'savage wind' and 'gathering storm'. The power of the hurricane is presented through religious references, as in 'divine' and 'rock of ages', but the hurricane does not appear a benevolent god; the suggestion of a 'divine game of hide and seek' offers on the face of it a childlike game, but the destructive force suggests that this is not a pleasurable and innocent game. The hurricane as more powerful than God is indicated by the ability to move so effortlessly the 'rock of ages', as often God is presented through the metaphor of 'rock', a solid object.

In the second paragraph [Text 20N(a)], Hortense describes Mrs Ryder's child-like excitement at the experience to come in the **collocation** of 'giddy girl' and the childlike verb 'skipped'. In fact her preparations seem unusual, as they are not concerned with protection against the destruction to come but show her concern with her appearance – she 'looks in the mirror, combing her hair'. As Michael arrives shortly after this and consequently Hortense realises the possible sexual relationship between him and Mrs Ryder, Levy indicates the specific metaphorical connection between Michael and a hurricane, as well as the broader metaphorical link between love and a hurricane.

Queenie's narrative [Text 20N(b)] draws again upon the connection between Michael and a hurricane. Michael's sexually suggestive interrogatives 'have you ever felt the force of a hurricane?' and 'would you like to?' are combined with the presentation of the physical power as all Michael's – shown in his actions of 'forcing', 'squeezing' and, finally, in biting Queenie. Queenie's use of the well-known saying 'In Hertfordshire ... hurricanes hardly ever happen' (made famous in the 1960s musical My Fair Lady in which a cockney girl is taught to speak like a lady using received pronunciation) foregrounds the unusualness of a hurricane in England, reminding us that a black Jamaican was not usual at this time in England either.

> **Key terms**
>
> **collocation:** words that are sequenced together regularly and therefore convey meaning through their association

First *Analysis* of the non-literary material

Now, by analysing lines from Arctic Monkeys' lyrics, specifically their 2006 hit, *I Bet You Look Good on the Dancefloor*, and their more recent (2013) release, *I Wanna Be Yours*, some decisions about the structuring of the *Analysis* section can begin to take place.

In both songs, lexical concepts from the domain of temperature appear: 'frozen', 'cold' in 'I bet...' and 'hot', 'portable heater' and 'cold' from 'I wanna be yours'. In 'I bet' the nouns 'explosion', 'dynamite' and 'fuse' all link semantically and perhaps connote the ideas of ignition, spark and flame associated with lust. 'I wanna be your' uses nouns of everyday objects 'vacuum cleaner', 'Ford Cortina', 'coffee pot' and ''leccy meter' to connote the speaker's desire to be essential to all aspects of his lover's life.

Currently the paragraphs of analysis read more like an essay than a research project. So, from this overall initial interpretation and analysis of the song lyrics, the following refinements are necessary.

- Key linguistic strategies need to be drawn out in order to devise some helpful sub-sections for the *Analysis* section; this will allow more focused (and less impressionistic) exploration.
- Links need to be made to relevant theoretical concepts (such as the ideas about metaphor explored earlier).

ACTIVITY 21

Metaphor

Review the analyses of Texts 20N(a) and 20N(b) and the Arctic Monkeys' song lyrics, along with your own observations.

1 Identify the metaphors in the extra Texts 20N(a) and 20N(b) from *Small Island* and the song.
2 What patterns can you find in the use of metaphor?
3 Using the language levels, what aspects of the writers' choices are interesting? For example, syntax, word classes, etc.
4 How can you link these to the linguists' discussion of metaphors as concepts we considered in the *Review*?
5 What sub-headings would help in examining particular aspects of metaphor?

Check your responses in the Ideas section on Cambridge Elevate

See 20.7.3 for the information on *Review*

As this potential investigation focuses on a concept (as well as a theme), the headings that would be suitable may be different from those you have looked at previously. Within each larger heading, small sub-headings could explore in more detail the separate features worth analysing, such as the metaphorical representations of love could be divided into target and source domains, conventional and unconventional metaphors or explore the ways that particular word classes such as nouns and verbs contribute to the metaphors.

20.17.5 Revised *Analysis*

Here's a part of the *Analysis* which builds upon the use of sub-headings as a means of honing into specific aspects of interest in the texts used, responding to the research focus. Here the literary texts and non-literary material are being considered together, but this is not essential. Look at the links between the linguistic aspects of the texts and the concepts explored in the *Review* that are now developed and integrated into the analysis.

Metaphors: target and source domains.

In Small Island and the song lyrics the target domain is the abstract concept of love and the writers use typical source domains to present these.

Kövesces (2002) identifies heat and cold as a way to talk about attitudes to other people and this is evident in the Arctic Monkeys' 'I wanna be yours' where the speaker desires to be a 'portable heater' to offer constant warmth to his lover and protect her from 'cold'. The use of heat and cold are also highlighted in 'I bet' as initially the potential lover is 'frozen' and 'cold' but the speaker's attraction to her turns her into a force as explosive as 'dynamite'.

Kövesces also identifies the use of forces as another common source domain as these 'effect various changes in the thing acted upon' (2004: 19–20). Levy introduces the hurricane as agent in the active aspect in the opening declaratives of the extract from Hortense's narrative [Text 20N(b)] but then shifts the focus on to human belongings in the passive 'A house can be picked up' and then to people themselves. In Small Island, the things acted upon are women – Mrs Ryder and Queenie. The consequences for Michael's force are devastating for Mrs Ryder, whose adulterous relationship is revealed as her husband is symbolically killed by the hurricane. For Queenie, the destructive consequence is a mixed-race baby, a visible symbol of her adultery.

20.17.6 Conclusions

The *Conclusions* need to offer a summary of the main points revealed by the study. This should be in the form of an overview of what has been revealed by bringing the textual sources together, showing how the understanding of each text has been enhanced by consideration of the other.

Using the *Small Island* (Text 20N) and song lyrics project we could imagine some potential conclusions that could be drawn.

- Metaphors to express the feelings of love in literary texts and song lyrics could be similar because the songs, by their very nature, have poetic qualities.
- Metaphors to express love could be used differently depending on the type of love being presented - eternal love could be presented differently from first love, illicit love or unrequited love.
- More varied metaphors could appear in the shorter lyrics, whereas the narrative genre could mean more extended metaphors and symbolism.

- Metaphors around love tend to draw on the same source domain but realise them differently, depending on the genre.

So, to conclude and link back to the investigation of the key concept of metaphor, there may be some discussion of the validity of the claim that there are conventional metaphors and that by looking at both types of source, this seems to be the case. There might also be a critique of the non-literary text choice and other material that could have been useful to compare. For example, had the non-literary material been ordinary people talking about love and describing it, the concept of using metaphor in everyday life could have been explored better than in the (arguably) semi-literary genre of song lyrics – although this too leads to a debate about literariness that you explored at the beginning of your study.

20.18 Bringing it all together

So, it's over to you to decide the content and focus of your investigation and the individual approach you will take. As it's a non-exam assessment, it'll be your teacher who will supervise and mark your work initially. What you need is to be confident that you have fulfilled the criteria for the written report and that you know how you will be assessed. By keeping the assessment objectives constantly in mind while you are drafting and redrafting your project until the final submission, you can reflect on where you are meeting them or where you need to make changes.

20.18.1 Self-assessment: check your learning

For each of the following statements, evaluate your confidence in that topic area:

Topic area	Very confident	Some knowledge	Need to revise
I know the required sections of the final report			
I understand the range of methods that I can choose from in order to collect my non-literary material			
I can explain and justify my choice of literary and non-literary material in the light of my chosen focus			
I can identify contextual factors that are significant to my choice of focus and my literary and non-literary material			
I can explore how relevant theories and concepts link to my chosen focus and my literary and non-literary material			

20.18.2 Word count guidance: written report

The total investigation should be between 2500–3000 words in length. You could for example use the following structure:

- *Introduction* and aims
- *Review*
- *Analysis*
- *Conclusion*
- *Appendix*: extracts and data
- *References*

20.18.3 Assessment objectives

There are four assessment objectives in the NEA. AO1 and AO2 are worth 15 marks each, AO3 and AO4 are worth 10 marks each. The following is a checklist of what each AO refers to and the strands assessed in each one. Often these relate to a section of your investigation, so again you can check these against the contents of your own project. The marking criteria are based on the assumption that you have included an investigation into a literary text and so you would get no marks (0) if there was no evidence of this.

- **AO1** (15 marks): Apply concepts and methods from integrated linguistic and literary study as appropriate, using associated terminology and coherent written expression

There are three strands, which are:
- an account of the source material
- a relevant methodology
- an effectively structured report.

- **AO2** (15 marks): Analyse ways in which meanings are shaped in texts

There are three strands, which are:
- the quality of analysis
- interpretation of features
- coverage of the literary text and non-literary material.

- **AO3** (10 marks): Demonstrate understanding of the significance and influence of the contexts in which texts are produced and received

There are two strands, which are:
- the relationship between texts and their particular contexts
- coverage of different aspects of context: for example, time, place, ideology, mode, purpose, audience, etc.

- **AO4** (10 marks): Explore connections across texts, informed by linguistic and literary concepts and methods

There are two strands, which are:
- the connections made between the texts and the exploration of relationships between the chosen texts
- a conclusion offering a critique and reflection on the rationale for comparison and the initial aims.

ACTIVITY 22

Using the assessment criteria

a *Before you start your investigation*
For each assessment objective, decide in which section(s) this is being assessed. Sometimes, the assessment criteria refer explicitly to the section(s) but sometimes you will have to suggest where this may be assessed.

b *As you write your research project report*
When you complete each section, return to the assessment criteria and self-assess. Have you met the assessment objectives required in that section? Using the marking criteria, place yourself on the levels of achievement for each AO. What suggestions for improvements do you have?

ENRICHING

21 Remembered places

21.1 Extension activities

21.1.1 Exploring quest narratives

You have studied Tim Youngs' (2013) idea that the quest narrative is hugely relevant to travel writing. The concept of a quest is more usually and obviously associated with adventure stories, or even the *bildungsroman*, than it is with travel narratives. Quest narratives are also referred to as 'hero's journey' narratives. In proposing the relevance of the quest narrative to travel writing, Youngs highlights the conventional quest narrative elements of the hero (the traveller), the search, the protagonist's point of view, obstacles and purpose in particular. Some of these aspects of quest writing can be found in Propp's morphology of the folktale, discussed in Unit 22. These and other aspects of quest narratives are worth exploring in more detail in relation to travel writing.

ACTIVITY 1

Travelling as questing

a Explore the similarities and differences between the kinds of travel writing you have studied in the anthology and the aspects of a questing narrative suggested by Youngs and by Propp. Where is the analogy Youngs proposes most analytically interesting and useful, and where is it most problematic – with what kinds of texts and genres (e.g. memoirs, travel guides, message board posts), and in what aspects (e.g. the 'obstacle', the 'purpose')?

b How far do you think the concept of a 'hero's journey' is masculine? What associations does it have for you with stereotypically masculine concepts in society (such as adventure, hunting and pursuit, conquest and colonialism, etc.)?

21.1.2 Genres of travel writing

The Paris anthology involves lots of different genres of non-literary texts. One of the best ways of exploring these genres is to practise writing texts using these genres yourself. Producing some original creative travel writing using different genres will reveal to you some of your expectations about the conventions, particularities, affordances and constraints of specific genres, and will show you how the genre influences the ways in which you use language and shape meaning.

ACTIVITY 2

Experimenting with and comparing genres

Think about the last time you went on a day trip or holiday, or do this activity next time you go on a day trip. Create three different pieces of travel writing about your experience using the genres listed here. Once you have created all three, compare and contrast the texts.

a Memoir or diary

b Letter or postcard

c Scrapbook or webpage.

21.2 Suggestions for small independent research investigations

21.2.1 Metaphors

You have looked at the metaphors 'LIFE IS A JOURNEY' and 'WRITING IS A JOURNEY' and investigated their use in different travel narratives. The metaphors we use can reveal a lot about culturally embedded ways of thinking. For example, because Great Britain is a group of islands, sea-faring journeys have played a prominent role in our past, for trade, exploration, travel and war. Despite the sea and sailing becoming a less prominent part of our lives over the centuries, except in times of war, sea-faring related metaphors are still embedded in our cultural lexicon, such as 'all hands on deck', 'three sheets to the wind', 'any port in a storm' and so on. This is a good example of metaphors from travel infiltrating and influencing everyday expression about other things. It is also illustrative of the ways in which, through metaphors, we use things we are familiar with and find easy to talk about and explain (often concrete things, like physical objects) to express things we find harder to talk about and explain (often abstract things, like ideas and emotions). In the 'LIFE IS A JOURNEY' and 'WRITING IS A JOURNEY' metaphors, the concept of a journey is the more familiar element, which we can be expected to have some similar experiences of, and 'life' and the process of 'writing' are the elements which are more abstract and complicated, hence the need for the concept of a journey as a vehicle for expressing them. 'LIFE IS A JOURNEY' is perhaps a more conventional metaphor (that is, common in everyday expression, and used to aid clarity of communication), whereas 'writing is a journey' might be an example of a more poetic metaphor (that is, unusual, and created for striking and defamiliarising effect).

It's worth thinking about these metaphors in more detail to develop insight into how the concept of a journey is being shaped and used in each. It's also interesting to explore other metaphors involving the concept of a journey.

ACTIVITY 3

Journey metaphors

a Table 15A in Section 15.6 broke down the metaphor 'SOUND IS CHOCOLATE'. Use the table template in Table 21A to break down the 'life' and 'journey' concepts: what elements of each concept of a 'journey' are foregrounded by their pairing? How does the metaphor change how you think of 'life'?

b What elements of the concepts of a 'journey' and 'life' are backgrounded in the metaphor?

c Repeat 3a and 3b for the metaphor 'WRITING IS A JOURNEY', and compare and contrast your conception of 'journey' in the two different metaphorical contexts.

d See if you can find or think of any other journey and journey-related metaphors and possible linguistic expressions of them, such as 'LOVE IS A JOURNEY' (expressed through phrases like 'the relationship isn't going anywhere' and 'my feelings have rather run away with me'), or, more generally, 'SUBJECTS ARE AREAS', 'LEARNING IS A JOURNEY', 'REASONING IS FOLLOWING A PATH', etc.

e Choose one of these metaphors involving the concept of a journey and write a short narrative (about 200 words) using it as an extended metaphor throughout your text.

Table 21A: The metaphor 'LIFE IS A JOURNEY'

Characteristics of a journey	Understood qualities of life through the metaphor

21.2.2 New technologies

New technologies enable the blending of different modes to communicate meaning. Increasingly accessible digital tools and growing digital literacy among younger generations are leading to new forms of recording and social sharing of travel experiences.

ACTIVITY 4

Narrative and new technologies

Explore some of the digital platforms and genres available and popular for digital travel writing (blogs, flickr albums, websites, etc.), and compare your experiences of the different affordances and constraints of these genres (consider, for example, how you are relatively free, guided or limited in navigating, engaging with and interpreting their content).

21.3 Wider reading list

21.3.1 Selected reading on key areas in *Remembered places*

Hulme, Peter and Youngs, Tim, eds. (2002) *The Cambridge Companion to Travel Writing*, Cambridge: Cambridge University Press.

This book includes essays by scholars from a variety of subject areas, from anthropology to literary studies, introducing and discussing travel writing in English from 1500 CE to the present day. The collection focuses on travel writing from six areas across the globe, provides a variety of tools for the study of travel writing, a survey of key cultural and theoretical issues, and an extensive list of further reading.

Rowlands, Penelope (2011) *Paris Was Ours: Thirty-Two Writers Reflect on the City of Light*, Chapel Hill, North Carolina: Algonquin Books of Chapel Hill

A collection of personal essays by well-known and less-known writers on Paris and its significance to them.

Thompson, Carl (2011) *Travel Writing*. Abingdon: Routledge.

Thompson's text provides an exploratory definition and deft historical survey of travel writing, engaging with canonical and marginal works, and shedding light on autobiographical elements of the practice.

Youngs, Tim (2013) *Cambridge Introduction to Travel Writing,* Cambridge: Cambridge University Press.

Youngs' book illustrates the various influences of a wide variety of literary and non-literary genres on travel writing, and surveys some of the most celebrated examples of the form.

21.3.2 Further useful resources - general

Anderson, Linda (2010) *Autobiography*, 2nd edn, London: Routledge.

George, Don, ed. (2011) *Tales From Nowhere: Unexpected Stories from Unexpected Places*, London: Lonely Planet.

George, Don (2012) *Better Than Fiction: True Travel Tales from Great Fiction Writers, London:* Lonely Planet.

George, Don (2013) *Lonely Planet's Guide to Travel Writing*, 3rd edn, London: Lonely Planet.

Foster, Shirley, and Mills, Sara (2013) *An Anthology of Women's Travel Writing*, Manchester: Manchester University Press.

Pettinger, Alasdair (website) *Studies in Travel Writing*.

Wheeler, Tony, ed. (2009) *Best of Lonely Planet Travel Writing*, London: Lonely Planet.

Yagoda, Ben (2009) *Memoir: A History*, New York: Riverhead Books.

Visit Alasdair Pettinger's site *Studies in Travel Writing* via Cambridge Elevate

21.4 Current research on key areas in remembered places

21.4.1 Avenues of research in academia

- **The Grand Tour, then and now:** The Grand Tour was the name given to a popular lengthy holiday around the cities of Europe, undertaken by the wealthy, to develop and demonstrate to others their cultural sophistication. It peaked in fashion between 1660 and 1820. Much more recently, the Gap Year tour of the Far East has become increasingly popular among middle and upper class youths. Both phenomena, increasingly in comparison, are of interest to researchers in the fields of cultural studies, history and literary studies, particularly with reference to understanding the role of travel in the development of identity and the self.
- **Travel writing and discourse communities:** The ease and boundlessness of online communication has enabled new collaborative forms of writing. Travel advice, blogs, guides and the like provide

a hub for cross-cultural sharing and discourse. New technologies are facilitating cyber-representations - virtual portrayals and creations - of geographic spaces and places, around which new discourse communities are centred. These texts and discourse communities are of great interest to scholars researching collaborative online discourse, cultural appropriation, digital memoirs and more.

21.4.2 Dr Carl Thompson, Reader in English Literature and Travel Culture at Nottingham Trent University, writes of his research into travel writing.

Any place – and every place – is as much an imaginative construct as a physical location. For portions of the material world to cohere into distinct 'places', humans have to mentally organize and name them, demarcating boundaries, specifying key identifying features. In this way, places are never perceived directly but always viewed through the mediating – and often simplifying – filters of language, culture and imagination.

These filters can shape what we see, or think we see, as we venture out into the world. They led Marco Polo, for example, to say he had seen unicorns when he visited the South East Asian island we now call Java. This was not a lie on Polo's part. In the medieval period such mythical beasts were thought to live in places like Java, which seemed highly exotic to Europeans. Polo arrived in Asia expecting to see marvels, and when he did encounter a single-horned quadruped – in fact, the animal we now call the Javan rhinoceros – he inevitably labelled it a unicorn.

Foreign peoples may be similarly viewed through a web of prior expectations, assumptions and mental categories. Yet as literary critic Edward Said argued in his influential book *Orientalism* (1978), when this happens the consequences can be profound and highly problematic.

In *Orientalism*, Said examined European and US depictions of the so-called 'Orient'. This was very much an invented region or 'imagined geography'. Supposedly embracing Muslim North Africa, the Middle East, India, South East Asia, China and Japan, this is territory encompassing a great variety of cultures, ethnicities and belief-systems. Yet for centuries both scholars and the general population in Europe believed that all these different places could be lumped together as the Orient. And their inhabitants were similarly to be classed as 'Orientals', with the assumption that they shared at some level certain key characteristics.

The characteristics routinely attributed to Orientals, Said demonstrated, were generally negative stereotypes, designed to foster a sense of European superiority by stressing the moral and intellectual inferiority of other cultures. Thus the Oriental was often depicted as lazy and passive, uninterested in progress or material improvement, and with a tendency to cruelty, despotism and sensuality. Once established as 'truths' about the many and varied peoples of the Middle and Far East, these stereotypes then became what travellers expected to find when visiting these regions. And so, like Marco Polo with his unicorns, this was what travellers frequently reported, as they singled out and described those aspects of their experience which conformed to their prior expectations.

In this way, travel writing has often served to both create and reflect a culture's imagined geographies of other regions. For this reason, no form of travel writing should ever be regarded as a wholly accurate, objective account of the world as it really is; rather, travel accounts record how one specific traveller, and by extension the culture he or she hails from, *perceives* another place or culture at a particular moment in time.

This is not to say that travellers are always completely in thrall to the imagined geographies dominant in their society. Many travellers have questioned these stock assumptions. Marco Polo thought the Javan rhinoceros was a unicorn, but he was also able to point out all the ways in which it contradicted traditional ideas about these creatures; it was very ugly, he noted, and couldn't be tamed by virgins. The best recent travel writers also usually try to complicate the stereotypes associated with the places they visit. Yet even as they write against one imagined geography, they necessarily bring another into existence. Their account can only be another impression, another perspective, as the traveller extrapolates from his or her personal experience to make larger claims about the entirety of a foreign culture. Those claims may not be false – yet at the same time they will never be the whole or only truth about another place or people.

ACTIVITY 5

Travel writing

Answer the following questions, in relation to Dr Thompson's text.

a How do you think your 'imaginative construct' of a place significant to your childhood is different from the real physical place? How do you think your childhood perception and the biases of your memory have shaped your imaginative construct in this instance?

b Can you think of, or find, any examples of art, television media, pop songs, comic books or literature which exhibit, or engage with and challenge, the stereotypes of 'Eastern' cultures discussed by Said in his work on 'Orientalism'?

c What imagined geographies are you aware of existing in other cultures in relation to England, and in relation to London in particular? For example, what do you believe to be popular schemas of England shared by Americans, or the French, or the Chinese?

d What do you think might be some of the most significant influences in cultural schemas of England and London, across the globe. Consider, for example, the following:

- trending cultural exports, such as the series *Downton Abbey*, popular in the USA, and the more world-wide popularity of the works of great writers such Shakespeare, Austen and Dickens
- the colonial history of the British Empire
- the typical tourist destinations of visitors to London (e.g., Buckingham Palace, Trafalgar Square, the Houses of Parliament, the Tower of London).

What other influences can you add to this list, and to what cultures might they be particularly significant?

21.4.3 Dr Ruth Page in video interview

Watch Dr Ruth Page, Reader in English Language at the University of Leicester, talk about her research into blogs and online discourse communities on Cambridge Elevate

ENRICHING

22 Imagined worlds

22.1 Extension activities

22.1.1 Modality extended

You have looked at modality, and the ways in which point of view can be expressed by a variety of modal linguistic forms (auxiliary verbs, lexical verbs, adjectives, etc.) in different modal domains (epistemic, deontic and boulomaic). The combination of particular types of narration (first or third person, etc.) and different modal domains create kinds of modal 'shading'. You looked at examples of Frankenstein's narration in which he expressed certainty and desire through the use of an array of epistemic and deontic forms.

ACTIVITY 1

Modal shading

In your chosen novel, choose one character, and explore the following questions.

a Does that character have a dominant pattern of modal shading?

b If the character's modal shading shifts, does his/her modal shading shift according to circumstances, and/or in relation to whom the character is addressing?

c If the character's modal shading shifts in relation to whom he/she is addressing, what does this suggest to you about that character and his/her relationships with other characters?

22.1.2 Places and perspectives

Some of the effects achieved by fantasy fiction are closely bound up with the presentation of particular (and peculiar) places and spaces that form the sites of the events. You have considered the ways in which locations can serve as motifs. You have also explored some uses of deixis to construct the perspective of a narrator or character and orientate you as a reader in and around the story world.

ACTIVITY 2

Exploring place

Analyse the ways in which perspectives and places are intertwined in your novel.

a Start by choosing a significant place in your text. Find and reread the first description of it. Now try to create a simple sketch of what you imagine the place looks like – how it is laid out, where it is light and dark, figures or furniture around the place, etc.

b Reflect on the relationship between the textual details and your imaginative construction of the place. For example:
- Through whose eyes (which deictic centre) do you see it?
- How, and how far, does the language through which the place is presented determine how you imagine and experience it?
- How much detail is coming from the text, the context and your own gap-filling?

c Now consider the various places and spaces in the text as a whole. Think about how your experiences of the significant sites of the novel are mediated through the perspectives of characters and the narrator. For example:

- Through whose eyes (which deictic centre) do you experience the different spaces?
- What locating, orienting and evaluative descriptive language is used to construct that perspective?
- Are there any dramatic shifts in perspective around each space?
- Is the same place presented differently from two or more characters' alternative perspectives?

d Finally, compare the presentation of different spaces within the novel, and think about this presentation in the context of the novel's genre. For example:

- Are different places presented in very diverse ways?
- How does the language used in setting the scenes contribute to the impressions you get of each place, and to your expectations of what might happen there?
- How do the ways in which these places are presented contribute to the relative prototypicality of this novel with respect to its genre?

22.1.3 Fantastic tellability

ACTIVITY 3

Tellability and structure

As you may recall, one of the characteristics of fantasy fiction identified by Brian Attebery is 'a basic narrative structure that begins with a problem and ends with a resolution'. Consider this characteristic in relation to Labovian notions of tellability and narrative structures.

For example:

a Does the narrative structure Attebery identifies fit the novel you are studying? If there is a problem, does it occur at the beginning of the story? If not, what events precede it, and how do they contribute to the plot? Are abstract and orientation sections included in the narrative?

b Is there a clear 'resolution' to the story, and if so what kind of resolution is it (escape, elimination, victory, change)? Does any section of narrative follow the resolution (if one occurs)?

c These questions involve an exploration of the relationships between the story (the chronological sequence of events) and the narration (the manner and order in which they are presented). Can you plot a very simple timeline for the story, and then mark the analeptic and proleptic path of narration across it? Where is the crux of 'complicating action', in Labov's terms ? If your novel's narration moves around a lot in a very non-chronological way, perhaps limit yourself to the section covering the complicating action.

d What makes this story 'tellable', in Labov's terms? Is it the problem, or the resolution, or something else? Is the nature of its tellability closely related to its genre?

e Retell the story of the novel to a friend in less than a minute and, if you can, record yourself doing so.

f Go back and listen to the recording, and analyse the ways in which you told it. For example:

- compare your retelling to Labov's narrative model
- review your retelling and in relation to Attebery's proposed characteristics of the genre
- note which events you included (as central to your retelling) and which you chose to leave out (as additional and not crucial to your retelling).

22.2 Suggestions for small independent research investigations

22.2.1 Exploring the relationship between unreliable narration and other-worldliness

Dystopian and gothic fiction, science and fantasy fiction, and magic realism go beyond the bounds of our world's reality. In doing so they test our capacity to suspend our disbelief, and our ability and willingness to temporarily accept and immerse ourselves in the strangeness of the story world. The relative reliability of the narrator, and the ways the language allows us to gauge this, play a significant part in our psychological and emotional engagement with the story.

ACTIVITY 4

Unreliable narration

There are many interesting questions to ask of the relationship between unreliable narration and the presentation of imagined worlds within the genres of fantasy fiction. While you are encouraged to think of questions of your own, some starting points might involve the following.

a Look closely at the first points in the narration at which the fantastical nature of the story world is communicated. Consider the ways in which this puts pressure on the presentation of the reliability of narrator, and how this pressure is handled, and is evident, in the language of the novel.

b How does the narrator of your novel react to the fantastical events of the story? Is it presented as a reality they are used to, or something that shocks them and which they themselves find hard to believe? How does this impact upon your own feelings about the story?

c Identify a range of novels within particular sub-genres of fantasy fiction. Locate the first moments of the fantastical in each (which may indeed be the first words of the first chapter). Conduct a comparative investigation of their narrators, applying the previous two questions to explore how reliable they are made to seem and how.

22.2.2 The *bildungsroman*, fantasy fiction and character development

You have tracked the characters in your novel, and explored how they change. You have learnt about the *bildungsroman*, a kind of novel which follows the progress and maturation of a character over time, usually from childhood to adulthood, following his/her 'coming of age', or similarly significant development. You have also learnt of two structuralist models of character roles: one based on Propp's morphology of the folktale, and the other on Greimas' actant model.

Along with his seven roles, Propp also proposed a model of thirty-one plot functions based on his work exploring the structure of folktales. You can research this online using a simple search – lots of resources are freely available. Propp's model traces alternative paths through which a character can face and overcome obstacles in his/her journey through life. You can therefore use it as a structuralist tool for the analysis of the *bildungsroman* qualities of some fantasy fiction. The *bildungsroman* and the fantasy genre can interact in interesting ways. Again, there are lots of avenues for exploration in this interaction, but Activity 5 lists some questions to think about in the first instance in relation to the novel you are studying.

See 22.3.2 for examples of the resources available

ACTIVITY 5

Tracking characters

a In most stories, the protagonist faces an obstacle or challenge: this is a crucial part of the story and of the character's development. In fantasy fiction, though, this challenge is often supernatural. How does this fantastical quality of the challenge impact upon the nature of his/her development?

b Which roles (in Propp's terms) and relationships (according to Greimas' model) do the different characters in your novel hold and move between, and at what points in the progression of the plot do these moves occur? How do these shifts in roles and relationships signal and/or contribute to character maturation and/or change?

22.3 Wider reading list

22.3.1 Selected reading on key areas in *Imagined worlds*

Curran, Stuart, ed. (n.d.), '*Frankenstein; or, the Modern Prometheus*, by Mary Wollstonecraft Shelley'.

A wealth of critical and other material on Frankenstein, including links to over 200 electronically available academic articles, put together by a team at the University of Pennsylvania.

Access the University of Pennsylvania archive via Cambridge Elevate

James, Edward and Mendlesohn, Farah (2012) *The Cambridge Companion to Fantasy Literature*, Cambridge: Cambridge University Press.

A collection of over twenty essays by academic experts covering the origins and development of fantasy literature since Enlightenment, and illustrating different critical approaches to it and its sub-genres.

Howells, Coral Ann (ed.) (2006) *The Cambridge Companion to Margaret Atwood*, Cambridge: Cambridge University Press.

A comprehensive collection of essays on Atwood's dominant themes and literary forms.

Hughes, William (2009) *Bram Stoker, Dracula. Readers' Guides to Essential Criticism*, London: Continuum.

A detailed analytical survey of critical reception of and approaches to Dracula *over the last century.*

McCrum, Robert (2007) 'Adventures in Disturbia', *The Guardian*, 14 October.

Find and read Robert McCrum's article for *The Guardian* via Cambridge Elevate

An in-depth account of The Lovely Bones, *its context and its appeal, through an interview with Alice Sebold.*

Semino, Elena (1997) *Language and World Creation in Poems and Other Texts*, London: Longman.

A clear introduction to deixis and other ways in which language is used in literature and other texts to construct imagined worlds.

Short, Mick (1996) 'Fictional prose and point of view', in *Exploring the Language of Poems, Plays and Prose*, London: Longman, pp. 255–287.

An engaging introduction to aspects of point of view. The chapter includes exercises to support understanding and closes with a useful check sheet to guide analysis. Other chapters in the book are also relevant to the construction of storyworlds.

22.3.2 Further useful resources – general

- 'Propp's morphology of the folk tale'.

Find and read more about 'Propp's morphology of the folk tale' via Cambridge Elevate

- 'Bildungsroman'

Find and read more about 'Bildungsroman' via Cambridge Elevate

- Abrams, M. H. (2014) *A Glossary of Literary Terms*, 11th edn., Stamford, CT: Cengage Learning.
- Gavins, Joanna (2007) *Text World Theory: An Introduction*, Edinburgh: Edinburgh University Press.
- Goldman, Alvin I. (2012) 'Theory of mind', in *The Oxford Handbook of Philosophy and Cognitive Science*, eds. Eric Margolis, Richard Samuels, and Stephen Stich, USA: Oxford University Press.

Find and read Alvin Goldman's paper 'Theory of mind' via Cambridge Elevate

- Hartley, George (no date) 'Point of view and narrative voice'.

Find and read George Hartley's paper 'Point of view and narrative voice' via Cambridge Elevate

- Leech, Geoffrey and Short, Mick (2007) *Style in Fiction: A Linguistic Introduction to English Fictional Prose*, 2nd edn, London: Longman.
- Lye, John (2008) 'Narrative point of view: some considerations'

Find and read more about 'Point of View and Narrative Voice' via Cambridge Elevate

- Nordquist, Richard (2014) 'Point of view (grammar and composition)'.

Find and read Nordquist's 'Point of view (grammar and composition)' via Cambridge Elevate

- Simpson, Paul (1993) *Language, Ideology and Point of View*, London: Routledge.
- Simpson, Paul (2014) *Stylistics: A Resource Book for Students*, 2nd edition, London: Routledge.

- Werth, Paul (1999) *Text Worlds: Representing Conceptual Space in Discourse*, London: Longman.

22.3.3 Further useful resources – genre

- Botting, Fred (2014) *Gothic*, 2nd edition, London: Routledge.
- James, Edward (2003) 'Utopias and anti-utopias' in James, Edward and Mendlesohn, Farah, eds, *The Cambridge Companion to Science Fiction,* Cambridge: Cambridge University Press, pp. 219–222.
- Smith, Andrew (2007) *Gothic Literature*, Edinburgh: Edinburgh University Press.

22.3.4 Further useful resources – set texts

- Botting, Fred (ed.) (1995) *Frankenstein. Contemporary Critical Essays*, London: Macmillan.
- Dopp, Jamie (1994) 'Subject-Position as Victim-Position in *The Handmaid's Tale*', *Studies in Canadian Literature*.

Find and read Jamie Dopp's paper 'Subject-Position as Victim-Position in *The Handmaid's Tale*' via Cambridge Elevate

- Franklin, Ruth (7 March 2012) 'Was *Frankenstein* really about childbirth?'.

Find and read Ruth Franklin's paper 'Was Frankenstein really about childbirth?' via Cambridge Elevate

- Hughes, William (2009) *Bram Stoker, Dracula. Readers' Guides to Essential Criticism*, London: Continuum.
- McComs, Judith (ed.) (1988) *Critical Essays on Margaret Atwood*, Boston: G. K. Hall.
- Miller, Elizabeth (1998) *Dracula: The Shade and the Shadow – A Critical Anthology*, Westcliff-on-Sea, Essex: Desert Island Books Limited.
- Miner, Madonne (1991) '"Trust me": Reading the romance plot in Margaret Atwood's *The Handmaid's Tale*', *Twentieth Century Literature*, 37(2): 148–168.

Find and read Madonne Miner's paper, '"Trust me": Reading the romance plot in Margaret Atwood's *The Handmaid's Tale*' via Cambridge Elevate

- Morton, Tim (2002) *A Routledge Literary Sourcebook on Mary Shelley's Frankenstein*, London: Routledge.
- Punter, David (2004) *The Gothic*, Oxford: Blackwell.
- Roberts, Steve (2006) *Dracula. York Notes Advanced*, London: Longman.
- Schoene-Harwood, Berthold (ed.) (2000) *Mary Shelley, Frankenstein: A Reader's Guide to Contemporary Criticism*, London: Palgrave.
- Whitney, Sarah (2010) 'Uneasy lie the bones: Alice Sebold's postfeminist gothic', *Tulsa Studies in Women's Literature*, 29(2): 351–373.

22.4 Current research on *Imagined worlds*

22.4.1 Avenues of research in academia

- **Text world theory:** This was developed by Paul Werth (1999) and Joanna Gavins (2007). It is a model of the dynamic process of story world construction that takes place as we build and move through time, space and various perspectives in fictional worlds.
- **Theory of mind:** This is the term given to the human ability to attribute states of mind to others – to deduce, suppose or project particular feelings and beliefs in or on to others based on the speech and behaviour of those others. Theory of mind is used in literary and narratological theory to explore the ways in which the minds of characters are presented and understood.

22.4.2 Professor Michaela Mahlberg on corpus linguistics

Michaela Mahlberg, Professor of English Language and Linguistics at the University of Nottingham, writes of her research into characterisation using corpus linguistic methods.

When reading a novel, readers construct impressions of characters in their minds. In this process, knowledge about people in the real world interacts with cues in the text. Textual cues can take a variety of forms. The narrator can give direct descriptions of characters or provide character information in more indirect ways, e.g. through the speech of characters. To study textual patterns that contribute to representations of character, we can employ corpus linguistic methods. 'Corpora' are large collections of electronic copies of texts. Corpus linguistic methods use specific software or computational tools to analyse these text collections. Corpus linguistic methods are increasingly used for the study of literary text. They can help, for instance, to count the occurrences of specific words or find patterns in texts (for a general introduction see Mahlberg 2013a).

The description of body language plays an important role for the creation of fictional characters (see Korte 1997). With a focus on Charles Dickens, some of my research shows how corpus linguistic methods can help to identify patterns of body language presentation. Examples include repeated sequences of words such as *his head against the wall* or *laying his hand upon his shoulder.* Such word 'clusters' can be associated with particular characters and highlight specific habits – Mr Jellyby in *Bleak House* is repeatedly shown to sit with his head against the wall, which reflects the state of exhaustion and resignation he is constantly in. Body language can also function to contextualise other textual information, as in Example (1). The cluster *laying his hand upon his shoulder* supports the character's speech: Nicholas tries to comfort and encourage his friend Smike both verbally and through his body language (see Mahlberg 2013b).

---

(1) 'Oh dear, oh dear!' he cried, covering his face with his cracked and horny hands. 'My heart will break. It will, it will.'

'Hush!' said Nicholas, *laying his hand upon his shoulder*. 'Be a man; you are nearly one by years, God help you.'

Charles Dickens, *Nicholas Nickleby*, Chapter 8

In addition to retrieving clusters, corpus linguistic methods also make it possible to search places in literary texts that are particularly likely to provide body language information. The online tool CLiC 1.0 has been designed to support the analysis of literary texts and is currently available with a corpus of texts by Charles Dickens and a selection of other nineteenth-century authors. CLiC has an option to search 'suspensions', i.e. stretches of narration that interrupt the speech of characters (cf. Lambert 1981), as in Example (2) where the suspension is italicised.

---

(2) 'I certainly, sir,' *returned Mrs. Sparsit, with a dignity serenely mournful*, 'was familiar with the Italian Opera at a very early age.'

Charles Dickens, *Hard Times*, Chapter 7

A concordance search for a character name in suspensions will find places in the text that are likely to contain character information. The screen shot in Figure 22A shows the results for a search for *Sparsit*. A 'concordance' is a display format that lists the occurrences of the search word (here *Sparsit*) aligned in the centre with a specific amount of context on the left and on the right. The settings for the search have been selected so that only places are found where *Sparsit* appears in suspensions. The concordance includes examples such as *rejoined Mrs. Sparsit, with decent resignation* (line 3) or *returned Mrs. Sparsit, almost with severity* (line 17) that describe the manner in which Mrs Sparsit speaks. Throughout the novel, the picture that such descriptions create contributes to forming an impression of the character. The concordance helps the analyst to identify relevant places in the text and display them in a format that makes it easy to see patterns.

Corpus linguistic methods can support the analysis of literary texts, but the results of corpus searches are only useful if they are appropriately interpreted by the analyst. It is important to select the right method for the question that you want to investigate and not every method will work equally for every text. See Mahlberg & McIntyre (2011), an open access article that you can download from the web, for an example of a different corpus linguistic approach tailored to the text under investigation.

References

Culpeper, Jonathan (2001) *Language and Characterisation. People in Plays and Other Texts*, Harlow: Pearson Education.

Korte, Barbara (1997) *Body Language in Literature*, Toronto: University of Toronto Press.

Lambert, Mark (1981) *Dickens and the Suspended Quotation*, New Haven, CT and London: Yale University Press.

Mahlberg, Michaela (2013a) 'Corpus stylistics', in Michael Burke (ed.), *The Routledge Handbook of Stylistics*, London: Routledge, 378–392.

Mahlberg, Michaela (2013b) *Corpus Stylistics and Dickens's Fiction*, New York & London: Routledge.

Mahlberg, Michaela, and Smith, Catherine (2012) *Dickens, The Suspended Quotation and the Corpus Language and Literature*, 21(1), 51–65

Mahlberg, Michaela, and McIntyre, Dan (2011) 'A case for corpus stylistics: Ian Fleming's *Casino Royale*', *English Text Construction*, 4(2), 204–227

Stockwell, Peter (2009) *Texture. A Cognitive Aesthetics of Reading*, Edinburgh: Edinburgh University Press.

ACTIVITY 6

Corpus linguistics and literature

Now that you have read Professor Mahlberg's words, complete tasks a–c.

a Create a definition of corpus linguistics in one sentence that you could use to explain it to a friend.

b Corpus linguistics projects tend to work with large corpora of many texts, and millions of words, which are analysed using sophisticated computer programmes. How could you adapt the ideas of corpus linguistics to be able to undertake smaller projects yourself, using the technology you have available to you?

c Professor Mahlberg describes a project looking at body language. Can you think of any other aspects of characterisation that you could study using corpus linguistic methods? What kinds of extracts of text would you need to be able to identify and focus on in order to study these aspects?

22.4.3 Professor Peter Stockwell in video interview

Watch Peter Stockwell, Professor of Literary Linguistics at the University of Nottingham, talk about story worlds in science fiction on Cambridge Elevate

Figure 22A
Screenshot of results for search of Sparsit in suspensions in *Hard Times* retrieved with CLiC 1.0

CLiC
A corpus tool to support the analysis of literary texts

The University of Nottingham
UNITED KINGDOM · CHINA · MALAYSIA

Concordance Keywords Clusters About

Concordance Results

KWIC Plot

Showing 1 to 23 of 23 entries CSV Print Toggle metadata Filter concordance:

	Left	Node	Right	Book
1	.a link to light you.' 'I certainly, sir,' returned Mrs	Sparsit,	with a dignity serenely mournful, 'was familiar with the Italian	Hard Times
2	.the lap of luxury.' 'I do not, sir,' returned Mrs	Sparsit	with a shake of her head, 'deny it.' Mr. Bounderby	Hard Times
3	.lords and ladies and honourables.' 'I trust, sir,' rejoined Mrs	Sparsit,	with decent resignation, 'it is not necessary that you should	Hard Times
4	.way!' 'I wish with all my heart, sir,' said Mrs	Sparsit,	in a highly superior manner; somehow she seemed, in a	Hard Times
5	.acknowledgments for past favours. And I hope, sir,' said Mrs	Sparsit,	concluding in an impressively compassionate manner, 'I fondly hope that	Hard Times
6	.consider, I will not consider, I cannot consider,' said Mrs	Sparsit,	with a most extensive stock on hand of honour and	Hard Times
7	.Sparsit. 'All is shut up, ma'am.' 'And what,' said Mrs	Sparsit,	pouring out her tea, 'is the news of the day?	Hard Times
8	.I do not pretend to understand these things,' said Mrs'	Sparsit,	with dignity, 'my lot having been signally cast in a	Hard Times
9	.eternity! I think he married Gradgrind's daughter?' 'Yes,' said Mrs	Sparsit,	suddenly compressing her mouth, 'he had that honour.' 'The lady	Hard Times
10	.I don't like his ways at all.' 'Bitzer,' said Mrs	Sparsit,	in a very impressive manner, 'do you recollect my having	Hard Times
11	.one another.' 'It is much to be regretted,' said Mrs	Sparsit,	making her nose more Roman and her eyebrows more Coriolanian	Hard Times
12	.personal dignity and claims to reverence. 'The clerks,' said Mrs	Sparsit,	carefully brushing an imperceptible crumb of bread and butter from	Hard Times
13	... impertinent curiosity,' pursued the stranger, fluttering over Mrs'	Sparsit's	eyebrows, with a propitiatory air, 'but you know the family,	Hard Times
14	.may be sometimes heard in Dutch clocks. Not,' said Mrs	Sparsit,	with a lofty sense of giving strict evidence, 'that I	Hard Times
15	...derby; 'when he shocked your feelings?' 'Yes, sir,' returned Mrs	Sparsit,	with a meek shake of her head, 'he certainly did	Hard Times
16	.to splendour, 'but it is my duty to remember,' Mrs	Sparsit	was fond of observing with a lofty grace: particularly when	Hard Times
17	.the trouble, I believe.' 'Don't say that, sir,' returned Mrs	Sparsit,	almost with severity, 'because that is very unkind to Mrs.	Hard Times
18	.expressed.' 'A singular world, I would say, sir,' pursued Mrs	Sparsit;	after acknowledging the compliment with a drooping of her dark	Hard Times
19	.small fry of business all the morning. 'Bitzer,' said Mrs	Sparsit	that afternoon, when her patron was gone on his journey,	Hard Times
20	.Your foot on the last step, my lady,' said Mrs'	Sparsit,	apostrophizing the descending figure, with the aid of her threatening	Hard Times
21	.speaking was not hurried. 'My dear child,' said Harthouse; Mrs	Sparsit	saw with delight that his arm embraced her; 'will you	Hard Times
22	.coachman. 'It's a Providence! Come out, ma'am!' then said Mrs	Sparsit,	to some one inside, 'come out, or we'll have you	Hard Times
23	.it appears to my poor judgment 'Oh! Pray, sir,' Mrs	Sparsit	interposed, with sprightly cheerfulness, 'don't disparage your judgment. ...	Hard Times

Source: The CLiC project, The University of Nottingham

ENRICHING

23 Poetic voices

23.1 Extension activities

23.1.1 Taking phonoaesthetics further

You have explored some of the relationships between sound and meaning in poetry. You've looked at the ways in which certain patterns of consonant and vowels clusters can seem more or less pleasant – euphonious or cacophonous – and have studied how sounds can be manipulated to convey the semantic content of words (e.g. the squelch of mud in the act of digging, in Heaney's poetry). This last matter – using sound to portray content – is a powerful tool, but it is also an area in which students sometimes make ill-thought through interpretative leaps and generalising claims. Here we're going to look at this aspect of phonoaesthetics in more detail.

ACTIVITY 1

Phonoaesthetic series

a List about ten words that you associate with light (e.g. bright, blinding, etc.)

b Go through your list, and see if there are any common clusters or consonants and/or vowels which appear in several words. For example, is there re-occurrence of the sounds 'bl', 'br' and the vowel sound 'i' (as in the sound made pronouncing 'eye')?

c Now write two more lists of five words each: one of words associated with light which don't contain any of the re-occurring sounds you noticed in 1b, and one of words which have nothing to do with light but do contain the re-occurring sounds you noticed in 1b.

d Repeat Activities 1a, 1b and 1c with the concept of mud and then with the concept of water (and/or the sea, waves, etc.).

As Activity 1 has been designed to illustrate, while there are indeed some patterns of consonant and vowel clusters within words of particular semantic fields, there are also exceptions. Often it is also the context of words and sounds – the semantics of preceding and subsequent words and phrases – which foregrounds particular associations. It's always worth paying close attention to the foregrounding effects of this context, and avoiding sweeping generalisations, when drawing links between particular sounds and meanings.

23.1.2 Deixis in detail

Person, spatial and temporal deixis played a significant role in your study of poetry in Unit 17. You explored the use of deixis in a range of poetry to construct a sense of space and time – location and atmosphere – as well as the roles and relationships between characters and the poetic persona.

Some scholars argue that deixis is largely responsible for the sense of immersion readers can feel when engaging with literary works, and the sense of empathy and connection that can be created with narrators and characters. Deixis tends not to work 'alone' in creating these effects, though. A careful analysis of deixis and other language in texts can extrapolate or disentangle quite which elements of language are working deictically, and which related spatial and temporal terms, for example, are not functioning deictically (e.g., 'in 1969' and 'at the door of the church', which provide temporal and spatial details, respectively, but are not deictic), and are also contributing to a sense of immersion and/or empathy.

ACTIVITY 2

Time and space

a Choose one poem from those you are studying for the *Poetic voices* unit and re-read it, thinking about the points at which you get a strong sense of the time and space of the text, and the relationships between participants (one of which is the 'speaking' poetic persona, and another of which is yourself, as the reader or addressee).

Below are some suggested poems. Some of these have been discussed in relation to aspects of deixis and perspective, so you have already done some of the groundwork: if you're not feeling very confident, you could work with one of these to start with, and then repeat this activity with another.

- John Donne: 'The Good-Morrow'; 'Air and Angels'; 'The Flea'; 'The Sun Rising'
- Robert Browning: 'My Last Duchess'; 'Christina (1)'; 'Home Thoughts, From Abroad'; 'Porphyria's Lover'
- Carol Ann Duffy: 'Stafford Afternoons'; 'Before You Were Mine'; 'First Love'; 'Never Go Back'
- Seamus Heaney: 'Death of a Naturalist'; 'Follower'; 'Blackberry-Picking'; 'Mid-Term Break'

b Go back over the poem, paying close attention to your sense of the location, temporality and relationships in/of the text.

- Are there particular junctures in the text at which you get strong impressions of vividness and immersion, or perhaps of distance and alienation?
- Do these impressions correlate with any concentration of deictic language at these junctures?
- Can you identify any particular features of person, spatial and temporal deixis at work at these junctures?

c What other language – language not functioning deictically, e.g. non-deictic spatial and temporal adverbial and prepositional phrases, verbs, metaphors, semantic fields – is also working towards these effects, and how?

23.2 Suggestions for small independent research investigations

23.2.1 Poetic syntax

One of the distinctive markers of poetry as a form is that it has special license to deviate from regular conventions of syntax and grammar to foreground particular words and phrases, and to fit lines to rhyme schemes and metrical patterns.

ACTIVITY 3

Words in unconventional orders

a Select five poems from those you are studying for this unit and identify any points at which the poet has arranged words in an unconventional order – for example, placing a modifying adjective *after* a noun (rather than in its more conventional pre-modifying position), or using a grammatically 'incorrect' word at a particular point (as in the title of Dylan Thomas's poem 'Do not go gentle into that good night', where the adjective 'gentle' would more properly be the adverb 'gently').

b Compare and contrast the interpretative effects of the manipulation of syntax and grammar in two of your five selected poems.

23.2.2 Poetic style in context

ACTIVITY 4

Poetic comparisons

Read and study the work of some poets who were writing and publishing poetry at the same time as the poet you are focusing on. Use Table 17B in Unit 17 to guide you, but try to find one or two more, ideally of a similar cultural background to your poet.

Compare the dominant thematic concerns and poetic techniques of your poet and the contemporaneous poets you have found.

- What similarities can you see between the work of your poet and other contemporaneous poets?
- What is distinctive about the work of the poet you are focusing on?
- What links your poet's work across different poems, and what makes his/her work identifiable as his/her own?

23.3 Wider reading list

23.3.1 Selected reading on key areas in *Poetic voices*

Allen, Michael, ed. (1997) *Seamus Heaney*, London: Palgrave Macmillan.

This is a wide-ranging collection of critical essays on, and reviews of, the work of Seamus Heaney, charting both Heaney's development as a poet and changing receptions of his poetry over time.

Hawlin, Stefan (2001) *Robert Browning*, London: Routledge.

Hawlin's guidebook surveys the main themes and notable stylistic techniques of Browning through discussion of his poetry. He presents the major critical debates within reception and interpretation of the poems, and provides biographical, social and cultural contextual information to situate Browning's work within the Victorian literary era.

Mallett, Phillip, (1999) *Selected Poems of John Donne: York Notes Advanced*, London: Longman.

Mallett's text offers an accessible overview of each of the poems published within, including summaries and critical notes, illustration of key themes, textual analysis and contextual information.

Short, Mick (1996) *Exploring the Language of Poems, Plays and Prose*, London: Routledge.

This is a really valuable textbook providing a wealth of stylistic tools for the analysis of poetry and other literary forms. The earlier chapters, particularly, offer illustrative analysis of the relationships between poetic devices and meaning, addressing foregrounding and deviation, sound patterning, rhythm, metre, accent and dialect, and more, in detail and with clear and instructive check sheets to support learning.

Woods, Michael J. (2005) *Selected Poems of Carol Ann Duffy: York Notes Advanced*, London: Longman.

An accessible overview of a range of Duffy's popular poetry, including summaries and critical notes, illustration of key themes, textual analysis and contextual information.

23.3.2 Further useful resources - general

Adams, Stephen (1997) *Poetic Designs: an Introduction to Meters, Verse Forms and Figures of Speech*, Peterborough, ON: Broadview.

Attridge, Derek (1995) *Poetic Rhythm: An Introduction*, Cambridge: Cambridge University Press.

Brownjohn, Sandy (2002) *The Poet's Craft: A Handbook of Rhyme, Metre and Verse*, London: Hodder & Stoughton.

Furniss, Tom, and Bath, Michael (1996) *Reading Poetry: An Introduction*, London: Prentice Hall.

Gregory, Helen (2012) 'Poetry Performances on the Page and Stage: Insights from Slam', in S. Gingell and W. Roy (eds.) *Listening Up, Writing Down, and Looking Beyond: Interfaces of the Oral, Written, and Visual*, 77–96, Waterloo, ON: Wilfrid Laurier University Press.

Hobsbaum, Philip (2006) *Metre, Rhythm and Verse Form*, London; New York: Routledge.

Jeffries, Lesley (2008) 'The role of style in reader-involvement: Deictic shifting in contemporary poems', *Journal of Literary Semantics*, 37 (1): 69–85.

Jeffries, Lesley (2000) 'Point of view and the reader in the poetry of Carol Ann Duffy', in Lesley Jeffries and Peter Sansom (eds.) *Contemporary Poems: Some Critical Approaches*, 54–68, Huddersfield: Smith Doorstop Books.

Lennard, John (2005) *The Poetry Handbook*, 2nd edn, Oxford: Oxford University Press.

Strand, Mark and Bolan, Eaven (eds.) (2000) *The Making of a Poem: A Norton Anthology of Poetic Forms*, London; New York: Norton.

Roberts, Philip (1991) *How Poetry Works*, Harmondsworth: Penguin.

Semino, Elena (1997) *Language and World Creation in Poems and Other Texts*, London: Longman.

Steele, Timothy (1999) *All the Fun's in How You Say a Thing: An Explanation of Metre and Versification*, Athens: Ohio University Press.

Verdonk, Peter (2013) *The Stylistics of Poetry: Context, Cognition, Discourse, History*, London: Bloomsbury.

Wainwright, Jeffrey (2004) *Poetry: The Basics*, London: Routledge.

23.3.3 Further useful resources - set texts

BBC Radio 4, (2008) 'The Metaphysical Poets', *In Our Time*.

British Council (2011) 'Carol Ann Duffy', *Literature*.

Listen to 'The Metaphysical Poets' on *In Our Time* via Cambridge Elevate

Read more about Carol Ann Duffy via Cambridge Elevate

Corcoran, Neil (1998) *The Poetry of Seamus Heaney: A Critical Guide*, London: Faber and Faber.

Dickson, Donald R., ed. (2007) *John Donne's Poetry*, New York: W. W. Norton & Company.

Guibbory, Achsah, ed. (2006) *The Cambridge Companion to John Donne*, Cambridge: Cambridge University Press.

Kennedy-Andrews, Elmer, ed. (1999) *The Poetry of Seamus Heaney*, Columbia, OH: Columbia University Press.

Loucks, James F., and Stauffer, Andrew M., eds. (2007) *Robert Browning's Poetry*, New York: W. W. Norton & Company.

Lucas, John (2001) *Student Guide to Robert Browning*, London: Greenwich Exchange Ltd.

Nutt, Joe (1999) *John Donne: The Poems*, London: Palgrave Macmillan.

Poetry Foundation (2014) 'Seamus Heaney'

Poets.org (n.d.) 'John Donne',

Find and read the Poetry Foundation's entry on Seamus Heaney via Cambridge Elevate

Read Poets.org's entry on John Donne via Cambridge Elevate

Poets.org (2004) 'A Brief Guide to Metaphysical Poets'

Find and read Poets.org's brief guide to the metaphysical poets via Cambridge Elevate

Swan, Robert, and Cox, Marian (2005) *AS/A Level Student Text Guide: The Poetry of Carol Ann Duffy*, London: Philip Allan.

The Guardian (2014) 'Carol Ann Duffy'

The Poetry Archive (n.d.) 'Carol Ann Duffy'

The Victorian Web (n.d.) 'Robert Browning'

Find and read *The Guardian's* profile on Carol Ann Duffy via Cambridge Elevate

Read The Poetry Archive's entry on Carol Ann Duffy via Cambridge Elevate

Find and read The Victorian Web's entry on Robert Browning via Cambridge Elevate

23.4 Current research on poetry and poetic voices

23.4.1 Avenues of research in academia

Performance poetry: Scholars such as Helen Gregory (2012) are increasingly engaging with poetry on the stage, on the street, on YouTube videos and on other performance platforms, exploring the relationship between the following elements:

- written and performed poetic craft
- the differences between recital and performance
- live and recorded, digital contexts
- sociocultural issues around performed identities and discourses
- anti-canonical and anti-prestige forms of art
- the relationship between performance poetry and other kinds of performance (including shared techniques such as gesture and movement).

Deixis in poetry: Deixis is an interesting area in the study of poetry, partially due to the common readerly identification of a poetic persona designated with the first-person pronoun – an 'I' speaker – with the poet. Elena Semino (1997) and Lesley Jeffries (2008, 2000) are two stylisticians who explore deixis, and pronouns in particular, in poetry, and the influence of deixis on a reader's interpretation and felt immersion/projection into participant roles in the literary discourse.

23.4.2 Poet Tony Walsh in video interview

Watch Tony Walsh, performant poet and writer, talk about poetic voices, performance and the role of places and memories in his poetry via Cambridge Elevate

ENRICHING

24 Writing about society

24.1 Extension activities

24.1.1 Intertextual reframing

Framing devices may be in the form of titles and author's introductions, and so on. There are yet further paratextual framing devices available to authors for the purposes of shaping interpretation. Fitzgerald opens *The Great Gatsby* with an epigraph. Summerscale uses epigraphs at the beginning of her text and at the beginning of each of the three 'parts' within it, and Krakauer uses them at the beginning of every chapter. Resituating a quotation from one text to within another brings the context and meaning of the quotation into the new work. Here, the quotation intertextually interacts with its new context. The meanings of the quotation, embedded in the new text in this way, can cast a new light on the new text, foregrounding particular themes. The intertextual interaction can also reflect back on the epigraph and the text it comes from: intertextual embedding of epigraphs can enable new interpretations of the quotation and its source context, in the light of its relationship to the new work.

Krakauer uses a range of epigraphs from different discourse types and genres, his sources including, for example, the novels *Doctor Zhivago* (1957) by Boris Pasternak, *The Call of the Wild* (1903) by Jack London and *The Adventures of Huckleberry Finn* (1884) by Mark Twain, but also the *New York Times* biographies of some of Alaska's adventurers, environmentalist lectures and treatises, and a wealth of non-fictional travel writing. Though Summerscale quotes a lot of documentary evidence, newspaper reports and other material presented as non-fictional in her book, her four epigraphs come from four novels: *The Moonstone* (1868) and *The Woman in White* (1860) by Wilkie Collins, *Bleak House* (1853) by Charles Dickens, and *The Turn of the Screw* (1898) by Henry James.

ACTIVITY 1

Reframing with epigraphs

a What impact do you think the kinds of discourse types and genres of epigraphs might have on your interpretation of a novel? Consider, in particular, your perceptions of the novel's relative fictionality and literariness.

b Find a novel you are familiar with which uses epigraphs (perhaps the novel you are studying for this unit), and analyse the relationship between one epigraph and the chapter, part or novel it frames (this exercise is easiest if you find a novel which uses epigraphs with each chapter, and if you study just one chapter and its epigraphs). Some questions you could start with are:
   - What are the themes and context of the text from which the epigraph came?
   - How does the epigraph shape your expectations of what might happen in the novel, part or chapter?
   - What aspects of the novel, part or chapter, as you read on, are foregrounded by the epigraph?

- What does this resituating of the epigraph do to its meaning?

c Using the novel you are studying for this unit, make a subtle, experimental re-creative intervention into its framing by playing with epigraphs. If the novel has no epigraphs in its original form, add some, and if the novel already has epigraphs, change them. Make this a two-stage process:
  - Firstly, find and add or swap in alternative epigraphs that are from the same genre and discourse type, and ideally also the same period, as the novel.
  - Then, swap in epigraphs from different genres and discourse types.
  - What impact do these changes have on the subsequent sections of the novel? For example, what is foregrounded and what is backgrounded? Is the sense of literariness changed? Are other effects created?

24.1.2 Deeper research into characters

Choose a character from the novel you are studying, and then complete *one* of the tasks in Activity 2.

ACTIVITY 2

Writing about characters

a Read some extended obituaries on significant figures in a newspaper (the kind of obituaries that are a page long, written by a professional obituary writer, not just the more standard few lines). Study what kind of structures and features are common to obituaries, and then try to write one for your character.

b *Profile* is a regular and long-running investigative documentary programme on BBC Radio 4. You can find it by going to the BBC iPlayer Radio homepage and doing a basic search for the name of the programme. Each episode is 13 minutes long, and focuses on providing a profile of someone significant to society. Most of the programmes do this through a combination of biographical description (by the presenter) and interviews with people who know the person, colleagues, friends, experts and others.

Imagine you are the producer of this programme, and you are constructing an episode on your chosen character. Draft a plan for the edition and consider the following questions.
- Who would you interview?
- What questions would you ask each interviewee?
- What would you expect them to say in response?
- What would you include in the biographical description?
- If you are feeling more ambitious, go on to then draft a script for the programme and transcripts of the interviews.

24.1.3 Re-plotting

ACTIVITY 3

Re-creative plotting

The plot of the novel you're studying offers opportunities for radical re-creative interventions. Without needing to write out a different version of the whole novel, you can easily develop alternative plot paths for the characters and events, and embellish these with detail as far as your interest takes you.

a Start by sketching out the plot of your novel along a timeline, in a very simple way, without much detail: just mark central and secondary events on the line. You might need to create several branches off a main line at points, where different events happen simultaneously.

b Intervene in the plot by altering the outcome of one of the events: start with an event which is minor (secondary), and track through the repercussions on future events and related character development. Next, alter a major event which is central to the plot, and repeat the process of going through the knock-on effects. What impact does each of these changes have on the themes and characters of the novel?

24.2 Suggestions for small independent research investigations

24.2.1 Recontextualising

Resetting a novel in a new context (geographic, historical, etc.) offers a radical new view of its working - the ways it is meaningful - and its relationships to its original contexts.

ACTIVITY 4

Resetting

a Lift the plot and characters out of the novel, and place them in a different continent (though keep to the same period in history). How far and in what ways would you have to change the nature of the events, the characters, and the story's themes and motifs for the story to continue to make sense in its new context?

b Do the same again, this time moving the story and characters to a different period in time as well as a different place. Again, how would you have to adapt the events, characters, themes and motifs for the story to continue to make sense? What kinds of changes do you need to make? How different from the original would the new story need to be?

24.2.2 Feminist re-creative writing

Feminism is a diverse movement which (broadly speaking) fights for women's freedom of choice in aspects of their lives, and for gender equality. Feminism informs some literary scholarship too: feminist literary theory explores oppression (including elision and misrepresentation) of women in literature.

ACTIVITY 5

Developing female characters and roles

a Explore how the female characters are represented in the novel you are studying. You can use various stylistic tools to do this including, for example, Genette's (1980, 1988) ideas about types of duration in representation of narrative events (summary, scene, descriptive pause and ellipsis), aspects of theories of politeness, turn-taking, verb processes and other concepts you've studied in the previous units. You could begin by asking some of the following questions, per character.
- How is she addressed by other characters?
- What are the dominant aspects of her identity and personality?
- How much does she speak, to whom, and what kinds of things does she say?
- How does she interact verbally with other characters?
- What actions does she take in the novel?
- What proportion of the novel is devoted to her story and character?
- What level of detail is used in illustrating her reactions to other characters and to events?
- Does she have more of an active or a passive role in the story?

b Reflect on how the representation of women in your novel might relate to the novel's themes, its genre and the period in which it was written.

24.2.3 Investigating character openness and empathy

At various points in this book you have explored the expression of point of view through, for example, different kinds of narration and modality. Readers vary in the empathy they feel for particular characters. The reasons for this are complex, and might include factors such as how open each character is - that is, to what degree a character's thoughts and feelings are revealed through the expression of point of view. The relationship between a reader's response to characters and the language of point of view is a rich area of enquiry.

ACTIVITY 6

Characterisation and reader empathy

a Do you think there is a direct correlation between how much insight you are given into the thoughts and feelings of a character, and the level of empathy you are likely to develop for that character?

b Identify some of ways a reader can be given insight into a character – the building blocks of characterisation. Here is the beginning of a list, with two different ways – try to add to these:
- direct representation of the character's speech
- description of the character's body language.

c Think about one or two characters in the novel you are studying that you have the least empathy with.
- Using the list you created in response to 6b, which of these ways of providing insight into characters are used most in the novel's portrayal of the one or two characters you are thinking about?
- How far do you think these ways of providing insight into characters influence your empathetic response?
- What else do you feel might be influencing your empathetic response?

d Think about which character you have the most empathy with in the novel you are studying.
- Why do you think this is?
- If you were to re-creatively intervene in the novel to alter the characterisation in such a way as to redirect your empathy to another character (that is, so that you would in this rewritten version develop more empathy with this other character), how would you do this?
- Find a paragraph in which the character you empathise with most and another character interact, and test out re-creative writing strategies to shift empathy to the other character.
- Reflect on the changes you made.

24.3 Wider reading list

24.3.1 Selected reading on key areas in *Writing about society*

Bloom, Harold, ed. (1996) *Bloom's Notes: F. Scott Fitzgerald's* The Great Gatsby, Bel Air, CA: Chelsea House.

A collection of essays written by leading academics on different characters and themes in Fitzgerald's novel.

Culpeper, Jonathan (2001) *Language and Characterisation: People in Plays and other Texts*, London: Longman.

A thorough and systematic investigation of characterisation, drawing on insights from psychology, and focusing on the roles of language and schema in readers' character construction.

Hansen, Liane (2003) 'The kite runner'.

An interview with Hosseini, exploring aspects of his childhood in Afghanistan and discussing some of the themes of his book.

Find and watch the interview with Hosseini via Cambridge Elevate

Kaplan, Cora (2007) *Victoriana: Histories, Fictions, Criticism*, Edinburgh: Edinburgh University Press.

A wide-ranging book providing a good grounding in the context of Summerscale's writing.

Krakauer, Jon (1993) 'Death of an Innocent', *Outside* magazine.

This is the article that forms the basis of Krakauer's book.

Find and read Jon Krakauer's article via Cambridge Elevate

Pope, Rob (1995) *Textual Intervention: Critical and Creative Strategies for Literary Studies*, Abingdon: Routledge.

An entertaining guide, full of exploratory activities, demonstrating textual intervention techniques and their analytical benefits: the most important work in this field.

Scott, Jeremy (2013) *Creative Writing and Stylistics: Creative and Critical Approaches*, Houndmills, Basingstoke: Palgrave Macmillan.

A detailed and practical textbook enabling you to further develop your stylistic skills and understanding for the purposes of more controlled and effective creative writing.

24.3.2 Further useful resources – general

- Swann, Joan, Pope, Rob and Carter, Ronald, (eds) (2011) *Creativity in Language and Literature: The State of the Art,* Houndmills, Basingstoke: Palgrave Macmillan.
- The Writer's Workshop (no date), 'Points of view in fiction'.

Find and read The Writer's Workshop article via Cambridge Elevate

24.3.3 Further useful resources – set texts

- Akbar, Said Hyder and Burton, Susan (2005) *Come Back to Afghanistan – Trying to Rebuild a Country with My Father, My Brother, My One-Eyed Uncle, Bearded Tribesmen, and President Karzai*, London: Bloomsbury.
- Anon. (2008) 'Kate Summerscale analyses the appeal of True Crime', *The Times*, 3rd Oct.
- Bloom, Harold (2004) *Bloom's Major Literary Characters: Jay Gatsby*, Bel Air, CA: Chelsea House.
- Christopher McCandless Memorial Foundation (2010) 'Back to the wild: the photographs and writings of Christopher McCandless'.

View the photographs and writings of Christopher McCandless via Cambridge Elevate

- Edwards, Janette (no date) 'Expatriate literature and the problem of contested representation: the case of Khaled Hosseini's The Kite Runner'.

Find and read Janette Edwards' article via Cambridge Elevate

- Flanders, Judith (2008) 'The Suspicions of Mr Whicher: or, the Murder at Road Hill House by Kate Summerscale', *The Sunday Times*, 6th April.
- Halfacre, Erik (2011) 'Hiking the Stampede Trail', Last Frontier Adventure Club.

Visit the 'Hiking the Stampede Trail' website via Cambridge Elevate

- Kohlke, Marie-Louise (2008) 'Introduction: Speculations in and on the Neo-Victorian encounter', *Neo-Victorian Studies* 1(1): 1–18.

Visit the 'Neo-Victorian Studies' website via Cambridge Elevate

- Malik, Muhammad Asghar, Shah, Syed Kazim, and Mahmood, Rashid (2013) 'The role of linguistic devices in representing ethnicity in The Kite Runner', *International Journal of Linguistics*, 5(1): 161–175.

Find and read the *International Journal of Linguistics* article via Cambridge Elevate

- Parkinson, Kathleen (1987) *Penguin Critical Studies: F. Scott Fitzgerald – The Great Gatsby*, London: Penguin Books.
- Rankin, Ian (2008) 'The birth of the detective', *The Guardian*, 12th April.

Find and read Ian Rankin's article via Cambridge Elevate

24.4 Current research in re-creative writing

24.4.1 Strands of research

- **Fanfiction:** This is a kind of fiction which is written by a novice or amateur writer in response to a published and popular work (including literature, film, cartoons, games and musicals). Fanfiction is often written in the form of prequels or sequels, or character spin-offs. As such, it is an interesting form of re-creative intervention. Fanfiction communities can develop around particular novels or series. Some authors welcome fanfiction responses, whereas others protest at the financial gains some fanfiction writers can make from reusing or developing the original plot ideas and characters. Fanfiction is often initially posted online. In the fields of literature and digital media research fanfiction, its relationship to original texts, the motives of its writers, etc.
- **Adaptation:** This is the representation of a work in the same or another medium (e.g. among novels, dance, opera, theatre, television, film, sculpture, comics.). A work may be adapted across genres (e.g. comedy to tragedy, romance to satire), in the form of imitation, appreciation, criticism, parody, etc. Whereas fanfiction adds to the original text, adaptation alters it. Adaptation theory is a fruitful area of literary and cultural criticism.

Find and read online fanfiction via Cambridge Elevate

24.4.2 Insights from creative writer Nicola Monaghan/Niki Valentine

Novelist Nicola Monaghan (a.k.a. Niki Valentine), of De Montfort University, describes her writing practice.

I write using two different names: gritty, urban stories as Nicola Monaghan, and others with a ghostly edge as Niki Valentine. I use pseudonyms to avoid confusing readers, because the books are very different. The writing process is the same, though. I start with characters, and a setting. Some authors create CVs for their characters, or answer questionnaires on their behalf. I've tried that, but what works best for me is to write them 'into' specific situations and see what happens. So my process begins with that. I stress test my characters, and write several thousand words where they go through some of the best and worst experiences I can imagine. After this, they feel fully formed, like friends I've known for years. I can imagine how they'd react to most things, although they still often surprise me. When I hear myself and other writers talk about their characters this way, as if they are real people outside of their control, I think we sound a little mad. But I think it's getting into this highly imaginative, almost hallucinatory state that helps us create characters that come off the page for the reader.

After this initial writing, comes the planning process. For a novel, I tend to plan in quite a bit of detail. I'll work from the inside out, starting with a sentence and building this into a paragraph, then a page, and grow this into a twenty-page summary of the story. Occasionally, I'll create a spreadsheet and plan chapter by chapter. I'll also do lots of research about the era or place where I've set my story, or my character's job or background. I'll print out pictures and memes from the internet, or create boards on Pinterest to set my mood. This part is a lot of fun.

For short stories, it's slightly different. I'll still do the research but I wouldn't plan in detail, or do the preparatory writing that might not make it into the story. Mostly, three or four starting sentences will be enough to get me going, to create a voice that will pull the story along. With a short story, you're trying to capture a moment, a microcosm of something bigger. This is ethereal and so it's difficult, but I've found it's all in the drafting. I wouldn't show anybody my early drafts because they're terrible!

I might write a first draft of 3000 words but I will redraft at least three or four times. This is how I get to know my characters better in a shorter piece, and how the themes emerge from the initial mess. Finally, I refine the language until I can't find a single word I would change. My editor always finds things that I can do better, even then. I can't stress enough that the most important part of writing is rewriting. Nothing ever comes out finished, nor does it ever really reach such a state. As DaVinci said, 'Art is never finished, only abandoned.'

ACTIVITY 7

Building characters and building stories

a Write down some of the strategies Nicola Monaghan uses to develop her characters.

b Try out one or two of these new strategies for a character of your choice from the novel you are studying for this unit.

c Create a short story, just a couple of pages long, around that character – what's called a 'spin off' in some media – based on your character development work in response to 7b. Either draft a plot and then embellish it, or draft three or four starting sentences and then continue. Which process do you find easier?

d Read over your short story and redraft sections which you feel are weak, or which are inconsistent in voice. Think carefully about the changes you are making and the interpretative effects you hope to achieve with your improvements.

24.4.3 Professor Rob Pope in video interview

Watch Rob Pope, Emeritus Professor of English at Oxford Brookes University, talk about textual intervention on Cambridge Elevate

ENRICHING

25

Dramatic encounters

25.1 Extension activities

25.1.1 Discourse structures

Figure 25A: Short's model of the prototypical dramatic discourse structure

Addresser 1 (Playwright) — Message — Addressee 1 (Audience / Reader)

Addresser 2 (Character A) — Message — Addressee 2 (Character B)

Figure 25A is the same as Figure 19A. It depicts conventional discourse structures in dramatic communication contexts. We can start to explore this model in more detail by considering how conflict situations can complicate the structure of communication in drama.

ACTIVITY 1

Conflict and the discourse structure of drama

a Choose a moment in a play in which two or more characters interact in a situation of conflict and sketch out Figure 25A, filling in the names of the characters and the nature of the messages. Are there multiple messages involved? Do any further communicative relationships need to be added to the diagram (perhaps between further sets of characters)?

b Think about the communication depicted at the highest level of Figure 25A. Does the message go from playwright to audience? Does the audience/reader contribute to the construction of meaning at all? What about fellow audience members in a live performance? If you were watching a play, how might the reactions of the audience around you impact upon your impressions and interpretations? Adapt and develop the diagram at this level as you see fit, in response to your thoughts on these questions.

c Look back at the list of stagecraft elements which contribute to performance. Where do roles such as director, producer and set designer fit into the discourse structure of drama? Can you add them into your diagram?

25.1.2 Conflict, tragedy and dramatic irony

ACTIVITY 2

Relationships between conflict, tragedy and dramatic irony

Do some research into tragedy and dramatic irony. Explore:

- the history of the terms
- early examples of each
- prototypical examples of each.

25.2 Suggestions for small independent research investigations

25.2.1 Speech realism extended

You have studied several linguistic and graphological techniques used by playwrights to represent speech, particularly non-fluency features and other signs of personal and interpersonal conflict in monologue and dialogue (including turn-taking, interruptions and the like).

ACTIVITY 3

Comparative analysis of written replication of verbal non-fluency features in dialogue

a Explore patterns and variation in the ways in which an individual playwright represents speech. Choose a play (not necessarily the one you are studying for this unit), and find some other plays written by the same playwright. Compare the linguistic and graphological representation of speech across the plays.

b Now explore how a particular playwright's choices in representing speech relate to those of other contemporaneous playwrights. Start with the play you are studying for this unit, and find two or three other plays written by different playwrights in the same period. Compare the linguistic and graphological representation of speech across the different plays. How do the techniques vary?

25.2.2 Behaviour in conflict

You have studied how writers use descriptions of different forms of body language (haptics, kinesics and proxemics) as part of characterisation. You have looked at how stage directions and, in particular, proxemics, body language and actions contribute to characterisation in drama, and have seen that the degree to which a playwright communicates character behaviour through stage directions varies significantly.

ACTIVITY 4

Depicting conflict through body language

a Think about how people move and gesture in situations of interpersonal conflict. Perhaps study the mimicry of this in TV and films, and write down some details you notice for different scenarios.

b Using the play text you are studying for this unit, select a scene in which two or more characters are in conflict.

- Think about how those characters might move and gesture in reaction to their own feelings, in response to each other, and/or to help communicate their thoughts and feelings to others.
- Use some of the skills you developed in Sections 19.2, 19.3 and 19.4 to adopt the role of the play's director: intervene in the text and add to the stage directions to very fully describe characters' behaviour in ways you feel fit the nature of the characters and this interaction.

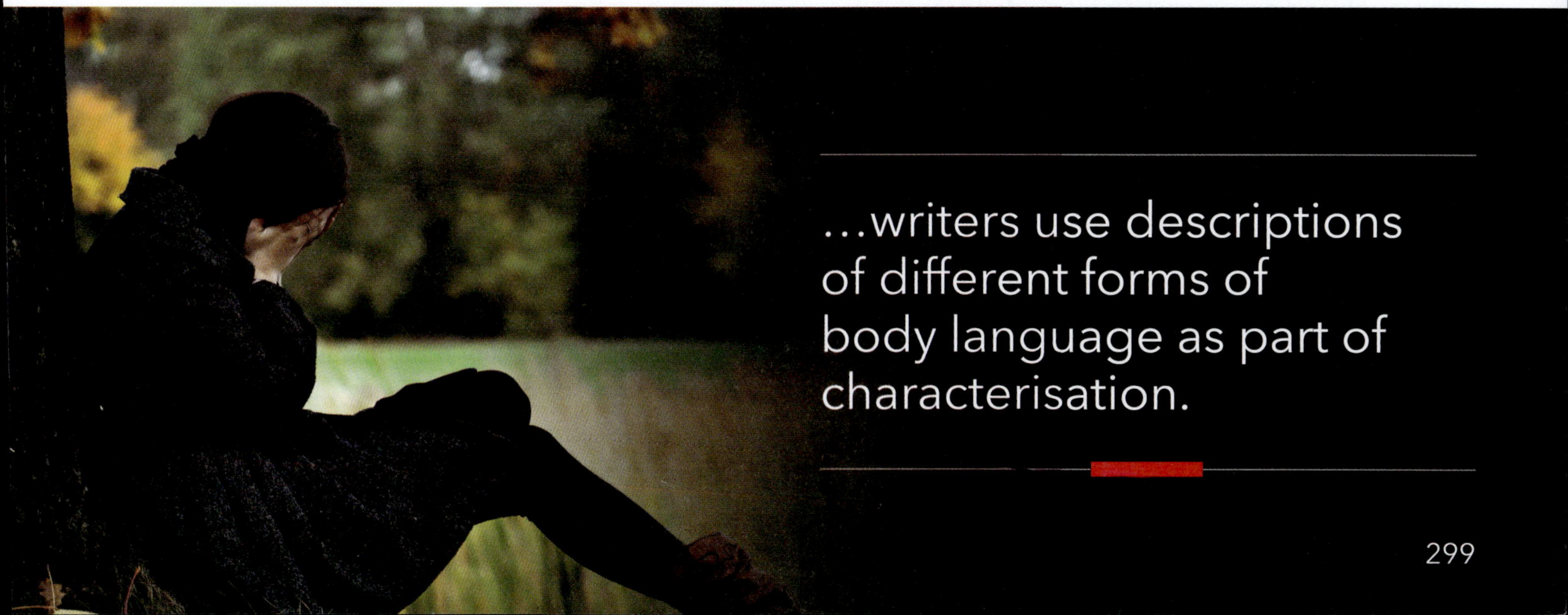

25.3 Wider reading list

25.3.1 Selected reading on key ideas in *Dramatic encounters*

Grundy, Peter (2008) *Doing Pragmatics,* 3rd edn, London: Routledge.

A clear and gently paced introduction to lots of pragmatic models and approaches to spoken communication, with many illustrative examples from everyday language.

Culpeper, Jonathon, Short, Mick, and Verdonk, Peter (1998) *Exploring the Language of Drama*, London: Routledge.

A useful and entertaining textbook demonstrating analyses of a wide range of stylistic features of dramatic texts.

Edgar, David (2009) *How Plays Work*, London: Nick Hern Books.

An exploration of the narrative patterns and other common strategies shared by many dramatic texts, with useful discussion of tragedy and dramatic irony, and a selective study of historical approaches to drama.

Wallace, Jennifer (2007) *The Cambridge Introduction to Tragedy*, Cambridge: Cambridge University Press.

A presentation of the canon of tragic drama, followed by an introduction to some of the dominant theoretical stances on tragedy, with further 'case studies' in fate, politics and gender.

Mason, Pamela (2002) *Cambridge Student Guide to Othello*, Cambridge: Cambridge University Press.

A thorough and extremely helpful guide to the play's relationship to its socio-historical context, with additional discussion of the play's language and a survey of popular critical approaches to the text.

Abbotson, Susan C. W. (2000) *Student Companion to Arthur Miller*, Westport, CT: Greenwood Press.

An accessible discussion of Miller's most significant plays, organised by theme, and cast in the light of his literary heritage and socio-cultural context.

Roudané, Matthew C., ed. (1997) *The Cambridge Companion to Tennessee Williams*, Cambridge: Cambridge University Press.

Thirteen critical essays by academic experts providing an extensive study of the life and works of Tennessee Williams.

Curtis, Nick (2013) 'Rory Kinnear on writing his first play', *London Evening Standard*, 4th Sept.

A detailed interview with Rory Kinnear exploring the themes of the play and its influences.

Find and read Nick Curtis' article via Cambridge Elevate

25.3.2 Further useful resources – general

- Black, Elizabeth (2005) *Pragmatic Stylistics*, Edinburgh: Edinburgh University Press.
- Clark, Billy and Chapman, Siobhan (2014) *Pragmatic Literary Stylistics*, London: Palgrave Macmillan.
- Poole, Adrian (2005) *Tragedy: A Very Short Introduction*, Oxford: Oxford University Press.

25.3.3 Further useful resources – set texts

- Billington, Michael (2013) '*The Herd* – Review', *The Guardian*, 19th Sept.

Find and read Michael Billington's article via Cambridge Elevate

- Bloom, Harold, ed. (1991) *Arthur Miller's* All My Sons, *Modern Critical Interpretations*, London: Chelsea House Publishers.
- Bradford, Wade (2014) '*A Streetcar Named Desire*, study guide and character outline', *About.com Education*.
- Cowen Orlin, Lena, ed. (2014) *Othello: The State of Play*, London: Bloomsbury Arden Shakespeare.
- Mabillard, Amanda (2014) '*Othello* study guide'.

Find and read the *Othello* Study Guide via Cambridge Elevate

- Maguire, Laurie (2014) *Othello: Language and Writing*, London: Bloomsbury Arden Shakespeare.
- Miller, Jordan Yale, ed. (1971) *Twentieth Century Interpretations of* A Streetcar Named Desire*: A Collection of Critical Essays*, London: Prentice Hall.
- Weller, Philip (no date) '*Othello* Navigator', *Shakespeare Navigators*.

Visit the *Othello* Navigator via Cambridge Elevate

25.4 Current research in *Dramatic encounters*

25.4.1 Strands of research

- **Politeness theory**: Academics working with politeness theory have developed it over recent decades. In particular, contemporary politeness theory challenges simplistic distinctions between intentions, politeness strategies, effects and acts. Current work looks more closely at the significance of contextual factors on face and politeness. These contextual factors include power hierarchies, cultural conventions and patterns of linguistic behaviours established between groups. Literary pragmatic scholarship is incorporating and furthering these insights to develop a more nuanced approach to politeness in literature.
- **Point of view**: Some academics have been investigating the means by which point of view is constructed in plays across its discourse structure, and the ways characters and audience members are positioned and oriented, with a focus on deixis. The differences between the variety of positions involved across the discourse structure and the range of methods of establishing point of view available to dramatic texts (in comparison to prose) have been of particular interest, as have the significance and manipulation of the perspective of the reader of the play text and the audience of live performances.

25.4.2 Professor Sara Mills on gender and power

You have explored the representation of power in language, and looked at how language can be used both to mark shifts in power and to help shift power. Sara Mills, Professor in Linguistics at Sheffield Hallam University, writes of gender and power in dialogue in relation to feminism. Feminist linguistics and feminist stylistics explore and question gender differences in men and women's use of language, and, more generally, the representation of women in language.

See Unit 24 for more information on feminism

Many early feminist writers assumed that gender and power have a close relation, that women are powerless and men powerful. They described the way that this power relation had an effect on women's and men's language, with women being hesitant, using indirect language, tag questions and avoiding swear words, and men being direct and assertive and using swear words. This stereotype of men and women's language has been challenged in recent years as it has become clear that power relations between women and men are not simply one of oppression and subordination. Baker (2008) has argued that we need to concentrate less on the way that women as a group and men as a group speak (sex difference), because this tends to be based on stereotypes of what women and men are like, and instead we need to focus on the way women and men negotiate these stereotypes in context (gender differences). Men and women do not speak in particular ways, but within contexts, they negotiate their gender identity as more or less masculine or feminine.

The effect in language of subordination is not as simple as early feminists thought. Instead, current feminists see women as not universally oppressed, because many women have jobs which have high status, and many women negotiate for themselves positions of status (local power/status) even when their place within an institution or family is not particularly high. This difference between the position you are allocated and the position you manage to negotiate for yourself is crucial, and it is largely achieved through the type of language you use. Thus, a woman who seems fairly powerless (think of someone like a working class woman who appears on a reality TV show) may in fact manage to negotiate a powerful position within that context, for example, through caring for others, acting on behalf of others, being assertive and using direct uncompromising language (Thornborrow, 2002).

However, speaking using the language which is normally associated with powerful people does not guarantee you a powerful position as a woman, because the way that people judge you is very important (Walsh, 2001). Within the business world, for example, women managers have quite a difficult path to tread. Mullany (2007) has shown that women may be judged as overly assertive and 'bossy' if they adopt the language which is seen to be appropriate to the business world. They often make the decision to temper this assertive business style with a more indirect style normally associated with femininity. Even a politician like Margaret Thatcher, well known for her brusqueness and assertiveness, occasionally used a much softer, feminine speech style. However, McElhinny (1998) has shown that women police officers have to make decisions about the degree to which they show emotion, typically considered feminine; in her research, most women police officers simply feel that they have to behave in a masculine way, being assertive and emotionless, in order to be seen as professional. This link between masculine speech (being direct, assertive, brusque) and professionalism is an important pressure on women in the workplace, for if speech which is categorised as feminine (indirect, caring, emotional) is used, then the speaker will be judged to be unprofessional, and if only masculine language is used then the woman will be judged as aggressive.

References

Baker, Paul (2008), *Sexed Texts: Language Gender and Sexuality*, London: Equinox.

McElhinny, Bonnie (1998), '"I don't smile much anymore"; gender, affect and the discourse of Pittsburgh police officers' in Coates, Jennifer., ed., *Language and Gender*, Oxford: Blackwells, pp. 309–325.

Mills, Sara and Mullany, Louise (2012), *Language, Gender and Feminism*, London: Routledge.

Thornborrow, Joanna (2002), *Power Talk,* Harlow, Essex: Pearson.

Walsh, Clare (2001), *Gender and Discourse*, Harlow, Essex: Pearson.

ACTIVITY 5

Gender and power in plays

a Choose one female character within the play you are studying, and find three points in the text where she interacts with others (select extracts of a couple of pages in length maximum). Analyse how her relative empowerment is expressed and controlled through her speech. For example:
- Can you identify any ways in which she uses stereotypically feminine or masculine speech strategies?
- Do you feel she holds, loses or gains a position of relative power through her speech style?
- Are her interaction styles different with different characters? If so, what roles do those characters have and what power relations exist between them?
- Do the reactions of other characters give any clues as to whether she is challenging or adhering to their assumptions about gender and linguistic behaviour?

b Repeat 5a focusing on a male character.

c Compare your responses to 5a and 5b. What does this suggest to you about the role of gender in the representation of these characters?

d How important do you feel the sex and gender identity of characters is to the reader/viewer's understanding of how they behave in situations of conflict?

25.4.3 Dr Billy Clark in video interview

You have explored Grice's maxims and their use in analysing the presentation of speech in literature.

Watch Dr Billy Clark, Associate Professor in English Language and Linguistics at Middlesex University, talk about neo-Gricean pragmatics on Cambridge Elevate

ENRICHING

26 Making connections

26.1 Extension activities

26.1.1 Developing research questions

The nature of your research question is very important to the ultimate quality of your report, and to how easy or difficult the report will be for you to write. A poorly considered question might leave you with little to say in response. Alternatively, you might inadvertently set yourself up to fail by asking yourself a question that is too big to answer in a project of this size. Obstacles to your process of analysis might arise a few weeks into your study, due to some hidden problems with the assumptions underlying your question. It is therefore very important to construct and consider your question very carefully before you embark on your project.

In Unit 20 you were asked to create some research questions related to a sample of literary and non-literary texts on sport. The ideas offered in response to this task suggested the following four examples of research questions.

1. How do the writers present successful and unsuccessful players?
2. Is there a difference in the ways that writers present male and female players?
3. Are there common metaphors associated with the presentation of sport and players?
4. How is negativity conveyed when presenting failure in sport?

ACTIVITY 1

Questioning research questions

a. What assumptions underlie these questions?
b. What is the scope of each of these questions in terms of the breadth of focus (the range of texts, themes, and significant linguistic levels, etc.)?
c. What might you need to take account of, in responding to each of these questions, in order to offer critically circumspect responses (i.e. not reductive, generalising or over-simplifying)?

26.1.2 Critical reading

You have looked at aspects of studying secondary sources, including evaluating your sources. In evaluating a source, its credibility is a good place to start, but there are further aspects worth considering. When reading secondary material, it's important to think about it carefully, and to analyse and question it. Think about what the author is saying, and why, and how far you agree and why. Reading critically involves not simply accepting all written material as fact, but recognising, questioning and comparing different viewpoints.

ACTIVITY 2

Understanding and analysing secondary material

For this activity, you need to select one paragraph from some written secondary material that you've identified as relevant and useful to your investigation.

a First, read through the paragraph without making any notes, just to reach a basic level of understanding of what the writer is saying in that paragraph.

b Now read through the paragraph more slowly, and try to identify the main point the author is making, and any sub-points he or she is making to support that point. Paraphrase the main message of the paragraph in one sentence.

c What kind of main point is the writer making? Is it a theoretical opinion? Or is it a factual detail (e.g. historical or biographical)?

d Critique the main point being made:
- Is it valid?
- Is it well-argued and supported with evidence?
- Does it reveal bias or problematic assumptions on the part of the writer?
- Do you agree with the point (wholly, partially or not at all)?

e How can you make productive use of this point in your report? Is it useful mostly as background reading, to help you understand the topic better (perhaps worth including in your *Review*), or is it something that you can cite to help you illustrate a point of your own (in your *Analysis*)?

26.1.3 Depth and breadth of analysis

Your *Analysis* should be 1250 words long. This might sound like a lot, but it's really only about eight or nine short paragraphs. In planning your *Analysis*, you will have to be selective in choosing which aspects of your primary material you focus on, and will need to think carefully about the depth of the discussion you can provide.

ACTIVITY 3

Scope and selectivity

Which do you think makes for a stronger investigation: an *Analysis* which presents a lot of points and examples but does not discuss them in much detail, or an *Analysis* which discusses only a very few examples, but does so in a lot of depth?

Your decision on how to balance depth and scope, for your own investigation, may be influenced by the nature of your question, your material and your interest.

26.1.4 Approaching different discourse types

You looked at different aspects of context when you compared *Small Island* and song lyrics. In order to produce a strong and well-reasoned investigation, you need to consider contextual factors influencing all of your material, and recognise the potential for very different contextual influences even within the same period or genre category.

ACTIVITY 4

Considering context

a Find two newspaper articles on the same story available on the internet today but reported in two different newspapers: *The Guardian* and *The Daily Mail*.

b Using the language through which the story is presented, and anything you know or can find out about the newspaper, compare the ideology, purpose and audience of each article.

26.2 Wider reading list

26.2.1 Selected reading on key areas in *Making connections*

- Copus, Julia (2009) *Brilliant Writing Tips for Students,* Houndsmills, Basingstoke: Palgrave Macmillan.
- Godwin, Janet (2009) *Planning Your Essay,* Houndsmills, Basingstoke: Palgrave Macmillan.
- Williams, Kate (2009) *Getting Critical,* Houndsmills, Basingstoke: Palgrave Macmillan.

These three books come from the same series of pocket-sized student guides. They are simple, short and clear with lots of examples and illustrations. These books are really useful tools to support development in critical reading and written communication.

- Wray, Alison, and Bloomer, Aileen (2012) *Projects in Language and Linguistics: A Practical Guide to Researching Language*, 3rd edn, London: Routledge.

This is a very popular book guiding students through the different parts of projects on language and linguistics in a step-by-step way. The book also has very useful and clear chapters on gathering and transcribing spoken data.

26.2.2 Further useful resources - texts exploring connections between language and literature

- Pope, Rob (2012) *Studying English Language and Literature*, 3rd edn, London: Routledge.

26.2.3 Further useful resources - guides on written communication

- Greetham, Bryan (2008) *How to Write Better Essays*, 2nd edn, Basingstoke: Palgrave Macmillan.
- Headrick, Paul (2014) *The Wiley Guide to Writing Essays About Literature,* Oxford: Wiley Blackwell.
- Stott, Rebecca, Anna Snaith and Rick Rylance, eds (2001) *Making Your Case: A Practical Guide to Essay Writing,* Harlow: Pearson Education.
- van Emden, Joan, and Becker, Lucinda (2003) *Effective Communication for Arts and Humanities Students*, London: Palgrave Macmillan.

26.2.4 Further useful resources - guides on research and critical reading

- Altick, Richard D. (1993) *The Art of Literary Research*, 4th edn, New York: Norton.
- Goatly, Andrew (2000) *Critical Reading and Writing: An Introductory Coursebook*, London: Routledge.

26.3 Current research on making connections between language and literature

26.3.1 Strands of research

- **Narratology:** Narrative is something which cuts across the divide between literary and non-literary discourse. Throughout this book you've explored the ways in which narrative appears in different shapes and structures, and in different genres and discourse types, across history and across the world, with interesting similarities and contrasts in its greatly varying contexts. Insights from the study of literary narrative offer a lot to the study of non-literary narrative, and vice versa. Narratology is a broad interdisciplinary field of study, in which integrated literary linguistic research in particular is making radical steps forward in our knowledge and understanding of the subject.
- **Stylistics:** Stylistic methods and approaches have been your tools throughout these units. Stylistics is a relatively new and flourishing field, and continues to go from strength to strength. Researchers are using it to explore new discourse types, broadening the stylistic toolkit. Stylisticians also continue to develop the nuances of the field's models and frameworks so as to penetrate the workings of texts further, and understand them and their interpretations in more acute detail. Stylistics is a very dynamic field.

26.3.2 Jessica Mason in video interview

Watch Jessica Mason, Research Associate at the University of Nottingham, talk about developing projects and writing non-exam assessments on Cambridge Elevate

References

Beginning units

Abbott, H. Porter (2008) *The Cambridge Introduction to Narrative*, New York: Cambridge University Press.

Baron, Naomi (2001) *Alphabet to Email: How Written English Evolved and Where It's Heading*, New York: Routledge.

Carter, Ronald and Nash, Walter (1990) *Seeing Through Language: A Guide of Styles of English Writing*, Oxford: Blackwell.

Goodwin, Charles (1984) 'Notes on story structure and the organization of participation', in J. Maxwell Atkinson and John Heritage (eds) *Structures of Social Action: Studies in Conversation Analysis*, Cambridge: Cambridge University Press, pp. 225–246.

Goffman, Erving (1955) 'On face-work: An analysis of ritual elements in social interaction, *Psychiatry: Interpersonal and Biological Processes*, 18 (3), 213–231.

Grice, Paul (1975) 'Logic and conversation', in P. Cole and J. Morgan (eds) *Syntax and Semantics III: Speech Acts*, New York: Academic Press, pp. 41–58.

Labov, William (1972) *Language in the Inner City: Studies in the Black English Vernacular*, Philadelphia, PA: University of Pennsylvania Press.

Lakoff, George and Johnson, Mark (1980) *Metaphors We Live By*, Chicago, IL: University of Chicago Press.

Short, Mick (1996) *Exploring the Language of Poems, Plays and Prose*, London: Longman.

Unit 15 *Remembered places*

Birkett, Dea, and Wheeler, Sarah (1998) *Amazonian: The Penguin Book of Women's New Travel Writing*, Harmondsworth: Penguin.

Crang, Mike (1998) *Cultural Geography*, London: Routledge.

Gee, James Paul (2012) *Social Linguistics and Literacies: Ideology in Discourses*, 4th edition, New York: Routledge.

Hyde, Janet (2005) 'The gender similarities hypothesis', *American Psychologist*, 60(6): 581–592.

Macionis, John (2008) *Society: The Basics*, Upper Saddle River, NJ: Prentice Hall.

Morris, Mary (2010) *The Illustrated Virago Book of Women Travellers*, London: Virago.

Page, Ruth (2012) *Stories and Social Media: Identities and Interaction*, Abingdon: Routledge.

Pomerantz, Anita (1984) 'Agreeing and disagreeing with assessments: Some features of preferred/dispreferred turn shapes, in J. Maxwell Atkinson and John Heritage (eds) *Structures of Social Action: Studies in Conversation Analysis*, Cambridge: Cambridge University Press, pp. 57–101.

Thompson, Carl (2011) *Travel Writing: The New Critical idiom*, London: Routledge.

Walvin, James (1988) *Victorian Values*, London: Cardinal Books.

Youngs, Tim (2013) *The Cambridge Introduction to Travel Writing*, Cambridge: Cambridge University Press.

Unit 16 *Imagined worlds*

Attebery, Brian (1992) *Strategies of Fantasy*, Bloomington, IN: Indiana University Press.

Forster, E.M. (1927) *Aspects of the Novel*, London: Edward Arnold.

Greimas, Algirdas Julien (1966) *Sémantique structurale*, Paris: Larousse.

Jackson, Rosemary (1981) *Fantasy: the Literature of Subversion*, London: Routledge.

Korte, Barbara (1997) *Body Language in Literature*, Toronto: University of Toronto Press.

Lambert, Mark (1981) *Dickens and the Suspended Quotation*, New Haven, CT: Yale University Press.

Leech, Geoffrey and Short, Mick (1981) *Style in Fiction: A Linguistic Introduction to English Fictional Prose*, London: Longman.

Madden, Matt (2006) *99 Ways to Tell a Story: Exercises in Style*, London: Jonathan Cape.

Propp, Vladimir (1928) *Morphology of the Folk Tale* (latest edition published 2003 by Texas University Press).

Queneau, Raymond (2013) *Exercises in Style*, revised edition, Richmond: Alma Classics.

Rabinowitz, Peter (2002) Reading beginnings and endings', in Brian Richardson (ed.) *Narrative Dynamics: Essays on Time, Plot, Closure, and Frames*, Columbus, Ohio: Ohio State University Press, pp. 300–313.

Simpson, Paul (1993) *Language, Ideology and Point of View*, London: Routledge.

Unit 17 *Poetic voices*

Aristotle (1996) *Poetics*, Harmondsworth: Penguin.

Unit 18 *Writing about society*

Genette, Gérard (1980) *Narrative Discourse: An Essay in Method*, tr. Jane E. Lewin, Ithaca, NY: Cornell University Press.

Genette, Gérard (1988) *Narrative Discourse Revisited*, tr. Jane E. Lewin, Ithaca, NY: Cornell University Press.

Unit 19 *Dramatic encounters*

Brown, Penelope and Levinson, Stephen (1987) *Politeness: Some Universals in Language Usage*, Cambridge: Cambridge University Press.

Culpeper, Jonathan (1996) 'Towards an anatomy of impoliteness', *Journal of Pragmatics* 25(3): 349–367.

Index

Note: Key Terms, and the page with their definition, are shown in **bold**. Glossary terms are in red.

Acknowledgements

The authors and publishers acknowledge the following sources of copyright material and are grateful for the permissions granted. While every effort has been made, it has not always been possible to identify the sources of all the material used, or to trace all copyright holders. If any omissions are brought to our notice, we will be happy to include the appropriate acknowledgements on reprinting.

Where unacknowledged in the text, all dictionary extracts are reproduced from Cambridge Dictionaries Online blog dictionaryblog.cambridge.org/© Cambridge University Press.

AQA examination questions are reproduced by permission of AQA

Text 2A, page 13: from *I Lick My Cheese and Other Notes from the Frontline of Flatsharing Sphere* by Oonagh O'Hagan, published by Little, Brown Book Group; Text 2B, page 14: Courtesy of Eurostar website, May 2015; Table 3A, page 16: adapted from *Alphabet to Email: How Written English Evolved and Where It's Heading* by Naomi S. Baron, 2001 Routledge (26 April 2001); Text 3B, page 17: adapted from a review of 'In the Night Garden - Live', Copyright © 2014 The Stage Media Company Limited; Text 3D, page 19: Virgin Media with permission; Text 4B, page 23: from *The Tiger Who Came to Tea* by Judith Kerr. Reprinted by permission of HarperCollins Publishers Ltd © 2006 Judith Kerr; Text 5A, page 26: from *The Suspicions of Mr Whicher, or The Murder of Road Hill House'*. © Kate Summerscale, 2009, Bloomsbury Publishing Plc; Text 5B, page 27: from 'The Duke and Duchess of Cambridge remember the fallen on ANZAC day',25/04/2014. With permission from HELLO! magazine; Text 5C, page 27: from *The Sociolinguistics of Narrative*, by Thornborrow, J. and Coates, Prof. J., (2005) John Benjamins Publishing Co; Text 6B, page 31: 'Bowers and Wilkins headphones' copyright B&W Group Ltd with permission; Text 6C, page 33: 'A new flavour of sound' with permission from Samsung; Text 7A, page 37: from Advertising Archive Limited; Text 7B, page 40: from *The Woman in Black* by Susan Hill, published by Vintage Books © Susan Hill 1983. Reproduced by permission of Sheil Land Associates Ltd; Text 8A, page 43: from the poem 'The Working Party' [From Siegfried Sassoon *The War Poems*, Published in 2012 by Faber and Faber, page 14 ISBN 978-0-571-24009-8] Barbara Levy Literary Agency with permission; Text 8B, page 45: from punoftheday.com; Text 9A, page 46: from *How to Catch a Star* by Oliver Jeffers published by HarperCollins Children's Books (25 Sep 2014). Reprinted by permission of HarperCollins Publishers Children's Books © 2005 Oliver Jeffers; Text 9B, page 48: showing key bus routes in central London © Transport for London; Text 9C, page 49: from 'How to Brush your Teeth' © 2012 Nottinghamshire Healthcare NHS Trust. All rights reserved; Text 10A, page 50: with permission from Stuff magazine; Text 10E, page 54: from 'Put your sneakers on!', Mad about Paris, with permission from Martina Meister; Text 12A, page 60: © Jon McGregor, 14/02/2013, 'I remember there was a hill', in *This Isn't The Sort Of Thing That Happens To Someone Like You*, Bloomsbury Publishing Plc; Text 12B, page 61: from 'Celia, Celia' in *Greatest Hits*, 1991 Bloodaxe Books Ltd , United Agents LLP with permission; Text 13B, page 65: Rt Hon. Michael Gove MP with permission; Text 15A, page 74: from *The Most Beautiful Walk in the World: A Pedestrian in Paris*. Permission granted by Short Books Ltd and the author John Baxter; Text 15C, page 78: from *Foreign Correspondent: Paris in the Sixties* by Peter Lennon, reprinted by permissison of Peters Fraser and Dunlop (petersfraserdunlop.com) on behalf of the Estate of Peter Lennon; Text 15E, page 82: from *Neither here, nor there* by Bill Bryson, published by Black Swan. Reprinted by permission of The Random House Group Limited; Text 15F, page 82: from 'Not For Parents Paris: Everything You Ever Wanted to Know' from *Lonely Planet Not for Parents Travel Book*, 2011, Reproduced with permission from Not For Parents Paris, edition 1 © 2011 Lonely Planet; Extract on page 84 from Macionis, John J., *Society: The Basics*, 13th Ed., 2015, p50. Reprinted by permission of Pearson Education, Inc, New York, New York; Text 15H, page 86: 'A new flavour of sound' with permission from Samsung; Text 15I, page 87: from Blurb: *The Sweet Life in Paris: Delicious Adventures in the World's Most Glorious–And Perplexing–City* by David Lebovitz, Broadway Books, with permission from Hill Nadell Literary Agency on behalf of the author David Lebovitz; Text 15J, pages 87-88: from 'Understanding chic' by Natasha Fraser-Cavassoni from *Paris Was Ours: Thirty-two Writers Reflect on the City of Light Algonquin Books of Chapel Hill*, with permission from Algonquin Books; Text 15K, page 89: from Ernest Hemingway on Paris American Bohemians in Paris The Toronto Star Weekly March 25 1922; Text 15L (a), page 91: from *The Most Beautiful Walk in the World: A Pedestrian in Paris* by John Baxter Reprinted by permission of Short Books Ltd; Text 15L (b), page 91: from *Neither here nor there* by Bill Bryson. Published by Black Swan. Reprinted by permission of The Random House Group Limited; Text 15M, page 94: from *French Milk* by Lucy Knisley, published by Touchstone Books; Text 15N, page 96: from Gransnet forum with permission gransnet.com; Text 15R, page 105: from 'Understanding chic' in *Paris Was Ours: Thirty-two Writers Reflect on the City of Light* by Natasha Fraser-Cavassoni, published by Algonquin Books with permission from Curtis Brown; Text 15S, page 106: from Tripadvisor.com, © 2014, TripAdvisor, LLC. All rights Reserved; Quotation from Mike Crang on page 80: from *Cultural Geography* (Routledge Contemporary Human Geography Series) by Mike Crang; Quotation from John Macionis on page 83: from *Society: The Basics* by John Macionis, published by Prentice Hall; Quotation from Dea Birkett and Sara Wheeler on page 87: from *Amazonian: The Penguin Book of Women's New Travel Writing* by Dea Birkett and Sara Wheeler, Penguin Books Ltd; Figure 15A, page 100: adapted from *Stories and Social Media: Identities and Interaction* (Routledge Studies in Sociolinguistics) by Ruth E. Page, published by Routledge; Extract on page 107: from *The Cambridge Companion to Fantasy Literature*, by Edward James and Farah Mendlesohn , 2012, Cambridge University Press; Extract on page 108: from 'Fantasy: *The Literature of Subversion (New Accents)* by Rosemary Jackson, published by Routledge; Text 16B, page 113: from *The Lovely Bones* by Alice Sebold, published by Picador. Reproduced by permission of David Higham Ltd; Text 16C, page 115: from *The Handmaid's Tale* by Margaret Atwood, published by Jonathan Cape. Reproduced by permission of The Random House Group Ltd and by permission of Curtis Brown; Text 16D, page 115: from *The Lovely Bones* by Alice Sebold, published by Picador. Reproduced by permission of David Higham Ltd; Text 16E, page 117: from *The Handmaid's Tale* by Margaret Atwood, published by Jonathan Cape. Reproduced by permission of The Random House Group Ltd and by permission of Curtis Brown; Text 16E, page 117: from *The Lovely Bones* by Alice Sebold, published by Picador. Reproduced by permission of David Higham Ltd; Text 16F, page 118: from *The Lovely Bones* by Alice Sebold, published by Picador. Reproduced by permission of David Higham Ltd; Text 16G, page 122: from *The Lovely Bones* by Alice Sebold, published by Picador. Reproduced by permission of David Higham Ltd; Text 16I, page 123: from *Analysing Police Interviews: Laughter, Confessions and the Tape* by Elisabeth Carter, published by Bloomsbury. Reproduced by permission of the author; Text 16J, page 123: from *The Lovely Bones* by Alice Sebold, published by Picador. Reproduced by permission of David Higham Ltd; Text 16K, page 124: from *The Lovely Bones* by Alice Sebold, published by Picador. Reproduced by permission of

David Higham Ltd; Text 16L, page 124: from *The Handmaid's Tale* by Margaret Atwood, published by Jonathan Cape. Reproduced by permission of The Random House Group Ltd and by permission of Curtis Brown; Extract on page 126: from *The Handmaid's Tale* by Margaret Atwood, published by Jonathan Cape. Reproduced by permission of The Random House Group Ltd and by permission of Curtis Brown; Extract on page 126: from *The Lovely Bones* by Alice Sebold, published by Picador. Reproduced by permission of David Higham Ltd; Extracts on page 126: from *The Lovely Bones* by Alice Sebold, published by Picador. Reproduced by permission of David Higham Ltd, Text 16M, page 127: from *99 Ways to Tell a Story: Exercises in Style* by Matt Madden published by Jonathan Cape. Reproduced by permission of The Random House Group Ltd and Creative Book Services; Text 16N & 16O page 128: from *99 Ways to Tell a Story: Exercises in Style* by Matt Madden published by Jonathan Cape. Reproduced by permission of The Random House Group Ltd and Creative Book Services; Extract on page 129: from *Snow Falling on Cedars*. © David Guterson, 2009, Bloomsbury Publishing Plc; Text 16Q, pages 129-130: from *One Day* by David Nicholls, published by Hodder and Stroughton; Quotation from Margaret Atwood on page 123: from *The Handmaid's Tale*, published by Jonathan Cape. Reproduced by permission of The Random House Group Ltd and by permission of Curtis Brown; Text 16W, pages 137-138: from *The Handmaid's Tale* by Margaret Atwood, published by Jonathan Cape. Reproduced by permission of The Random House Group Ltd and by permission of Curtis Brown; Text 16X, page 138: from *The Lovely Bones* by Alice Sebold, published by Picador. Reproduced by permission of David Higham Ltd; Text 16AA, page 142: from *The Handmaid's Tale* by Margaret Atwood, published by Jonathan Cape. Reproduced by permission of The Random House Group Ltd and by permission of Curtis Brown; Text 17A, page 144: from *Birthday Letters* by John Carey and Seamus Heaney, Faber and Faber Ltd; Text 17B, page 146: from *First Day at School* by Roger McGough with permission from United Agents; Text 17C (b), page 146: from 'Digging' in *Death of a Naturalist* by Seamus Heaney, Faber and Faber Ltd; Text 17C (d), page 147: from *Mean Time* by Carol Ann Duffy with permission from Rogers, Coleridge and White; Text 17D, page 147: from 'Poetry is a form of dissent' by Simon Armitage © Guardian news and media, 2011; Text 17E, page 148: from *How To Eat A Poem* by Merriam, Eve. HarperCollins US Children's Books with permission; Quotation from Billy Collins on page 148: excerpts from *Introduction to Poetry* from 'The Apple That Astonished Paris'. © 1988, 1996 by Billy Collins. Reprinted with the permission of The Permissions Company, Inc., on behalf of the University of Arkansas Press, uapress.com; Text 17F, page 149: from 'Small Female Skull' from *Standing Female Nude* by Carol Ann Duffy, published by Anvil Press Poetry; Quote on page 150: from poetryarchive.org by Carol Ann; Quote on page 150: by Seamus Heaney from goodreads.com, Faber and Faber Ltd; Text 17G, page 152: from 'Strange Fruit' in *North* by Seamus Heaney, Faber and Faber Ltd; Text 17I, page 155: from 'Originally' in The *Other Country* by Carol Ann Duffy published by Picador with permission from Rogers, Coleridge and White; Text 17K (c), page 156: from 'Valentine' in *Love Poems* by Carol Ann Duffy, published by Picador with permission from Rogers, Coleridge and White; Text 17K (d), page 156: from 'Punishment' in *North* by Seamus Heaney, Faber and Faber Ltd; Text 17L (a) & (b) pages 156-157: from 'The Otter' in *Human Chain* by Seamus Heaney, Faber and Faber Ltd; Extract on page 158 from Caprice in Consonants. *Blinkies: Funny Poems to Read in a Blink* by Alma Denny, with permission from Lamb & Lion Studio; Table 17D, page 159: from *English Today 42, Volume 11* (2). by David Crystal, Cambridge University Press; Extract on page 160 from 'The Otter' in *Human Chain* by Seamus Heaney, Faber and Faber Ltd; Text 17N, page 160: from 'Digging' in *Death of a Naturalist* by Seamus Heaney, Faber and Faber Ltd; Extract on page 161: from *A Student's Guide to Seamus Heaney* by Neil Corcoran, Faber and Faber Ltd; Text 17O (c), page 162: from 'The Biographer' in *Mean Time* by Carol Ann Duffy published by Picador with permission from Rogers, Coleridge and White; Text 17O (d), page 162: from 'Night Drive' in *Death of a Naturalist* by Seamus Heaney, Faber and Faber Ltd; Text 17Q, page 164: from *A Glossary of Literary Terms* by Abrams, Meyer H., reproduced with permission of Holt, Rinehart & Winston Inc in the format Republish in a book via Copyright Clearance Center; Extract on page 167: from 'Stafford Afternoons' in *The World's Wife* by Carol Ann Duffy, published by Picador; Text 17S (a), page 168: from *Death of a Naturalist* by Seamus Heaney, Faber and Faber Ltd; Text 17T (c), page 169: from 'Stafford Afternoons' in *The World's Wife* by Carol Ann Duffy, published by Picador; Text 17T (d), page 169: from 'Personal Helicon' in *Death of a Naturalist* by Seamus Heaney, Faber and Faber Ltd; Text 17U, page 170: from 'Before You Were Mine' in *Mean Time* by Carol Ann Duffy, published by Picador with permission from Rogers, Coleridge and White; Text 17V, page 170: from 'Mid-Term Break' in *Death of a Naturalist* by Seamus Heaney, Faber and Faber Ltd; Quote on page 172: by Jackie Kay, The Poetry Society: poetrysociety.org.uk; Text 17W (b), page 172: from 'Mid-Term Break' in *Death of a Naturalist* by Seamus Heaney, Faber and Faber Ltd; Extract on page 176: from 'Follower' by Seamus Heaney, Faber and Faber Ltd; Text 17Y(c), page 177: from 'First Love' in *Mean Time* by Carol Ann Duffy, published by Picador; Text 17Y (d), page 177: from 'Punishment' in *North* by Seamus Heaney, Faber and Faber Ltd; Extract on page 178: from 'Blackberry Picking' in *Death of a Naturalist* by Seamus Heaney, Faber and Faber Ltd; Text 18C, page 194: from *Into the Wild Pan* by Jon Krakauer. © Jon Krakauer 1998 , published by Pan Macmillan Publishers with permission from Pan Macmillan; Text 18D, pages 194-195: from *The Suspicions of Mr Whicher, or The Murder of Road Hill House*. © Kate Summerscale, 2009, Bloomsbury Publishing Plc; Text 18E, page 196: from *The Kite Runner*. © Khaled Hosseini, 2011, Bloomsbury Publishing Plc; Text 18F, pages 200: from *The Suspicions of Mr Whicher, or The Murder of Road Hill House*. © Kate Summerscale, 2009. Bloomsbury Publishing Plc; Text 18G (a), page 206: from *Into the Wild Pan* by John Krakauer, published by Pan Macmillan Publishers with permission from Pan Macmillan; Text 18G (b), page 206: from *The Suspicions of Mr Whicher, or The Murder of Road Hill House*. © Kate Summerscale, 2009. Bloomsbury Publishing Plc; Short extracts within table on page 209: from *The Suspicions of Mr Whicher, or The Murder of Road Hill House*. © Kate Summerscale, 2009. Bloomsbury Publishing Plc; Extract on page 214 from *Into the Wild Pan* by John Krakauer, published by Pan Macmillan Publishers with permission from Pan Macmillan; Extract on page 214 from *The Suspicions of Mr Whicher, or The Murder of Road Hill House*. © Kate Summerscale, 2009, Bloomsbury Publishing Plc; Figure 19A, page 214: from *Short's model of the prototypical dramatic discourse structure in Exploring the Language of Poems, Plays and Prose*, published by Longman, used with permission from Taylor and Francis; Text 19B, page 217: from *A Streetcar Named Desire* by Tennessee Williams, published by Penguin Classics with permission from New Directions Publishing Corp; Text 19C (b), page 217: from *All My Sons* by Arthur Miller. © 1947, renewed © 1975 by Arthur Miller. Used by permission of Penguin Books, an imprint of Penguin Publishing Group, a division of Penguin Random House LLC and with permission from Wylie; Text 19D, page 218: from *All My Sons* by Arthur Miller. © 1947, renewed © 1975 by Arthur Miller. Used by permission of Penguin Books, an imprint of Penguin Publishing Group, a division of Penguin Random House LLC and with permission from Wylie; Text 19G (a), page 219: from *All My Sons* by Arthur Miller. © 1947, renewed © 1975 by Arthur Miller. Used by permission of Penguin Books, an imprint of Penguin Publishing Group, a division of Penguin Random House LLC and with permission from Wylie; Text 19G (b), page 220: from *The Herd* by Rory Kinnear with permission from Nick Hern Books; Text 19G (c), page 220: from *A Streetcar Named Desire* by Tennessee Williams published by Penguin Classics with permission from New Directions Publishing Corp; Text 19H (a) & (c), pages 220-221: from *All My Sons* by Arthur Miller. © 1947, renewed © 1975 by Arthur Miller. Used by permission of Penguin Books, an imprint of Penguin Publishing Group, a division of Penguin Random House LLC and with permission from Wylie; Text 19I, page 221: from *All My Sons* by Arthur Miller. © 1947, renewed © 1975 by Arthur Miller. Used by permission of Penguin Books, an imprint of Penguin Publishing Group, a division of Penguin Random House LLC and with permission from Wylie; Text 19J, page 221: from *The Herd* by Rory Kinnear with permission from Nick Hern Books; Text 19L, page 222: from *A Streetcar Named Desire* by Tennessee Williams, published by Penguin Classics with permission from New Directions Publishing Corp; Text 19M, page 224: from *All My Sons* by Arthur Miller. © 1947, renewed © 1975 by Arthur Miller. Used by permission of Penguin Books, an imprint of Penguin Publishing Group, a division of Penguin Random House LLC and with permission from Wylie; Extract on page 226 from *All My Sons* by Arthur Miller. © 1947, renewed © 1975 by Arthur Miller. Used by permission of Penguin Books, an imprint of Penguin Publishing Group, a division of Penguin Random House LLC and with permission from Wylie; Text 19N, page 225: from *The Herd* by Rory Kinnear with permission from Nick Hern Books; Extract on page 229 from *The Kite Runner*. © Khaled Hosseini, 2011, Bloomsbury Publishing Plc; Text 19O & 19P, page 228: from *A Streetcar Named Desire* by Tennessee Williams, published by Penguin Classics with permission from New Directions Publishing Corp; Text 19Q (a), page 230: from *The Herd* by Rory Kinnear with permission from Nick Hern Books; Text 19Q (b), page 230: from *All My Sons* by Arthur Miller. © 1947, renewed © 1975 by Arthur Miller. Used by permission of Penguin Books, an imprint of Penguin Publishing Group, a division of Penguin Random House LLC and with permission from Wylie; Text 19Q (c), page 230: from *A Streetcar Named Desire* by Tennessee Williams, published by Penguin Classics with permission from New Directions Publishing Corp; Text 19S, page 232: from *A Streetcar Named Desire* by Tennessee Williams, published by Penguin Classics with permission from New Directions Publishing Corp; Text 19T, page 233: from *All My Sons* by Arthur Miller. © 1947, renewed © 1975 by Arthur Miller. Used by permission of Penguin Books, an imprint of Penguin Publishing Group, a division of Penguin Random House LLC and with permission from Wylie; Text 19U, page 235: from *A Streetcar Named Desire* by Tennessee Williams, published by Penguin Classics with permission from New Directions Publishing Corp; Extract on page 240: from *All My Sons* by Arthur Miller. © 1947, renewed © 1975 by Arthur Miller. Used by permission of Penguin Books, an imprint of Penguin Publishing Group, a division of Penguin Random House LLC and with permission from Wylie; Extract on page 240: from *A Streetcar Named Desire* by Tennessee Williams, published by Penguin Classics with permission from New Directions Publishing Corp; Text 19Z, page 241: from *The Herd* by Rory Kinnear with permission from Nick Hern Books; Text 19AA & Text 19AB, page 241: from *A Streetcar Named Desire* by Tennessee Williams, published by Penguin Classics with permission from New Directions Publishing Corp; Text 20A, page 250: from *Wise Children* by Angela Carter, published by Vintage Classics; Text 20C (a), page 252: from *We Need to Talk About Kevin* by Lionel Shriver, published by Serpent's Tail with permission from Profile Books; Text 20C (b), page 252: from *Birdsong* by Sebastian Faulks, published by Hutchinson. Reproduced by permission of The Random House Group Ltd; Extract on page 256: from *Trainspotting* by Irvine Welsh, published by Secker. Reproduced by permission of The Random House Group Ltd; Text 20F(a), page 259: from 'A whole different ball game: Meet the women aiming to win the World Cup' by John Koski, Daily Mail 2011 with permission; Text 20F(c), page 259: from *A Prayer for Owen Meany* by John Irving with permission Black Swan, Bloomsbury; Text 20N, pages 270-271: from *Small Island* by Andrea Levy, published by Tinder Press 2014; Figure 22A, page 286: for search of Sparsit in suspensions in Hard Times retrieved with CLiC 1.0 http://clic.nottingham.ac.uk/concordances/ The CLiC project is supported by the Arts and Humanities Research Council [AH/K005146/1] Centre for Research in Applied Linguistics with permission; Figure 25A, page 298: from Short's model of the prototypical dramatic discourse structure in *Exploring the Language of Poems, Plays and Prose,* published by Longman, used with permission from Taylor and Francis.

Photo acknowledgements

Splash image on front cover: Copyright 2013 Fabian Oefner www.fabianoefner.com

p. 4 (T): blueskies9/Fotolia; p. 4 (C): diversepixel/Fotolia; p. 4 (B): Viacheslav Iakobchuk/Fotolia; p. 8 WavebreakmediaMicro/Fotolia; p. 9 LeitnerR/Fotolia; p. 12: kamiwro/Fotolia; p. 16: A.B.G./Fotolia; p. 17: image/Alamy; p. 18: Sebastian Gauert/Fotolia; p. 20: LuminaStock/Thinkstock; p. 21: bertys30/Fotolia; p. 24: Dmitry Pichugin/Fotolia; p. 24: Photographee.eu/Fotolia; p. 28: blueskies9/Fotolia; p. 29: iPics/Fotolia; p. 35: Les Cunliffe/Fotolia; p. 37: Advertising Archive Limited; p. 39: Wanchi/Fotolia; p. 41: Sergey Sanin/Fotolia; p. 42: gamjai/Fotolia; p. 44: freshidea/Fotolia; p. 46: Minerva Studio/Fotolia; p. 50: DrHitch/Fotolia; p. 50: Stuff magazine 2014; p. 52: Monkey Business/Fotolia; p. 54: rdnzl/Fotolia; p. 55: markrubens/Fotolia; p. 57: Anioł/Fotolia; p. 60: Photographee.eu/Fotolia; p. 62: Oleg Zhukov/Fotolia; p. 64: felix/Fotolia; p. 65: SolisImages/Fotolia; p. 66: djama/Fotolia; p. 68: Remains/Fotolia; p. 69: Maksim Kostenko/Fotolia; p. 70: Robert Kneschke/Fotolia; p. 72: djama/Fotolia; p. 74: neirfy/Fotolia; p. 78: sas/Fotolia; p. 80: pixarno/Fotolia; p. 81: Beboy/Fotolia; p. 82: Ekaterina Pokrovsky/Fotolia; p. 89: pab_map/Fotolia; p. 93: keithburn/Fotolia; p. 107: diversepixel/Fotolia; p. 108: Andrey Kiselev/Fotolia; p. 111: Zacarias da Mata/Fotolia; p. 115: weseetheworld/Fotolia; p. 121: milanmarkovic78/Fotolia; p. 127, 128: Matt Madden, 99 Ways to Tell a Story: Exercises in Style, 2006; p. 129: Remains/Fotolia; p. 140: Sergey Nivens/Fotolia; p. 142: Serhiy Kobyakov/Fotolia; p. 144: librakv/Fotolia; p. 145: Rainer Albiez/Fotolia; p. 146: Pascal Huot/Fotolia; p. 149: coffeemill/Fotolia; p. 157: Cosmin Manci/Fotolia; p. 161: Kruwt/Fotolia; p. 162: David Stuart/Fotolia; p. 166: Valena Soraja Image/Fotolia; p. 171: Robert Hoetink/Fotolia; p. 178: Pavla Zakova/Fotolia; p. 183: kmiragaya/Fotolia; p. 184: Ezio Gutzemberg/Fotolia; p. 185: xalanx/Fotolia; p. 186: blvdone/Fotolia; p. 188: eugenesergeev/Fotolia; p. 193: Elena Schweitzer/Fotolia; p. 214: bananna/Fotolia; p. 229: Ella/Fotolia; p. 230: Dorling Kindersley/Getty; p. 235 (T): Interfoto/Alamy; p. 235 (B): United Archives GmbH/Alamy; p. 247: ktsdesign/Fotolia; p. 259: snaptitude/Fotolia; p. 275: Giorgio Clementi/Fotolia; p. 280: sdecoret/Fotolia; p. 283: stuart/Fotolia; p. 287: ProMotion/Fotolia; p. 291: BillionPhotos.com/Fotolia; p. 298: Viacheslav Iakobchuk/Fotolia; p. 299: Photographee.eu/Fotolia; p. 303: Amgun/Fotolia.